ALSO BY CHARLES LEERHSEN

Blood and Smoke: A True Tale of Mystery, Mayhem, and the Birth of the Indy 500

Crazy Good: The True Story of Dan Patch, the Most Famous Horse in America

TY COBB

A TERRIBLE BEAUTY

CHARLES LEERHSEN

Simon & Schuster

New York   London   Toronto   Sydney   New Delhi

Simon & Schuster
1230 Avenue of the Americas
New York, NY 10020

First Simon & Schuster hardcover edition May 2015

SIMON & SCHUSTER and colophon are registered trademarks of Simon & Schuster, Inc.

For information about special discounts for bulk purchases, please contact Simon & Schuster Special Sales at 1-866-506-1949 or business@simonandschuster.com.

The Simon & Schuster Speakers Bureau can bring authors to your live event. For more information or to book an event contact the Simon & Schuster Speakers Bureau at 1-866-248-3049 or visit our website at www.simonspeaker.com.

Interior design by Joy O'Meara

Manufactured in the United States of America

10   9   8   7   6   5   4   3   2   1

Library of Congress Cataloging-in-Publication Data

Leerhsen, Charles.
    Ty Cobb : a terrible beauty / Charles Leerhsen.—First Simon & Schuster hardcover edition.
        pages   cm
    1. Cobb, Ty, 1886–1961. 2. Baseball players—United States—Biography. I. Title.
    GV865.C6L44   2015
    796.357092—dc23
    [B]   2014041478
ISBN 978-1-4516-4576-7
ISBN 978-1-4516-4580-4 (ebook)

PHOTO CREDITS:
1–3, 14: Detroit Public Library
4–9, 11, 12, 17–18: National Baseball Hall of Fame and Museum
10: Getty Images/Pictorial Library
15, 16: Library of Congress

For Sarah

He, too, has resigned his part
In the casual comedy;
He, too, has been changed in his turn,
Transformed utterly:
A terrible beauty is born.

—*Easter 1916*, by William Butler Yeats

"Those who really possess sensibility ought early to be taught that it is a dangerous quality, which is continually extracting the excess of misery or delight from every surrounding circumstance. And since, in our passage through this world, painful circumstances occur more frequently than pleasing ones, and since our sense of evil is, I fear, more acute than our sense of good, we become the victims of our feelings, unless we can in some degree command them."

—*The Mysteries of Udolpho* by Ann Radcliffe

"When Cobb is on first base and he breaks for second, the best thing you can do, really, is to throw to third."

—Hall of Fame catcher and manager Ray Schalk

— CONTENTS —

TY COBB

— PRELUDE —

The Opie and Anthony Show

Opie: Was he a wife-beater, that Ty Cobb?

Jim Norton: Ty Cobb was an everything-beater. He beat up everything. Ty Cobb was a horrible racist. I think he was a Demoral addict. . . . I want a Cobb jersey, because he was such a brutal guy.

Opie: I want to know if this is true. There is a myth that Ty Cobb killed a man with a baseball bat and then hit a home run with it the next day.

Jim Norton: That's probably nonsense but his mother did murder his father. I think the real story . . . is that Ty Cobb's father suspected his mother of cheating, and came home and . . . it maybe it wasn't the mother who shot him, maybe it was the lover . . . but I think that Ty said that the last thing my father saw was the man who was effing his wife.

Opie: Wow . . . How did he die?

Jim Norton: I think he died of old age. It may have been morphine he was hooked on. He was injecting something into his stomach.

Opie: People say he died of a codeine overdose.

Jim Norton: Oh, really? So it was codeine he was hooked on?

Opie: How old was he when he died?

Jim Norton: He was in his seventies.

Opie: That's old for back when he died. Not many guys living past seventy in Ty Cobb's time.

Jim Norton: Only four people from baseball attended Ty Cobb's funeral.

(Laughter)

Opie: He slept with a loaded pistol under his pillow, he was so afraid.

(Laughter)

Jim Norton (Reading): In spring training in 1907 Cobb fought a black groundskeeper over the condition of the Tigers' spring training field in Augusta, Georgia, and ended up choking the man's wife when she intervened.

(Laughter)

Opie: What a maniac . . . just a maniac! I don't think I saw the Ty Cobb movie. Is this stuff in it?

Jim Norton: Him being a racist absolutely is in it. Tommy Lee Jones, as an actor, I would for free do the lines he got to do. He was really good as Ty Cobb. Robert Wuhl was okay as the guy Stumpy who plays the reporter who . . . Cobb wanted him to write his life. And the conflict was, Cobb was like "I want this to be like I am the great Ty Cobb." Meanwhile this guy is taking notes on what an awful human being Ty Cobb is . . . just a racist and is terrible and is rotten.

Opie: Cobb had no clue what an ass he was?

Jim Norton: He knew. He just didn't care.

Opie: He didn't care.

"Take Me Out to the Ball Game" begins to play.

Jim Norton: And this guy is in the Hall of Fame?

PART ONE

— CHAPTER ONE —

LEANING INTO THE FULL-LENGTH MIRROR, and using a stick of stage makeup, Ty Cobb painted a jagged crimson line above his eyes of robin's egg blue. Meant to resemble a battle wound incurred at a moment of gridiron glory, it looked, alas, more like the fever chart for a failing business concern: cosmetology as practiced by a twenty-four-year-old, heterosexual Detroit Tiger. Next came the burnt cork. Black maintained a prominent place on the theatrical palette in 1911—Cobb himself had several times been called on stage to receive the semiofficial "Champion Batsman of the World" trophy from a minstrel dressed in full darkie regalia—but now he required just a smidgen, for the right side of his chin, a fake scuff to balance the bright greasepaint gash.

"My only problem," he said, leaning closer still to the looking glass and mussing his thinning strawberry blond curls, "is that I ain't got any football hair."

"Say, Ty, who taught you how to do that?" said one of Cobb's two dressing room drop-bys that evening, Harry Matthews, a squat, cigar-chomping ex-minor-league teammate who managed the Albany Babies of the South Atlantic League.

"Nobody," said Cobb. "I just had to learn how myself. All you got to do is make up natural, see?"

But it was hard to see through the smoke Matthews was emitting, and the fat old catcher turned aside and coughed on Cobb's makeup pots. "So you're a painter, too, eh?" he said finally, chuckling and choking. "Ain't I pretty!"

The other visitor to Cobb's cramped quarters that evening, the person who recorded this sparkling dialogue for posterity, was Howell Foreman, a cub reporter for the *Atlanta Constitution*. To the then new Atlanta Theater on that long-ago Saturday, Foreman had brought a large supply of mostly inane questions ("How do you think the acting of a game of football compares with the playing of a real game of baseball?")—but also, it would turn out, the admirable instinct, or maybe it was just the journalistic naïveté (he was only seventeen), to leave his notes largely unprocessed rather than shaping them into a conventional newspaper piece. The somewhat serpentine result, while not exactly a pleasure to read, provides something like raw security camera footage recording what it was like to be Tyrus Raymond Cobb as the Georgia Peach neared the height of his baseball prowess.

It was damn disconcerting. Cobb, who had no acting experience and who, despite being the son of a renowned orator, always felt ill at ease when required to speak in public, was nevertheless spending his early off-season touring the country, or at least a large swath east of the Mississippi, in *The College Widow*, a well-known comedy in three acts by the celebrated Hoosier humorist George Ade. He played Billy Bolton, a handsome halfback tempted to transfer from Bingham to Atwater College by the latter's coach's conniving blond girlfriend. Although Cobb surprised some people with his almost adequate acting skills, especially those who had expected him to hook-slide in from the wings, snarling, and spike his fellow thespians where they stood, and though tickets were selling briskly in venues North and South, the venture was turning out to be not as enjoyable as George M. Cohan, the famous "Yankee Doodle Boy," had assured him it would be over a long, boozy dinner one very complicated (and eventually bloody) night in Cleveland two years earlier. Touring, instead, was strenuous and stressful work performed at a season when he would rather have been tramping through the north Georgia hills with his hunting dogs and his friends—say, George Stallings, the former New York Highlanders manager, and Honus Wagner, the star shortstop for the Pittsburgh Pirates, companions on previous bird-shooting trips.

But Cobb had made a commitment and because he wanted desperately to avoid disappointing both his audience and his promoters, he devoted much psychic and physical energy to what is supposed to be "the art that conceals itself." From a seat near the footlights, you could see him sweat, and those who had spent as much as $1.50 for a ticket (about three times what it cost to watch him play the Cleveland Naps, the St. Louis Browns, or the Philadelphia Athletics) appreciated the sincere effort. In some of the same cities where, in the warmer months, he was booed and barraged with Moxie bottles for being such a danger to the aspirations of the beloved home team, audiences gave him a standing ovation at the end of each act and, as surely as if it was part of the script, shouted "Speech! Speech!" at the final curtain. But that only maximized Cobb's misery.

On the field, he was an extraordinary improviser, and off it, in small groups, a raconteur of the first rank (the veteran catcher Moe Berg, a New Yorker who graduated from Princeton and Columbia Law school and was a frequent houseguest of Cobb's in Augusta, would call him "an intellectual giant"). Yet at the podium—or beneath a proscenium, sans script— he lost his composure, and could sound like a typical tongue-tied jock. To avoid the nightmare of extemporaneous curtain-call oratory, Cobb would gesture extravagantly toward his heaving chest, the result of a 105-yard touchdown Billy Bolton had supposedly scored (offstage) in the play's climactic moments, and mime a hero all too willing but alas far too winded to speak. His lame joke always worked, yet the groundlings' groans of disappointment wore on him and made him envy the other ballplayer in the original cast, Joe Jackson of the Philadelphia A's, who, despite being a raw rookie, had realized during rehearsals that he was not exactly born to tread the boards and had put on his walking shoes just before the *Widow* had opened in Trenton.

Cobb, who was making $500 a week, or more than twice as much as the relatively large sum he got to play baseball, had kept going, though, and by dint of strenuous concentration and dumb luck avoided disaster— until the players reached Pittsburgh, and in the upper right balcony, at the moment of the star's opening night entrance, his twenty-two-month-old son, Ty Jr., had stood up and squealed "Daddy! Daddy!" The sea of twisting heads and waves of unexpected laughter had nearly capsized Cobb; Ade's lines tapered to a palpitating point in his cortex, then vanished. They came back as soon as the house settled, thank goodness, and the show went on, but of all the nerve-racking moments he had endured in five-plus years of major league baseball—and these included fistfights, strained tête-à-têtes with President William Howard Taft ("Greetings, Citizen Ty!"), "black hand" letters threatening assassination (Cobb's, not Taft's), an endless presentation of watches, trophies, medals, books (he was known as a constant reader), and funereal flower-wreaths, as well as, of course, the occasional arrest for assault and battery—none was worse than that momentary Steel City meltdown.

Ty Cobb didn't need this kind of aggravation. Getting invited to appear in cold-weather vaudeville was, after all, no particular honor. Ballplayers of every stripe had been dabbling in what George M. Cohan would have called "the show business" since the 1890s, when Adrian "Cap" Anson, the longtime Chicago White Stocking, then down on his luck, performed a depressing baseball-themed act with two of his grown daughters (he actually did slide into a base secured at center stage). In the months after the 1911 World Series (won by Connie Mack's Athletics over John McGraw's Giants in six games), while Cobb was appearing in *The College Widow*, Rube Marquard of the Giants was doing stand-up; the Pirates' Marty O'Toole had a part in a Wild West show; three A's ("Chief" Bender, Cy Morgan, and Jack Coombs) were appearing with the singing Pearl Sisters; Leonard "King" Cole of the Cubs, the inspiration for Ring Lardner's "Alibi Ike" stories, was making the rounds in Chicago doing something vaguely theatrical, and Herman "Germany" Schaefer, one of Cobb's former Tiger teammates and now a Washington Senator, was touring, with Cobb's apparent blessing, with a satirical recitation called "Why Does Tyrus Tire Us?" For his acting talents, Cobb was probably pulling down much more than any of them, but by exploiting his fame in that fashion he was aligning himself with a crew composed mostly of prodigals, mediocrities, has-beens, and clowns. (Perhaps all one needs to know about Germany Schaefer is that he was personally responsible for major league baseball's rule 7.08i, which forbids running the bases in reverse.)

Cobb in 1911 was still a young man wrestling with the question of what it meant to be this new thing called a celebrity—that is, when he was not down under the grandstand, postgame, wrestling with an umpire, teammate, or rival. If he was in fact the greatest player in the history of baseball, as no one less than Charles Comiskey, the president of the Chicago White Sox and one of the founding fathers of the modern game, had declared recently in a syndicated newspaper essay that was the talk of the sports world, then how did that status translate to his day-to-day existence? Cobb could not figure out whether, in real life, he should play the ultrasensitive Southern cavalier or the courtly, gregarious Georgia gent, and he wavered between the two roles his whole career. Yet coming off the 1911 campaign, he was fairly certain that the annual festival of postseason stunt casting was beneath his dignity.

Some people, some Sabermetricians, will tell you that 1911 was not the best of Cobb's 23½ seasons, and it's true that in such esoteric categories as "run production" and "batting average relative to the rest of the league," it demonstrably wasn't. But you needn't be a baseball nerd to know it was pretty wonderful. Cobb batted .420 that year, and set records for RBI (127), hits (248), runs (147), stolen bases (83), and longest hitting streak (40 games), all despite suffering for much of the summer from a hacking cough and stomach problems, which he thought might be typhoid but which were more likely nerves, and often playing against doctor's orders. The numbers, naturally, never tell the full story and in Cobb's case they fail to convey what an exciting player the haunted-looking, light-hitting rookie of 1905 had become: part Wee Willie Keller ("Hit 'em where they ain't"), part Freud, part Puck. Art history majors might also compare him to Caravaggio, the conflicted, creative firebrand of whom it was written in 1604, "he will swagger about . . . with a sword at his side, from one ball-court to the next, ever ready to engage in a fight or an argument, so that it is most awkward to get along with him." Cobb, though, never had to go looking for people to tussle with; they usually came (to speak like Cobb for a moment) a-calling.

In his prime Tyrus Raymond Cobb was a good-looking man—six feet tall and 190 pounds—who believed something fairly revolutionary for his time: that success in baseball went to the smart. He held the bat with a split-hands grip—unusual but not unique—that allowed him to make a last-second decision, to choke up and poke the ball over an infielder's head—or slide his top hand down and swing for the fences (which, in the deadball era, were roughly a million miles away). Employed over the course of nearly two dozen major league seasons, this technique allowed Cobb to achieve a lifetime batting average of .366, amazing in his day and still the highest ever. But it was his philosophy of the game, not the bat-grip he shared with Honus Wagner and a few others, that accounted for his greatness.

That philosophy could be pared down to two words: pay attention. "He didn't out-hit the opposition and he didn't outrun them," Cobb's longtime teammate and onetime tormentor "Wahoo" Sam Crawford said. "He out-thought them!" Cobb spent his days studying his baseball rivals and mentally cataloging their tendencies, strengths, and faults, both as players and human beings, since he felt he could exploit both to his professional advantage; many evenings, while his teammates hung out in the hotel lobby (the pastime within the pastime in those potted-palmy days) or hoisted beers, he would sit in his room making notes and sketching plays while listening to classical violinist Fritz Kreisler on the gramophone. His "personal batboy"—Cobb could be more than a bit of a diva—Jimmy Lanier, said, "Cobb would lay awake in bed engrossed in plots to out-smart opposing members of other American League clubs." "Some of my best ideas," Cobb himself said in a syndicated newspaper series that appeared in 1914, "have come to me at night just before I fall asleep, when, they say, great poems often come to their authors. I get up and write them down."

He was intrigued by the unpredictability of baseball, he often said, but it was perfecting ways to influence the proceedings and control the out-comes of various game situations that gave him the most satisfaction. He loved, for example, to find himself on third against the Highlanders (who were just starting to be known also as the Yankees in those days) because he knew that by dancing off the bag he could almost always draw a risky cross-diamond throw from their first baseman Hal Chase after a routine putout—and dash for home if the peg went awry. (It was pliable rivals like Chase that allowed Cobb to steal home 54 times in his career, another record that still stands.) Stepping into the box, Cobb liked to see a catcher staring at his feet to determine if he was thinking "pull" (feet spread wide apart) or "opposite field." When under such scrutiny, Cobb would often assume one kind of stance, then hop to another as the pitcher released the ball, a fake-out move that some old-timers considered dirty pool.

Nothing pleased Cobb more, though, than the way he was able to handle the future Hall of Famer Walter Johnson, ace of the Washington Senators, the hardest thrower in the American League. After he noticed how upset the good-hearted Big Train got when he beaned batters, Cobb stood in against him as he did against nobody else, hunching over the plate and sticking his head into the strike zone. He could have gotten killed; instead, very often, he got walked.

But the Peach's "pay attention" approach worked both ways. As much as he studied *you* he wanted you to think about *him*, so he could mess with your composure and your expectations, exploit your laziness or lack of focus, expose your particular and perhaps very personal fears. The hyperbolic sportswriters of the day credited Cobb with bringing psychology to a game previously packed with Bunyanesque bumpkins swinging rough-hewn clubs at saliva-sodden spheres—and hailed what he was doing as "scientific baseball."

Or at least some of them did, some of the time. Journalistic standards were different then, and wildly inconsistent. Scandalous or embarrassing off-the-field incidents might be overlooked or played down as a favor to one of the participants. That Cobb's mother had shot and killed his father a few days before Ty's major league debut, that the minor league player the Tigers wanted over Cobb, Clyde Engle, was hampered by gonorrhea, that Cobb missed time early in the 1906 season because he had what was then called a nervous breakdown—such things were obscured by euphemisms if they were written about at all. In other cases, though, controversies might be concocted or exaggerated to please the sports editor and the reading public. Quotes were frequently manufactured, or so polished you could see the writer's face in them; throw-pillow-worthy aphorisms and corny jokes, sometimes corny coon jokes, were credited to players who had never said such things, and almost everyone seems to have shrugged this off as just the way things worked.

On a slow news day, some of the same scribes who usually showered Cobb with hosannas might depict him as a maniacal base runner who preyed upon innocent infielders and hapless catchers with his feloniously filed spikes. His own hometown paper, the *Detroit Free Press*, once said that he was "dangerous to the point of dementia" (which is exactly what he wanted his opponents to think), and at least one editorial page writer opined in all seriousness that by tearing around the base paths in such an aggressive manner he was exacting revenge for General William Tecumseh Sherman's bloody march through his beloved home state fifty-something years before.

The relationship between Cobb and cleated shoes, is, like most things Cobbian, complicated, and will be explored in greater depth, but let us say for now that Cobb denied the charges and many of his coevals backed him staunchly, saying he was merely playing the game the way it was meant to be played—and, by the way, so were they when they squashed their own spikes into his in-coming shins, ankles, and calves. "Cobb is a game square fellow who never cut a man with his spikes intentionally in his life, and anyone who gets by with his spikes knows it," said Germany Schaefer, whose testimony must however be weighed against the fact that Cobb once gave him a $1,500 Chalmers sedan just because Schaefer, affecting ignorance of how things worked in the automobile age, asked Cobb if he might have it, since Cobb had two.

But whatever you called Cobb—sadist or scientist, cracker or Peach— he was unquestionably the biggest draw in baseball, the only player worth $100,000 to his team each season at the gate, in the opinion of the esteemed weekly *Sporting Life* (though he was never paid nearly that much). If one steers wide of the best-known biographies—Charles C. Alexander's 1984 *Ty Cobb* and Al Stump's 1994 *Cobb*, both of which tend to depict their subject as a crabbed, sad soul—and instead homes in on letters by and to Cobb, the testimony of eyewitnesses, and contemporary newspaper accounts, the reasons for his popularity quickly become obvious. "The greatness of Ty Cobb was something that had to be seen," said George Sisler, a Hall of Famer who played from 1915 to 1930. "And to see him was to remember him forever."

Even if we confine ourselves to 1911, a year so productive that you'd think it would contain a minimum of irregularities and distractions, colorful and controversial episodes abound.

Consider an incident that occurred at Detroit's Bennett Park on May 12 of that year. The Yankees were in town on that unseasonably warm Friday. In the seventh inning, with his team down 5–3, Cobb came to bat with runners on first and second—and hit a line drive off "Slim"

Caldwell that smacked against the wall of the left field bleachers for an opposite field double. (Cobb, though naturally right-handed, always batted left.) The man on second, Tex Covington, scored easily, but Donie Bush, the trailing runner, barely slid in safely under catcher Ed Sweeney's tag. Not surprisingly, given the closeness of the play, Sweeney turned to the umpire and, said the *New York Times*, "began a protest" while "all the members of the infield flocked to the plate to help."

In other words, in the heat of the moment the Yankees forgot that Cobb was standing on second.

> *Under such circumstances it is the custom of the base runner to sit down on the sack and wait for something to turn up* [*the* Times *continued*]. *But Cobb, observing that third base was unguarded, trotted amiably up there. No one saw him. So he tiptoed gingerly along toward the group at the plate. He did not come under the observation of the public until he was about ten feet from the goal all base runners seek, where for a few seconds he stood practically still, peering into the cluster of disputants before him, looking for an opening to slide through. He found one and skated across the plate with the winning run under the noses of almost the entire New York team, Sweeney touching him with the ball when it was too late.*

It has been said by many that Cobb lacked a sense of humor, and he himself said, "I have never been able to see the humorous side of baseball," but on the base paths he showed a brand of physical wit that sometimes made people laugh out loud. His Chaplinesque seventh-inning score that day in Detroit would put the Tigers ahead for good. It was the fourteenth time he had stolen home plate in his still young career, and the second time he'd done it that month. "When I am on the bases," he said, "I try continually to get as close to the home plate as possible, overlooking no opportunity." Mere inches meant a lot to him. As he waited on base for a teammate to take his licks, he would constantly kick the loose sacks of those days in the direction in which he was headed, trying to gain every possible advantage. Two months later, on July 12 in Detroit, Cobb would steal second, third, and home on *three consecutive pitches* by the A's Harry Krause. "He was like compressed steam," said his fellow American

League star Eddie Collins, later a manager and team executive. "Cobb was always exerting pressure, always searching out a weak spot here and there to display his seemingly inexhaustible and tireless energy." Casey Stengel said that Cobb was the only player he ever saw who could score from third on a weak infield pop-up—he would tag up, then break for home as soon as the fielder began to lob the ball back to the pitcher. "His constant chiding, deriding, tantalizing demeanor when on a base has done more to upset the morale of the opposing infield than the mere taking of forbidden sacks, costly as those usually prove to be," wrote Sverre O. Braathen, in his 1928 book, *Ty Cobb: The Idol of Baseball Fandom.* General admission—50 cents—was still a half day's pay for many Americans, and yet surely here was a man who was worth four bits to ogle.

If the first half of Cobb's life were a novel it would be a ripping page-turner, at times almost too heavy on incident. Not long after the Yankees left town that spring on May 24, he was sitting in someone else's car in Detroit's Cadillac Square when he noticed, about 100 yards away, in front of the Pontchartrain Hotel, a man cranking up the black Chalmers 30 sedan that he had won for leading the league with a .383 batting average in 1910. As the thief, a nineteen-year-old named John Miles, hopped in and took off, Cobb pursued him on foot, caught the car, vaulted into the topless tonneau, and, according to the *Atlanta Constitution*, turned off the engine and "hurled the youth into the street." The next morning, after hearing out Miles's sniffling bride of eight months, Cobb told a judge that "things had not been breaking well for the couple" and added, "I would be in favor of letting him go"—but the magistrate gaveled down his mercy plea, and ordered Miles to be arraigned.

Cobb—as surprising as it may sound to those who base their opinion of him on the ever-darkening myths that float through today's popular culture—was not always the crankiest person in the room. The current-day conventional wisdom about him as encapsulated in the line mouthed by the Shoeless Joe Jackson character in the movie *Field of Dreams*—"No one liked that son of a bitch"—simply isn't accurate. Many (including Jackson, Tris Speaker, Walter Johnson, and other greats of Cobb's era) liked him, a lot. "He had his enemies, sure," Lou Brissie, a major league pitcher in the late 1940s and early 1950s, and an acquaintance of Cobb's, told me over lunch one day at a restaurant in downtown Augusta. "But with a man like Cobb, for most other guys on the team, it's not a matter of like or dislike. He's up there on another level, in terms of who he is in the world and how he thinks of himself and how he's treated, the way Ruth and DiMaggio and Ted Williams later were. You might play ball with those guys every day, you might travel with them all over the country for years, but somehow you don't think in terms of them being your *friend*. You didn't think about how much you *liked* each other."

Charles Alexander in his book tells us that Cobb usually got a warm welcome from opposing players, even if they were trying to hide their feelings of intimidation. "When Cobb came on the field," he writes, "players on the other team would call out 'Hello, Peach! How are you, Peach!' and otherwise behave affably." Cobb sometimes engaged with them, but on other occasions appeared aloof, as part of his nonstop psychological warfare. ("Baseball is 50 percent brain, 25 percent eye and 25 percent arm and leg," Cobb said in 1912.) As a consequence of such behavior, some of his colleagues considered him a jerk. Heywood Broun, writing in the *New York Morning Telegraph*, said Cobb was "perhaps . . . the least popular player who ever lived" because "pistareen ball players whom he has shown up dislike him, third basemen with bum arms, second basemen with tender skins, catchers who cannot throw out a talented slider—all despise Cobb. And their attitude has infected the stands."

And yet to many average fans, who did not feel competitive with him or threatened (or humbled) by his talent, he was simply an idol. They may have booed or feared him for the havoc he could wreak on their team. But they also sent him bushels of letters asking how they or their children might break into the game, or posed questions about hitting, fielding, or base running, And he almost always wrote back (eventually) in his trademark green ink with advice, and sometimes a pamphlet full of pointers he'd worked up for a sporting goods company, and sometimes a picture. Occasionally he would apologize for sending two pictures when the writer had only requested one, and he never failed to mention how flattered he was when someone asked for his autograph. The recipients of these letters would treasure them for the rest of their lives, and pass them along as

family heirlooms. Ty Cobb was a deep pool of brackish water. The son of
a bitch had many partisans.

That Cobb fans would come to number in the millions was made certain
by an accident of timing. He wasn't just the most super of the sports
superstars; he was also, chronologically, the first. Cobb became the biggest
draw in baseball—surpassing Honus Wagner, Tris Speaker, Nap Lajoie,
and Christy Mathewson—just as the game was becoming, as Steven A.
Riess tells us in his important book *Touching Base: Professional Baseball
and American Culture in the Progressive Era*, "an integral part of American
life and not just a frivolous misuse of valuable time better spent in more
gainful pursuits." According to the myths fashioned by the magnates who
owned the teams in the early 1900s, passed along by the journalists eager
to justify their existence and slurped up by an increasingly sports-mad
public, baseball built character by stressing team play, fast thinking, and
acceptance of authority in the form of the fallible but ultimate ump. It
also supposedly encouraged civic pride, discouraged juvenile delinquency,
and helped the immigrants of the Great Wave to assimilate. In the popular
imagination, or at least in the mind of newspaper editorial writers, it func-
tioned, somehow, as a safeguard of democracy. In 1907 the *New York Evening World*'s Allen Sangree wrote, "As a tonic, an exercise, a safety valve,
baseball is second only to death as a leveler. So long as it remains our national game, America will abide no monarchy, and anarchy will be slow."

To be widely recognized as the greatest living master of this still new,
nation-saving art put the young outfielder in a position of power without
precedent. No wonder President William Howard Taft went in for the
man-hug whenever he shook Cobb's hand, and tried desperately to bond
with the ballplayer over their connection to Augusta, where the bumbling one-term Republican sometimes summered. In the rapidly evolving
popular culture, a radical possibility had come to pass: that under certain
circumstances, an athlete could eclipse a sitting U.S. president. Indeed,
when Cobb started touring with *The College Widow* some sportswriters
speculated that what we were seeing was merely the second chapter in the
life of a Renaissance Man, and that Cobb would conquer the stage the
way he had conquered baseball and move on from there to God knows

what—maybe medicine, the field his father had wanted him to pursue, or driving in auto races, which was something he frequently talked about doing—before finally deciding to settle down and perhaps even *be* president. Baseball was the bee's knees, people felt, but baseball couldn't hold him. It was to check out the rumor that he might soon "desert the dusty diamond to join the high-brow contingent and tread the Thespian boards" that the *Atlanta Constitution* sent Howell Foreman to interview Cobb backstage on a Saturday night in November of 1911.

Cobb found Foreman sitting in his dressing room when he rushed back during the first act to make a quick costume change—and he was too polite to turn the eager young reporter away. "He greeted me," Foreman wrote, "with a broad beaming smile showing that he was trying to say 'Glad to see you.'" (Note the "trying.") When Harry Matthews, the big Albany (Georgia) Baby, appeared moments later, Cobb shook his hand and told him to have a seat, then, Foreman wrote, "he hooked on a 'ready-made' white bow, and ran out of the door. He went on stage, had a few dances with 'the widow' at the faculty reception, and in five minutes came back in the room." Surveying the scene warily, Cobb said, "Well, I won't have anything to do for a while yet . . ." and indicated he could chat some. But when the second act started and his visitors stayed put, he was forced to change costumes in tight quarters and endure Foreman's Chinese water drip of questions while keeping an ear cocked for his cues.

"How do you like this acting business, Mr. Cobb?"

"Oh, it's very good. I just started this show in September, you see, so I haven't had so much experience. [But] I never get nervous on stage; I didn't even have the stage fright the first night. Of course, I felt a little funny when the time came for to hug the widow and me, a married man, but I got away with it. I like the soft stuff, the loving business, better than the rough stuff. I've had more experience, you know."

Missing Cobb's amusing self-reference, Foreman plunged ahead: "Mr. Cobb, do you ever get this horsehide-pigskin-buckskin business mixed up?"

"Nope. I manage to get along all right, I think; but of course, that's for you fellows in the audience to judge. I can't tell whether I'm getting 'em mixed up or not."

"How does Mrs. T. R. Cobb like this love-making part of the play?"

"Oh, she doesn't like this acting business much anyway. I don't guess she likes me making love to others even on the stage."

Once or twice, no doubt because of the conditions in his dressing room, Cobb missed a cue, Foreman wrote, and "the hoarse voice of the stage manager bellowed forth from behind the scenes." Then Cobb, with a whispered "Excuse me," would dash out to dance with a roomful of adoring coeds, or converse with his stern stage dad, or perform a love scene with the woman who played the temptress. At one point in the third act, after again begging his guests' indulgence, Cobb left to jog in the corridor, so as to appear breathless from making his crucial touchdown. When he returned, Foreman was finally ready to broach the subject of whether Cobb was going to quit the green pastures of baseball for—one can imagine him making a sweeping gesture to indicate the smoky, windowless room full of mirrors and face paint and tedious visitors—"all *this*."

Cobb shook his head. "Give me baseball every time," he said. "This acting stuff is just the same thing over and over again. There's no excitement to it. But in baseball, ah! That's different. Baseball always excites me. Every day there's something new to learn, something else to see. You never can tell just what's going to happen. I can't to save my neck sit still in a ball game. Give me baseball every time."

Two decades later, retired and with no formal connections to the game, he had changed his mind. In a radio interview with an old friend, the sportswriter Grantland Rice, that was recorded in the early 1930s, he spoke of being thoroughly tired of baseball. "It's a great game," he said, "but I feel like a prisoner who's been set free."

"How do you mean, Ty?" Rice asked.

"Baseball to me was more work than play—in fact it was *all* work," Cobb said. (He had a surprisingly high-pitched voice, and in his north Georgia accent "all" comes out sounding like a cross between "awe" and "oil.") "I was lucky enough to lead the league [in batting] when I was twenty years old, and after that I wanted to lead it *every* year. I never thought I was any genius, so I gave my life to the game for twenty-five years. It was a constant battle, and it wore me out."

That he was far from being a natural talent, like, say, Shoeless Joe Jackson, and thus had to work diligently at being successful is a constant theme over the years in Cobb's public discourse. To maintain what he considered his ideal weight of 190, he ate only two meals a day, which meant he was hungry most of the time. To protect his surprisingly finicky eyes, he avoided coffee, milk, chewing gum, and movies. The off-season was no vacation for Cobb. On winter days he wore heavy boots and tried to stand and walk as much as possible; when spring training started he put lead weights in his shoes—all in the name of building up his legs for the championship season. Many of his contemporaries agreed that he was never very fast on his feet, just always in shape and brilliantly opportunistic.

The strategizing alone was exhausting, "I must have been in about 30,000 plays and I tried to think about every play and how it should be made," he told Rice. "I believed in putting up a mental hazard for the other fellow. Every play was a problem of some sort. That's what I mean by the strain and grind of twenty-five years."

In another radio interview done a few years later, he sounded even more burnt out (and even less like a prisoner "set free"). The unidentified questioner starts off by referring to Cobb as "the roughest and toughest" ballplayer ever, then rambles on for what feels like minutes before finally arriving at a surpassingly dumb question, something about how he and Cobb both live in Augusta, isn't that right, Mr. Cobb? The first time I listened to this old recording, I wondered if Cobb would brush off the inane icebreaker and go right back to the "roughest and toughest" reference. As much as he liked his opponents to believe that he was half crazy and capable of almost anything on the base paths, he was also, I knew, terribly sensitive about being described as an uncouth, violent person, and he might punch you in the nose if you even hinted at such a thing.

Cobb didn't let me down. His first words back to the radio guy, who had just asked him where he lived, were, "Now, I appreciate what you say about me being the roughest and toughest . . ."

I thought: Okay, here we go! It sounded like Cobb was fixing to set this poor man straight, to explain to him and to the listening audience that to call him the roughest and the toughest is like describing Hamlet as "upset"—that is, to oversimplify matters to the point of misrepresentation.

But then he changed direction. Why, I of course can't begin to say. Maybe he realized he had arrived very quickly at a crossroads in the conversation. Either he poured his whole life into this microphone by way of explanation, and tried to convey the nuances and subtleties of what it meant to be the Georgia Peach—or he took an easier path through what was essentially just another stupid interview (and since the advent of radio, fairly late in his career, the questions had gotten increasingly similar and stupider). In any case, he stopped objecting before he really got started, and went with the flow.

"The Good Book says, 'Turn the other cheek,'" he said, trying to sound chipper, "but you know I never believed in that much. It doesn't prove out. I happen to have believed more in 'An eye for an eye' when I played baseball," he said with a forced chuckle.

He was playing a role, just like he'd played Billy Bolton. I could forgive him for this. The truth was complicated and he was a very tired man. Truth wasn't necessarily what people really wanted, anyway. Cobb didn't live long enough to see *The Man Who Shot Liberty Valance*, but he understood the most famous line from it: "When the legend becomes fact, print the legend."

Cobb never ran for president or became an actor or anything more than an occasional race car driver. His post-baseball life went, in most ways, pretty much the way you might expect. When the Hall of Fame came along in 1936, he was the first man selected for enshrinement. He did a lot of charity work, such as starting an education fund for Georgia boys and girls who wouldn't otherwise be able to afford college and founding a hospital in his hometown of Royston. And he became a go-to guy for quotes when the game of baseball changed in some way. In 1952, when the Texas League was finally getting around to realizing that Jackie Robinson had broken the color barrier five years earlier, and let in a black player, he told a reporter who asked him about it that the integration of mainstream baseball had been long overdue. "I see no reason in the world why we shouldn't compete with colored athletes as long as they conduct themselves with politeness and gentility. Let me say also that no white man has the right to be less of a gentleman than a colored man. In my book, that goes not just for baseball but for all walks of life."

He lived out his life, in other words, doing what retired baseball stars do: accepting awards and acting like the wise and sometimes cranky old oracle. But what set Cobb apart from so many others was that myth of roughness and toughness. It didn't just endure, it picked up momentum at a certain point after his death and started to grow and change. However much truth it did or didn't contain at any point in its evolution, it took on a life of its own. Ty Cobb was replaced—overshadowed might be a better word—by "Ty Cobb," a fully posable figure. Consider the issue of race. In making his statement about the Texas League, and in praising the play of Willie Mays and Roy Campanella on other occasions (the Dodger catcher, he said, was "the player who reminds me the most of myself"), Cobb didn't just "clout a verbal home run for the Negro player," as the Associated Press said in 1952; he set himself apart from fellow Southerners like Dixie Walker and Enos Slaughter, who had nothing good to say about the black men in their game, and openly resented their arrival. Two of the many men with whom he engaged in physical combat were black, it is true, but in his lifetime Cobb was not known as a bigot (few people not dressed in bedsheets were). He had black friends and fans, and on at least one occasion threw out the first ball of the season at a Negro League park.

And yet . . .

Try this: Go into a bar that has at least one working television. Sidle up to some beer sipper and, after a decent interval, say, "Ty Cobb, right?" The most common response, I've found in my several years of research, will be, "Oh my God! Tell me about it," delivered with the obligatory eye roll. The second most common response is "Worst racist ever"—said with varying degrees of disapproval.

It is hardly just barflies who hold this opinion. "The mere sight of black people so filled Cobb with rage," wrote Timothy M. Gay in his biography of Tris Speaker, "that on several occasions he brutally pistol-whipped African American men whose only offense was to share a sidewalk with him." In the 1994 Ken Burns series *Baseball*, the respected writer and historian Dan Okrent called Cobb "an embarrassment to the game" because of his racism, and Burns treats Cobb as a dangerous miscreant: the anti–Jackie Robinson. Indeed, to the authors of the 2004 book *American Monsters*, Cobb fits squarely alongside Charles Manson, John Wilkes Booth, and the owners of the Triangle Shirtwaist Factory (considered responsible for the deaths of 146 garment workers in 1911) in the pantheon of America's most despicable villains.

American Monsters is not by any definition an important or influential work, yet it accurately reflects the conventional wisdom. More than fifty years after Cobb's death, it is not difficult to find people who, though they might describe themselves as casual baseball fans, have never heard of him. Of those who recognize the name, though, most think of Cobb as a singularly horrible man, a murderer, even, of one or more black people.

"Are you going to tell the story of how he stabbed the black waiter in Cleveland?" someone asked me about halfway through my research on this book.

The answer is, Yes, well, sort of.

The book you hold in your hands is not meant to change your mind about "Ty Cobb." For the most part, it is not about him; sorry.

This is, rather, the story of Ty Cobb.

— CHAPTER TWO —

EVERY STORY MUST BEGIN SOMEPLACE, and the story of the actual Ty Cobb began in Banks County, Georgia, on December 18, 1886. Many people assume (or assert) that Cobb grew up in a shotgun shack on the wrong side of the tracks from Dogpatch; that is hardly the case. He was born in a nicely appointed thirteen-room house—built low to minimize storm damage—on the property of his maternal grandfather, a fairly well-to-do former Confederate Army captain named Caleb Chitwood. Cobb's parents lived elsewhere in the county but "I was taken there to be born," he said, possibly because the unoccupied house, set apart from nearby towns, provided privacy and peace. Local people, for a reason now lost to history, called the area "the Narrows." It looks today like any ill-defined, nondescript portion of semi-woods along the side of a highway. I tramped around in the brush there for about an hour one fine spring morning and could find no evidence of the Chitwood house, though there is a modest sign off what is now the Ty Cobb Parkway telling the traveler that he is in the vicinity of the ballplayer's birthplace.

Cobb's mother was the very pretty Amanda Chitwood, his father a tall, thin, North Carolinian named William Herschel Cobb, who had first met her when he was a farmhand, working his way through school, on the Chitwood plantation. In some books and articles, Amanda is said to have been twelve years old when she married the twenty-two-year-old W.H., but those tend to be the same sources that try to put a sordid, Southern Gothic spin on the tale. Their marriage license clearly shows that she was fifteen when they wed in February of 1886, a very young but still respectable age for a bride back then, even in the North. What is possibly true is the rumor that Amanda had for a while been one of her husband's students (he also taught school on his way to getting a bachelor's degree). That certainly would have raised a few eyebrows, but then so, in nineteenth-century rural Georgia, would the very act of providing a daughter with a formal education, something only "progressive" parents like the Chitwoods did.

Tyrus Raymond Cobb was the baby's full name. Where his parents got "Raymond" from is anyone's guess. "Tyrus," though it doesn't sound so strange now (thanks largely to Tyrus Raymond Cobb), may well have been a name of their own invention. (It was only after he started hitting above .300 that people stopped calling him "Cyrus.") W.H. apparently fashioned it from "Tyre," the ancient Phoenician city that in 332 BC gallantly held out for seven months before finally falling to Alexander the Great. The Narrows may have put the history maven in mind of that episode for it was there, twenty-two years earlier, that a small but passionate militia had dealt General Sherman an annoying but ultimately meaningless setback on his march to the sea. Though there are significant gaps in our knowledge of "Professor" Cobb, as the locals called him, he clearly placed pluck among the virtues. He would name his other son after John Paul Jones and his daughter after Florence Nightingale.

The window when Tyrus Raymond could honestly say "I have not yet begun to fight" was small indeed. By the time the family had moved to Royston, Georgia (pop. 550), in about 1895—after stops in Lavonia, Harmony Grove, and Carnesville, as W. H. Cobb climbed the ladder of pedagogical success, progressing from general instructor to high school principal in a handful of semesters—the skinny lad who always seemed to be tossing up stones and whacking them with sticks had become known as a bare-knuckled battler. "You saw it the minute you set eyes on him," said a childhood friend of young Ty's hair-trigger temperament. For decades afterward, Cobb's former neighbors, today his neighbors once again at Royston's Rose Hill Cemetery, loved to tell visiting journalists how they had fought with him at various locations around town, and with varying degrees of seriousness. In 1950, Cobb's friend Joe Cunningham recalled that "we had no sooner met than we were having playful scraps in the office of the local newspaper, *The Sentinel*—and a destructive time we had, too, doing far more damage to the defenseless printers' tables than we did to ourselves. The door would be locked from the inside, leaving those on the outside in fear and trembling lest we kill each other."

A local legend had it that Cobb once beat up a fat classmate whose mistake had caused their team to lose a spelling bee to the fifth-grade girls. In a testy little town such as fin de siècle Royston, where, according to the *History of Franklin County Georgia*, "peace officers were selected for brawn as it was quite common to have them challenged by community 'bullies' for wrestling, etc.," the townsfolk thought that story reflected well on young Tyrus. To them, it meant that he combined a classically Southern penchant for swift justice with the admirable if somewhat anal Yankee habit of spelling words exactly the same way every time. It may even have been true. Cobb in later years denied the most outrageous yarns about his youth, like the one advanced by the noted dressing room interloper Howell Foreman in the March 1912 issue of *Baseball Digest*, saying that Ty as a child "used to vent his spleen on ebony 'pickaninnies' when he was too thoughtful of the Caucasian race to pummel the countenance of a white boy." ("Just made up," the elderly Cobb would say about such yarns. "Just. Made. Up.") But even Cobb admitted in one interview to having "a vying nature." And in a seemingly heartfelt memoir, serialized in newspapers in 1914, he allowed that he had "a terrible temper in my younger days, and it got me into a lot of trouble."

There is no denying that Cobb was a born battler, just as some people seem to come into the world as jokesters, wimps, loners, or bores. This quality was striking to those who knew and liked him. As his friend Grantland Rice wrote in his memoir *The Tumult and the Shouting*, "When I first met Cobb I found him to be an extremely peculiar soul, brooding and bubbling with violence, combative all the way, a streak, incidentally, he never lost."

It wasn't easy to get a reputation as a fighter in a time when people used to fight so damn much. (By "fight" I mean swing and poke their fists at each other, like you see in the movies. By "people" I mean men.) Violence was the lingua franca of the day. The president of the United States from 1901 until 1909, Theodore Roosevelt, "invited new acquaintances to wrestle and box with him, or to fight with wooden swords" wrote the journalist

Nicholas Lemann. "His rhetorical flourishes often included invocations of violence, including jocular threats to have his opponents killed."

Reliable statistics about spontaneous violence are impossible to come by; prior to Nat Fleischer's *Ring Record Book*, first published in 1942, no one bothered to keep official records of even formal matches. Still, the anecdotal evidence—references in newspapers and popular literature— suggest that fisticuffs were once an everyday way to settle disputes or assert one's alpha male status. (In Ring Lardner's classic epistolary novel of 1916, *You Know Me Al*, the narrator, a pitcher named Jack Keefe, continu- ally threatens to bust various people in the jaw.) Fights were apt to erupt at any time or anywhere human beings interacted. Boys were supposed to start fighting young, the way Cobb did. J. Adams Puffer, a kind of Edwardian Age Dr. Benjamin Spock, maintained that to stay morally and mentally fit, male children should fight once a day on average, and more often during their first week at a new school. The "sensitive, retiring" lad "needs encouragement to stand his ground and fight," Puffer wrote in his 1912 opus *The Boy and His Gang*, and though it may sound shocking today, in a world where a kid can fail a pre-K interview if he gently shoves a Styrofoam shape in the general direction of a fellow applicant, the self-appointed expert was backed up on this point by the founding pres- ident of the American Psychological Association, G. Stanley Hall, who believed that when it came to young boys "better even an occasional nose dented by a fist . . . than stagnation, general cynicism and censoriousness, bodily and psychic cowardice."

Fights that didn't stem from boys being boys could often be traced to men being drunk. Early-twentieth-century boozing is, like fighting, hard to quantify, but numerous studies show that alcohol-related death and violence were much more frequent then. In big cities and country towns, barroom brawls occurred as frequently as barrooms, owing not just to the mixture of aged whiskey and eternal questions such as "John L. Sul- livan or Paddy Ryan?" but to the absence, generally speaking, of women, who when they finally started drinking socially in great numbers during Prohibition proved far superior as a civilizing force to a shillelagh placed prominently by the cash register or an elegantly lettered enamel sign say- ing "Take It Outside." But before ladies, mayhem prevailed. In the early

1900s, several "black eye repair shops" operated along New York's Bowery, their proprietors offering to gingerly apply pancake makeup for a fee of 5 or 10 cents to facial discolorations incurred at the many nearby taverns.

Besides spontaneous tiffs, the South had semi-ritualized ones, with two aggrieved parties agreeing to retire presently to an open patch of level ground, often referred to as "over yonder," before going at it like rutting gazelles. Getting into a fight—or a duel—down in Dixie was as simple as flipping a switch, or, more precisely, pulling a nose, for under the elaborate gentleman's code then prevailing, that was the way a ticked-off fellow formally challenged a foe. "The nose was the part of the face that preceded a man as he moved in the world," Kenneth S. Greenberg explains in his book *Honor and Slavery*. "It was the most prominent physical projection of a man's character, and it was always exposed to the gaze of others. . . . One of the greatest insults for a man of honor, then, was to have his nose pulled or tweaked."

Ty Cobb's maternal great-grandfather Thomas Anderson Mize possessed quite the prominent proboscis yet he was by reputation rather less a fighter than a prototypical promoter of fights, the Don King of his day. When tempers and nostrils flared around his hometown of Flintsville, Georgia, in the mid-nineteenth century, Mize provided the space where matters could be settled—a nicely cleared quarter acre out behind his dry goods store. Men, women, and children would gather there to watch the fisticuffs, creating a kind of human ring, and when it was over find themselves feeling good about life, the spectacle being, according to a sketch of Flintsville mores that ran in the *Atlanta Constitution* in 1921, reliably cathartic. "When anyone got angry, a circle would be made, and the contestants would roll up their sleeves and fight with bare fists," the article said. "After the fight they would shake hands and be friends. There were no grudges in those days between friends and neighbors." Mize believed the communal afterglow put gawkers in the mood to shop, and as fighters toed the line in the red Georgia soil and squared off in anticipation of the referee's nod, he assumed his stance behind the strongbox. If matters didn't get settled so cleanly every time—if, say, the ill will caused by an ambiguous finish only festered and spread—he could, it was said, get an ugly crowd to calm down by old-fashioned physical intimidation. From the single photograph of him that survives, it is hard to gauge his physical stature and yet as the great-grandpa of arguably the greatest hitter of all time, and a somewhat more distant ancestor of Johnny "Big Cat" Mize, another Hall of Famer who batted .312 over 15 seasons for the Cardinals, Giants, and Yankees, Tom Mize was probably strapping for a storekeep.

Cobb's mother—though she would be tried for first-degree voluntary manslaughter one day—was never known to be a quarrelsome or aggressive person. So we must ask: was it from his daddy, William Herschel Cobb—born on February 23, 1863, a time when the smell of gunpowder and rotting corpses fouled the Southern air—that Ty got his fighting ways?

That, too, does not seem likely.

In most books and biographical sketches of his famous son, W. H. Cobb makes a cameo appearance as the stern old-fashioned nineteenth-century dad, utterly stock in his celluloid-collar stiffness. *That* W. H. Cobb surely would have been fanning the flame of Ty's pugnaciousness, and showing him how to stick and move and keep his elbow in when he threw the left hook. *Son, I just heard the fifth-grade girls won the spelling bee—someone is going DOWN!* But that W. H. Cobb never existed. The real Professor was something very different. From his speeches and writings and the testimony of his contemporaries—resources that have never been examined in much depth before, perhaps because they lead to inconvenient truths—we can see the outlines of what looks like a tall, dark, handsome humanist, or at the very least a well-turned-out, physically imposing man out of sync with the fighting spirit of his times. In the Cobb household, the mother, Amanda, was the disciplinarian. "I'd always heard that she carried around a sapling switch," Ty's grandson Herschel Cobb told me, "and used it on the children whenever she felt it was needed." W.H. was a more typical twentieth-century parent. "He had," said Joe Cunningham, his student for six years, "a very cosmopolitan mind." The only letter of W.H. to Ty that survives is sweetly affectionate, and obviously concerned about his elder son's quick-tempered ways. "Be good and dutiful," W.H. wrote in early 1902, when his fifteen-year-old boy was visiting his beloved "Grandpa Johnny" Cobb in North Carolina, and the Professor was looking out on a January snowfall from his writing desk ("It is two inches, I reckon. . . . Hardly a sound has been heard today. It is six o'clock."), and missing him so. "Conquer your anger and wild passions that would degrade your dignity and belittle your manhood. Cherish all the good that springs up in you. Be under the perpetual guidance of the better angel of your nature. Starve out and drive out the demon that lurks in all human blood and [is] ready and anxious and restless to arise and reign. Be good."

The paternal side of Ty Cobb's family tree can be traced ultimately to Ireland, but it has deep roots in America, and many tangled branches. One section, known within the clan as "the Georgia Cobbs," produced Howell Cobb, speaker of the U.S. House of Representatives, secretary of the treasury under James Buchanan, and governor of his state, as well as his younger brother Thomas Reade Rootes Cobb, a Confederate major general. But William Herschel Cobb descended directly from a different and fairly distant line, which ran back into the hills of North Carolina. His people were more iconoclastic than their fancy Georgia kin, especially regarding the Peculiar Institution. W.H's grandfather, William Alfred Cobb, was a Methodist minister who tested the patience of his parishioners by preaching to Indians and whites alike, then pushed the congregation around the bend by preaching against slavery. In 1848 he and his family were run out of Haywood County for their abolitionist beliefs; they resettled in Union County, a more mountainous region where slaves, being less vital to the economy, were not such a hot-button issue.

The one child of William A. Cobb whom we know much about, John Franklin Cobb—Ty's beloved "Grandpa Johnny"—was an antislavery Republican who joined Robert E. Lee's army when his state seceded, but failed to consistently report for duty. He seems to have exuded a palpable air of intelligence, a certain oracular presence which conveyed to his Cherokee County neighbors that he was a man of principle, a conscientious objector rather than a common deserter. Indeed by his middle years John had become known as "Squire Cobb," for his service as an all-purpose sage and adjudicator of local disputes. Although not an educated man, he strongly believed in book-learning and made sure all four of his sons and both of his daughters went to college, at least for a while, an amazing feat of nineteenth-century parenting.

His firstborn, Ty's father, W.H., got the furthest in school, taking a

BA in liberal arts in 1892 from North Georgia Agricultural College in Dahlonega, the first coeducational college in the state. Although he was already a married man with three children and a full-time teaching job, W.H. graduated first in his class. In an unpublished family memoir Ty's Aunt Norah remembered that as her older brother W.H. received his diploma, she felt "her mother's tears splash upon her hand" and saw her father "run his finger around his collar to give the lump in his throat more room to dissolve." Amanda, wearing "white satin with filmy lace like moonbeams around her neck," waited stage right to present her husband (whom she would shoot and kill one day) with a bouquet of budded roses. Six-year-old Ty, she said, slept through the ceremony.

Ty Cobb's father was ambitious in the modern way: eager to better himself through education and willing to relocate. He was also religious in the modern way, which is to say not terribly (Royston in general was not known as a particularly pious place), although, seeming unable to turn down any job involving blackboards and desks, he did serve as super-intendent of the Baptist Sunday School. Like many in the postwar gen-eration who took part in the great migration from family farm to city or town, he felt . . . well, a bit disoriented, no doubt, but also liberated from eons of ignorance. Said Cunningham: "He lived before his time." W.H. had no interest in singing the same old hymns, and making the same old mistakes, until he expired in the bed where he'd been delivered. He was especially outspoken about race. "History teaches that three systems of controlling the people have been tried: slavery, serfdom and education," he said before a meeting of the Georgia Agricultural Society in 1901, "and that the first two have been dismal failures." Like his father, he saw education as the key to individual and societal progress, and disdained Jim Crow brutality. He once turned up in a local hardware store where a small mob had gathered to discuss the lynching of a Negro then in the town jail. Reminding them that they lived in a country of laws, and that he would personally make sure they answered to those laws if they con-tinued with their plotting, he sent his neighbors home grumbling. In the same speech he made to the state's most prominent farmers in '01, W.H. said, "As a way of teaching people to control themselves, schooling is the greatest political discovery of the ages. . . . The slate and pencil are more efficient implements of true weal than the hangman's knot and the police-man's club."

When W.H. spoke like this—which is to say a bit like Atticus Finch from *To Kill a Mockingbird*—few people in Franklin County, Georgia, jumped to their feet and shouted, "You're damn tootin'!" Still, his ideal-ism and personal magnetism led him to believe for a while that he might have a future in politics. "All my efforts shall be exerted toward harmony among our people," he said when he announced his intention of running as a Democrat for a seat in the State Senate in late 1899. If that was code for "I'm not anti-Negro," it went over most folks' heads because he won election to the Atlanta House by a wide margin. During his time in the Senate he fought doggedly for school funding and, on the politically tricky question of alcohol prohibition, drew a wavy line, saying gin mills were fine for big cities, but not in places where farmers had to get up early and stand in the sun.

The defining issue of the Professor's two-year term, though, was a bill introduced by one of his Senate colleagues that would have meant the death of Negro schools in segregated Georgia. Cranky old Confederate Army captain Hiram Parks Bell, saying he was tired of seeing white chil-dren laboring in the field while black kids "traipsed" by them on their way to their publicly funded schools, called for an amendment to the state constitution that forbade tax revenue generated by Caucasians from being used to support Negro education. Of course the black population, having been systematically denied education and employment opportu-nities, was not generating enough tax money to support even its inferior schools. Bell's proposal was yet another example of post-Reconstruction cruelty—and Cobb's father would have none of it. Rising to showcase his impressive physical stature (he stood a shade under six feet, tall for the times), he called the measure "Unnecessary and unjust," and, said the *Atlanta Constitution*, produced "figures that showed that the negroes did not get more than their just proportion now." He also pointed out that "the negro had contributed to the upbuilding of the state, and that he had an interest in our government. He said that the negro had been loyal to the white man and that the white man ought to be grateful to him for what he had done. He said that we ought to be generous with the negro and help him to become a useful and helpful member of society." When it was called to a vote, Hiram Park's mean-spirited proposal was defeated by a narrow margin.

Putting his Senate colleagues in occasional touch with their better angels was no doubt satisfying for the Professor. "Even my boyish mind," said Ty's childhood friend Joe Cunningham, "realized that the Professor had a keen and enlightened mind which caught a vision of the future." But despite (or perhaps because of) the blow he struck for Negro education, his long-range political prospects looked grim. W. H. Cobb was out of necessity a Democrat (Republicans simply didn't win elections in those parts), and the Southern Democrats were essentially the party of men like "Pitchfork" Ben Tillman, the South Carolina governor who said of black voters, "We have scratched our head to find out how we could eliminate the last one of them. We stuffed ballot boxes. We shot them. We are not ashamed of it." Daunted by the prospect of thriving in that environment, in 1902 the Professor returned to the business of education, and was soon elected commissioner of the Franklin County schools, a position he held while serving as principal of Royston High School and teaching classes there. A few years later he ran successfully for mayor of his town, and at some point also became its postmaster. In 1905 W.H. added yet another job: editor of the *Royston Record*. No copies prior to 1939 seem to have survived, so we can't speak with certainty about the *Record*'s political bent. But based on the beliefs of those most closely associated with the weekly we can guess at it. The paper was owned by the Universalist minister J. M. Bowers, who forty years after Appomattox still described himself as an abolitionist, and it was printed on a press owned by J.M.'s older brother, "Uncle Billy" Bowers, who boasted of having been "the only man in Georgia who voted for Abraham Lincoln."

By now it should be clear that while plenty of North Carolina hills and hollers featured in Ty Cobb's family history, there was no hint of the hillbilly, as other biographers and journalists have suggested or outright said. Rare indeed is the redneck whose mother descended from relatively genteel, upper-middle-class stock and whose father was, in Ty's words, "a scholar, state senator, editor and philosopher," not to mention an advocate for the oppressed. With allowances for time and place, the household run by Amanda and William Cobb appears much more yuppie than yokum. The couple strove ever upward, obsessed about their children's education, and tended to view local events as a function of real estate values. As Cobb himself said, "I knew which fork to use."

Still, the environment in which he was raised can tell us only so much about who Ty Cobb was. The question is, how far did the Peach fall from the family tree? Did young Ty emulate his father, whose status as a community leader and something of a public intellectual made the family special? Or did he resent and rebel against a parent who might just as easily be seen as every adolescents' worst nightmare—a man who represented the ultimate authority figure in Ty's own high school, who called attention to himself when he ran for public office, and who brought at least a measure of disapproval on the family for his softhearted views on Negroes. W.H. was not the sort of man who settled matters with his fists, and that is admirable. Yet it's easy to imagine that with a more "normal" and less Negro-friendly father, Ty might have gotten in a lot fewer fights. He might have had a very different self-identity and, in turn, a very different life.

The average adolescent views his parents with a mix of pride and embarrassment that is subject to daily, unpredictable tides, and there is no reason to suspect Cobb did not have the usual feelings in the usual proportions until the very last days of his youth. But when Amanda shot and killed W.H. on the evening of August 8, 1905, a little more than halfway through Ty's eighteenth year, all normal relations with his parents abruptly ceased and a curtain fell heavily on the first act of Cobb's life. Whatever their relationship had been before, from that day onward, Ty's devotion to his father burned, to borrow Walter Pater's perhaps over-borrowed phrase, with a hard gemlike flame, and he became very suddenly a man with certain strong characteristics. Still, let's not rush past turn-of-the-century Royston, the way most trains once did. One cannot fully understand Ty Cobb without considering the happy but sensitive boy who preceded the wary, nervous hero.

— CHAPTER THREE —

TY COBB ALWAYS INSISTED THAT he had been a normal boy, from "a small country town of the old type," and in fact the more reliable stories from his early years support a character not unlike that literary sensation of 1885 Huckleberry Finn—a seemingly carefree, somewhat school-averse child content to live in the dogwood-scented moment. Both Ty and Huck liked to fish and hunt and otherwise be outdoors incessantly, and from both the fictional and real child we can learn something about the interaction between the races in the nineteenth-century American South. Among the chief differences between the boys are that Cobb's father was a pillar of the community, and not the town drunk, and that while Huck was almost impossible to corral in a classroom, Ty would go more often than not, but spend the day with his hands down below his desk, furiously winding twine around hunks of old ink erasers to make baseballs.

Little Royston, incorporated in 1879 and situated in the northeast corner of the state, was a bustling agricultural hub in Ty's youth. The peaches hung so heavy in a good year that they broke all but the very biggest branches of the trees, it was said, the sharp cracks resounding like gunshots—and yet peaches weren't where the real money was. Royston's success was as a center of the cotton and corn trade, and the home of the Ginn chicken, a toothsome but feisty bird—even the poultry was pugnacious in Royston—bred by the Cobb family's friend, Stephen A. Ginn. With two hotels, the Johnson and the Royston House, and numerous shops and eating places, the town typically contained more traveling salesmen and farmers' daughters than your average joke book. Downtown streets were often gridlocked with wagons full of cotton bales, although by the 1890s cattle was already starting to push out crops. A survey in 1904 showed that not one house in Royston was vacant. Farmland went for about $5.32 an acre circa 1900, which was not bad.

There were plenty of peach baskets but no basketball hoops in Royston when Cobb was a kid, not surprising since James Naismith didn't invent the game until 1891. No one played football then in Franklin County, either. Apart from competitive running and what Cobb called "hop, skip and jumping races," it was all ball, though not necessarily the kind involving four bases arranged in a diamond pattern.

When Tyrus first showed interest in sports in the early 1890s, Franklin County kids still played town ball and cat, as well as the more evolved game of base-ball, as it was then rendered. Cat, or old cat, was a relatively simple pastime based on an English game called tip cat in which the batter struck a wooden spindle—probably detritus from the textile mills—instead of a ball. It could be played with just two bases, if only a few players were available, or as many as four bases if school was out, no one had chores to do, and eighteen or so boys could be conscripted into a match. "In this crude game, you could hit two balls without running if they did not suit you," Cobb wrote in a newspaper article. "You could hit them anywhere, too, there being no foul lines or anything of that sort, but on the third smash you were forced to run." Although it seems in some ways like a benign game—instead of an opposing pitcher there was a kind of neutral expediter who stood near home base and gently tossed the ball up for the batter to strike on its descent—cat was considered dangerous because to get a runner out you had to hit him with the thrown ball. The practice was called "soaking" or "plugging," and players often used the opportunity to drill an opponent in the head or ribs, hoping, as a matter of strategy, or personal vengeance, to put him out for the game or even the season.

Town ball, which descended from another English game called rounders, and tended to look more like baseball, was flexible enough to accommodate as few as four and as many as twenty players per side, and allow between one and nine outs per half inning. It borrowed from cat the concept of soaking the (of course, helmetless) runner, as opposed to throwing to a baseman who would execute a force-out or tag. Said Cobb: "I became very proficient at dodging [and] I laid a foundation for my Major League career." He would also note that Southern boys, who played a lot of cat and town ball, showed extraordinary "pepper" as big leaguers, simply because sampling the full spectrum of ball-and-stick games, and not worrying about being baseball purists, meant you "got on the field every day and got more exercise."

Cobb got so much exercise as a kid that he looks, in team pictures from that era, as gaunt as an urchin out of Dickens. "I used to grind away at it from the time I got up in the morning until darkness put a stop to it, using every spare moment I could get when out of school," he said. "I would play catch with every player who would condescend to notice me," and when there was no one else around he would throw the ball against the brick wall of a building that housed a grocery store "with all the strength at my command, and catch it on the rebound." Besides being skinny he was also strikingly short, especially for someone who would blossom into a six-footer; some people in Royston referred to him as "the midget." At the age of eleven, when he held a marginal spot on the Rompers, a kind of junior varsity that served as a feeder for the "official" town team, the Royston Reds, he could barely lift the bats that Joe Cunningham's father, William, the local coffin maker and the Cobbs' next-door neighbor, fashioned for him and his own son from scrap wood—though Ty cherished those big black bolts of mountain ash nevertheless.

Marching down Main Street with his casket-shard propped against his shoulder and his fancy, store-bought mitt dangling from the knob, Cobb was a relatively carefree child. He always was, he said, notably "timid around adults," to the point where some people thought they detected a slight stammer in his speech, and he could be cocky with his peers in a way that led to frequent combat, yet on the whole Ty seem to have been well adjusted and popular, perhaps because he was, even then, so darn *entertaining*.

In his highly fictionalized 1994 biography of Cobb—which is not to be confused with the highly fictionalized *auto*biography he wrote in partnership with the dying Cobb in 1961—the sportswriter Al Stump says that the thirteen-year-old Tyrus once walked across a high wire strung twenty feet above Royston's Main Street by a traveling circus. That may

not be true—Stump sources the story to a newspaper that did not exist
at the time, and it appears nowhere else in the Cobb literature—but it
was indeed the *kind* of thing the young Cobb might do to amuse himself
and onlookers. He was a fun-loving kid who liked an audience to amaze
with physical feats. In Royston, playing baseball was a good way to get
one. One day in the spring of 1894 or so, Amanda Cobb looked out
her kitchen window and saw Tyrus and a bunch of Negro boys merrily
hauling a cart laden with scrap metal, broken furniture, and other things
they'd found in backyards and vacant lots around town. They were headed
toward the junkyard to try to make a few dollars, and Mrs. Cobb knew
for what. "He was always thinking up ways of earning money to buy baseball supplies," she would tell a writer for the *Springfield* (Massachusetts)
Sunday Union and Republican in 1928. "He was always playing when he
was a child. In fact, we had a hard time getting him to go to school. I remember that the first money he earned he spent for a mitt. He couldn't
have been more than six years old when a neighbor asked him to take his
cow to the pasture and gave Ty some change for doing it. Ty didn't buy
candy or ice cream. He knew what he wanted, and he got it—a baseball
glove.

"He must have been thinking baseball all the time," she went on, "because when he wasn't actually playing, he was swinging his arms about as
he threw or caught an imaginary baseball. I can remember seeing him on
the way home from school, fanning the air the whole way. He played on
all the school teams, whether he was asked to or not."

In later years—probably to burnish his image as a hero and a spokesman
for his sport—he and his boosters went out of their way to note that
his early encounters with the Negro race were either inconsequential or
benign. A 1909 editorial in the *Charlotte Observer* said, "Cobb, born
with the prominence that is universal among white persons in Georgia,
sought no further prominence by buckshotting his compatriots. So far as
is known, he never attended a lynching." Faint praise indeed, but baseball
was just as racist as the rest of the society. Just a few years earlier, in 1904,
the supposedly saintly Christy Mathewson and his fellow New York Giants had taken a break from spring training in Birmingham, Alabama, to

witness "the hanging of a negro murderer named Stone" at the invitation of the local sheriff, according to *Sporting Life*. Cobb's own statements about black people can by today's standards sound cliché or politically incorrect. In the 1952 newspaper interview in which he applauded the belated breaking of the color barrier in the Texas minor leagues, Cobb said, when asked about his own history with Negroes, "I like them. When I was little I had a colored mammy. I played with colored children." On and off during his youth, Cobb worked alongside black men on the family farm, not as the owner's son, he swore, but as just another laborer under the supervision of an elderly black man he called Uncle Ezra, a longtime Cobb family employee. In 1924, he told H. G. Salsinger, the sports editor of the *Detroit News*, that a black man (presumably not Ezra) had taught him to swim. Seeing that Ty was "timid of the water," Salsinger wrote, the Negro told Cobb to climb on his back and brought him out to the middle of the swimming hole. "The negro swam about with Cobb's arms around his neck, his legs pinned to his sides. He repeated this the next day, and the next. Then one day he carried Cobb to midstream on his back. There he made him release his hold. Cobb, forced to swim or sink, discovered he could swim."

As idyllic as his days in Royston seemed to be, Ty was always delighted to visit Grandpa Johnnie, the antislavery Reb, in rural Murphy, North Carolina. For a while Tyrus went there each summer and on every winter school vacation, smuggling his dog, Bob, on the short train trip, though the conductors probably knew what was chuffing beneath the newspapers tented at Ty's feet. Referring to the wintry landscape he had tramped in his own youth, W. H. Cobb wrote to his sorely missed son in January of 1902, "I am glad you have been receptive of its austere beauty and solemn grandeur. . . . That is a picturesque and romantic country with solitude enough to give nature a chance to be heard in the soul." Perhaps, but what Ty liked best about Murphy was the action and the camaraderie. Grandpa Johnnie took him on hunting trips for small game like possum and at night told him tales of big game, like "slavering" bears who stood twelve feet tall on their hind feet and showed their "corncob size" teeth. ("If I'd missed him, Tyrus, you wouldn't be here today!") Ty often came back with stories of his own. At his grandfather's urging he wrote up "Possums and Myself," a true tale of treeing, shooting, and skinning an animal to make a "fine hat"; W.H. proudly ran it under Ty's byline in the *Royston Record*.

Ty had some indoor adventures in North Carolina as well. Once, when he was about eleven, he accompanied Johnnie Cobb to Asheville, where the "squire" was serving as the foreman of the county grand jury in a civil matter, probably a dispute over land. When the verdict was announced by his grandfather, the loser in the case ran up and grabbed Johnnie by the shirt, an act that caused Ty to also come charging out of the audience and attempt to boot the man in the shins. The angry litigant, unaware of what a pair of Cobb-kicked pants might bring one day on the memorabilia market, swatted him away, but when he turned back to Johnnie Cobb the squire had drawn his pistol. "Be on your way," Ty's grandpa said, and the man left peaceably.

On the trip back to Murphy, Ty may well have gotten a lecture about the dangers of impulsive behavior, but like many children before and since, he suffered few consequences for the indiscretions he committed while in his grandparents' care. Nor did John and his wife, Sarah, monitor how much ball he played, an increasingly significant issue at home as he grew older. During his summer stays, Cobb's Aunt Norah (his father's youngest sister), a "wonderful woman," according to Cobb, would drive him in a horse-drawn buggy to the equivalent of Little League games around Murphy, where the preference was still for town ball. As the perennial new kid, Cobb was always at risk for a particularly hard plugging and he seems to have accepted pain and the occasional minor concussion as the price of admission. In his 1961 autobiography, Cobb told about a Murphy-area game in which he hit a hopper back to the box, then tore down the line toward first base, screaming all the way in anticipation of the soaker that was surely coming. He awoke moments later with his head in Aunt Norah's lap and her handkerchief in his ear to staunch the blood flow. (Just as he wasn't always the grouchiest person in the room, he was not always the orneriest player on the field. A medical student who saw his naked corpse laid out on a gurney just after he died in 1961 noted that it was covered with knots, dents, scars, and lumps, the souvenirs of soakings, spikings, beanballs, and falls caused by strategically discarded catcher's masks, and hip checks from shortstops as he rounded second base. The game—the world—was different then.)

Hits were hard to come by when the midget started out—a right-hander who batted left, perhaps because it gave him a two-step head start toward first, or because most pitchers are right-handed; it seems that no one ever asked him, and he never addressed the issue, so we'll never know for certain why. (When questioned on this topic by your author, Yogi Berra, another righty who hit left, said that if he himself ever had had a particular motivation for switching over he'd forgotten it—"I guess it was something a lot of kids just did back then," he said, though his "back then" was forty years after Cobb's.) Too proud to go back to the silly-looking elongated paddles he had first used for bats, and too weak to get around like the big boys with his hefty "custom made" models, Cobb was at first of no real use to the Rompers, who may have taken him on as a benchwarmer, solely for his skill at making baseballs, or, to be precise, ball cores. Every so often, he would deliver a batch of the stringy things to another boy on the Rompers who couldn't play very well, either, but could cut and sew leather, Cobb said, "as well as a harness maker" and thus was adept at stitching on the tanned horsehide used for covers. The system worked well enough—until the day a classmate noticed Cobb winding string beneath his school desk (again), and, still ticked off about a soaking Ty had given him in a game of town ball, tattled to the teacher. Cobb remembered getting "a whipping in front of the whole school," after which his ball core production dropped dramatically. Clearly, he had to look for other ways to make himself valuable to the Rompers. For a while, he served as the designated retriever of foul balls, a chore that kept him close to the action, and technically on the team, yet only made him appear more pathetic. When he tried to talk his way into the lineup, pointing out to the manager and some of the more influential players that in Carnesville, the town where he had lived previously, he had made the first string at the age of nine, "they just laughed at me," Cobb recalled.

If you understood the pecking order of north Georgia town teams of that era, you'd know why. Though roughly the same size in terms of population, Carnesville was the bushes compared to Royston, where a number of well-paid mercenaries played for the men's squad, the Reds, and minor league scouts regularly came through on the Elberton Air Line Railroad to see, in the parlance of the trade, "if there was anything in the lake." The team wore bright red suits and, said Cobb, "Believe me, whenever the Royston club went on the field they attracted attention—you could see that club a mile." In a 1904 article, the *Augusta Chronicle* commended Royston, about seventy miles to the northwest, for its "push and pluck" as compared to other Franklin County whistle-stops and noted that it was "baseball crazy." Partly because some of the choicest spots on the senior squad were taken by semiprofessionals, both the Rompers—who billed themselves as "the little potatoes that are hard to peel"—and Reds were tougher to make than your average small-town team, but the accomplishment was correspondingly more meaningful, a rosette on the résumé of anyone who wanted to go further in the game.

Cobb said that "so great was my anxiety to play" for Royston that he spent many hours concocting a methodical make-or-break plan. Though he was not especially fleet of foot, "How to Sprint," a 25 cent pamphlet he saw advertised in the back of *The Police Gazette*, would help him run the bases, he believed, if he could ever figure out a way to get on in the first place. As for his defensive ability, that would be aided immeasurably, he felt, by trading in his tattered and freakish homemade leather fielder's glove ("A disgrace," he called it, "something betwixt a catcher's mitt and a first baseman's glove") for a model that he had seen at the local dry goods store and had decided that "I couldn't live without." How he managed the $1.25 purchase price is, among Cobb scholars, such as they are, a matter of dispute. His mother, as noted, said he saved up the pennies he made in the junk business to buy it, but in the only slightly reliable *Ty Cobb: My Life in Baseball*, Cobb says that he stole two "expensive" volumes from his father's library and traded them for the mitt. (Why didn't he just ask his parents for the money? In still other versions of the tale, he does, but W.H., who was starting to worry that his eldest boy was devoting too much time to baseball and not thinking seriously enough about the University of Georgia—or the other schools W.H. thought he might be able to help get him into, West Point and Annapolis—responded with a firm no.) Cobb goes on to suggest in *My Life* that he was punished for the theft after it was discovered, but he doesn't say how severely. (A severe punishment for the Cobb boys in those days was being made to muck out the several cow stalls on the fifty-two-acre farm W.H. maintained just outside the Royston town limits.) In his 1994 biography of Cobb, however, Stump, without saying how he came upon the new information, or even acknowledging that he was changing his story, says that Ty earned the money for the new mitt by baling hay.

Transforming himself into a consistent hitter was Ty's toughest task, as it would be for almost anybody. Hitting is a mysterious skill. Some seem to be born with the gift. Some hit well until they reach a certain level of organized baseball, at which point they stop suddenly, confounded by the curveball or fear of success (see Billy Beane in Michael Lewis's *Moneyball*). Whether a coach can make a weak hitter or headcase into more of an offensive threat remains an open question—note that Dusty Baker's 1992 treatise is not called *How to Hit Better*, but, rather defensively, *You Can Teach Hitting*. Ted Williams liked to talk about hitting and cheerfully told many young players that their approach was "horseshit." In 1984, Williams published *The Science of Hitting*, a book that collects his primary thoughts on the subject, and which still sells fairly briskly. But whether Williams ever actually improved anyone's batting average is debatable. His book, like the works of Stephen Hawking, is probably more dusted than read. Most struggling hitters feel *their* way is best, for them at least, and wish to be left alone so they can further ingrain the habits that have not served them well.

For hitters, advice, like grappa, is always taken with a premonition of regret. The esteemed baseball writer Roger Angell, when interviewed for this book, remembered how Rod Carew had once complained to him that he was deeply frustrated as a hitting instructor for the Minnesota Twins because players were reluctant to change the techniques they had been using since Little League—even though their numbers were anemic, and the doctor sent to cure their ills, Carew, had a pleasant plateside manner, and a career batting average of .328. It just may be that when it comes to hitting, people either teach themselves—the way Williams (a .344 lifetime hitter, and by the way another righty who hit left) did—or they don't learn. As the author of *The Science of Hitting* felt compelled to admit in an early chapter, one of the best pieces of baseball advice he ever got was from Cobb's friend Lefty O'Doul, who, when Williams, then a Pacific Coast Leaguer, approached him for tips, said, "Son, whatever you do, don't let anybody change you."

Cobb changed himself dramatically as a hitter in the early months of 1898. "I had the gift of being able to appraise myself, even at that age [twelve]," he said two decades later. "It has been the greatest asset of my life." All of his life, in articles and after-dinner introductions, people would describe Cobb as "a natural," thinking they were paying the supreme compliment—and he would respond that he was anything but. A natural, he would say, is someone like his friend Shoeless Joe Jackson. "Joe just busts 'em," Cobb said, "and hopes for the best." (Those hopes were often realized; Jackson, yet another left-handed batter who threw righty, hit .356 for his career.) Cobb would over time refine and trick out his approach to batting, adding, among other things, foot fakes meant to deceive the catcher, bursts of chatter, and—this was his true brilliance— a way of carrying himself that clearly conveyed that he was the pitcher's problem to solve, and not the reverse. But in his desire to gain a spot on the Royston Rompers, Ty tried to put aside all impulses to employ "psychology." He suppressed the urge to imitate the swaggering older boys—and reinvented himself as kind of rudimentary hitting machine, the patent application for which might say "A device for poking baseballs into unoccupied portions of the playing field." His only desire was to make contact with the ball and reach base safely; how he looked doing it didn't matter.

What he did was simple and straightforward. ("Ah, please never forget," Christopher Hitchens wrote, "how useful the obvious can be.") Ty's first adjustment was to choke up severely on the bat and employ what he called "a snap swing." Because there are only a few seconds of film showing Cobb at bat, we can only assume this looked the way it sounds—a short, fast swipe meant to put the ball just beyond the reach of an infielder. "I don't recall whether it was by accident or study that I developed [the snap swing]," Cobb said. But "after that the pitchers never fooled me much." Facing right-handers he stood far forward in the batter's box, believing this allowed him to strike a curveball before it broke. Against southpaws he did the opposite, setting up as far back as possible so he could hit the ball post-break. (Many other players from the deadball era employed a variation on the snap swing, but virtually no one else moved around the box the way he did.)

Cobb's other modification, the split-hands grip, for him a necessary and inseparable part of the snap swing, was, despite what some people think, not borrowed from Honus Wagner, who, though twelve years older than Cobb, was in 1898 still an obscure shortstop with the Louisville Colonels of the National League, and thus unknown to most people outside Kentucky. In later years, Cobb liked to note that he and Wagner, by then a Pittsburgh Pirates star, were leading their respective leagues with a technique considered by most instructional books to be as sacrilegious as the headfirst slide. The split grip, however, was merely a starting position that let a hitter make a last-second decision to slide the lower hand upward or the upper hand down toward the knob—to place the ball, Wee Willie Keeler–style, "where they ain't," or drive it for distance. His new swing allowed Cobb to meet the ball in front of the plate, where he could *almost* but not quite see it making contact with his bat; as a result, he seldom swung and missed. "I did not have the physical prowess to drive the ball far," he said of those early times, "but I would usually keep my strikeout record down to two, three or possibly four times a season." He swore that one year, over the course of the 25- to 30-game town league season, he avoided strikeouts completely.

Cobb's revised approach to hitting, coupled with a simultaneous growth spurt that added about four inches in height, as well as about twenty pounds in weight, did for him more or less what the devil did for Robert Johnson, down at the crossroads. No records of the Royston teams have survived, and remembered accounts get muddled, but it appears that a few games into his 1898 season with the Rompers, the shortstop on the Reds was injured in a farming accident, or had to go buy a mule or something, and the twelve-year-old Cobb got called up to the town team, where some of the players were in their twenties and several of the ringers were understood to be thirty or older. They needed a shortstop, and Ty, who had started out as a catcher and subsequently played every position except pitcher for the Rompers, was more than willing to give it a try.

This was a bold and risky move, though. The Reds, after all, were an elite group, having already produced, in the person of Thomas Vandiver "Van" Bagwell, a pitcher who'd been given a tryout with the Nashville Volunteers of the revered Southern League.

The Royston Reds "were regular demigods to me," Cobb said in 1913, but the admiration wasn't mutual. "Come back when you grow up a little!" the older players told him when he first reported for duty with his big black bat. "Where's his nurse?" someone shouted from the stands. "Have you got his milk bottle in that grip?" Cobb, ultrasensitive to any slight, even then, remembered that taunt for the rest of his life ("Unfortunately," he once noted, "it is a human trait to remember the unkind things after the nice ones are forgotten"), but he didn't act on it, as he would act on—and overreact to—so many insults and perceived insults in the years ahead. Like Joe Gans, the crackerjack lightweight champ of that era, he was willing to take a few shots to get inside. "I was met with parental opposition and rebuffs from managers and players," he said, "and I permitted nothing to swerve me from that determination."

Yet even in the faster company of the Reds, he stood out from the start, not just for his ability to get hits, but also for his base running and fielding. "When I was 12 years old I knew pretty well what I could do as a ballplayer," he said at age thirty-nine. Besides the snap swing and split grip he now had confidence—by far the single most important attribute for any athlete, he would always maintain. ("He can conquer who believe they can," Virgil told us.) When he talked to Stump for *My Life in Baseball* in 1960, Cobb recalled the moment that certified him as "a boy hero." It happened in the ninth inning of a game against Elberton, when he came to bat with the score tied and a man on second. Stroking—or more likely poking—his third hit of the afternoon, and knocking in the winning run, he heard the cheers and felt "bewitched," he said. Once a young man receives that kind of public adulation, Cobb noted on another occasion, "something happens in him."

His fascination with fame was further inflamed by a letter Van Bagwell had sent, addressed to the Reds as a whole, from the Volunteers headquarters in Nashville. In it the blacksmith's son spoke, Marco Polo–like, about his encounter with the colorful world of early organized baseball. He had seen in the flesh Davy Crockett—the one who played first base—as well as "Batty" Abbaticchio, "Deerfoot" Bay, "Hub" Perdue, "Snapper" Kennedy, "Scoops" Carey, "Punch" Knoll, and "Foxy" "Newt" "Ike" Fisher, the catcher who also served as the Vols' manager, perhaps because he had the most nicknames. Bagwell wrote, Cobb said, "all about the professional league, how the players acted, what was expected of them, and so on. He told about the life in the hotels. Every line of this letter was fascinating. I read it and reread it. I didn't realize it for a long time, but my future had been mapped out for me." Although he was still too modest to think of the Southern League as being within his capabilities, or so he claimed, "nothing could keep me from satisfying my ambition of showing that I could be as good as any of them."

Cobb joined the Reds during a period of great upheaval. Their new manager (and catcher), a bank clerk named Bob McCreary, had recently dismissed the ringers and added a residency rule—now you actually had to live in Royston to play on the team. But though the roster changed considerably, Cobb was still the youngest player on it—and the only one whose father wouldn't allow him to travel for away games. Young Tyrus led a sheltered life; when he reached the Detroit Tigers at age eighteen he would be shocked by the coarse language he heard from the professional players. But it wasn't just to shield him from the temptations of Elberton, Georgia, the "Electric City" of Anderson, South Carolina, or the other small towns the Reds visited that W.H. insisted he eschew road trips; it was to limit his playing time while simultaneously exposing him to more reputable professions. In 1898 or 1899, he arranged for Ty to visit Colonel W. R. Little, a prominent Carnesville attorney. The boy found the middle-aged man mildly amusing—"one of the old-fashioned barristers who grew his hair long," he called him many years later—and he took him up on his offer to browse his library. But there was no initial chemistry between Cobb and the law. "I cracked those books three or four times and they were dry as hell," he said in a 1958 interview with sports columnist Furman Bisher. "I knew I didn't want to be a lawyer." At around the same time a group of Franklin County physicians, at the behest of the Professor, invited Ty to watch them perform an operation. The patient was a black teenager who had been shot by a white man under circumstances that Cobb didn't mention. He said that at one point he was urged "to feel around inside" the young man's intestines for the bullet, which he did without hesitation but also without luck, though the shooting victim survived. Cobb liked telling this story, to make the point that he was not squeamish about blood and guts, but the experience did not make him think seriously about medicine.

Ty also got a taste of farming in his youth, but that was out of necessity. W.H. needed help on his fifty-two acres, and as time went on Ty found the tasks not so distasteful. He liked the fresh air and sunshine, as well as being asked his opinion of which livestock to buy, and how much corn to plant in which field, and discussing with his father "the English import of cotton which competed with our Georgia output." Cobb said "I never felt closer to [my father] than when he said of the cotton crop, 'Do you think we should sell now or hold on for a better price?'" Even after W.H. relented, in Ty's second season with the Reds, and allowed his son to travel with the team on the condition that manager McCreary, a fellow Mason, keep a fatherly eye on him, Ty found time for farmwork.

On January 5, 1904, when he was up at the place butchering hogs with Uncle Ezra, Ty managed to shoot himself with his "parlor rifle," a .22 caliber firearm designed for indoor target practice at a gallery or arcade. The gun had been lying in a tangle of brambles, and when he picked it up a twig tripped the trigger. The bullet entered near the collarbone, and lodged in his left shoulder. Ezra provided first-aid, and although the wound was (as his father would write in a letter to his own parents several weeks later) "not much more than a big thorn scratch," W.H. spirited Ty by train to Atlanta, where the hospitals had X-ray machines. The doctor there found the bullet on his film, and showed it to W.H., but suggested they take a wait-and-see approach, as probing might do more harm than the initial injury.

It was either on this trip, or more likely during a follow-up doctor's visit in Atlanta several weeks later, that the Cobbs, *père et fils*, took in an exhibition game at Piedmont Park featuring the Atlanta Crackers of the Southern League versus the barnstorming Cleveland Naps, as the American League team was known in those days, after their second baseman

Napoleon Lajoie. This was Ty's first exposure to the conglomeration of commedia dell'arte troupes that was turn-of-the-century big league ball, and he was mesmerized. In addition to "The Frenchman," the Naps that year featured the heedless headfirst slider Terry Turner, the convicted umpire beater Fritz Buelow (for "tuggling" an ump to the ground the previous season the German-born catcher had received a five-day suspension and a $10 fine), and Claude Rossman, an outfielder who had a psychological problem that prevented him from throwing the ball when he became excited. Every side, circa 1904, had its sideshow. During batting practice, Cobb went down to the field and asked the Naps' Bill Bradley if he could take a snapshot of him; the brilliant third baseman—whose 29-game hitting streak of 1902 was a major league record until Cobb hit in 45 straight games in 1911—not only posed for the gangly, wide-eyed lad with the Pocket Brownie, he hung around and chatted. ("I kept those pictures until they turned to dust," Cobb said.)

In some ways Cobb's day at Piedmont Park resembles the portentous encounter between the sixteen-year-old Bill Clinton and President John F. Kennedy in 1963, or the famous photograph that captures a six-year-old Theodore Roosevelt staring out his Manhattan window at Abraham Lincoln's funeral cortege. For here were players who would figure meaningfully in Cobb's future: Lajoie, pitcher Addie Joss, and catcher "Handsome Harry" Bemis (who would three years later repeatedly beat Cobb over the head with a ball that Ty had just knocked from his hand while sliding in to complete an inside-the-park home run). The sight of the debonair Naps only made him yearn even harder for the baseball life. "Players in practice were performing wonderful antics," he wrote in a serialized 1914 newspaper memoir. "I saw things that opened my eyes, that sowed in me the seeds of determination to emulate those major leaguers some day." (The bullet, in case you're wondering, remained permanently in Cobb's body, and, although he later developed a hypochondriacal streak, caused no complaints beyond an occasional "burning sensation" on chilly mornings.)

As Ty passed through his teen years with the Royston Reds, it became increasingly clear that he was the best ballplayer anyone in that hotbed of baseball had ever stood and cheered for, better even than Van Bagwell (who returned to the Reds after getting a look-see from the Savannah Pathfinders). One day, in a game against Harmony Grove, when he was about sixteen, the locals effectively forced professionalism upon young Tyrus. After a rising line drive tipped off the glove of a fellow outfielder and Cobb, who'd been running for the same ball, made a fully extended flying catch "that all my life I have never thrilled to more," a total of $11 in coins—about ten days' pay for the average rural Georgian—came raining down upon the diamond, and he gathered them up gratefully. In its next edition, the *Royston Record* broke with its policy of ignoring sports and ran a page-one story about the game written by the editor, W. H. Cobb himself.

— CHAPTER FOUR —

THE VAUDEVILLE COMIC EDDIE CANTOR, born in 1892, once said that his grandmother employed "ballplayer" as a synonym for "lazy bum," as in "Don't lay around the house all day like a ballplayer." To pack one's pancake mitt and head toward a possible position with the Muncie Fruit Jars of the Interstate Association, the Des Moines Prohibitionists of the Western League, the San Jose Prune Pickers of the California League, or, as in Cobb's case, the Augusta Tourists of the South Atlantic League, was tantamount to running off with the carnival in those days when almost no one asked an athlete for his autograph, and many big leaguers made only $1,800 for a season, or $2,000 if they kept their promise to stay sober—in other words, a romantic and often rebellious gesture that didn't exactly enhance one's bank account or reputation. Just as the *thea-tah* had long been a highbrow art form populated by randy vagabonds known as actors, baseball was a wholesome national pastime brimming with, as Cantor's Grandma Iskowitz would say, ballplayers. One needs to remember that a father in 1904 was almost certainly pointing his son toward relative respectability and financial security when he steered the boy *away* from professional ball.

The conflict between Tyrus and his father over the former's career choice should not be breezed by too quickly, but we oughtn't make too much of it, either, as have others who wanted to paint W.H. as overly severe, and his children the damaged products of a dysfunctional hearth. The issue of Ty's career path was ever-simmering in the Cobbs' rented wood-frame home at 95 Franklin Springs Street, but the debate seems never really to have reached a rapid boil. Cobb wedged a reference to his father's baseball phobia into almost every extended interview he ever did—to make the point, it seems, that he had a caring dad, and one who in his skepticism toward the then groundbreaking notion that a grown man could make a living playing a mere game, was typical of the times. "It has struck me as odd that of all the baseball autobiographies I have read not one of the successful players ever started out with the full consent of his father," he said in 1925. "Parents are unanimously against baseball as a profession." Indeed, Lawrence S. Ritter's great oral history of the deadball era, *The Glory of Their Times*, begins with the story of Rube Marquard, who was born the same year as Cobb, telling his father that he wanted to become a ballplayer, and Papa Marquard belittling the idea and saying, "I don't understand why a grown man would wear those funny-looking suits." Young Rube had to sneak out of his house in Cleveland in the wee hours and hop a freight train to Iowa for a tryout. Later in the book, another masterful pitcher, Smoky Joe Wood, says that the only reason his father allowed him to attempt a career in baseball was that "it must have appealed to his sense of the absurd."

If W.H.'s patience started to wear on occasion, it was because Tyrus was Yankee-pushy about his plans, going so far at age fifteen or sixteen as to accept $3 to play two games as a ringer for the Anderson, South Carolina, town team. While this may seem quaint and inconsequential, it was, in fact, a stubbornly defiant gesture that, even more than the shower of loose change from Roystonians mentioned in the previous chapter, effectively ended his amateur status, and scotched any hope of a compromise between father and son whereby Ty might play all the baseball he wanted, but for the University of Georgia (which of course permitted no $1.50-per-game pros). Never one to let the matter of his aspirations rest, Ty even sent a parade of friends to pay a call on the Professor and, with initially charming but ultimately tedious little lectures about how travel broadens a person and athletics opens the lungs, attempt to wear down his resistance. One evening post-supper not long after they saw the Naps play in Atlanta, as W.H. was working at his desk, Ty sucked up the courage to show his father the carbon copy of a contract he had recently received from the semi-famous Con Strouthers, part-owner and manager of the Augusta Tourists.

Young Cobb had written to all six skippers in the brand-new South

Atlantic League, which envisioned itself as one small step down from the Class A Southern League, enclosing letters from prominent Roystonians attesting to his character and baseball talents. Only George "King" Kelly of the Jacksonville Jax, and Strouthers had responded, and only the latter held out any hope of a job. The provisional boilerplate contract he included—apparently after Cobb, undeterred by his initial silence, had begged a Royston preacher named John Yarborough to write to his Augusta friend W. S. Sherman, asking Sherman to write on Cobb's behalf to *his* friend Strouthers (like I said, Yankee-pushy)—stipulated that Cobb would get $90 a month during the season *if* he made the team. Before consulting his father, Ty had signed the original and sent it back addressed to Mr. John Cornelius Strouthers, Warren Park, Augusta.

The offer was specious—Tyrus would have to make the roughly 200-mile round-trip for a tryout of open-ended duration at his own expense—but even a noncommittal contract left Cobb feeling "intoxicated," and, he said, it "shocked" his father by finally bringing matters to a head. Having turned seventeen the previous December, Cobb was, by the standards of the day, in a position to leave home anytime he pleased, but he wanted his father's permission to undertake his great baseball adventure, as well as, perhaps, a bit of money for train fare. "Never in my life had I had an argument with my father," he once said, and, from the way he most often told the tale, he didn't exactly have one that evening, either, though the beleaguered W.H. may have spoken emphatically at first. "We discussed it fully an hour," Cobb said of a conversation that in many accounts is tortured into something out of *Long Day's Journey into Night*. At about the sixty-minute point his father took the position that he was probably coming around to anyway, at his own pace—namely that Ty should go and get professional baseball out of his system. Cobb said his father ended their discussion by calmly writing him a check for $50, and saying, "This will carry you through for a month. Now go down there and satisfy yourself that there is nothing in this baseball business. Then come back to your studies. I'm sure you will be back by the end of the month, if not before." To the teenage Ty, this grudging concession resounded like Isaac's blessing to Jacob in Genesis 27; he was packed and gone the next morning.

Ty set off for Augusta in early April of 1904 with his friend and Reds teammate Stewart Brown, who had written to and received back from Con Strouthers the same unbinding agreement. Five years older than Cobb, Brown was a pitcher of some local renown, but of his experience with the Tourists we know almost nothing, except that he failed to make the grade and wound up playing briefly for the Vienna, Georgia, town team before returning to his medical studies. In 1950 his son Stewart Jr. would be named the first chief physician at Cobb Memorial, the hospital his fellow Tourist prospect founded in their hometown.

Cobb in some ways fit demographically into the community of professional ballplayers he aspired to join. Most major leaguers of his day were middle-class natives of English-Irish stock, 75 percent had some high school, and quite a few (only 10 percent of the total, but more than three times as many as the general population) had fathers who were professional men. Yet as a lad from the Southern provinces Cobb was an outlier in key ways, too, since the vast majority of National and American Leaguers came from the Northeast and, although every team seemed to have at least three guys called Rube, had grown up in cities. From the moment he started working out with the Tourists, Tyrus, the rawest of raw recruits, showed that he either didn't know or didn't care how professional athletes comported themselves on and off the diamond.

That was not necessarily a bad thing since in those early years of the game professionals often comported themselves abysmally. So many of our great-granddaddies' heroes played drunk or hungover, or were on the DL with STDs, or gambled on games in which they participated, that the championship seasons were to a great extent shaped by sin. (From the 1892 *Spalding Guide*: "Season after season have clubs become bankrupt solely through the failure of their teams to accomplish successful field work owing to the presence of two or three drunkards in their team.") Rules were to men like King Kelly and John McGraw—and there were a *lot* of men like Kelly and McGraw—as the melody line was to Parker or Gillespie. Third baseman McGraw—who had at least twice as many fights as Cobb ever did, and was called "mean and vicious" and "ready at any time to maim a rival player or umpire" by the president of the National League—kicked, tripped, pushed, elbowed, hip-checked, or, on days when he was feeling merciful toward his fellow man, merely held the belts of opposing runners who were trying to dash home. Kelly, in the era when the league provided just one umpire for each game, would, when he noticed that the ump was keeping his eye on the bouncing ball, go from first to third by cutting across the pitcher's mound, or so it was often said.

Hall of Famer Rogers Hornsby—who had a much worse reputation than Cobb for being an SOB—once wrote a magazine article called "You've Got to Cheat to Win" in which he contended that cheating occurred in each of 2,259 major league games in which he participated, starting in 1915. (He wasn't even talking about the use of spitballs, which were legal until 1920.) Diving into a pitched ball was perhaps the most common illicit practice; "Kid" Elberfeld, a short-fused shortstop for six major league teams, managed to get about 165 trips to first that way. "They didn't care," Sam Crawford said in *The Glory of Their Times*. "They had it down to a fine art, you know. They look like they were trying to get out of the way, but they managed to let the ball just nick them." Sensitive about his acting skills, Elberfeld once responded to being called out for interfering with the pitch by flinging a handful of mud into the umpire's open mouth.

How these men got away with rule breaking and umpire abuse—fines seldom exceeded $50 and suspensions rarely lasted longer than three days—is easy to explain: cheating and fighting were believed to be central to the game. When Chicago sportswriter Hugh Fullerton wrote that "in baseball almost anything short of maiming and injury are permissible," he forgot that maiming and injuring were permissible under certain circumstances, too. In a 1909 Zane Grey novella called "The Shortstop," the protagonist stabs a base runner with a horseshoe nail to slow down his progress toward the plate. The action "embodied the Great Spirit of the game," Grey wrote. "Ball playing is a fight all the time." According to W. O. McGeehan, who covered sports for the *New York Herald Tribune*, baseball wasn't a polite game by nature—"and that's *why* it is the National Pastime." "Wake up the echoes at the Hall of Fame," wrote Bill Veeck, the owner at different times of the Indians, Browns, and White Sox, "and you will find that baseball's immortals were a rowdy and raucous group of men who would climb down off their plaques and go rampaging through

Cooperstown, taking spoils, like the Third Army bustling through Germany."

Things were often no less unruly away from the stadium, as the beleaguered innkeepers along the circuits could readily testify; the better hotels often refused to accept ballplayers. The poster boy for profligacy was . . . well, here we could easily get into a debate. Some would say Edward Delahanty, a fluid-gaited forerunner of Joe DiMaggio who patrolled left field for the Philadelphia Phillies, Cleveland Infants, and Washington Senators, an early power hitter who also drank for the fences, often to forget his racetrack debt. (When he was sober, said Crawford, Delahanty was "the best right-handed hitter I ever saw.") After being put off a train in extreme upstate New York in 1903 for being crazy-drunk and brandishing a razor, "Big Ed" somehow wound up tumbling into Niagara Falls, where he both drowned and got mangled by the propeller of the *Maid of the Mist*. "Way to be remembered, Delahanty!" you might reasonably say. Yet others contended that his flashy demise obscured an otherwise run-of-the-mill SOB story, and that the distinction of being a baseball commissioner's worst nightmare more rightly belonged to "Turkey" Mike Donlin, pride of the Santa Cruz Sand Crabs.

Donlin, darkly handsome despite a long knife scar on his left cheek, was a terribly talented and extremely popular figure with self-destructive habits, a kind of Peoria-born, line-drive-stroking Sir Richard Burton. A major vaudeville star when he felt like it—he and his wife, the actress Mabel Hite, had a smash hit with a one-act play he wrote called *Stealing Home*—and an oft-sidelined outfielder who hit .333 for eight major league teams when he didn't have the DTs, Donlin combined public adoration with public urination in ways that would not be seen again until the advent of Charlie Sheen. The St. Louis Perfectos should have sensed something was amiss when they had to address his first contract to a drunk tank outside San Francisco, but they, too, were smitten—until he beat up a couple of chorus girls. The Perfectos then traded him to the Orioles, where he began to shuttle between show and baseball business, parole and incarceration, moodiness and madness, coming close to being the worst role model in early professional ball.

I'm going to give that distinction—which let us not forget has been so often bestowed upon Cobb, who spent so many nights listening to violin records and diagramming plays on the hotel stationery—to Ned Garvin. If you combine Delahanty and Donlin and add in a little gunplay, you get Virgil Lee "Ned" Garvin, whose other nickname was the "Navasota Tarantula," after the vice-ridden stagecoach stop in Texas from which he hailed. In his essential *Baseball Abstract*, Bill James says Garvin may be the hard-luck pitcher of all time because his terrible won-lost record (58–97) belies an elegantly low ERA (2.72). He also, fittingly, invented the screwball, which he called "the reverse curve," and Christy Mathewson rechristened the fadeaway. Yet despite undeniable skill and interest in advancing the twirler's art, Garvin managed to be blacklisted by the National League at the very moment it was being accused of being far too tolerant of miscreants. To do this he had to shoot a Chicago cop (nonfatally, but still) in the head, severely beat the traveling secretary for his team, the Brooklyn Superbas, in a St. Louis saloon, and then break the nose of an insurance salesman who "wouldn't engage me in conversation" in a New Jersey hotel lobby, the desire to initiate conversation with an insurance salesman being in most people's books prima facie evidence of depravity.

You may think I exaggerate the amount of eccentricity in baseball circa 1900 for comic effect. Although there can be no way to count the crazies, the game surely had a higher percentage of them in the early 1900s, when it was to a degree a fallback for those who could not find more respectable employment, and no one knew exactly the correct way for a professional athlete to behave. In *The Glory of Their Times* various deadball stars, interviewed in the early 1960s, nostalgically and diplomatically refer to their mentally and emotionally disturbed colleagues as "characters," but at the time more normal players grumbled that the "magnates," as team owners were known, were signing up people without regard to their conduct or character, and making the respectable men look bad by association. Indeed the American League was founded in 1901 largely because Ban Johnson, a straitlaced former sportswriter, saw the need for a brand of baseball that was safe for family consumption, a game that did not include fistfights and bottle tossing, where the hurlers were pitchers, not ashen-faced alcoholics vomiting up last night's beer in plain view of the kiddies. The AL met with instant success, but its pool of players just as quickly became less than pristine (NL-reject Ned Garvin resurfaced with the New York Highlanders in 1904), and its product indistinguishable from that of the senior circuit.

It is thus hardly surprising then that someone with Ty Cobb's finely honed sense of propriety would not make a smooth entrance into this world.

— CHAPTER FIVE —

UNLIKE HIS FRIEND STEWART BROWN, who seems to have simply not been up to South Atlantic League (Sally League) standards, Ty Cobb made a kind of funky and complicated first impression with the Augusta Tourists, intriguing, perplexing, and amusing their manager all at once. Well, maybe not amusing the cranky Con Strouthers so much. A tall, skinny, pimply kid still growing into his own body, he reported for duty wearing his bright red Royston togs—the look of dismay Strouthers fixed on him in particular suggests that Brown was not similarly clad—and carrying a cloth bag holding several of his odd-looking black bats (the *Augusta Chronicle* said that they were "spliced," presumably at the handle, like cricket bats, to give them "spring"), which he referred to strangely, in the singular, as "the Biffer." Ty was the antithesis of the grizzled and jaded vets who tended to set the tone on the Tourists. He wasn't perpetually hungover or too cool to appear enthusiastic. The wide-eyed kid from Royston couldn't wait to show people an Indian-head penny with the words "Army and Navy" stamped on the reverse, where "One Cent" would normally be—a then still fairly common "commercial token," produced by private companies during the Civil War, when coins were scarce, but to his mind a true collector's item. He also told anyone who'd listen that his father was coming on opening day to watch him play.

The Ty Cobb of 1904 was, in other words, both young for his years and wildly presumptuous. Opening day? Who said he would still be around then? Preseason tryouts were still in progress at that point, and not shaping up terribly well for the hill-country youngster, owing to his bizarre behavior. While running the bases during intra-squad drills, Ty waved his arms wildly, barreled into infielders, and otherwise gave observers a foretaste of the man whom Germany Schaefer would describe with admiration a couple of years later as "the craziest runner I've ever seen." In fielding practice, the local paper said, Cobb would puckishly cut off grounders and "fun-goes" that Strouthers was smacking to others. Was this just nervous bravado on the part of a crimson-clad bumpkin who might see this as his one big chance? It doesn't seem so. Cobb said he felt "just full of life and pepper," and it's clear from the newspaper coverage that it pleased him to behave that way, even if he could tell, as he said later, that the manager "did not seem to look upon me with favor."

The other would-be Tourists appeared to like him just fine, if their mild joshing is any indication. "Back to the plow for you!" Tommy McMillan, a fifteen-year-old aspiring shortstop yelled at him one morning when he muffed a catch. (You don't hear that one much anymore.) By mid-April, Dave Edmunds, a veteran utility man, had christened Cobb "Sleuth," "probably because that worthy 'cops' everything that comes his way," said the correspondent for the *Chronicle*. Around Warren Park, Sleuth sprinted at top speed everywhere he went: to the plate for practice swings, to the outfield to shag flies, back to the dugout when the manager waved him in for a conversation—about not being such a maniac. "Don't *run* like that!" Strouthers told him. "Save some of that pep! You'll need it for later on!" Cobb heard him out but stubbornly refused to slow down.

Strouthers and the other Tourists—a motley mix of young prospects and older men who'd been kicking around the low minors since the days when foul balls were not strikes, and some fielders went without gloves—could not figure where, or if, the contumacious kid fit in. At the plate, during practice, he appeared formidable, "swatting 'em out," said the *Chronicle*, "with his black bat. . . . He will make a big leaguer in a year or two." But offsetting this, to some degree, was his inability, or refusal, to take direction, which for Strouthers, a burnt-out case at thirty-eight, was, either way, no small matter. A few days before the season opener, the paper reported that Sleuth "slid in home yesterday and one could hear his body grating against the ground. He came up all right, but out." That Cobb's rumbustious behavior caused the *Chronicle* to pay so much attention to him, a "yannigan" (or rookie) from a place, said that paper, that no one in Augusta had ever heard of, may have also irritated the manager. Cobb figured to be sent packing before the April 26 opener, if only because the fledgling Sally League had decided to go with mingy thirteen-man rosters. And yet in mid-April, Sleuth was still hanging around, taking up locker space and sapping Strouthers's small reserve of patience.

The manager was probably glad to say yes when Cobb requested a day off in mid-April to go on a kind of educational excursion. At seventeen, Ty was a regular reader of Grantland Rice, later one of America's premier sportswriters, but then a fledgling columnist for the *Atlanta Constitution*. Rice, proud of his ability to spot baseball talent in the rough, had lately been peppering his pieces with mentions of one Harry Hale of Happy Hollow, Tennessee, a six-foot-seven-inch deaf-mute with a killer fastball. Hale was trying to catch on with the Atlanta Crackers of the Southern League, and Cobb, "who never lost an opportunity to study his craft," as Rice said in his memoir, *The Tumult and the Shouting*, desperately wanted to see him pitch and observe how opponents adjusted to his heater. The Crackers were playing the Shreveport Sports at Piedmont Park the day that Ty arrived by train from Augusta. For four innings Hale lived up to Rice's hype, throwing smoke and holding Shreveport hitless. Then one of the Sports laid down a bunt and exposed the pitcher's weakness: he was a painfully awkward fielder. One bunter at a time, Shreveport loaded the bases. Stumbling after the fourth consecutive bunt, Hale spiked himself in the hand; two runs scored and he had to leave the game for stitches. Years later, after they had become friends, Cobb kidded Rice about his great "discovery"—but in 1904 Shreveport's dismantling of Harry Hale fascinated him. Three years later, when the even harder-throwing Walter Johnson came up with the Washington Senators, Cobb remembered the lesson well. We've already seen how Ty rattled Johnson by leaning far over the plate daring the Big Train to hit him, but in 1907 Johnson, besides being squeamish about plunking opponents, was notably slow off the mound. Cobb was among the first to spot the weakness, and he and the other Tigers laid down so many bunts against the tall, ungainly rookie in his major league debut that they made him realize he needed to work harder on defense. Once he improved his fielding, his place as an immortal was assured.

On the train back to Augusta that day, Cobb had an encounter that would mean little to him, but which had an enduring effect on the other party. Norvell "Oliver" Hardy, later the film partner of Stan Laurel, was then a chubby, precocious twelve-year-old who would frequently go AWOL from military school in Milledge, Georgia, to find work in Atlanta theatricals. Heading home after just such an adventure, he struck up a conversation with Cobb, who allowed that he was going to Warren Park to rejoin the Augusta Tourists. "Are you the bat boy?" said Hardy.

Cobb was indignant. "Bat boy?" he said. "You come to the game today; I'll show you."

Hardy, telling the tale to Rice forty years later on the Hal Roach Studio lot, and perhaps embellishing it a bit, said he took up Cobb on his offer to see him in what probably was a preseason intra-squad game. "He was something at that," the comedian said with a chuckle. "Cobb hammered a single, two doubles, a triple and a home run—and stole two bases."

If Cobb was too annoying for manager Strouthers to embrace wholeheartedly, he also was too promising, in his untamed way, to cut. On April 20, with the first regular season game, against the Columbia (North Carolina) Skyscrapers, less than a week away, Strouthers told him to go into the clubhouse and find himself a baseball-uniform-colored uniform, for Chrissakes, and the next day's *Chronicle* reported that "Cobb has discarded his red suit" and referred to him as a "fixture." But none of that meant that he had officially made the team.

Strouthers was not the best judge of talent, or the best anything. A portly fellow who resembled the stereotypical barbershop quartet bass, with handlebar mustache and hair parted dead center, he had what might generously be called a checkered past. Before his turn with the Tourists, he had been cited by various newspapers as an "utter failure" (as manager of Detroit in the Western League in 1895), the "hardest kicker [biggest whiner] in the Interstate League" (when he managed the Mansfield Haymakers in 1897), "about the worst that has happened" (as an umpire in the Interstate League), and "disgusting" (for his cursing and bullying of "Umpire Cline" while managing the Chattanooga Lookouts in 1902). To supplement his baseball income, he sometimes managed bad boxers and flop musicals. Solvency eluded him. In December of 1902, Strouthers was arrested in Columbus, Ohio, for stealing an iron coin bank containing $50 from one Bertha Chase, a boardinghouse owner who said that he'd also reneged on his promise to make her his third wife.

Things started off auspiciously for Strouthers in Augusta, where he got an opportunity to exhibit his modest flair for promotion. His "Name the Team" contest, meant to stir interest in the new franchise, which he and his partner, an Augusta railroad manager named Harlan Wingard, had each paid $500 to purchase from the league, would be the high point of his brief tenure in that city of 40,000. What the prize was, beyond the thrill of seeing one's suggestion immortalized in felt and flannel on the players' uniforms, is not known, but around April 1, 1904, just before Cobb arrived, Strouthers announced that he had identified the best and worst submissions. The worst was Augusta Grave Diggers, a reference to Magnolia Cemetery, the resting place of many a Confederate soldier, just across Third Street from Warren Park. The best suggestion in Strouthers's opinion, Tourists, made reference to what was still an important industry in Augusta in those years before Florida tempted the snowbirds farther south.

As opening day approached, Cobb's status with the team was vague at best. He was not named in the starting lineup that Strouthers submitted to the *Chronicle* on the morning of the first game—but he *was* in the open horse-drawn wagon that carried the Tourists on a circuitous route, through a light, cold drizzle, to Warren Park, preceded by the soggy Sacred Heart Cadets Band, for their encounter with the Skyscrapers. Cobb's fate as a Tourist, as it turned out, was tied to backstage machinations involving Augusta catcher Andy Roth, whom the Nashville Vols were claiming was contractually obligated to play for them. Roth, a Pennsylvania boy who'd honed his skills with the Lancaster Chicks and the Harrisburg Senators, was understood to be the best player on the team, if not in the entire league: the *Atlanta Constitution* said he "bats like a fiend and throws like a Japanese rapid-fire gun." Strouthers was confident he could prevail, but on the morning of the game, Sally League commissioner Charles Boyer ordered him to hold Roth out until the matter could be adjudicated, and the manager had to refigure his lineup, putting Cobb at center.

He would bat seventh, behind a leadoff man whose name is rendered in the record book as "William Spratt?" and a cleanup hitter, Harry Truby, who was trying to catch on with his twenty-third minor league club.

There was something quintessentially American about the Augusta Tourists first-ever opening day, Tuesday, April 26, 1904, which was also Confederate Memorial Day in the South. The first two fans to pay the 10 cent admission fee, said the *Chronicle*, were "M. J. Murphy, of North Augusta, and Charles Love, colored." (Murphy, for his dime, got to sit wherever he pleased; Love was limited to the Negro section in right field.) The Catholic school band played "Dixie" for the mostly Protestant crowd and a prominent lawyer named Henry Cohen threw out the first pitch (bouncing the ball three feet in front of home plate, and exiting to good-natured razzing). The president of the Augusta Rooters Club, Mexican-born music teacher José Andonegui, was offering $10 in gold to any Tourist who hit the ball over the center field fence that day. Even the parking was egalitarian: the city announced that it was putting in "hitching posts for horses, buggies and automobiles," with a security guard present to discourage joy riders, a much discussed problem in those days. Just before game time, the sky brightened and the drizzle all but ceased. About 2,000 turned out and during batting practice "got up on their hind legs" to cheer the Tourists and "show that they could be counted on." Two thousand was a decent crowd even for a midweek major league game in those days, and it certified the Tourists as the most popular attraction in town since a traveling show reenacting scenes from the Boer War had passed through a month earlier. In a matter of months, Con Strouthers would be begging for an umpiring job in a lesser league, and the skipper of the opposing Skyscrapers, Jack Grim, declared legally insane. But for now, hope reigned. Even though it was 3:30 p.m. when the home team finally trotted onto the muddy field, it was morning in Augusta.

The Tourists failed to keep the good mood going, losing a seesaw battle 8–7, but Cobb, after making out in his first two "organized ball" at-bats, finished the game in what would become his signature style. Leading off the eighth inning, he stroked a double over the center fielder's head. He then immediately stole third and, two batters later, scored on a slow roller to the second baseman, coming into the catcher, Dennis

Shea, like the Wabash Cannonball. "Cobb was enthusiastically cheered," said the *Chronicle*. "His opening of the fireworks [the Tourists would score four more runs that inning] gave him a warm place in the hearts of the fans." In the ninth he led off once more, and this time "slammed the ball over the ridge in left for a clean home run." In its game notes, the paper prophetically called the opposite field blast "a peacherina" that drove the crowd "bughouse," and added that Tyrus "was going to make a good man."

Strouthers, though, seemed oblivious to Cobb's popularity. The next afternoon, after Sleuth had gone hitless but scored a run in an 8–3 Augusta win, the manager cut his teenage center fielder, saying only, in a brief meeting in his office beneath the bleachers, "I don't need you anymore." Cobb was so surprised that for a instant he thought the older man was kidding, in the rough way ballplayers did. Ten years later, Cobb recalled that Strouthers also said that he wasn't fast enough for the Class C Tourists, though that may be a flourish he added later, to make the manager look doubly foolish, since Cobb was by 1915 a base stealer of wide renown. In any case, Ty was devastated both by the news and by the coldness with which it was delivered. He expected more from adults. He expected courtesy. "Evidently," Cobb said of Strouthers in 1914, "he didn't understand a boy's mind."

I have on my desk a photocopy of the first real contract our sensitive young subject ever signed. It was not with the Tourists, whose roster he was on and off too quickly that spring for such formalities. Rather, the document bears the letterhead of the Anniston, Alabama, Base Ball Association, a franchise in the independent (a euphemism for Class D) Tennessee-Alabama League—a team I so wish I could tell you was called the Jennifers, but which in fact was known as the Steelers or the Nobles or sometimes the Noblemen, when it was called anything at all. (Team nicknames in those days were usually left to the imagination of sportswriters and fans, who changed their minds perfidiously.) It is dated April 29, 1904, two days after Cobb was cut from the Tourists. In that brief span, Ty, though reeling from rejection, was able to a) get a lead on another job from a fellow Strouthers castoff named Fred Hayes, b) call his father to explain to him what had happened, c) make his way to Anniston, a noisy mill town of 10,000, 240 miles west of Augusta, and d) hash out a new deal. The Professor agreed that Ty should not quit while he was down. "Don't come home a failure," he said, trying to help his son avoid a psychological scar. Cobb, it seems, negotiated levelheadedly with the Anniston team owner, a druggist named L. L. Scarborough. The two-page agreement called for him to be paid $50 a month for the season, down considerably from the $90 the Tourists would have given him, but either he or Scarborough used a fountain pen to draw a line through the clause that said "and when not so traveling the party of the second part [Cobb] will pay all of his own expenses." That meant he would get board and meal money when he was "home" in Anniston—a considerable concession.

Horseplayers might apply the word "formful" to Ty's experience with the Anniston Steelers. Dropping down a notch in class, he immediately stood out more than he had at the C level, hitting .357, if you believe the accounts written nearly twenty years later by *Detroit News* sports editor H. G. Salsinger, or .457 if you believe Cobb's own newspaper memoirs. (It is really anyone's guess; the Tennessee-Alabama League did not keep cumulative statistics.) But the months he spent in Anniston were not all ice cream sodas at Scarborough's drugstore and huzzahs at Zinn Park. His teammates made his life difficult by riding him hard, partly out of jealousy, no doubt, but also because he played in such a raw and untamed way, jumping and shouting when on base, so as to distract the opposing pitcher, barreling into defenders, and chattering constantly. Instead of "Sleuth," a nickname he had rather cottoned to, his fellow Steelers mockingly referred to him as "Scrappy." It was in the clubhouse at Anniston that he first battled physically with teammates.

Homesickness added to his woes. Years later, an Anniston businessman named Ed Darden recalled that his parents, who were also from the north Georgia hills, put up Cobb that summer in the third-floor bedroom of the Quintard Avenue house that Ed normally shared with his younger brother, Wesley. It had two double beds; Cobb, the talk of the town, slept in one, and the two bedazzled boys, ages thirteen and ten, attempted to sleep in the other. Some nights nobody got much shuteye. Their distinguished guest, it soon became clear, suffered from an unquiet mind. Cobb still simmered with rage at Con Strouthers for letting him go, and also felt lonely being 200 miles from home and at the bottom of the baseball barrel. "I'll never forget that first Sunday," Darden told the *Anniston Star* in 1961. "Ty moped around the house all day. My mother did the best she could to bring him around, but it just wasn't any use. And the following weekend, after getting his first paycheck [for $12.50], he packed up and went home. Mr. Scarborough had to catch the train and bring him back." In time, though, with the help of the Steelers' kindly manager, George "Dad" Groves, a man to whom, Cobb said, "a life of hard knocks had given a broad understanding of human nature," he settled down a bit and became easier to be around. Darden chuckled when he recalled "Ty's method of getting me and Wes into the ball game. He would hand me his glove and Wes his bat and we would trail him into the park, carrying his equipment."

Ultimately, Cobb really didn't really want to go home, of course; he wanted to get to the major leagues, and as quickly as possible. On off days in Anniston, he spent hours at the counter of Scarborough's store writing postcards and letters to Grantland Rice, trying to trick the columnist into doing for him what Rice had done for Happy Harry Hale—that is, tout him as the Next Big Thing. Each note Cobb wrote contained a rave review of his abilities over a fictitious signature. *"Ty Cobb is really tearing up the horsehide in the Tennessee-Alabama League—Jack Smith."* Instead of sending off these pieces right away, Ty would drop them in mailboxes at various points along the Steelers' circuit, the better to create the impression of a grassroots movement. In *The Tumult and the Shouting*, Rice recalled getting dozens of such counterfeit testimonials. Although Cobb's pseudonyms—Brown, Jackson, Jones, Smith—were suspiciously common, Rice fell for the ruse, and feeling "under pressure" from his readers, finally inserted a note into his column saying "a new wonder had arrived, the darling of the fans, Ty Cobb."

The idea of a groundswell for Cobb wasn't so preposterous. The fans in Augusta certainly wanted him back. While Cobb led the Steelers to the top of the Tennessee-Alabama League, the Tourists were playing ineptly and nearing financial collapse. Some days as few as fifty people came out to witness what had become a sad excuse for a team. In a 4–2 loss to the Savannah Pathfinders on June 6, Harry Truby refused to leave second base after being called out on a close play, and had to be "melodramatically removed" from Warren Park by a mounted policeman, said the *Chronicle*. Later, Strouthers was arrested by another Augusta cop when he wouldn't stop "kicking" at an umpire's decision. By early July, some people were accusing the manager of "queering" games—that is, conspiring to lose so he could cash a bet. Meanwhile, every time Cobb stroked another game-winning hit for the Steelers, he made Strouthers look stupider for sending him packing. In early July, a contrite Strouthers wrote to Cobb asking if he would consider returning to Augusta. Ty, savoring the moment, said in response that he would never be a Tourist again as long as Strouthers remained in charge, and also made his precondition known to the *Chronicle*. Those reports sealed the skipper's fate. By mid-July, Strouthers had sold his 50 percent interest in the franchise to a consortium of business-men and hightailed it out of town just ahead of a tornado that blew the roof off the grandstand at Warren Park. Even before repairs were started, his once silent partner, Harlan Wingard, now the field manager, publicly summoned Cobb back to the Tourists.

This time Cobb agreed to return, but it was never easy to get him quickly from one place to another. Five days after telling Wingard he was on his way, he still hadn't arrived in Augusta. The problem, he explained in a telegram from Anniston, concerned his need to track down team owner Scarborough to collect several weeks' back pay. But when a new deadline for his arrival was set, and he again failed to show, "this did not suit the manager," said the *Chronicle*, and the angry Wingard "wired instructions that Cobb need not report at all." Nevertheless when Ty finally turned up the next day, Wingard immediately inserted him into the lineup.

Ty went 0-for-4 in his first game back with the Tourists, the start of a rough couple of months. As good as he was, he still had a lot to learn—about the hit-and-run play, about breaking from the batter's box after a bunt, about the line between creative disruption on the base paths and pointless yannigan shenanigans. On top of that he got sick with what he decided was malaria. He stayed in the lineup but struggled for weeks, and when the season ended, with the Tourists finishing fifth out of six in the Sally League standings, he was hitting just .237.

— CHAPTER SIX —

PLAYING ORGANIZED BASEBALL FOR A full season temporarily took some of the edge off Cobb's enthusiasm for the game. The Augusta Tourists, whether managed by a dyspeptic baseball gypsy (Strouthers), or a career railroad man (Wingard), were an unsettled amalgam of current and former hopefuls, the latter content to spend a few sin-soaked seasons playing games for pay before settling into the short, brutish lives that awaited many men born before the turn of the century. United by a sense that they were just passing through town on their way to something better (besides Cobb, the future major leaguers included pitchers Eddie Cicotte and Nap Rucker, and outfielder Clyde Engle) or worse, the Tourists collectively constituted what was known in those days as "a joy club." They drank in the unlicensed "blind tigers" that were both a bane of and a source of side income for the corruptible Augusta police, and frolicked with the disreputable ladies who hung around the Warren Park grandstand, smoking cigarettes and drawing cross looks from spectators, and stern warnings from the *Chronicle*. ("Women of questionable character will save themselves the humiliation of being turned down at the gate by staying away from the park.") Cobb couldn't help being at least a little intrigued by his circumstances, and, yielding to the peer pressure, he got nonchalant about the game at times, a choice that always left him feeling crummy.

Andy Roth, the good-hitting catcher who became the Tourists' third manager in their tumultuous first season, had led Ty to believe that, despite his lackluster batting average, a position on the 1905 team was his to lose. But Ty didn't see Roth as the leader the Tourists needed—he was too unimaginative as a baseball man and too lenient as a babysitter, he

felt, and by the time Cobb returned to Royston in the fall of 1904, exposure to the profession's grimmer realities—not the least of which was that
baseball was a game played by ballplayers—had tempered his passion.
He wasn't over baseball by any means, but he needed a break from the
cynicism and vulgarity of the locker room, as well as from the constant
losing. So he threw himself into small-town life, working on his father's
farm alongside Uncle Ezra, going for runs on the still unpaved roads, and
catching up with old friends, like Clifford Ginn, a former teammate on
the Reds and Rompers who was married to his mother's kid sister and
who in later years would serve as his accountant. What they talked about
while sitting on Ty's front porch on Franklin Springs Street we'll never
know for certain, but Topic A in town that winter was the Jones sisters,
the Cobbs' next-door neighbors.

Annie and Vinie Jones had been a source of controversy in Royston
for about fifteen years by then, since before W.H. and Amanda Cobb
and their children had moved to Royston in 1897. The unmarried sisters,
both in their mid-thirties in 1905, claimed to be dressmakers as well as
"teachers of a certain system of dressmaking," but everyone knew they
were prostitutes. Not wishing to call attention to themselves, they were
careful to live quietly, but they could not always control their customers.
Late one night in the spring of 1903, Stephen Ginn, Clifford's father
and the breeder of the famous Ginn chickens, barged into their house
in a drunken state and began smashing their possessions with a stick.
When Annie called in another neighbor, Sanford Hulm, to help them,
Ginn told him "in a maudlin fashion," that he had paid Vinie $600 for
a year's worth of sexual privileges, but was disappointed to discover the
arrangement was not exclusive. The police came and it was a mess. Ginn
was no stranger to public humiliation. In 1892, he was startled from
sleep by what he thought was an intruder, fired the pistol that he kept
on his nightstand, and shot off one of his fingers. The police came and it
was a mess—but that time in a kind of darkly comic fashion. The Vinie
Jones incident—which took place just a few doors down from the house
where Ginn lived with his wife and eight children—sent a chill through
Royston because it threatened the social fabric. It made townsfolk wonder
how many other fathers might be out there fooling around and falling in

love. In short order, a summons was served on the women, and despite very little hard evidence, prosecutors managed to get an indictment, or as they said in Georgia, a "true bill." It wasn't until two years later, though, around the time that Cobb was packing for his second season with the Augusta Tourists, that their case finally showed signs of coming to trial.

We'll get back to that matter, which, it could be argued, played a key role in the Cobb family's tragic summer, but let us say for the moment that in the early months of 1905, Ty was certainly aware of his notorious next-door neighbors—and yet still more interested in baseball. Refreshed after several months in the fields and on the roads of Royston, he eagerly anticipated the coming Tourists' season. With training camp set to open at Warren Park, he packed two bags—a leather one for clothes, a cloth one for his beloved bats—and was among the first four players to check in for what were technically tryouts on Sunday, March 19, 1905. It was a rare instance of his being early for anything. Manager Roth, perhaps surprised, as others were, to see that he had over the winter completed the transition from midget to "big, raw-boned hulking kid," greeted him warmly and penciled him in to the lineup for an exhibition game the next day against the Detroit Tigers—"the kings of the diamond," as the *Chronicle* called them, erroneously.

The Tigers—who got their nickname back in the 1890s, when they were part of the Western League, from their yellow-and-brown-striped socks—were actually one of the less imposing teams in the four-year-old American League. They were training in Augusta for the first time ever, having spent their previous two springs in Shreveport, prepping for campaigns that ended with fifth- and seventh-places finishes, respectively. Detroit's secretary-treasurer, Frank Navin, had arranged the switch to Augusta because its Albion Hotel, an officious-looking edifice just across Broad Street from the Confederate monument, promised to put up each player at the bargain price of $15 per week, and the Turkish bathhouse next door offered its facilities for just $2.50 per man, including one's choice of "colored or white rubbers," meaning masseurs. For Navin, running a ball club was always about getting a bargain; the Great Nickel Nurser, as he was sometimes known, had a reputation for being the most miserly man in the game.

He did, it was true, have some excuses for his stinginess: Detroit (population 300,000) was the smallest city represented in the eight-team American League and it had the smallest ballpark in the majors (seating capacity: 8,500). With a grand total of only 118,000 attendees the previous season it had the second-slowest turnstiles in the AL, ahead of only the hapless Washington Senators. The Tigers also suffered from the unique problem of "wildcat bleachers": rickety wooden stands thrown up by entrepreneurs on the corner of Cherry Street and National Avenue that allowed people—for a 15 cent fee that the franchise never saw a penny of—to look over the Bennett Park fence and literally steal a peek at the action. Large swatches of the outfield walls went begging for advertising despite the bargain rate of $25 per season per panel, and the renting of seat cushions, a lively side business in some big league outposts, was a total bust in the nascent Motor City. That year the Tigers were also being sued by their former popcorn man for wrongful dismissal, and there was concern in the front office that a substantial settlement—meaning anything over a few thousand dollars—could capsize the financially tenuous franchise.

And yet those who worked with Navin knew he would have been just as tough with a buck if he'd been managing Standard Oil or Carnegie Steel. For the pale, bald, poker-faced son of an Irish railroad worker—he looked a bit like a thumb with glasses—pinching owner Bill Yawkey's pennies was the game within the game, and he delighted in it. Reading through the letters he sent to his players each January, telling them to sign the enclosed contract and be quick about it, one gets a sense of the joy he took in sparring with men who because they were bound by the reserve clause (which kept them from becoming free agents) and had no agents or lawyers to represent them, were fighting with their hands tied. "I wish to call your attention to the fact that outside of [Ollie] Pickering, who has been released to Columbus, you were the lowest hitter in the American League of the regular outfielders" Navin said in a typically pleasant note to Sam Crawford in the early days of 1905 (the usually productive outfielder had had an off year due to an injury). The secretary hated writing checks, even for the small sums the Tigers paid for necessities: $72 for a gross, or one year's worth, of baseballs; $429.32 annual rent for Bennett

Park. His obsession with saving money sometimes tempted him across moral lines. Writing to a manufacturer of turnstiles in 1906, he asked if the company made a model with a concealed counter—an inquiry that would seem to support Cobb's later contention that the Tigers under-reported ticket sales so they could cry poverty to their players and lower the tithe they paid the league.

Navin's tightness might have gone less remarked upon if it wasn't juxtaposed so blatantly with his profligate personal ways. Letters in the Ernie Harwell Collection at the Detroit Public Library show that in the midst of arguing with players about three-figure raises, he would be ordering expensive lingerie from a fancy New York shop, presumably for his wife; promising to "stake" a friend in Boston "to a nice young lady" when he, Navin, next came to visit; and bantering about big investments in madcap ventures like an early forerunner of the parachute jump attraction then being considered for Coney Island. It was his gambling, though, that set him apart as a spendthrift. The working-class boy from Adrian, Michigan, had once toiled as a croupier in a Detroit casino, and he played a lot of poker, but horses were his métier, and he was frequently on the phone with his bookie. This Frank Navin resembled the cheaper model only in his emotionless demeanor. One day when he had $500 down on an 8–1 shot in the first race at some out-of-town track, his jockey bumped into the starting barrier and tumbled to the turf. Upon hearing the bad news, Navin without so much as a sigh, said, "I wonder what looks good in the second."

That attitude would serve him well with the Tigers, who seemed to be a star-crossed team, especially after their manager, Win Mercer, who displayed a more rational reaction to gambling losses, committed suicide in January of 1903 by inhaling illuminating gas at a San Francisco hotel. Navin was a minor front-office figure then, but he had what Frederick G. Lieb, in his comprehensive and colorful history of the Detroit club, called "the ability to make figures stand up and say Uncle," as well as a knack for pleasing his boss of the moment. When Tigers owner Sam Angus brought him over from his insurance business, Navin served him loyally, quickly becoming more than just a glorified bookkeeper. As the owner ran low on operating capital in the middle of '03, and American League president

Ban Johnson threatened to move the franchise to Pittsburgh, Navin deftly engineered the sale of the Tigers to William Clyman Yawkey, an old iron and lumber baron who was probably the richest man in Michigan. And when W. C. Yawkey died of a heart attack just before the contract could be signed, Navin even more deftly sold the millionaire's only son on the idea of assuming the $50,000 obligation even though William Hoover Yawkey was a rudderless trust-fund kid who cared little about sports. The younger magnate (who was both the uncle and adoptive father of future Red Sox owner Tom Yawkey) was delighted to let Navin and manager Ed Barrow run the club while he fulfilled the duties of an Edwardian-era playboy.

Barrow, though paid less than Navin, was probably the club's most valuable asset, owning to his gimlet eye for talent. History knows him better as the general manager who presided over the transformation of Babe Ruth from pitcher to outfielder, then built a Yankees dynasty around him and Lou Gehrig in the 1920s. But Barrow's work with the Tigers was no less remarkable considering that he was forced to operate within Navin's severe financial constraints. His greatest single acquisition was the aforementioned Wahoo Sam Crawford, a future Hall of Famer whose rights he acquired from Cincinnati in 1903, but his best year with the franchise was 1904, when he brought in outfielder Matty McIntyre, shortstop Charley O'Leary and third baseman Bill Coughlin, forgotten names today but productive role players who would help turn the Tigers into league champs.

The one criterion that Barrow seems not to have considered too closely when assembling a team was chemistry. Even though men of color were not an option in those days, the talent market was diverse—"We had stupid guys, smart guys, tough guys, mild guys, crazy guys, college men, slickers from the city and hicks from the country," Davy Jones, who joined the Tigers in 1906, told Lawrence Ritter in *The Glory of Their Times*—and the potential for trouble when those types came together to form a ball team was substantial. But Barrow either didn't notice or didn't care about such things. It could be that, like many baseball men of his vintage—he was born in 1868 while his parents were rumbling through

Springfield, Illinois, in a covered wagon—he wasn't sensitive or sympathetic to the concept of group dynamics. Or maybe his budget simply
prohibited the acquisition of players who weren't huge pains in the ass.
But for whatever reason, the Tiger team he assembled was a hodgepodge
of sour and contentious personalities, awash (it almost went without saying) in alcohol—as unlovable to each other as they were to the citizens of
Detroit.

No one personified this discordant pre-Cobb club more than Norman
"Kid" Elberfeld. "Tabasco," as the fiery shortstop was sometimes known,
once wrestled the famous umpire Silk O'Loughlin to the ground after a
disputed call and held the unofficial record for being ejected, no mean
feat in that day when at least one umpire (Andy Gifford) carried a knife
because he was so often set upon by angry players. Barrow, knowing how
much Elberfeld hated being a Tiger, once accused him of indulging in
"loaferish behavior" to force a trade. But, interestingly, I think, Barrow
was not shocked by Elberfeld's attitude. He didn't even dislike the (usually) aggressive Kid, whom he recognized as a stock character in the pag-
eant that was early organized baseball: the Hothead—a role that Barrow
had himself played over the years. Barrow's players trembled at his wither-
ing performance evaluations and expletive-flecked advice. Once outfielder
Jimmy Barrett screwed up the courage to say, "Mr. Barrow, your methods
take all the individuality away from a ballplayer." Barrett immediately
regretted the remark. "If you ever speak to me that way again," Barrow
told him, "I will take more than your individuality away from you. I will
knock your block off!" Barrett actually got away easy. Barrow's usual
method for dealing with a troublesome player was to invite the man to his
office, lock the door, and then pounce on him with both fists. It truly was
a golden age of grouchiness.

Both Barrow and Navin hated it when owner Bill Yawkey would swan
in from his pampered high-society life and bequeath $50 and $100 spot
bonuses to players who had performed in ways that he adjudged to be
above and beyond the call. But the two Tiger leaders didn't agree on much
else, and in fact came to dislike each other deeply. Navin needed a more
malleable man in the skipper's spot if his influence over the franchise was
going to increase, and Barrow could not abide his boss's constant med-

dling in player transactions. In December of 1904, after a particularly bitter squabble over a third-string catcher, Barrow quit and took a job in the American Association as manager of the Indianapolis Indians.

The Tigers weren't at Augusta's Warren Park the day Cobb reported for duty with the Tourists in March of 1905. They were involved in a publicity stunt at the local zoo, riding Lil the elephant as well as an unnamed camel or two and "gazing into the yellow eyes of caged lions" (there were no tigers available) while writers from the *Augusta Chronicle* and the Detroit dailies followed them around and observed their carefree and confident behavior. The message that the ticket-buying public was meant to take from this apparently unphotographed photo op was that the team's 62–90 season of 1904 was a rapidly receding memory. Strengthened by several off-season moves, they were ready to take a run at the mighty Boston Americans, AL champs for the last two seasons. But for all their swagger in spring training, the Tigers did not really seem primed for happier times. While they had taken several steps forward under Barrow, his departure, combined with the advent of Bill Armour as manager, amounted to a substantial net setback.

Armour, whose career as an outfielder for the Paterson Silk Weavers, the Toledo Mud Hens, and other minor league clubs had been hamstrung by his morbid fear of butterflies, simply didn't inspire confidence as a skipper. Fired by Cleveland for his failure to get along with the team's beloved star, Napoleon Lajoie, he came to Detroit at Navin's request—and hit the ground bumbling. It took him a couple of months just to find Germany Schaefer's home address in Chicago to send him a contract; he alienated his best players by belittling their abilities in letters he sent them during their annual negotiations; and he amused rival managers by writing to them to ask if they happened to have any extra pitchers "of Cy Young caliber" available for trading. (They did not.) He might have been better cast as the team's traveling secretary; he obsessed about every detail of the Tigers' accommodations at the Albion in Augusta and, in lieu of landing hot pitching prospects, devised a system whereby each Tiger player would retain the same number sleeping car berth for the entire season, thus saving valuable moments at the start of every road trip. Connie Mack he was not.

Armour did *dress* like Connie Mack, though, wearing a suit and tie in the dugout, the way Mack did as manager of the A's from 1901 through 1950, in hopes of commanding respect. (He was also, it would appear, the last man in the major leagues to sport a mustache until Rollie Fingers came along in the 1960s.) Armour's players, however, were not impressed. It was only when he wielded the cudgel of the reserve clause, in letters that channeled his boss's heartless tone, that they acknowledged his superior position.

"Dear Sir," Armour wrote to Matty McIntyre in January of 1905 after the left fielder had threatened to jump to the Eastern League rather than accept the Tigers' offer,

> *I have always wondered why you didn't make a better showing last year, and now I have discovered the cause. Any young player that stays one year in the American League and then wishes to go back to the Eastern League shows what he is made of. . . . There have been hundreds of failures for the same reason that you will be a failure and was [sic] a failure practically last year. We hung on to you and kept bolstering you up, but I can now see it is of no use. As far as the Detroit Club releasing you, we have not the slightest idea of so doing. You will play ball if you play in organized base ball with the Detroit Club at a salary of Two Thousand Dollars, and you can report or not, as you see fit. I don't see that you tore things loose so much on any of the American League Parks last year.*

Such nastiness is what passed for normal discourse with those early Tigers. Former manager Ed Barrow had set the tone by pulling together players who didn't get along well, with the world or with each other, and keeping them in line by means of threats and corporal punishment. Armour would continue the tradition, even managing, via his inept impersonation of a martinet, to make matters worse. And no one would remember what happened back then in the bowels of Bennett Park if the planets weren't aligning in a way that put Ty Cobb and the Tigers on intersecting paths.

CHAPTER SEVEN

IF THERE WAS ANYONE WHO could put the swagger back into the browbeaten Tigers, it was the decidedly Class C Augusta Tourists. There were several ways that Warren Park would never be confused with a major league venue, starting with the fact that its infield remained unsodded, and thus in its very lack of lushness served as an ironic reminder that the place was severely bush. Then there were the not-so-uniform uniforms of the home team; manager Andy Roth had found himself six suits short at the start of the Tourists' second season, and had put out a call for donations, which arrived by the bundle but naturally did not match. Newcomers to Augusta baseball also had to adjust to the singular way the spectators behaved. Instead of reacting instantly to something that happened on the field, they would sit in silence, noted *Detroit Free Press* correspondent Joe S. Jackson, the way playgoers might pause to ponder "a subtly humorous line," and then, a long moment or two after the fact, "burst into a manifestation of appreciation that lasts twice as long as a similar ovation does elsewhere." Both the ground and the groundlings set the place apart. But the Tourists and their ballpark never looked more backwater than when they played host to what everyone then called "fast company"—a major league club.

Detroit played Augusta five times that spring and won four times, whacking the ball through the barren, brown infield seemingly at will while stymieing their opponents with sparkling glove work and sparrow-like curves. In every game but one the Tigers reached double digits in hits while the Tourists could only scratch out a handful. They executed double steals, hit-and-run plays, and sacrifice bunts, all at a speed that left their audiences of 300 or so agog. On defense, Detroit shortstop Charley

O'Leary was especially impressive, "cabbaging" grounders on the short hop (one correspondent wrote) and whipping them to Crawford, who was being tested that spring, said the *Chronicle*, at "the initial sack." The fawning (and fickle) hometown paper said that young Tyrus especially should pay attention to the master class the Tigers were conducting. "Cobb is showing up well," said the *Chronicle*'s "Diamond Dust" column of March 24. "Only one word of caution to the clever sticker in running bases, to wit: You are not in the amateur game now, and reckless endeavors to steal a sack on an experienced pitcher, when he has the ball, is a failure nine times out of ten. Fast sprinting, clever sliding and neat swings around the basemen, well practiced, will pay you better in the long run, Cobb." It wasn't just the *Chronicle* that thought Ty should tone down his flamboyant play. When George Leidy, a veteran outfielder, joined the Tourists a couple of months later, he noted the Royston kid was "the butt of all the would-be comedians on the club" for his overly aggressive style. Ty wouldn't stop running wild, though, until Andy Roth finally forbade him from stealing—and then he sat and sulked.

Before the Tigers broke camp and headed to Detroit, Germany Schaefer and pitcher "Wild Bill" Donovan took time during batting practice to say goodbye to Cobb, who had hit about .300 against their club, and to offer him a few pointers. "Always slide feet first," Schaefer said. Donovan advised Armour to keep an eye on the overzealous redheaded kid, because he was "going places." Ty later admitted that he fantasized about joining the big leaguers for the trip north. Once the Tigers left town, his spirits sagged, and his average reverted to what it had been the previous autumn, when he had finished in a funk. Then it fell even lower. On the first of May, Cobb was hitting .243 and a week later .235. For the first time in his career, he was failing even to make contact—"Cobb did his fanning act again" became a *Chronicle* mantra. His problems were not confined to the plate. In right field, where he played most of the time, line drives slithered through his hands and fly balls plunked to the earth all around him. He pretended he didn't care, and often it seemed like he truly didn't. In a home game against the Savannah Pathfinders, he missed a routine fly ball because he had been munching on a wheel of caramel popcorn while standing in the outfield.

• • •

Perhaps it is no coincidence that Cobb at the moment was falling in love. The object of his affection, Charlotte Marion Lombard, was the eldest daughter of one of the wealthiest men in Augusta, a magnate whose money came from two distinctly nineteenth-century enterprises: an iron-works and a grist mill. When Ty met her, though, through a boyfriend of one of her classmates at Sacred Heart Academy, she gave her name as Charlie: a sign, or so it would seem, of proto-flapper, modern-gal spunk. She was only fifteen at the time but she started showing up regularly at Tourists games and her presence, in the ladies section, was hardly lost on Tyrus. They began seeing each other, at dances and other organized func-tions, and before long they were talking marriage. Her father, Roswell O. Lombard, thought she was too young and Ty's profession too undepend-able, though, and so for the time being they made no firm plans.

Lombard was more correct about baseball than he knew. The Tour-ists, tired of Ty's antics, and short on cash, were exploring the possibility of selling him to another team hundreds of miles distant. Ed Barrow, in his lively autobiography, *My Fifty Years in Baseball*, says that Roth at that juncture reached out to him to propose a deal: Cobb and utility man Clyde Engle for $800 as a package or $500 for either man alone. He ne-glected to mention that the latter—a talented player who would make it to the major leagues a few years later—had a sexually transmitted disease that would soon put him out for a long spell. But Barrow in any case was in no mood to deal. "I was not in a happy mental state" as manager of the Indianapolis Indians, he wrote. "I was still rankled when I thought of Navin and Detroit . . . further, I had Fannie Taylor up in Toronto on my mind and wanted to get back there. Indeed, I have told her many a time through the years that she cost me Ty Cobb." Barrow's book makes no previous or further mention of Ms. Taylor, and that's a shame because the Ontario-based enchantress changed baseball history. By helping to scotch a trade that would have sent Cobb to Indiana, she put the trou-bled eighteen-year-old on a path to encounter George Leidy, the man he would always credit with saving his career from a premature demise.

George O. Leidy never made it to the major leagues, and he cut such a narrow swath through the bushes that it's impossible to describe him in great detail. Contemporary reports note that he was of medium height with gnarled knuckles, for whatever that may be worth to your imagination. Even I, at this point probably one of America's foremost George O. Leidy experts, cannot tell you what the O. stood for. He is an enigma wrapped in an Augusta Tourists uniform. Cobb said he had a Southern drawl, but Leidy was born and raised in New Jersey. His manner is rendered, in the traditional Cobb literature, as even-keeled and mild, but that's probably just an assumption based on the stabilizing role he played in Cobb's life. The facts, few as they are, suggest a more complicated man, who, though valued for his leadership skills, had flashed a temper from time to time and once been suspended from the Pennsylvania League (where he played on the same Harrisburg team as Roth) for "insubordination." In 1904, when he managed the Monroe Hill Citys of the Cotton States League, *Sporting Life* described him as "cranky"—and in those days, as we've seen, you had to be practically a serial killer to register as such.

How this man of mystery came to join the Tourists in April of 1905 will perhaps never be known. Owner John B. Carter had been feuding with Roth over his inability to impose discipline, so it's possible that Leidy, an experienced manager with a reputation for strictness, was brought in by the front office to help in that regard. What we do know is that no sooner had Leidy arrived than he announced his departure, saying that the Tourists were more unruly than he had expected, utterly beyond help. After some discussion with Carter and Roth, however, he calmed down, agreed to stay on, and was designated team captain, which made him the heir apparent to Roth.

Leidy had his first talk with Cobb on the evening of the day that Roth benched him for snacking in the outfield. "The wonderful old man," as Cobb remembered his thirty-six-year-old teammate, took him on a streetcar ride to an amusement park on the outskirts of Augusta, where they strolled the gas-lit grounds and talked. Leidy "wasn't angry, just disappointed," Cobb recalled. "Baseball [he said] was a great game. It had unlimited opportunities for a boy who knew how to play. Eating popcorn in the outfield was all right if you thought the game was just a joke. But suppose you were too ambitious for that kind of horseplay? Suppose you kept your eye on the ball, studied, practiced, learned to make the most of what nature had given you. You could go to towns that would make Augusta look like a crossroads. You could be famous, you could make a fortune. And every boy in America would idolize you. Your name would go down in the history books. That night was the turning point," Cobb said. "I made up my mind to be a big leaguer if it killed me."

Leidy's gospel was nothing more complicated than practice makes perfect, but he thought in terms of hundreds if not thousands of hours of repetitive drills. "Christy Mathewson wasn't always a great pitcher," he told Cobb that evening at the amusement park. "When he started out he had very poor control, so he'd go to the park early and take along a catcher. He'd have the catcher hold his glove in one position and try to hit the hollow of the glove with every pitch. In the winter he cut a hole about twice as big as a baseball about the height of an average man's waist in the side of his barn, and he'd pitch for hours trying to throw the ball through the hole." Moving on to Honus Wagner, the era's other major star, Leidy recounted a strange story about how the burly shortstop, eager to get a better jump on ground balls, would "dig trenches and set himself in those trenches in his stocking feet to get a better start." Even if some of Leidy's lessons left Cobb scratching his head, the moral of every tale he told was: "You gotta keep pegging at one certain thing until you got it down pat."

At the conclusion of that life-changing lecture, Leidy advised Ty to meet him early next morning at Warren Park and to bring a sweater. Cobb, for all his desire to explore the limits of the game, was not yet a good bunter, so the older man put the plumped-up cardigan just inside the first base line, about forty feet from home plate, and tossed Cobb baseballs so he could practice drag bunting into it. This went on for at least an hour, after which they transitioned to drills involving the hit-and-run play and stealing bases. Cobb also practiced sliding in loose dirt he dug up in a remote corner of Warren Park, hooking and fadeaway-ing and figure-fouring until blood from his leg wounds seeped through his uniform pants. Day after day, alone together on the field, not stopping until other Tourists started filtering in at around 11:00 a.m., he and Leidy repeated their lessons, sometimes putting the sweater on the third base side, at other times stopping the exercises and talking about common-sense things like getting enough sleep and eating lighter meals at midday. Cobb had once routinely enjoyed a platter of roast pork and sweet potatoes before heading to the ballpark; after hearing Leidy describe the digestive process as only a minor league baseball manager could, he cut back to soup, then eliminated lunch entirely. He knew he needed help, and he liked Leidy's holistic approach, which posited a right and wrong way to live and play.

"Up to that time, I had been running hog wild all over the field. I was a bundle of springs. . . . I would run bases harum scarum and would gallop all over the field trying to get into every play. . . . In some ways my speed and energy were a handicap. I would frequently muss things up." A change, he saw, was necessary, but being publicly chastised by men like Strouthers and Roth, and teased by his teammates, had only driven him deeper into his "harum scarum" approach. With Leidy's help he found a face-saving way out. Leidy knew how to criticize Cobb without hurting his feelings, and spoke as a fellow hothead, a man who couldn't suffer fools, a role Cobb could relate to and respect. Cobb didn't become a conventional player by any means, but he became determined to channel his exuberance. "I began to find myself," Ty recalled.

He began to find the ball, too, with almost scary consistency. On May 29 he was hitting .290, and two weeks later, .312. As his average improved, he began to carry himself with a little swagger. It was around this time that Ty began his trademark ritual of swinging all three of his beloved black bats while waiting in the on-deck circle. The routine rarely varied. He would start with a trio of biffers, then switch to one (which he twirled over his head), then pick up another, then swing with all three again before dropping two rather dramatically and striding to the plate. Today almost every player performs some variation on this routine, usually using a weighted club or a lead donut instead of multiple bats. For most if not all it is simply a matter of limbering up. But Cobb from the start saw it as more than just that. He thought of it as a way to intimidate the pitcher, who he knew was probably watching him out of the corner of his eye as he juggled his weapons like a samurai preparing to fight. "I was always doing something," Cobb recalled years later, "always trying to rattle the other side any way I could."

Toward the end of June, to the surprise of no one, Leidy became manager of the Tourists, while Roth stayed on as the starting catcher. Days later, *Sporting Life* congratulated "Cyrus Cobb" for becoming the first player in the South Atlantic League to reach 100 hits that season. The team wasn't winning any more often than it had been a few weeks earlier, but the mood around Warren Park had at least temporarily brightened. On July 23, the *Chronicle* published a poem, the latest installment of its Augusta Tourists "alphabet book":

> *G is for grouchy*
> *Which is how we all feel*
> *When Cobb gets a start*
> *And then fails to steal.*

Meanwhile up north, the Tigers were taking their by now customary midsummer swan dive through the AL standings. After losing nine out of 10 to Boston, Washington, and Philadelphia in late July and early August, their record stood at 43–47–1, and even their cadre of loyal cranks (as fans were called in those days) had started to grumble. "The boys have not been getting the support their record calls for," Joe S. Jackson wrote in the *Detroit Free Press*, "the crowds having been slim and the applause frequently stronger for the visitors than for the home team," who indeed received "loud guffaws for every slip that is made." The pitching was "unreliable" Jackson conceded, the catching "far from the strongest in the league," and the outfield had a "patched up" feel. That was putting it mildly; all but one of their six outfielders had some kind of serious complaint. Matty McIntyre was out indefinitely with a "paralyzed hand"; Bobby Lowe and Jimmy Barrett both had leg injuries; Duff Cooley had a perpetual hangover, and Charlie Hickman quit the team in a huff, saying Armour was blaming him for everything that was going wrong, and he couldn't bear being the scapegoat.

The manager was indeed showing signs of desperation, begging men who had never played in the big leagues (and never would) to join his team. On July 7, he wrote to one Henry Melchior, a twenty-five-year-old outfielder for the Grand Rapids Orphans of the Central League, urging him to reconsider an offer Melchior had spurned a few days earlier. "What seems to be the trouble? There is an elegant opportunity for you with our team. My outfield is in pretty bad shape and I would be able to put you in and use you right along." Melchior, unimpressed, chose to remain an Orphan. Armour next addressed a letter to "Mr. James, Ball Player, Lancaster, Ohio." "Dear Sir," it said, "I understand through a friend of mine that you are a left-handed pitcher. Would like to know what your age, height, and weight are, and whatever experience you have had in baseball."

Armour also dispatched his chief scout Henry "Heinie" Youngman, a portly German immigrant, to comb the country for prospects. It is sometimes said that Youngman was told to "Go get that Cobb kid we saw in Augusta last spring!" But after trying and failing to recruit an outfielder in Massachusetts, the scout, it seems, hopped an Augusta-bound train to check out the Tourists on a whim. If anyone was drawing him there it was pitcher Eddie Cicotte, a Michigan phenom whom the Tigers had optioned to the Sally League team after a spring tryout. Cicotte was throwing almost nothing but knuckleballs and spitters, Armour had heard, and he was worried about the twenty-one-year-old prospect hurting his arm with the "freak pitches." Neither Youngman nor Armour appears to have had Cobb—the player that pitcher Donovan advised them to watch out for—on his mind when his trip began. "Let me know when you will start South," the manager wrote his scout on July 14. "I think the weather would do you a whole lot of good as you carry a little extra superfluous flesh with you anyhow. You will find the southern country mighty fine in the summer time. Do not be afraid to make a deal for any player that looks good enough for this company but do not let him hold you up." It wasn't easy to be clueless about Cobb—who was then batting about .315, leading the Sally League in hits, and getting write-ups in *Sporting Life*— but both Armour and Youngman somehow managed.

Youngman may have first heard the name Ty Cobb shortly after his arrival, when he ran into Leidy on an Augusta street. In a nicely evocative interview with a *Washington Post* reporter six years after the fact, the Tourists' manager said that he had written to Fred Clarke, the manager of the Pittsburgh Pirates, and Connie Mack of the Philadelphia A's, urging them to take Ty in the annual early-September draft, and was waiting to hear back from that illustrious duo, when he turned a corner and bumped into Heinie Youngman. I'll let Leidy tell the tale.

"Anything in the lake?" Youngman asked, after we had shaken hands.

"Yes," says I, "there is. I've got a 'dinger' here. He can throw the ball just as far as anybody else, get down to first quicker than any man who ever lived, hit just as hard and fast as he wants to, can lay it down in a five-foot ring anywhere if you want to mark it off—"

"What you been smoking?" interrupted Youngman.

"That ain't no smoke talk," says I. "It's the truth."

"Tell me about him again then," said Heinie.

"No, you come out to the park this afternoon and see him work," says I.

The first time Tyrus came to bat in that day's game he smashed one at the pitcher that liked to have tore his ear off. The next time up he hit one about as high as a street car, and it went dang-ity-ding-ding up against the pickets in center field, for three bags. Then came a bunt, about three feet from the plate, and in spite of the quick fielding by the pitcher, Tyrus was on his way back to first when it was picked up. The last time up, he hit one so hard that nobody knew where it was until they heard it hit the fence in right field.

"Well, how do you like him?" I asked Scout Youngman, after the game.

"Oh, he did pretty good today," said he.

"Well, come out tomorrow," says I, sarcastic like.

He only made two hits the next day. We left that night for Jacksonville, but when I woke up there the first person I saw was Heinie Youngman, who had come about 200 miles to see Tyrus again. In the three games at Jacksonville, Tyrus made eleven hits. Shortly after this, Cobb was sold to Detroit, and when he left me, he said,

"George, if I make good up there, you've got something coming to you."

"Well," says I, "if you keep your word, I've got it in my pocket, for you'll make good."

And sure enough, at the end of the season, he came through, like the thoroughbred he is, and always will be.

PART TWO

GEORGE LEIDY DIDN'T LIE ABOUT the role he played in Ty Cobb's ascent to the majors. If anything, Leidy was overly modest about his contribution, to the point where we probably wouldn't know his name if Cobb hadn't brought it up so often. But at the same time Leidy's recall was hardly flawless, as the passage at the end of the previous chapter demonstrates. For one thing, he referred there to Youngman as "Young," a slipup I took the liberty of correcting. For another, Cobb didn't get eleven hits in three games against the Jacksonville Jays, as Leidy claimed; he got seven hits in four games—still good for a .438 series average. And then there is the fact that those games weren't played in Jacksonville's Dixieland Park, a turn-of-the-century wonderland that—besides an exquisitely manicured baseball diamond—featured a collection of clockwork rides and a small oval track where ostriches raced to sulky. No, the Tourists faced the Jays at Augusta's dusty Warren Park just prior to Heinie Youngman's arrival. Indeed by the time his team set off for its next series in Jacksonville, in early August of 1905, Ty didn't travel with it, owing to a family emergency.

We have come to another it-is-impossible-to-say-with-certainty moment in our tale. While I am able to bring to the discussion of W. H. Cobb's murder a number of facts and considerations that haven't seen daylight since the tragedy, if ever, no one can state with certainty why Ty's father was tramping around in his own side yard at about 11:00 p.m. on August 8, 1905. Ostensibly he had left home for a few days to visit some schools in the district that he supervised. He departed on a Tuesday, telling Amanda and others that he'd return that Thursday evening. But that's not what happened. His itinerary can't be reconstructed precisely at this remove, but we do know that in addition to any other calls he may have made he went to see his friend Judge W. R. Little in Carnesville (the jurist to whom he had earlier sent Ty to whet his interest in the law), and that he came back to Royston not two days later but late that same night. Why did he say one thing and do another—and upon his return, why didn't he go directly into his house? And how come, as the coroner's report showed, he had a pistol and a rock in the pockets of his suit jacket?

One possible explanation is that he was sneaking in a little spying on the scandalous sisters next door before turning in for the evening. Keeping an eye on Annie and Vinie Jones had become something of an obsession for W.H.—not for any voyeuristic reason, it seems, but because he liked to play detective, surveying their property and tracking their behavior while he built a case against them as a public nuisance. The women's trial had finally happened a month before, with Judge Little presiding, in the ancient, crumbling courthouse at Carnesville, the county seat. A verdict should have ended the matter but didn't. Annie and Vinie got such an obviously raw deal from Judge Little in terms of what was admissible evidence and what was not—he told the jury that the sisters' silence in the face of someone calling them whores could be considered an admission of guilt—and filed an appeal so quickly after they were found guilty of "running a lewd house" that everyone knew that nothing really had been settled and that the case would be back in court presently. More evidence would be needed to get a conviction that would stick, and W. H. Cobb eagerly resumed his role as amateur Pinkerton. It's conceivable that he returned early from his business trip—perhaps because some meetings were canceled (a malaria epidemic had hit the South that summer)—and on the way back dropped by Judge Little's place to strategize about the Jones case. Then, arriving at Franklin Springs Street at about 10:30, he may have decided to check for signs of activity next door; stirrings of any kind at that hour would be suspicious. In this scenario, the pistol and rock in his pocket could be accounted for as weapons he might need in case of a confrontation with a Jones client who was angry about being spotted.

Whether that is what happened on the fateful night we cannot say, but it's a reasonable scenario that you won't find in any previous Cobb book. The reason is that Cobb's two main biographers, Charles Alexander and

Al Stump, did not seem to be aware that the Jones sisters existed. Both writers accept without question the much repeated rumor of the day—that W.H. was spying on Amanda, whom he had for a while suspected of being unfaithful. In this version, those "school visits" were merely a trap W.H. set for his wife; his plan from the start was to double back and catch her in the act. Such a simple and titillating tale had great appeal to the tabloid-inflected spirit of the times. "Mrs. Cobb is a very beautiful woman," said the *Washington Post* in the wake of the tragedy, "and there has been gossip about her for some time." Another daily said that W.H. had been advised by one neighbor to forget the Joneses and "keep his eye on his own house." Still others suggested that Amanda, always a little shrewder than her husband, was well aware that he planned to return early, and that she knew exactly whom she was shooting that night.

Amanda was known for being tough and unflappable—"She could chew nails and spit them out," one family member, who asked not to be identified, as if he were still afraid of her, told me—but at the coroner's inquest the morning after the shooting, the thirty-four-year-old widow sobbed as she told the story of hearing a "rustling sound" outside her bedroom, going "from window to window, two or three times, maybe more," and finally firing off two shots. (Ty's two younger siblings, John Paul, who was usually referred to by his middle name, and Florence, were staying with friends that night.) In her overwrought state, she described the scene somewhat confusingly. Alexander and Stump took her references to "upper and lower windows" and a figure disappearing "around the chimney" to mean that the master bedroom was on the second floor and Amanda shot W.H. while he was walking on the roof. That was not the case. If the authors had looked at an easily found photo of the house (which was demolished in the 1950s to make space for a funeral parlor parking lot) they would have seen it was a one-story structure and that W.H. was standing on terra firma when his wife saw his outline and opened fire. Alexander and Stump made other errors as well. Both also say that Amanda used a shotgun to kill her husband when the corner's report clearly indicates it was a pistol. ("I went up and got my pistol," said Amanda. "After shooting, I threw the pistol down.")

Cobb came home the day after the killing to a house wracked by grief and shame. A burial date had been set for his father, and his possibly adulterous mother had been indicted for voluntary manslaughter, meaning there would be a sensational trial and she might spend twenty or thirty years in prison. News of the tragedy—"Former State Senator Shot"—was turning up in papers from coast to coast; that Amanda had a son named "Cyrus" who was a professional baseball player was sometimes mentioned. Cobb never talked publicly about the death of his father or its immediate aftermath, but the accident (if that's what it was) must have been made grotesquely painful for him by the attendant whiff of scandal. What would life be like now? Was he suddenly, at eighteen, the man of the house? Should he console his mother, or accept consolation from her, after what she had done?

While his mind reeled, the press wuthered like an idiot wind against the Cobbs' suddenly much discussed windows. Cobb avoided or turned away the newspapermen who came to Royston in search of dirt, but a *Washington Post* reporter managed to interview his younger brother, Paul, and wrote a piece that made him look as pathetically naive about adult relationships as, at the age of sixteen, he probably was. Paul and the twelve-year-old Florence, the story said, "were very much surprised to see the sensational reports in regard to family differences between their father and mother. Paul said that the domestic relations between his father and mother were the most pleasant, in that they lived together in perfect harmony." Yes, indeed, the reader was left to think—until the minute she blew his head off.

Amanda was formally arrested at the funeral, as she stood crying over her husband's still-open grave. Her bail was set at $7,000. (Stephen Ginn signed the bond, as he had signed the Jones sisters'.) She was temporarily free and presumed innocent, but faced the wrath of W.H.'s brothers, who wanted to see her get the maximum punishment. Although not wealthy, the Cobb men hired four lawyers to help the state's solicitor general prosecute the case. They intended, they said, to call to the stand the chief of the Atlanta police, who would tell how one of his officers had rushed to quell a disturbance involving W.H. and Amanda that had taken place at the Jackson Hotel a month before the killing. The Cobb brothers promised that in due time they would reveal the name of the man with whom Amanda was allegedly sleeping.

• • •

Ty was missed and pitied in Augusta, where the shooting and its aftermath were covered thoroughly but sensitively by the *Chronicle*. "A team without Cobb," one unidentified player said, "is like an army without Washington or Lee." He was first set to rejoin the Tourists the day after his father's funeral, on August 12. But after several last-minute changes of travel plans—all too typical for him, yet excusable under the circumstances—he arrived back in Augusta on August 16, in time for a doubleheader against the Charleston Sea Gulls. In terms of hitting he picked up where he left off, smacking two singles in the first game (and going 0-for-3 in the second before bowing out with a minor finger injury). Much had happened with the club, however, in the eight days he'd been away. C. D. Carr, the owner since July 23, had dismissed George Leidy (whose sternness seems to have played poorly with everyone except Cobb) as both a manager and outfielder—and reinstated Andy Roth as the Tourists' skipper. Carr, a prominent wholesale grocer, stated bluntly that Leidy had "unquestionably done his best and failed." He also expressed the hope that his Tourists would not relapse into their previous undisciplined state. Alas the unruly "joy club" assembled by Strouthers was soon back in session. Two days into Roth's second tenure, first baseman Ed Lauzon, a well-known wag, came to bat at Warren Park wearing, said the *Chronicle*, "a very large false nose and a brush of whiskers"—his way of mocking Savannah Pathfinders pitcher Harry "Klondike" Kane (born Cohen). The paper said the stunt made Kane "dance with rage"—though he may have segued into a celebratory horah after he held Lauzon hitless in four at-bats.

Cobb couldn't be bothered with such nonsense—he was finally headed for fast company. He'd learned about the Tigers' interest in him, unofficially, from Youngman, who needed to see him in only three games—the aforementioned doubleheader and the next day's meeting with the Macon Brigands, in which Cobb hit two singles and a double, and put down a nice sacrifice bunt—before working out a deal with the Tourists to acquire his rights. The price for Cobb's contract was $500, "payable," said the awestruck local paper, "in a lump sum." Under the terms of the agreement, Cobb was to finish out the season with Augusta, then report to Warren Park for spring training as a Tiger the following March.

But no sooner had the scout left town than Tigers manager Armour changed his mind and decided that he needed to have Cobb in Detroit as soon as possible. Duff Cooley was drinking himself out of his center fielder's job as fast as he could, the sportswriters were running out of polite ways to describe what was causing his inability to chase down fly balls, and the bench was devoid of reasonable substitutes. So debilitated was the team that Armour had to turn down lucrative midseason exhibition games with Michigan schools and semipro squads ("We are too crippled to play," he wrote to the Mt. Carmel Athletic Association), something that must have troubled Navin. The manager, midway through his first season, seemed worried about his job—and rightly so. The injuries were not his fault but the Tigers had lapsed into in a state of mental, if not moral, disarray. Many men were showing up drunk or seriously hungover. In mid-August the manager made the unusual move of leaving the team to search for players up and down the East Coast. The trip was not productive and owner Yawkey told the *Detroit News* he was confused by what was going on. "Our team is a mystery to me," he said. "I go out and see them play the finest ball in the land, and the next day I feel like coming down the back streets to my hotel."

His embarrassment would only increase. After what the *Free Press* called a "disastrous road trip" during which they lost four straight to Washington, Detroit again faced the last-place Senators at home in a game that ended, or rather came asunder, in the 11th inning when the Tigers, incensed by a call made by umpire Bill Sheridan, refused to resume their field positions, and fans chased him across the outfield and into the street—where a panting Sheridan declared Detroit losers by forfeit. Over the next several days the Tigers dropped three more games and their despair deepened. Said White Sox manager Fielder Jones: "The Tigers are a minor league bunch."

Cobb was hardly seen as a savior—the South in general was thought to produce inferior talent—but his arrival would provide at least a brief distraction and perhaps a glimmer of hope. In a flurry of telegrams, Armour and Carr negotiated a codicil in which the Tigers would give the Tourists an additional $200 to have Cobb report immediately, bringing his total cost to $700. Navin, however, thought that was a lot for an unproven teenager and he nixed the deal—forcing the desperate manager to pay the expedited delivery fee out of his own pocket. Cobb didn't know he'd been put on a fast track to the Big Show (as it was already called) until August 19, when he hit a single in a game against the Brigands, and the first baseman, making chitchat while trying to keep him close to the sack, said, "So I hear you're going up."

Soon after the game was over that day Cobb wired Armour asking what the Tigers had paid for his contract. From a legal standpoint this was none of his business, and he almost certainly knew the answer already from talking to Carr—the inquiry was really an attempt to open negotiations. Cobb wanted a cut of what the Tourists were getting for him, a not uncommon request in those days when organized sports was still new and men were startled to find that they could be sold like chattel. If he didn't get something from the Tigers, he told Carr, he just might not go north. (Though it was illogical to ask the team *paying* for your contract to kick something back to you, players naturally thought in terms of where they had the most leverage.)

When Carr relayed the news that Cobb was balking, Armour said, "I anticipated some trouble when I received his telegram," and added, "there is not one ball player in fifty that is sold to a Major League Club who receives any portion of the purchase price whatever." Yet Cobb wasn't finished making demands: he wanted the Tigers to pay his $78 round-trip train fare to Detroit and back home to Royston at the end of the season. Armour wrote to him patiently explaining that providing such transportation was "against team rules." The Tigers would give Cobb a salary of $225 a month, but no more.

While Cobb and Armour stood their ground, 800-odd miles apart, the Tourists went ahead with their farewell tribute. "Ty Cobb was the recipient of a handsome gold watch and a large bunch of roses yesterday during the ball game, as tokens of esteem from fans and a lady friend," said the *Chronicle*, which chose not to identify Charlie Lombard by name. The whole ceremony was a bit mystifying. Rather than schedule it before the first pitch, or after the game, the team said goodbye to "the town's favorite player" (as the *Chronicle* called him) prior to his third at-bat. With two out and the Tourists trailing the Brigands 2–0 in the sixth inning, the game was halted and Charlie Lombard and several local dignitaries proceeded from the grandstand while Ty, flanked by his teammates, fidgeted at home plate, thinking of the speech he'd have to make. After getting the watch and the flowers, he was brought front and center, and as always in such situations, the son of the founder of the North Georgia Oratorical Association groped for words. "Cobb replied in a couple of sentences, assuring all of his appreciation," said the paper. "Every time he hesitated for a word, some of the players, who were lined up on either side of him, had a suggestion of a comical nature to make." When the game resumed, he struck out—"as is usual" in such situations, the *Chronicle* said. For the afternoon—it was Friday, August 25—he had two singles and a stolen base as the Tourists lost 3–0 to Macon before 1,400, the biggest turnout at Warren Park since opening day.

As a *Chronicle* story noted, the hoopla might well have been all for naught, since Ty and the Tigers hadn't yet made a deal. Over the weekend, though, the impasse was broken, and on Sunday the 27th the *Detroit Free Press* ran a story saying that "the fastest man in the South," and the "sort of swatsman who can be called a 'natural born hitter'" (the phrase that Cobb detested) would be "joining the Detroit aggregation at once." Behind the scenes the big league club had caved. Cobb's acquisition appears to have been recorded, disingenuously, as a draft, so the Tigers could slip him the $150 that draftees traditionally received without setting a distasteful precedent. He also won the battle for round-trip train fare, in August and again in October, a perk offered to no other player.

It was late in the morning of Tuesday, August 29, when Ty finally put his cloth bag of bats and his leather satchel of clothing down on the platform of Michigan Central Station in downtown Detroit. He seems to have staggered out of the train, thoroughly exhausted. It was his first time north of the Mason-Dixon line and he had not had an easy crossing. Missing his connections in both Atlanta and Cincinnati (in true Ty Cobb fashion) he had added more than twelve hours to what was under normal summer circumstances a sweaty thirty-hour slog. During his layover in Cincinnati, still known as "the Queen City of the West," he had hopped a trolley to see the sights, which included the Ivory Soap factory and the neoclassical Cincinnati Reds' stadium, called the Palace of the Fans. At that point in the journey he still was relatively fresh, with curiosity to satisfy and energy to burn. In Detroit, deprived of sleep and wearing the same August-wrecked suit he had put on as a minor leaguer, he did not appear fit for fast company.

The team functionary who met Ty at the station and drove him to the ballpark in a horse-drawn carriage must have wondered how Armour was going to react to the sight of this strung-out, bedraggled Georgia lad. Would he put him into that afternoon's game, the first in a three-game series against the New York Highlanders? Cobb wasn't just travel-worn; he had lost weight and acquired a sunken-eyed look after dealing with all that was going on in Royston. In one of the first photos of him taken in a Detroit uniform—which already had that distinctive Old English "D"—he seems to have reverted to the nervous, stuttering, too-skinny man-child from the Royston Reds. Armour took one look at Cobb and decided he needed at least one good night's rest before going into the lineup. It wasn't a difficult decision. Neither the cranks nor the writers would be clamoring for his participation because no one expected a kid from the Sally League to make much difference. More likely, he'd be a total bust, gone and forgotten by the following spring. One *Free Press* story announcing the arrival of Cobb said "If he gets away with a .275 mark, he will be satisfying everybody."

Bennett Park didn't have dugouts yet, so Cobb watched the first major league game he ever saw—a 2–0 Tigers victory, made possible by the golden left arm of "Twilight" Ed Killian, a man who was poetry on the mound, but poison in the clubhouse—from the exposed bench on the third base side of the infield, where the other Tigers sat. No one much noted the arrival of perhaps the greatest player of all time. "The glances of the players as I went to the bench were not unfriendly," Cobb wrote in a 1925 serial first published in the *New York Evening Journal*, "but they were decidedly impersonal. No particular interest was taken in my presence. I had a feeling of being a spectator." The situation would change—but not right away. Ty had arrived on a team that desperately needed healthy bodies, so at first he was accepted and even appreciated by his teammates for the function he served. He wasn't in those final weeks of the 1905 season barred from the batting cage, denied a locker, or ignored when he asked a question, the way rookies of that era so often were. As a result Cobb felt like he had been "mustered in," he said. Except he hadn't; he had only been overlooked, for the moment, by a dysfunctional group of men grimly focused on earning their sobriety bonus, or improving their numbers a bit so they might argue more effectively next winter for a $200 raise, as they played out the schedule. This would be another pennant-less season for the Tigers, and the veterans would get back to him, they figured, in the fullness of time, and in what they deemed the appropriate manner. "I didn't realize it then," he wrote, in 1925, "but I was in for the hardest struggle of my life."

When Cobb returned to Bennett Park the next day, Armour told him to "go get a glove and go out there," pointing toward the *Detroit Tribune* billboard in center field. He'd be batting fifth. Scheduled to pitch for the Highlanders was the formidable righty Jack Chesbro, a specialist in the spitball, which was legal then and would remain so for another fourteen years. The future Hall of Famer, yet another well-known grump, never claimed to be a showman. With no need to be especially secretive about his "saliva pitch," Chesbro would stand on the mound and lick his fingers, then apply his "tobacco juice" to the ball. The brownness made his pitches difficult to see; the moisture lent them a maddening unpredictability. Chesbro called the spitter "the greatest invention of the baseball age." For catchers, whose mitts were mitten-sized, it was difficult to handle, and of course disgusting to touch. Highlanders backstop James "Deacon" McGuire objected to it on sanitary grounds, but his opinion didn't matter in light of Chesbro's phenomenal results. In 1904, using the spitter in combination with a mysterious "slowball," "Happy Jack," as he was ironically known, had gone 41–12, still the most wins ever compiled in a single season. As the *Free Press* said of Cobb the next day, "For a young man anxious to get along in the world it was not an auspicious occasion."

About 1,200 turned out for the Tigers-Highlanders matchup of August 30. Many years ago I met a man—my theater professor at Fordham, Vaughn Deering—who claimed to have been one of them. "You could tell right away Cobb was going to be special," he said, in the same gravelly but pear-shaped tones he had employed as a member of Otis Skinner's theatrical troupe. Deering, who talked more about baseball than drama in class, was old enough to make his attendance at the game possible—and ads in the *Free Press* show that Skinner's company did indeed stop in Detroit at the time. So I may very well have shaken a hand that pushed a turnstile or shelled a peanut on the historic occasion of Cobb's major league debut. I only wish now I had probed Deering for details, especially about Bennett Park, which seems to have been a most quirky venue. Built in 1896 on the site of the city's hay market, and named for a beloved old minor league catcher, Charlie Bennett, it was the smallest and most eccentrically shaped park in the league, thanks to stands that extended almost all the way down the left field foul line but on the other side barely made it halfway around to first base. The cobblestone floor of the hay market occasionally breached the playing surface, causing balls to take freakish bounces. *Aha*, you might say, *the ghost of the buried nineteenth century breaking forth to bedevil the twentieth!* But the infielders who played there just said, "*Shit*, it hit a cobble!"—an excuse you didn't hear anywhere else.

Cobb would later say that he was nervous, but not as much as he thought he'd be as he trotted out to a spot between left fielder Matty McIntyre, a belligerent New York City boy constantly at odds with the front office, and Wahoo Sam Crawford, at twenty-five one of the game's best all-around players. As eager as he was to succeed, Ty was delighted, he said in one newspaper memoir, not to get any chances in the outfield that first half inning.

When it was time for the Tigers to hit they likely surprised themselves by getting to Jack Chesbro early. No sooner had Silk O'Loughlin, the sole umpire on duty, shouted "Baa-a-rup!" than leadoff man McIntyre was on with a line drive double to left. (O'Loughlin, the inventor of the seal-bark way of speaking that umpires still employ today, had an uncanny knack for being present at critical moments in Cobb's career.) Then light-hitting first baseman Pinky Lindsay knocked in the runner with a single, and Germany Schaefer got Lindsay over to second with a sacrifice bunt. Crawford was next up, to be followed by Cobb. Before handing him the big homemade biffer he'd use in his first major league plate appearance, Tigers batboy Frank Brady kissed it for good luck.

As strange as that may sound, it was no big deal at the time. Baseball in 1905 was just getting started as a big business, but it was already rife with superstitions and weird rites. No peanuts in the clubhouse, never walk between the pitcher and the umpire, don't let the ump toss his little whisk broom onto your side of the field, and for God's sake don't step on the foul line. Tigers pitcher Bill Donovan believed it bad luck to strike out the first batter, so he went out of his way not to. Connie Mack, often thought of as the game's greatest sage, carried the right hind foot of a rabbit that had been killed in a graveyard at midnight by a hunchbacked Negro, and so on. If kissing a bat sounds odd, consider that Jack Fournier, when he played for the 1912 Chicago White Sox, kissed teammate Russell Blackburne before each plate appearance. What batboy Brady did on the Tigers bench would not have turned many heads in 1905. But Cobb's next move—which was to take his bat and put it with two others and step into the on-deck area swinging the bouquet of black lumber back and forth and then above his head—*that* surely caught the attention of the Tigers. One can imagine them, with eyebrows cocked, making a mental note: Kid thinks he's something special.

Crawford gently knocked one back to the box.

Cobb came to the plate then with two outs and Lindsay on third. Chesbro's first pitch was a high spitter that Ty lunged at amateurishly.

The next pitch he took—a curve that dropped straight down over the plate. "*Stee*-rike *Tuh!*" said O'Loughlin. Then came another fastball, this one not so fast and waist high, which Cobb, letting both hands slide down toward the knob of his bat, drove smoothly into the gap in left center. "Believe me," he said many years later, "it was some proud kid who sped around to second amidst the cheers of the crowd."

— CHAPTER NINE —

IT WAS A GOOD DEBUT. Besides the double in his first major league at-bat Cobb also drew a walk in four trips to the plate as the Tigers, behind the stolid pitching of George Mullin, who had just rejoined the team after burying his brother, beat the Highlanders 5–3. The few balls that came Cobb's way in the outfield that afternoon he handled cleanly, though he appeared not always certain of what to do with them next. The Detroit sportswriters publicly acknowledged his promising start, as did his manager, privately. "Tried Cobb out yesterday and he did first-rate," Armour wrote to his scout Heinie Youngman on August 31. "He looks like he might make a pretty good man with the proper kind of training." To C. D. Carr, owner of the Augusta team, Armour allowed in his next letter of the day that his new man "did very nice work" but "was a little slow in getting the ball away from him at two or three different times in the game, which I think was due to the fact that he was somewhat afraid of making a bad throw. He could have completed a nice double play [outfielders tended to play not far behind the infielders in those days and often participated in double plays], and another time caught a man at the plate, but of course, this will come to him when he is a little more experienced."

Cobb's advanced education had already started in the fifth inning of his first game, when he tried to steal second following the walk. Sensing that he'd gotten off a step too slowly, and that he stood a good chance of being thrown out by the Highlanders catcher, Deacon McGuire, Cobb lost his composure and dove into the bag headfirst, like he did in his early days with the Augusta Tourists. This was not considered the wisest way to slide, and shortstop Elberfeld showed him one reason why. The always cantankerous Kid, refreshed after an eight-day suspension for "grabbing umpire [John] McCarthy by the blouse and shaking him," didn't just tag Cobb with McGuire's perfect peg; he brought his knee down on the back of Cobb's neck and pushed his face into the barely concealed hay market cobbles. "My forehead and face were shoved into the hard ground and the skin peeled off just above the eyebrows," Cobb recalled in his 1925 memoir (republished in book form as *My Twenty Years in Baseball*). But as painful as the experience was, he did not come up swinging; his *feelings* were not injured. "The clever way in which he moved completely blocked me," Ty wrote. "When I got to my feet I was much subdued. I had run into a real big leaguer. I realized that he knew much of what I would have to learn." The encounter turned out to be the beginning of a friendship with Elberfeld, who while hardly as talented as Cobb, shared his penchant for always going hard and exploiting every opportunity an opponent unwittingly provided. Strong-willed, seat-of-the-pants players like Elberfeld may play a brand of baseball that can leave rivals beaten and bleeding, Ty once said, "but they were rarely malicious."

On the way back to the bench, Cobb says in *My Twenty Years*, he had what sounds at first like an epiphany. "I began to think 'that is no way to slide into a base! I'm all wrong.' By going in there head first the baseman has all the advantage. From then on I watched closely. I noted how Elberfeld and other stars went into the bag—feet first, spikes shining. 'By going in that way,' I said to myself, 'the advantage is with the slider. He is testing the other fellow's nerve. Why let him test mine?'" It's a nice story, and perhaps to a degree a true one, but it also feels like a too tidy version of reality. Cobb, by this point, had already been warned off the headfirst slide by both George Leidy and Germany Schaefer, and in fact he would, despite what they and Elberfeld advised, retain the move in his repertoire for the remainder of his career, convinced that in certain situations it provided a critical advantage. Cobb had great respect for anyone who played the game passionately and well, and he enjoyed learning from the masters. At the same time, he studiously avoided becoming a textbook player. He wanted to blend the best of the received wisdom into a refined version of his crazy-seeming "harum scarum" style. He wanted to play a slightly different game than everyone else was playing, to be out of sync with the anticipated rhythms, protocols, and conventions. Hit 'em where they ain't, run when you really shouldn't, keep going when you ought to stop. It was the modern age and his game was the baseball equivalent of modern art. It was at once a dramatic break from the past and a comment on it. It made people nervous. His game looked ugly until it looked bold and smart.

On the day of Cobb's second major league game, August 31, 1905, the Highlanders made things easier for the Tigers by putting forth pudgy right-hander Jack Powell, who was known during his 16 seasons in the major leagues as a "nothing" pitcher, because he had neither a true fastball nor a breaking curve. Rather than being flummoxed by Powell's vacuousness, as some apparently were, Ty stroked two singles. Neither figured in the Tigers' 5–0 victory, but getting three hits in his first two games, said Cobb, "did more I believe than any other thing to restore my complete confidence and send me on my way for a major league career." Confidence was 50 percent of baseball, Cobb often said—and that is why he cultivated the quality in himself and concentrated so hard on undermining it in others.

Overall, though, this was a weird time for Cobb. He was still grieving for his father, and the papers back in Georgia were ardently following his mother's manslaughter case and working the unfaithful-wife angle awfully hard. On the evening of his second game with the Tigers, a reporter from the *Columbus* (Georgia) *Ledger* spotted Amanda back at the Jackson Hotel in Atlanta with "a man said to be her cousin." Police knocked on her door "shortly after midnight" looking for one Joshua Chambers but found only Mrs. Cobb and her frightened daughter, Florence. "Arrests will follow the finding of Chambers," the paper promised, leaving readers to imagine what the charges might possibly be.

Amanda was something of a mystery herself. It was hard to tell what was going on beneath that schoolmarmish hive of bright red hair. Was she the archetypal black widow, or an innocent victim of circumstances? The morning after the police came to her door, she and Florence moved from the Jackson to the Aragon Hotel, a fancier place farther from the train station—and into the sights of the *Macon Telegraph*. Amanda, "the mother of Cy Cobb, a professional ballplayer," told that reporter she didn't know yet when she would be tried, but felt "I have been done an injustice, a very grave injustice. For the sake of my children, however, who would suffer from going through so much notoriety, I will refrain from offering any explanations."

If anyone was really looking for him, Joshua Chambers should not have been hard to find. He was in fact Amanda's distant cousin, and, like her late husband, a prominent educator in Franklin County. He had worked with W.H. over the years, sometimes as co-principal of the same school. Whether Chambers was the cause of the loud argument between Amanda and W.H. that brought the police running in early July we cannot know. He would soon vanish from the newspapers' narrative, flotsam in the scandal's wake. But the larger story of the shooting and its aftermath would not go away. A few weeks later Amanda, for technical reasons, had to be rearrested and reindicted and her bail was raised to $10,000, a fantastic amount for someone who was not really a flight risk. The system seemed stacked against her and, overcome with hopelessness, she cried freely in the courtroom as the judge set her bail, or so the dailies noted with their usual overweening concern.

No doubt mortified by the melodrama being played out in the papers, Cobb tried to lose himself in the baseball life. Being a major leaguer meant frequent train travel, and many open evenings suitable for long summer walks in interesting cities that had recently started smelling more like automobiles than horse flop. As a flaneur and a constant reader (he especially liked biographies of Jefferson and Napoleon) Cobb was often away from his teammates, though he sometimes played cards with Germany Schaefer, Bill Donovan, and a few others. Some veterans resented Cobb's apparent aloofness, but perhaps because he *was* so infrequently around those men, he didn't immediately sense their feelings. He felt things were going fairly well, even if, as September wore on, his batting average hovered around .250 and his fielding was less than stellar. On September 24, the *Augusta Chronicle* ran an article saying that "a gentleman of the city" had received a letter from Cobb, who seemed in excellent spirits and was "enjoying the many interesting sights on the present road trip." He had toured "the largest iron works in the world" in Pittsburgh when the Tigers played an exhibition game there against an "outlaw" team from Homestead, Pennsylvania. On a swing through Washington for a series against the Nationals he had visited the Library of Congress.

Such behavior in a rookie was not normally tolerated. Cobb was probably spared from harassment or worse in that first half year by the utter mediocrity of his play. If he had been hitting .320 and fielding brilliantly, his taste for high culture might have been impossible to tolerate. But the best you could say about Cobb in the latter part of 1905 was that from time to time he appeared promising. On September 12 at Bennett Park he went 2-for-4 and scored the winning run in the ninth inning in what would later be seen as typically Ty Cobb fashion—coming home all the way from second on a bobbled infield grounder. Looking like the Rookie of the Year at D.C.'s National Park on September 22 (the distinction was not actually awarded until 1947), he had two singles and a double, scored two runs, and stole a base in a 6–5 Tigers' victory. A few days later in *Sporting Life*, Detroit writer Paul H. Bruske said that despite being "a bit green to the fast game" Ty was an "infant prodigy." Manager Armour showed his satisfaction by penciling him into the lineup virtually every day, and Cobb was starting to feel at home in Bennett Park's vast center field, between billboards for President Suspenders and LaVerdo Havana Cigars ("Couldn't Be Better If You Paid a Dollar").

But there was much to offset the good news. He went 0-for-5 in a September 3 game in which the rest of the Tigers feasted on St. Louis Browns pitching, combining for 16 hits in a 10–1 victory at Sportsman's Park—one of many occasions on which he, as they used to say, took the collar. He also had more problems with the sun than your average outfielder, and at least once, at National Park, Armour had to move him from center to left field in midgame. (A few years later, Cobb would be one of the first players to smear his cheeks with black soot to diminish the glare.) Meanwhile, when he *was* in center his natural overaggressiveness often caused him to stray into Matty McIntyre's left field workspace. One incursion in a home game against the White Sox was especially egregious and led to his first confrontation with a fellow Tiger—though it doesn't seem that he and McIntyre exchanged blows. The way the sportswriters told the tale, Ty was clearly in the wrong. "McIntyre called for [Lee]

Tannehill's fly in the ninth and got the ball in his glove," the *Free Press* reported on September 6. "Cobb interfered with him, despite the call, and the ball was dropped." The paper couldn't resist a bit of finger-wagging: "When Mr. McIntyre tears loose the call for a ball, it is the best policy of the other fielders to step aside."

Still, Cobb's crazy energy continued to intrigue some observers, such as American League president Ban Johnson, who told Clark Griffith, the manager of the Washington Senators, he thought the unheralded young Tiger was an unpolished gem and a future star. Griffith begged to differ. "You are dead wrong," he said. "Wait and see—Cobb won't survive one swing around the circuit once the pitchers get wise to him."

His words initially seemed prophetic. Cobb was at first highly vulnerable to a left-hander's curve, as left-handed batters usually are. As a result he saw a lot of them, and did more than his share of fanning. The year 1905 was a bad one for hitters in general. When Cobb came up at the end of August, only three American Leaguers were hitting above .300: George Stone of the St. Louis Browns, Willie Keeler of the Highlanders, and Nap Lajoie of the Naps. Sam Crawford would come close for the Tigers, finishing the season at .297. But Cobb ranked far beneath them in the batters' standings. While the team played much better after his arrival, and won 19 of their final 30 games, finishing third in the AL behind the pennant-winning Athletics and the White Sox, it is hard to make a case for his causing the surge, since he ended up hitting just .240.

Cobb could have gone home immediately following the final game of the season, a 7–1 win over the Naps in Cleveland on October 7, but, enjoying the distance from Royston, and no doubt wanting to pocket a bit more cash, he chose to stay with the team for two exhibition contests. The second of these, played on October 10, was billed as a "thank you" game. Fans expressed their appreciation to the players not just by buying a ticket (each man wound up realizing "a nice little bit of money"—$80—from the gate, according to the *Free Press*) but also by breaking into a "warm ovation" each time a Tiger made his first appearance at the plate. Cobb received prolonged applause, the papers noted, and later told the fans, through the press, that he was looking forward to seeing them again next season. The advent of Davy Jones, a highly touted outfielder whom

Armour had procured from the Minneapolis Millers of the Class A American Association, seemed to leave him unfazed. When a reporter from the *Atlanta Constitution* ran into Ty at a Georgia Tech–Clemson football game in early December and conducted an impromptu interview, "Cobb intimated," the paper said, "that he would get the position on the 1906 Tiger lineup without having to fight it out with another candidate."

Why was he so sure that he could bounce back from a lackluster season? No one ever asked him, so we'll never know, but perhaps it was because he had done it before. Two-forty was only three points higher than the batting average he had wound up with at the end of 1904, as a seventeen-year-old Augusta Tourist. A few months later he was leading the Sally League with a .326 average. Granted, he was in the majors now, his father was gone, and his inner life was so roiled he didn't know how to feel about his own mother. But this much he did know: he was Ty Cobb and Ty Cobb was no .240 hitter.

CHAPTER TEN

TY COBB HAD SEVERAL GOOD reasons for feeling like he'd been accepted by the veteran members of the Detroit Tigers in the autumn of 1905, starting with the fact that the season had ended and he hadn't been harassed, abused, and made to feel like he should go someplace else—back down to the Sally League, say, or out of baseball entirely: in other words, he hadn't been given a good old-fashioned hazing. Except for the brief flare-up with fellow outfielder Matty McIntyre over territorial rights, the Georgia kid had gotten virtually no guff from any of the interlocking cliques of cranky Yankees that constituted the Detroit Base Ball and Amusement Company. True, it's not as if they hung around his locker asking if he'd read any good books lately (if they had he would have said *Les Misérables*, a lifelong favorite he was once again working through just then), but they treated him like just another one of the boys, sacrificing him over to the next base when the situation called for it, sliding in hard to make it difficult for a fielder to throw him out on the back end of a double play, and, on at least one occasion, interfering (artfully) with the catcher so he could more easily steal second. Such things were not done automatically for every rookie in that golden age of bullying. Yet they were done for him and as a result he felt like a full-fledged member of the ball club.

The men in the Tigers front office did more than just tolerate their youngest player or take him for granted—they actively *liked* him. On January 6, 1906, Bill Armour sent Cobb a contract for 1906 that would pay him $1,500, "$300 more than I talked to you of before leaving," the manager noted. "Before Mr. Navin left for California, we had a long talk on the subject," Armour added, "and we both liked you and felt as we would rather have you satisfied than otherwise, have decided to do our part to make everything satisfactory to you." To spend just a few hours in the Ernie Harwell Collection at the Detroit Public Library paging through the old letters is to know that the manager and team secretary, Frank Navin, did not talk to the other Tigers in such a kindly and supportive fashion. Armour, who typically sent players a contract with a cover letter saying, essentially, Take it or leave it, sounded almost paternal when he wrote to Cobb, whom he knew would be occupied during the off-season with his late father's estate, and who had told some people that he wasn't completely certain he would be coming back; his family might need him and, besides, he could easily make more money than the Tigers were paying, even in a small town like Royston. "I trust you will be able to round up your business affairs in such shape that you can give your attention to baseball," Armour said. "Think you would be very foolish to pull away from the game at present as you have a bright future in front of you if I am any judge of a player." Cobb felt kindly toward the manager in return. He quickly signed the contract and, though he was still among the lowest-paid players on the team, sent it back with a note of gratitude.

Reaching out again in a way that showed his affection and trust, Armour in early February asked Cobb if he could make an advance trip to Warren Park to inspect the playing field, which was reputed to have been ravaged over the winter by a traveling carnival. Glad to be asked and happy for an excuse to get away from Royston and visit his girlfriend Charlie Lombard's hometown, Cobb went to Augusta and reported back that the rumors were true: the field was indeed a mess. "Last year it was generally conceded that Augusta had the best diamond in the South," he told the *Chronicle*, which covered him as a visiting dignitary and described him as "the idol of [local] baseball fans." "But now we have the worst. Only a semblance of the real diamond remains while the outfield is boggy, full of holes and covered with trash. I was greatly surprised, not to say shocked, when I saw how matters were."

Though the name of the Warren Park groundskeeper did not surface in the report of the controversy, Cobb was in effect criticizing the work of Henry "Bungy" Cummings, a twenty-five-year-old black man who lived with his wife, Savannah, and their eleven-year-old son, George, in a small house adjacent to the Negro section of the grandstand, in far right field. Cummings was officially the janitor of the facility, but his prime responsibility was the maintenance of the strikingly grassless playing surface. After a few years on the job, he was well liked, and his work was occasionally complimented by the *Chronicle*'s sportswriters, yet he was also known around town as a hopeless if harmless drunk. Cummings didn't lose his job over Cobb's scathing assessment (he would remain the Warren Park groundskeeper for at least another ten years), but he must have been mortified—or enraged—when, in response to it, local volunteers formed a crew and went to work getting the field into shape for the Tigers' early-March arrival. Whether Cummings tried to save face by directing their efforts or humbly made amends by working along with them we don't know. But we should keep his name in mind because this otherwise forgotten man, misidentified in previous books and articles as Bungy Davis, will resurface as a key figure in Cobb's story.

With the family breadwinner suddenly gone, money, for the first time in Ty's life, was a concern. The Cobbs had a small financial cushion in the form of property in the Narrows that had been bequeathed to Amanda and her siblings after their father, the Confederate captain who made good, died in 1893. Her share was worth a few thousand dollars, enough in those days to pay for the quintet of lawyers who would defend her from the charge of first-degree voluntary manslaughter, and allow the family to build a modest house elsewhere in Royston. Moving from Franklin Springs Street was absolutely necessary, Ty felt, because of the bad memories the house now held and because of the dynamite that townsfolk had starting putting around the Jones sisters' place next door. The ladies usually found the scary red sticks before they could be detonated, but one day when they were away from home their porch was blown to smithereens. Later, the house would be set on fire by an unknown person or persons. Ty knew that he couldn't be away for months at a time playing baseball while his family stayed fifty or so feet from an active war zone.

To bring in a few extra dollars for day-to-day expenses, Ty took a temporary off-season job as a baseball coach at University School, a University of Georgia prep academy in Stone Mountain. It was only a two-week engagement, but it didn't end until the third or fourth day of the Tigers' preseason training camp. In mid-January he wrote to Armour asking for permission but mostly telling him that he would come to Augusta on or about March 11, three days after the official start date. Given his good stead and that so many Tigers were holding out for better contracts that year, ensuring that spring training would get off to a stutter-start, he didn't think that would be a problem. The manager, however, quickly denied his request. "It will be to the advantage of yourself and our club to be with us during our training period as there are a few points in the game that I am anxious for you to get next to," Armour wrote back. Why he took this strict position is hard to say, though he liked having Cobb around and may genuinely have felt his youngest player needed to bone up on some basics. In the end it didn't matter. Whatever his motive for saying no, Cobb ignored his response and took the job anyway—and Armour ignored his late arrival. The manager rarely backed up his stern talk with strong actions, and by then everyone on the Tigers—including Armour's boss, Frank Navin—knew it.

Armour would spend the coming season gradually losing control of the club. His paralyzing butterfly phobia never seems to have become an issue, but his lack of leadership skills did. He had gotten off to a bad start the year before, sounding strident about salaries in his very first letters in January and February, then leaving his struggling team during the dog days and dashing about the country, desperately trying and mostly failing to recruit halfway decent players. As time went on it became ever clearer why the Cleveland Naps had fired Armour at the end of the 1904 season, and installed Nap Lajoie as player-manager. Apart from his poor instincts for personnel management, Armour simply made too many mistakes, such as, at the start of his second year with the Tigers, forgetting to order new uniforms. When the Tigers scattered for home in October of 1905, he had told them to "see a good tailor" and send along their current measurements by the first of the year. Then he seems to have woken up one morning in February of '06 and realized that he'd never followed up. As a result he had to sheepishly survey the players by mail, asking anyone who had taken his uniform home to please bring it back—sometimes while in the midst of testy salary negotiations with those same men.

In 1906, Armour's second year with the club, those negotiations seemed more problematic than ever. When the Tigers' train pulled into Augusta on the evening of March 4, it had only twelve players, less than half the roster, almost all of them pitchers. This presented some obvious problems. Who exactly would these men pitch *to* and how would this remnant of the club play intra-squad games? The manager's short-term solution was to order the construction of a life-size dummy that would be propped up on a stake at home plate, presumably so the pitchers could have a sense of the strike zone, a target at which to aim. Armour was said to be quite proud of his creation, but most everyone else seemed a bit embarrassed by the silly-looking effigy—which said more about the Bill Armour era than the manager had intended.

With Navin away for the winter, touring the racetracks of California, first winning a fortune and then losing two or three, the Tigers, as they at last signed their contracts and dribbled into camp, took to either bullying Armour or ignoring him. "Not even a troupe of emotional actresses presents any greater difficulty to management than a modern baseball club," *Detroit News* reporter Paul Bruske wrote. Sam Crawford, Germany Schaefer, Charley O'Leary, Bill Coughlin, Charlie Schmidt, Bob Lowe, Tom Doran, Pinky Lindsay, and a few others all had refused to sign the first contracts Armour had sent them, or report for duty, or hop to his orders when they did arrive, and even the hot prospect Davy Jones, who had already signed for $2,400, took a shot at getting a little more of what the players sometimes called "tease." If you followed Jones, this was not surprising; he had jumped so many contracts early in his career that the writers dubbed him "The Kangaroo." (Armour denied his request, assuring him that he was getting "the club limit"—then later the same day offered Crawford $3,000.)

Besides wanting more money, the Tiger players wanted more respect. Holdouts who had been sent what Navin called "booze contracts" (the vast majority of the team that year) said they were offended by the idea that $200 to $500 of their annual salary would be set aside pending a postseason judgment by management regarding their "good habits." *Drinkers? Them?* To a man they wanted these "sobriety clauses" struck, and the booze-bonus money folded into their regular paychecks. They didn't have much of a case, though. Rare was the day when the Tigers clubhouse didn't smell like stale hops. This was, after all, a team hampered by perpetual headaches and sometimes even intra-inning imbibing; their backup catcher, Jack Warner, at least once had to be led off the field drunk. (Even the chief baseball writer for the *Detroit Free Press*, Joe S. Jackson, was known as a "nipper" who would habitually sip from a flask during the course of a game.) "You know drinking was carried to an extreme last year," Armour wrote to third baseman Bill Coughlin, the team captain, in early 1906. "The club owners as well as myself are broadminded enough to know that a glass of beer will not hurt anyone, but ten or twelve will, and this is what we are aiming to remedy." He reminded Schaefer of a contrite promise about drinking that the second baseman had made to him one day the previous year after an exhibition game in Columbus, Ohio, but had failed to keep. He told McIntyre that he would give him $2,200 for the year, "and $200 additional providing you go to Hot Springs for a course of baths before reporting time" in order to "boil" the winter's alcohol residue from his body. Cobb was one of the few whose contract had no sobriety clause; instead of temperance lectures he got back-pats. "Was glad to hear that you've been [practicing] bunting," Armour wrote to him on February 19, "as you will find that it will be a lot of good to you." Ty was a good boy, and for the time being, anyway, he liked being one.

When there were finally enough men in camp for intra-squad games, Armour posted lineup cards that should have removed any lingering doubts about Cobb's status. In contests between the Yannigans and Regulars, as the practice teams were called, Ty was always listed among the latter group. The message in this was unmistakable because, while some veterans were usually needed to round out the Yannigans' lineups, the Regulars always remained rookie-free, the team of Crawford, McIntyre, Captain Bill Coughlin, and a few other stalwarts who could be considered the faces of the franchise. "The answer to one subject may be regarded as given, and that is the outfield proposition," wrote Joe S. Jackson from the Tigers' training camp on March 18. "Ty Cobb, the ambitious young Georgian who made a hit with the home fans last fall, will be with the club through 1906."

That was true only as far as it went, however. Cobb would be a fix-ture, but mostly on the bench: he wouldn't be starting in center field, as he had the year before. That job would go to twenty-five-year-old Davy Jones, who, said Jackson, "unless he meets with some accident" would be a first-stringer when the Tigers played the Chicago White Sox at Bennett Park on April 14, opening day. Jones, who'd grown up poor in the tiny Welsh community of Cambria, Wisconsin, and had a law degree from Dixon College in Illinois, was a fine hitter and probably faster than Cobb, though nowhere near as unpredictable or inventive (who was?). Like al-most everyone else on the Tigers, he had a temper and a tendency to settle disputes with his fists, yet he was certainly the more polished of the two prospective center fielders in 1906, having spent considerable stretches in the major leagues already, mostly with the St. Louis Browns and Chicago Cubs. He was also coming off a season in which he'd finished second in the American Association, a league far more esteemed than Cobb's South Atlantic, with a .346 average.

About the only knock against Jones was that he was prone to mishaps and illness. He'd sat out many games early in his career due to typhoid fever, a broken leg, and assorted other miseries. When Joe S. Jackson wrote that Jones would be in center field barring an accident, he wasn't just employing a figure of speech. Indeed on the train trip north from Augusta that spring, Jones incurred the kind of injury you just don't hear about anymore: while attempting to hang his hat on a hook outside his sleeping car berth, he hit his head on an (unlit) gas lamp, opening a siz-able wound on his scalp. Since he was already suffering from tonsillitis, he felt especially miserable.

By then, though, a sea change had occurred on the Tigers, making the innocent days of late winter seem far away indeed. Cliques were constantly forming and disbanding in that cranky, cotton-mouthed clubhouse, but it was the dramatic realignment of certain players in op-position to Cobb in the early spring of 1906 that would have a dramatic effect on the team for years to come—and on Cobb himself forever. The conspiracy first revealed itself, appropriately enough, on or very near the Ides of March. When Cobb trotted onto the field for batting practice at Warren Park one morning, he found Matty McIntyre waiting for him, and blocking his path to home plate. What was this about? Six years older than Cobb, a fair left fielder and a solid .260 hitter, McIntyre was a darkly handsome, and decidedly gruff, Staten Island Irishman, yet another Tiger who liked to express himself with his fists. But that day his anger seemed to have no precipitating cause (Cobb said he was "shocked" by McIntyre's behavior), and employing the most obscene terms ("It was unbelievable to me that men could use some of those epithets and be manly"), he informed Ty that he wouldn't be taking any batting practice, not that day, perhaps not ever. If Cobb wanted to occupy himself, McIntyre said, he could run around in the outfield and shag fly balls hit by the veterans, or, better yet, pack his bag and return to the second-rate Southern minors from whence he'd slithered. A half year behind schedule, but with no power lost for being pent up for so long, the hazing of Ty Cobb had begun.

Not surprisingly, those Tigers brought to the dark art of bullying the requisite fierceness but little imaginative flair. Barring a yannigan from batting practice was a cliché move in those "olden days," Cobb said, when ballplayers were not yet the "higher class of men" they would become, in his estimation, just a few years later. So was running into a rookie trying to field a ball, or, if the hazee was a pitcher, playing purposely porous defense behind him to help tarnish his record. It didn't matter if you were hurting your own club with such tactics as long as you were hurting the new guy's chances and thus helping a veteran keep his job. Nor did baseball hazing have much pretense of being an outlandish practical joke that perpetrator and victim would one day laugh about and bond over. For the most part, it was just mean.

Hazing didn't happen to every new player—the less talented ones, especially, didn't seem worth the time, trouble, or thumbtacks—but if you were selected for the process you were supposed to take your punishment humbly and without complaint—to ride out the storm. Cobb, however, seemed constitutionally incapable of doing that. Before McIntyre could finish cursing him out, Cobb moved through stages of outrage. His first instinct was to enlist support, but when he appealed to other men milling in the on-deck area—his friends, he thought—they literally turned their backs on him. Even the graying, forty-year-old Bobby Lowe, a paternal figure at whose house Cobb had at least once eaten dinner, succumbed to the peer pressure, and said nothing. (Cobb would never forget that.) Ty's next move was to stalk over to the dugout and demand redress from Armour. The manager, who tended to shy away from face-to-face confrontations with his men, tried to laugh off the matter as the sort of thing every ballplayer goes through. "Go up there and take your turn," he told Cobb, according to the 1925 memoir. "If they say anything, shove 'em out of the way. They're kidding you." So Ty did just that, pushing his way to the plate and getting in his swings, as he said, "despite their looks."

When he came back to the clubhouse a few minutes later, he discovered what he described as "a tragedy." The black ash bats that Joe Cunningham, the Royston coffin carpenter, had made for him and that he'd been hauling wherever he went for the past several years, had been sawed into pieces—"and," he added, "parts of them thrown away." After that the indignities just kept coming. Cobb would on many occasions find his street clothes tied in knots and at other times his uniform missing. When he retrieved his hat from a restaurant checkroom—usually after dining alone—he sometimes found it twisted out of shape, or punched through at the crown. On train trips some of the Tigers seated behind him threw wads of wet newspaper at his head. The bathroom on his hotel floor (the johns were communal in those days, at least in the kinds of places ballplayers stayed) was always occupied or locked when he tried to use it. At one point, Cobb's enemies pressured his roommate, pitcher Ed Willett, into asking Armour to move him out, leaving Cobb as the only Tiger without a partner on road trips. Speaking of this time years later to Grantland Rice, Cobb said that ostracization didn't bother him so much "because it gave me more time by myself to think about baseball." In any case, he did not, for the most part, fight back with his fists when harassed and abused in this way—to do so would have been futile because he was always outnumbered—but his defiant attitude was enough to keep his tormentors at their task. Some, like Sam Crawford, thought any excesses on the part of the anti-Cobb clique were basically Cobb's fault. "He took it the wrong way," Crawford said in *The Glory of Their Times*, sounding what was at the time a popular refrain. "He came up with an antagonistic attitude, which in his mind turned any little razzing into a life-or-death struggle."

The reporters assigned to cover the Tigers could see what was happening, but wrote nothing about it until months later, when Armour finally gave them an excuse to violate the unwritten rule about not airing a team's dirty laundry by suspending McIntyre for his role in the harassment of Cobb. How much of a scandal they were sitting on, how much sympathy there might be on the part of the general public for someone in Cobb's position, would be hard to say. Some people were starting to see the stupidity in hazing, especially after a famous 1898 case in which a West Point Cadet named Oscar Booze died after being held down and forced to drink Tabasco sauce. Yet most still believed, as Senator Albert Beveridge of Indiana did, that the practice had roots in healthy male aggression. "A young man is like a male animal after all," Beveridge said, "and those who object to his rioting like a young bull are in a perpetual quarrel with nature." Charles Foster Kent, head of the department of biblical literature at the Yale Divinity School, said that the book of Genesis proved that Joseph has been "eft'ectually hazed" by his brothers, and came away from the experience "less fresh [as in impudent]. We all look back on the hazing incidents of our college days," Kent added, "as a pleasant memory."

The extent of Cobb's hazing—its exact duration and the depths of its severity—is not known. Although he mentioned it a few times in his various memoirs, he didn't dwell on the subject, mostly because he didn't want to depict himself as a victim. The fact that Al Stump, his ghostwriter, featured the period prominently (and inaccurately) in chapter one of his autobiography is a key reason Cobb was preparing to sue to stop publication of the book when he died in July of 1961. (*Ty Cobb: My Life in Baseball* came out that September.) What seems certain is that Cobb's hazing was harsher and went on for far longer than the typical rookie's. It also felt colder—more premeditated—since it started at an arbitrary point in the season *after* he arrived in the majors. One imagines a group of grown men sitting together somewhere, in the days before the initial batting practice episode, probably with drinks in hand, working themselves up over an oblivious if somewhat cocky teen, who was just then sitting in his room listening to Fritz Kreisler recordings. Why did Cobb upset them so much, and why did they erupt just then, after tolerating him the year before?

One thing that annoyed them was his Southernness. More than just another detestable attribute—like his bookishness or his popularity with the Augusta fans—this fact magnified and colored everything about him. Southerners were exoticized by their boreal brethren in those days—for their elaborate codes of conduct, their odd cuisine (possum? really?), and their feelings in regard to race (or rather the more open, or one might say less hypocritical, way that many expressed those feelings). For some of the Tiger players, Cobb's Southernness played out most maddeningly in his air of aristocracy, his sense of being in some ineffable way *better* than them, an attitude they sensed, to their dismay, had a basis in fact. Writing fifty-five years later, on the occasion of Cobb's death, E. A. Batchelor, a longtime sports editor for the *Detroit Free Press* and *Daily News*, said, "that Ty came from a higher social plane than had spawned the bullies made them all the more determined to drive him off the squad." In the North in those days, Southerners who failed to display sufficient deference were often said, as Crawford said of Cobb, to be "still fighting the Civil War." In *The Glory of Their Times*, Crawford added, "As far we were concerned, we were all damn Yankees before he met us." Cobb wasn't the only Southern ballplayer to hear this accusation. A few years later, Shoeless Joe Jackson, in his rookie season, was twice driven back to his home in rural Pickens County, South Carolina, by teammates on the Philadelphia Athletics who teased him mercilessly for being an illiterate hillbilly. Unable to stop the harassment, manager Connie Mack finally traded Jackson to Cleveland—where in his first full season with the Naps he hit .408. ("It don't take school stuff to help a fella play ball," Jackson said.)

Of course, Cobb had been Southern—and almost all the other things he was in 1906—the previous summer, when he had gotten along fine with everyone except Matty McIntyre. It wasn't until the following spring that he added his only truly unpardonable sin, the one thing worse than being Southern: being good. When he showed up in Augusta that spring he was broader across the shoulders, having added about twenty-five pounds of muscle over the winter, in the estimation of the *Free Press*. Meanwhile, he seemed, at the age of nineteen, both faster and more powerful: from the start of spring training the ball jumped off his bat, and he would be halfway to first base before it bounced. He'd been working out hard during the off-season, he told the sportswriters who marveled at his condition—and reported that he seemed to be in midseason form while the other, older Tigers were, as usual, slowly and creakily working their way into playing shape, an observation that certainly did not increase his popularity among the veterans. In his first intra-squad game, Cobb hit an inside-the-park home run, immediately justifying his selection as a Regular. In his first official preseason game about a week later, against the Brooklyn Superbas, he got a triple and single. Against the Macon Brigands of the Sally League a few days after that, he was 3-for-4. The only game that month in which he went hitless was the one the Tigers played against the Augusta Tourists on the night before his mother's trial for manslaughter. This is a small sample of performances, to be sure, but there was something about the way Cobb *looked* getting those hits that confirmed the initial impressions of those who thought he'd be first-rate. Despite a surfeit of outfielders, Navin and Armour turned down several offers for Cobb that would have allowed them to add a badly needed catcher to their staff. "I think we'll keep Cobb," the manager wrote to Ed Barrow, his counterpart on the Toronto Maple Leafs of the Eastern League, "at least until [Jimmy] Barrett comes around."

Cobb was certainly playing like a keeper. In 1906 he came out of the gate hitting .300, a far better number than that of any of the teammates—Crawford, McIntyre, Jones—he was supposed to be understudying. Joe S. Jackson wrote in the *Free Press* that if the Tigers starting outfield was picked "on what they have shown thus far, Cobb would be the first selected of the four now in harness." He wasn't just a promising rookie anymore; he was . . . (drum roll, please) "the Georgia Peach," or so Jackson wrote in the March 18 *Free Press*. At least one other player, pitcher Nap Rucker, a native of the Atlanta suburb of Crabapple, had been dubbed that in the past, but once Cobb got the nickname, it stuck.

A basic question arises: was Cobb thriving *despite* the turmoil that surrounded him—the ostracism, the broken bats and hats, the wads of wet newspaper—or *because* of it? This is not a simple question, and whatever the answer we do know that he was not a man able to block things out. It is impossible to talk to people who knew him and come away with the sense that he ever slipped and rolled with life's punches; rather, he led with his chin. This tendency may have been rooted in the same Southernness that aggravated his fellow Tigers. Historian Ted Ownby, in his book *Subduing Satan: Religion, Recreation, and Manhood in the Rural South, 1865–1920*, says that the men of that region have never been good at letting a wrong roll off their backs. "They have always felt a need to exert their will over any enemy as directly and immediately as possible," Ownby says. "The driving influence is not primarily a taste for blood but rather a consistent readiness for confrontation. Southerners have long been quick to take offense, quick to go to war, and, when at war, quick to mount a direct assault." Cobb's defenses, though constantly up, were anything but impermeable. Indeed—and this I think is key to understanding Ty Cobb—his defenses stunk. Sticks and stones broke his bones *and* names would always harm him. "We Cobbs cry a lot," he said many years later, breaking into tears as, at the age of sixty-three, he announced his intention to build a hospital in Royston in honor of his father. He was hypersensitive.

One didn't have to be as emotionally fragile as Cobb, though, to be hurt by what Matty McIntyre and his ilk were doing. The hazing he received in 1906 was long and brutal. Cobb thought about it night and day and later recalled that it left him with a "heavy burning" inside. "They sort of formed a gang which kept aloof from me," he wrote. "They clearly made me feel my position—that of a recruit. I had no place in their counsels. I had to go about alone." He was still technically a teenager, newly fatherless, far from home. "Other players have gone through struggles as hard," he wrote, "but none harder."

And yet for all that he was not worn down or weakened—at least not immediately—by either the hazing or the worry about his mother's impending trial. He was, rather, at the peak of physical condition—on the verge, just as he suspected, of a historic comeback from his crummy .240 half year.

Cobb was learning something about himself that spring: despite his Irish bloodlines he was the kind of person who would rather have the wind in his face than at his back. "I *like* opposition," he would observe years later. The many extra challenges he endured that spring and beyond seemed to help bolster his will and focus his mind. His great talent was not blocking out adversity but letting it come through, unfiltered, and turning it into fuel. As Cobb's favorite historical figure, Napoleon Bonaparte, said, "Adversity is the midwife of genius." Connie Mack once put it another way: "Don't get Cobb mad." Anger made him better. "When the hazing players would get me angry and upset by some petty act," Cobb said, "I often gritted my teeth and declared to myself that I would get a base hit the next time up or die in the attempt." In this way he made his enemies, and his worries, complicit in his quest for greatness. Whatever did not kill Cobb would make him a .350 hitter—and some years a .400 one.

Cobb was not entirely without support on those 1906 Tigers. One particularly difficult day the pitcher Bill Donovan called him aside. "Kid," Cobb recalled him saying, "don't think you haven't a friend on this ball club. The fellows may razz you and give you that bush stuff, but there are some here who are your friends and who are going to [give you] an even break. Don't let those fellows keep you from being a good ball player." One night that spring, Cobb went with Donovan and two or three teammates to an Augusta theater where a female fortune-teller was doing a stage act that involved questions from the audience. Cobb couldn't resist. The *Free Press* reported that he "called on the lady to ask what position the Tigers would hold at the close of the 1906 season."

"Fifth place," was the reply and, said the paper, "this crushed the Georgian, who thinks he's aboard the flag-getter, and he refused to remain in the theater, hustling back to the hotel and seeking the seclusion of his room and the solace of slumber."

A sensitive lad he was.

The trial of Amanda Cobb took Ty away from the Tigers, but only briefly. The vagaries of the Georgia Circuit Court system were such that everyone involved got just one day's notice that the proceedings would begin on Thursday, March 29, in Livonia. Cobb caught a train from Augusta that morning and arrived late as usual. Due to the sensational coverage, the courthouse was packed with the overflow milling on the steps. "This case is the most important one that has been tried in this court for a number of years," said the *Atlanta Constitution*, "owing to the prominence of Professor W. H. Cobb and his wife in this community." Everyone wanted to see the pretty widow who would, said the *Macon Telegraph*, be cited for "alleged improper conduct during a visit to Atlanta" just prior to her husband's death. Cobb was ushered inside during his mother's hours-long, teary, sotto voce testimony about her relationship with the late W.H., including an account of the accident. That was about the only aspect of the trial that went as anticipated.

Instead of being a week-long battle royal among the ten lawyers, with much dirt dished, as many had hoped, both sides made their cases relatively quickly and the all-male jury began deliberations at 4:00 p.m. the next day. No transcript of the trial was ever produced, and the newspaper reporting is strangely detail-free, but it appears that in the end the Atlanta police chief was never called to the stand. From the opening gavel the case seems to have shifted dramatically in Amanda's favor—as if for the sake of propriety, by gentlemen's agreement, the key issue of adultery was left unmentioned. Perhaps W.H.'s angry brothers, or the prosecutors themselves, did not in the end have the heart or stomach to make a case for Amanda's defamation and incarceration. In any case, the proceedings were almost perfunctory, and the jury took only an hour to find her not guilty. Cobb immediately telegraphed the news to Bill Armour, who tipped off Joe S. Jackson, who wrote about the verdict in the next day's *Free Press*. In the end, Cobb spent only a decent interval away from the team, taking a day or so to get his mother resettled in Royston, and travel with his brother back to Georgia Tech, where Paul was enrolled that semester. He caught up with his teammates at the Slag Pile, the 600-seat home of the Birmingham Barons, as the Tigers barnstormed their way north from spring training, and despite physical and emotional fatigue and an increasingly sore throat, got three hits in his first game back.

In light verse, the *Augusta Chronicle* sent a message to Bill Armour on behalf of Cobb's Georgia fans:

Ty is a Georgia laddie,
you took him north, we know.
And if you love us dearly,
you'll give him a chance to show.

There may be big leaguers able
to beat Tyrus out of a job,
but promise us, Armour,
you won't make a farmer,
out of our Georgia Tyrus Cobb

Cobb's sore throat became unbearable by the time the team reached Toledo a few days later. He told Germany Schaefer he felt feverish and couldn't swallow. The second baseman found a doctor and went with Cobb to see him. "Malarial tonsillitis" was the diagnosis, and Cobb immediately began two or three days of ham-fisted surgeries from which he was barely able to make it back to the hotel. He always maintained that the doctor who performed the procedure was later committed to an insane asylum. Whether or not that was true, he lost so much blood he had to spend a few days confined to his hotel room. When he rejoined the team, McIntyre and company were waiting.

CHAPTER ELEVEN

IN LATE JUNE OF 1906 Bill Armour decided he had to do something about the ongoing hazing of Cobb—who was then, by all the traditional methods of measuring baseball performance, the best player on the team—and so, on the 23rd, while the Tigers were in Chicago for a three-game series against the "Hitless Wonder" White Sox (they would win the world championship that year despite a team batting average of .230, the lowest in the league), he suspended Matty McIntyre "indefinitely and a little longer," according to Joe S. Jackson of the *Detroit Free Press*. Other teammates might have been banished along with McIntyre, as the manager told his men in what must have been a tense clubhouse meeting the day before the announcement came down. But if Armour had punished everyone who was guilty of harassing Cobb, he said, he couldn't have put a team on the field.

"And so it came to pass," wrote Jackson, that Matthew McIntyre, up from the potato fields of Staten Island, New York, was cast "in the role of Horrible Example."

Readers of the *Free Press* could be excused from at first wondering as they skimmed the sports pages for the latest news of their beloved "Tiges" that morning: a horrible example of *what*? Cobb's hazing had been happening away from public view. Unless he chanced to be riding in a Pullman car with the club when Cobb was being pelted with wads of wet newspaper, or staying in a hotel where he roamed the hallways in search of an unlocked lavatory, no regular crank, as devoted as he might be to the team, knew anything about it. Armour, still thinking he could keep secret this particular example of his failure to maintain order, had tried to frame the suspension as his reaction to simple player recalcitrance.

"I asked McIntyre if he wouldn't ginger up his work," the manager said in his official statement. "He said he wouldn't hustle, and I told him he had put on a Detroit uniform for the last time." His offense, technically, was "indifferent play." Armour's account was so far from reality, though, so patently ridiculous, that the beat reporters saw it as an excuse to tell the more interesting truth about how the team had been crippled by dissension since spring training, and that Cobb, the youngster everyone was talking about, was at the center of the civil war.

Armour may have done McIntyre a favor by suspending him just then. After several months of fixating on Cobb, the outfielder was showing signs of unraveling mentally and needing a "time-out," as the kindergarten teachers say, to get a grip and gather his wits. What became the last straw for Armour was an action not even directed at Cobb, but at one of Matty's own co-conspirators—a sign, thought the manager, that the overwrought hazers were starting to turn on each other, and that the war on Cobb might be devolving into a mad free-for-all. With the bases loaded in the fifth inning at South Side Park on the afternoon of June 22, White Sox catcher Billy Sullivan—the second-worst hitter in baseball history among players who had at least 3,000 at-bats (lifetime average: .213)— stroked a soft liner in the direction of McIntyre, who acted like it was too hot to handle and let it roll to a patch of no-man's-land in deep left center. Before the ball could be fielded by Davy Jones (Cobb was out of the lineup that day), Sullivan had a rare triple and three RBI, which went to the discredit of pitcher Ed Siever. What McIntyre had against Siever, a workmanlike lefty who shared his strong aversion to Cobb, can only be imagined, but when the inning was over, the two had words about the incident and nearly came to blows on the bench.

McIntyre had already shown he was the sort of player who didn't mind hurting the team if he could advance a personal vendetta. For the last few months he'd been ignoring hit-and-run signals and declining to lay down sacrifice bunts when Cobb was on base, and he had failed to heed Armour's repeated admonitions to knock it off and be mindful of the common cause. About a week before McIntyre's suspension, Cobb had finally repaid his slights in kind, letting a ball hit off Matty's pal and roommate, Twilight Ed Killian, get by him in right field and go for a

triple. (He and Killian also had words at the end of the inning.) As trai-
torous as this was—the hit knocked in a run that helped the Highlanders
win the game—Armour remained staunchly on Cobb's side, and blamed
McIntyre for bringing the feud onto the field in the first place.

In some ways, McIntyre must have known he had already lost the
battle with Cobb, who would always be favored over him as long as they
both were Tigers. He was disgusted, and his immediate reaction to his
suspension in late June was a demand to be traded or released. "I will
never play for the Tigers again!" McIntyre told Jackson. Armour, as much
as he would have liked to get rid of him, declined the trade request, preferring to punish his problem child by keeping him in a state of forced,
unpaid leave. To add a little extra sting to the suspension, he also moved
Cobb into McIntyre's position, where the youngster seemed at home and
remained potent with the bat, going 3-for-5 in his first game as a left
fielder and bringing his average close to .350.

It had been an exhilarating few months for Cobb. Coming out of
spring training, almost everyone, including Armour, believed to some
degree what Clark Griffith had said the year before: that once the league's
smarter pitchers got a second look at him, they would contrive through
slow curves and outside-corner-nipping pitches to bring his preseason
batting average back down to earth. Cobb, in fact, sat on the bench for
that entire first week of the regular season, not playing a single inning.
But then on April 22 Crawford "strained his side swinging at a high
one in the ninth," said the *Free Press* (the problem was probably a pulled
oblique muscle), and the next day Cobb got a chance to play against the
Browns in St. Louis, where he beat out a sacrifice bunt and eventually
made it around to score. After that he hit safely in every game but one for
the next five weeks.

By the time of McIntyre's suspension, Cobb's rise was more than just
a Detroit story. *Sporting Life* called him "a find of the first water" and
Jimmy Collins, manager of the Boston Americans, inquired about his
availability, but in vain; the Detroit club would entertain no offers. Washington Senators manager Joe Cantillon, who'd been in organized baseball
since 1878, said he had never seen a player quite like Cobb. "Listen, the
next time he pokes a bunt at you," he told his overmatched third base-

man, "run back to third base and try to head him off there!" Cobb wasn't just good, he was exciting, the kind of player who sold tickets—who made the otherwise mediocre Tigers, said Paul W. Eaton of *Sporting Life*, grasping for a wildly futuristic figure, "worth four dollars to see." Whether the Tigers won or lost, Cobb was always a topic of conversation. On May 17 he had the only hit in a masterpiece tossed by Rube Waddell of the Philadelphia A's. A few days later, in a dramatic victory over Boston, he made what might have been the catch of the season, diving for a sinking liner, first swatting the ball into the air with his mitt, then snatching it bare-handed.

If there had been an ESPN in those days, Cobb would have hogged the daily highlight reel. Besides making noteworthy plays, he seemed to figure into every baseball controversy. On May 5 the Tigers played at home against the Browns in a game that started at 3:00 and was to be ended by mutual agreement at 5:00, if still ongoing, no matter what the score, so both teams could catch a train to St. Louis for a rematch there the following day. Most games in those days took less than ninety minutes to complete, and such cutoff times, though at odds with the proudly clockless spirit of the sport, were fairly commonplace (and provided for in the league by-laws), but in this case the crowd for some reason was not informed of the conditions in advance. Trouble might have been avoided if the score had remained as lopsided as it was with two outs in the bottom of the eighth inning, when the Tigers were trailing 7–3. But then Cobb hit a bases-loaded triple, and Detroit scored another run in the ninth, which meant that when the game reached the two-hour mark, and was declared over, the score was tied. Agitated fans poured onto the field by the hundreds to demand an explanation from (lone) umpire Tom Connolly. Violence was avoided but the incident made national headlines.

Nine days later in Washington, Cobb was at the center of another squabble. With the game tied with two out in the top of the tenth, and men on second and third, he came to bat—and hit what looked like a routine roller to the second baseman. However, by busting out of the batter's box and sliding (feet first), he was able to beat the throw, at least in the opinion of umpire Tom Connor. One runner scored, and the man on second advanced to third. Many Senators fans booed heartily and Washington manager Jake Stahl ran out to argue. As soon as things settled down in the stadium and the umpire said "Play ball!" Cobb broke toward second. The Washington catcher wisely threw to third to hold the runner there, but in his haste wound up launching the ball into left field. (If there was a stat for Causing Errant Throws, Cobb would hold another record.) Another run scored and the Tigers won that day, but the result was overshadowed by reports of D.C. police storming the field after the game to save umpire Connor, who was being "treated roughly" by spectators still livid about his calling Cobb safe at first the previous inning.

Cobb was on his way to becoming the best hitter the game ever saw, but it was his adventures on the base paths, the way he fooled with the already well established rhythms of the pastime while making his way from one of the era's loosely secured, puffy white sacks to another—exploding down the first base line, bolting at odd moments, not stopping when virtually all others would—that made him a curiosity and, before long, a star. He was a true original, a young man with one cleated foot in the newfangled "psychological" era, and the other planted firmly in the unfashionable pre-1900 past, a time when raucous teams like the National League Baltimore Orioles dove and tumbled 'round the diamond like circus acrobats. (As Louis Menand said of T. S. Eliot, "It is often impossible to tell which direction he is pointing in.") For the press, the irresistible temptation was to talk about his speed; *Sporting Life* compared him to the Thoroughbred champion Sysonby, and the *Philadelphia Press* reported that an "expert watch holder" positioned near first base at Columbia Park, the Athletics' home field, on May 17, caught him beating out a bunt in three and one fifth seconds, a time that if accurate would still rank among the fastest ever.

Cobb always denied being especially fleet afoot, just as he resisted the label of "natural hitter." For him, progress on the base paths was all about studying a pitcher's habits, confounding expectations, and intimidating the opposition—giving the impression, through body language, chippy chatter (*"I'm going on the next pitch! Watch me! Watch out!"*), and his own past performances, that he had no hesitation about coming in very hard. Almost everything he did on the field was a considered, conscious decision based on his theory of the game. As both a lightning rod for con-troversy and a man of ideas he stood apart from baseball's other premier players, who were either Goody-Two-shoes like Christy Mathewson or stolid, poorly educated, lunch-bucket types like Honus Wagner and Nap Lajoie. To gauge the true distance between Cobb and Lajoie, a player he resembled statistically, consider that as a signing bonus one year Lajoie received a mule. Decades later, when they were old men and Cobb vis-ited Lajoie in Daytona Beach, they sat together on his porch and Lajoie told that story, shaking his head in wonderment at his own docility and saying, "I took a mule, Ty, a *mule!*" Cobb, though he hailed from what he called "a small town of the old fashioned sort," was not the kind of player to whom you would ever think of saying, "Instead of money, how about a nice mule?"

Because Cobb, with his colorful style and obvious intelligence, was a blessing to a baseball writer, he received not just attention but also sym-pathy from Joe S. Jackson, the most influential scribe in Detroit. "Cobb is burning up the outfield and base paths with his speed," Jackson (the founding president of the Baseball Writers' Association of America) wrote back in spring training, soon after he'd christened Cobb the Georgia Peach. In Jackson's accounts, "Tyrus" never merely hit a double; he "deliv-ered a huge drive to center for two bases." When the story of McIntyre's suspension broke and reporters finally felt free to write about the feud between Matty and Ty, Jackson made it clear to the public that the club was on the Peach's side. He often praised the performances of other Ti-gers, and like all writers of that day could always find excuses for why the team was underperforming—but Cobb, it seemed, was the only player he liked to hang around with, to sit next to on trains, and accompany to the theater to see a fortune-teller's show.

Cobb would always get along well with most writers; during and after his playing days he invited many to his home (a not uncommon practice in the days when reporters and athletes resided in the same socio-economic class). But then in 1906, innocent and ostracized and often at loose ends, Cobb would chat up almost anyone who was friendly and polite, including fans who called to him as he stood in the outfield. In his

1913 memoir, serialized in the *Atlanta Constitution* and later republished by the Ty Cobb scholar Wesley Fricks as *Inside Baseball with Ty Cobb*, he said, "Frequently a bleacherite will ask, 'Who is that pitching now or who is that pinch batter?' [There were no uniform numbers in those days, and the only public address system was an announcer or umpire shouting through a megaphone from around home plate.] It is very easy to turn and tell him who it is or to say honestly you don't know if it happens to be a youngster on an opposing club you have never seen before. However, there are players who will either keep their back turned on spectators or make some sarcastic reply. Then they wonder why they are jeered constantly."

In writing about the young Cobb, Jackson often liked to portray him as a backwoods exotic, the classic rube (à la Gomer Pyle or Jethro from *The Beverly Hillbillies*) who often spouts wisdom or folksy humor. While the characterization may, in Cobb's early times with the team, have contained a germ of truth, some of Jackson's anecdotes, such as the story of Ty's aggrieved reaction to the Augusta fortune-teller, seem obviously exaggerated. Almost all of what Jackson's bumpkinesque Cobb caricature says and does is innocuous stuff, stretched or concocted to fill a column on days of rain or travel. But in the *Free Press* of April 1, 1906, one finds an item of special interest, because it turns on the subject of race. On this occasion Jackson wrote about himself as a put-upon New Englander (he was born in Rhode Island) who couldn't step outside in the South without getting his briefcase toted, his coat whisked, or his shoes shined by some tip-seeking "Afro-African boy." Upon hearing the writer's complaint, young "Tyrus," his traveling companion, notes that when down in Dixie a white Northerner need not dispense abnormal gratuities in the hope of getting better service or assuaging one's guilt about the plight of "the menials." Cobb is not quoted directly in the brief item ("the menials," it should be noted, is Jackson's phrase, not Cobb's), but we are reminded by Jackson (albeit not very coherently, so brace yourself) that he was "born and bred in the South" and "understands the negro perfectly and is ever ready to prove that the colored man more readily responds to the requests and demands of those of the South who maintains the old relation of master and man between the races, than to those of the Northerner, who proceeds on lines that indicate that he believes that the fourteenth amendment means just what it says."

The run-on nature of the writing suggests that Jackson is bluffing his way through a few column inches on a day when the Tigers didn't play. Perhaps Cobb did say something like he is indirectly quoted as saying— that over-tipping can lead to feelings of resentment, and that an extra nickel here and there will not rectify the damage wrought by Jim Crow. Or maybe not. In any case, let the record show that this inconsequential little blurb is the only example of Cobb even *purportedly* talking about race relations until the 1950s, when he hailed the advent of Jackie Robinson.

For all the venom he seemed to be packing in his spleen, Matty McIntyre came around quickly. He never even stopped coming to the ballpark. Though his paychecks were on hold he showed up every day and took batting practice, saying to the reporters that he wanted to make the point that he was available for duty. The team wouldn't put out a uniform for him, so he wore an old navy blue road uniform he happened to have. Since the Tigers were at home at this time, his outfit only made him seem like more of an outcast.

The indefinite suspension lasted about a week. With Cobb hitting .355 (the third highest batting average in the American League), and Navin and Armour backing their prized youngster in the newspaper, McIntyre understood he had to kowtow to the front office or return to the potato fields of his youth. The manager had said that Matty could regain his place on the club at any time by telling him face-to-face that he intended to play hard and focus on baseball. So on the morning of Saturday, June 30, McIntyre went hat in hand to the Tigers offices in the Hammond Building, a steel-framed, ten-floor "skyscraper" on the corner of Griswold and West Fort, sought out the skipper, and said the right words, however grudgingly. Armour put him back in left field that afternoon, moved Cobb to center, and kept Crawford in right. Davy Jones, who'd been struggling at the plate, was now officially the second-stringer that Ty had been at the season's start. It was late June, the season was only half over, and there was still time to make a run at the pennant—if McIntyre's apology signaled a true change of heart.

No such luck. Tension and gloom still permeated the Tigers clubhouse. Though he stopped openly taunting and abusing Cobb, McIntyre continued to seethe at the sight of the team's best hitter, and Twilight Ed Killian became downright enraged by the way the front office was making an example of his roommate, to the point of one day being drunk and disorderly at the ballpark. Although it is difficult to pin down the dates, it is likely Cobb had the second of his several fights with Charlie Schmidt, the catcher being groomed to replace the oft-inebriated Warner, at around this time. The first, which had occurred early in the regular season, "arose," Cobb said, "over some trivial incident on the bench. He was a much bigger man than I but we mixed it up. In the struggle he fell over a barrel and I pounced on top of him as he lay on the barrel. They pulled us apart but the felling had started."

The second fight happened because Schmidt was being teased by his teammates for his failure to subdue his much less bulky opponent in the first one. "As I turned around the corner of the bench [one day]," Cobb said, "he soaked me with a hard one right on the jaw. There wasn't any fight after that. I simply hit the ground."

On July 3, the tension broke momentarily when the Tigers played in Cleveland before 1,400 fans and amid a shower so persistent that, said the *Free Press*, "players slid about as if they were on roller skates, bats slipped from the hands of batsmen and sailed fifty feet, and base running was made possible only by the runner keeping on the grass and leaping to the sack." In the sixth inning Germany Schaefer, trying to send a subtle hint to umpire Billy Evans that the game ought to be called, appeared at second base wearing a yellow rain slicker, and actually played with the coat on, though he got tangled in it while taking a relay from Cobb, and his fashion statement cost the Tigers a run. It didn't matter. When Evans finally called the game in the top of the seventh, Detroit was down 5–0 and even more securely in fifth place. The brief catharsis was over and the unhappy caravan moved on.

Baseball statistics don't always reflect a team's true reality. The Tigers went 11–14 in July, but their record was that balanced only because they played some truly dreadful clubs, like the Boston Americans, who would go on to lose 105 games that season, and whose manager, Jimmy Collins, kept going AWOL (he was fired, but his successor, Chick Stahl, committed suicide), and the reliably incompetent Senators, whom Charley Dryden of the *San Francisco Chronicle* would dub "First in war, first in peace and last in the American League." Detroit felt and looked more like a 5–20 team. Everyone's batting average except Davy Jones's plummeted in July. Cobb's fell more than 20 points in the first week and kept falling. A mini-epidemic of illnesses and injuries swept over the club. The Tigers had made it this far on anger and adrenaline, but now they seemed worn down. Almost every man complained of some kind of antique deadball era ailment, like a sore finger (Warner), a sore neck (Donovan), "neuralgia of the head" (Fred Payne), a thumb smashed by "the descent of a sleeping car window" (Charley O'Leary), a rupture (Jones), or lumbago (Killian), but Ty seemed to be troubled by something vaguer and more virulent—more modern, too. When he couldn't take the field at the Huntington Avenue Baseball Grounds in Boston on July 17, the *Herald* said it was because of "all-around complaints." Armour was not always sympathetic when players said they were sick, especially if they wanted the team to pay their doctor bills. Schaefer once told him he thought he needed a stomach operation and the manager told him to "Just take a big teaspoon of the best olive oil you can find before each meal and you'll be fine." But Cobb was a more precious commodity than Schaefer and so was treated differently. On July 18, with Ty still out of the lineup and the Tigers scheduled to move on to New York for a series against the Highlanders, Armour sent him home. The morning of the 19th, Cobb, with his bag of clothes in one hand and his bag of bats in the other, got on a train bound for Detroit—and disappeared.

— CHAPTER TWELVE —

THE OFFICIAL EXPLANATION FOR COBB'S absence was that he was in the hospital for an operation. That statement, provided jointly by manager Bill Armour and secretary Frank Navin, was so brief and so vague as to obviously be code for "Don't ask us where Cobb is, okay, fellows?" If the beat writers did follow up nevertheless, and if they were confided in by the Tigers' front office, it apparently was on condition that they keep the answer secret. Not only was information about Cobb scarce immediately following his July 18 departure, but until he returned forty-four days later, on the 2nd of September, the scantest references to him, a brilliant young player who'd hovered among the top five hitters in the league, were hard to come by. Tiger cranks might have rubbed their eyes and questioned their sanity. Had there really been a tall young redhead who walked every day down Woodward Avenue from his rooming house to Bennett Park, got a hit or three, stole a base or two, then strolled back home for an early dinner—a fresh, sober face on a squad dominated by dour drunks—or had Detroit just dreamed him?

It is left for Cobb historians to puzzle out what happened. Some consider his sudden absence in the heart of the 1906 season to be among the game's great unsolved mysteries—and it is true that privacy laws, the passage of time, and the then prevailing standards of propriety, as well as the severe misfortunes that have since befallen the city of Detroit, do combine to daunt the modern scholar searching for truth. A lot of Michigan medical records have been destroyed just because it was too expensive to move or keep them. But let us see by applying what *is* knowable how far we can get.

The first thing I will suggest is that we eliminate the *Augusta Chron-*

icle's theory, which was that Cobb's problem was dietary in nature and stemmed from a lack of good Southern cooking. "Ty Cobb can't digest the food that's been given him in the North," the paper said, in an editorial that at least acknowledged his absence, and which urged Armour to get him back in the lineup by "feeding him blue-stemmed collards and corn bread." Cobb might have appreciated those victuals, assuming he had an appetite, but the *Chronicle* failed to grasp the gravity of the situation. When a star ballplayer drops from sight, and his hometown papers tiptoe around his absence, the cause can be assumed to be beyond the powers of even pork chops or fried catfish. Still, in a general way—in the sense, that is, that Cobb's stomach was the source of his troubles—the *Chronicle* might indeed have been on to something. So let us for a moment ponder that.

To assume gastrointestinal problems made sense. You can only feed off psychological abuse and physical intimidation for so long before you start feeding off yourself. Cobb's ultrasensitivity, coupled with his circumstances, would seem to put him at a high risk for disorders like irritable bowel syndrome or ulcers—things that might need to be addressed with the "operation" he was in fact said to be having. Intestinal ills can sometimes have inconvenient, embarrassing consequences—which might explain the secrecy surrounding his leave. But with all the polite, scientific, and pleasantly imprecise terms available for use in those decorous times, would someone really maintain a lifelong information lockdown about a six-week interval (as Cobb did, avoiding any mention of his 1906 absence in his several serialized memoirs and autobiography) if the problem was basically a bad bellyache? That does not seem likely.

Something stronger than embarrassment—and more akin to shame—probably drove the silence. Could Cobb have been experiencing a disorder of the emotions or of the mind? As fodder for gossip, a nervous breakdown certainly beats diarrhea. And Cobb was a candidate for psychological problems. Apart from his particular personal issues in Royston and Detroit, he was a brittle man living in a tilt-a-whirl time, a period, as historian Philipp Blom shows in his book *The Vertigo Years*, when the automobile, the airplane, the typewriter, and mass entertainments like movies (and organized baseball), were transforming society—and throwing all kinds of people off their stride. Just being alive in 1906 America, as women joined the workforce and hundreds of thousands migrated from farms to cities, starting life anew, stressed the nervous system and roiled the mind. The concurrent rise of psychoanalysis (and alcoholism) and the numerous newspaper advertisements for patent medicines that relieved "neurasthenia" showed that millions who had never met Matty McIntyre, or learned that their mother had killed their father, were actively trying to maintain a sense of mental serenity. The writer and advice giver Margaret E. Sangster, in an article published in the *Detroit Free Press* later that year, said, "The prevalence of nervous disease cannot be ignored by anyone who is familiar with social conditions in America. It is no longer an extraordinary occurrence in life," she added, "to be obliged to spend a period of retirement at a rest cure or a sanitarium."

It would seem that as a strapping young Southern man, given to athletics and the outdoor life of hunting and fishing, Cobb would rank, in the popular imagination at least, as an unlikely mental patient—and yet his confinement in a psychiatric facility is the most common explanation of his 1906 dropout among biographers and buffs. Al Stump, in his largely fictitious yet generally unquestioned biography of 1994, *Cobb*, says merely that Ty was sent to a "sanatorium" "on the outskirts of Detroit." The more trustworthy Richard Bak, in his 2005 book, *Peach: Ty Cobb in His Time and Ours*, writes that "the club quietly arranged for his convalescence at a sanatorium in rural Oakland County, north of Detroit. There, with the aid of medication, he slept long hours, giving his mind and body a chance to rest. He fished, swam, and hiked in the woods. . . . Visitors and newspapers were forbidden." Bak no doubt means the Pontiac Asylum, a Gothic, archetypically Gilded Age facility in Pontiac, Michigan, which was demolished in 2000—but he does not say where he gets any of his (curiously detailed) information. Charles Alexander, in his 1984 biography, *Ty Cobb*, says only that "A close reading of contemporary press coverage suggests that Cobb suffered some kind of emotional and physical collapse." He also notes that "Joe H. [*sic*] Jackson" nine days later wrote that Cobb was at "a sanitarium" and "probably will be there for some time." Unmentioned by Alexander or anyone else is that the *Detroit News* also reported that Cobb was "laid up in a local sanitarium," and though "still very weak" was expected by his doctor to return before the season's end.

"Sanitarium" was not always synonymous with "mental ward." It could mean a long-term-care facility for tuberculosis or postsurgical patients, a place for anyone who could be said to be convalescing. It could also be a kind of health spa, like John Harvey Kellogg's famous Battle Creek Sanitarium, where rich folk took recreational enemas. But the word "sanitarium" alone, with no brand name or modifiers, sounds (and sounded) like a euphemism, and inevitably conjures up a psychiatric facility.

Many who closely followed Cobb's game would probably not be shocked to learn that a player had cracked up. In more ways than one, baseball was bedlam. The pressures of the public arena were intense, the lack of role models and precedents destabilizing (professional ballplayers were not heroes, and in some places not even a topic of conversation when Cobb and his contemporaries were growing up), as all the fighting and drinking suggested. Boxers, it was true, had preceded ballplayers as celebrated athletes, but they didn't need to stay in the spotlight over the course of a 154-game season, getting publicly berated by their managers, being urged by their daddies to come home and help with the harvest, heckled and, sometimes, hazed. Yes, they lived with every prizefighter's worst nightmare—being knocked unconscious and having their wives and girlfriends rush simultaneously into the ring—but overall they didn't face the same daily level of stress. It almost goes without saying that baseball, that most statistic-minded of pastimes, kept a semiofficial list of player suicides going back to Frank Ringo of the Phillies in 1889 and including the aforementioned Tigers manager Win Mercer, who in 1903 left behind a note about the false promises of the baseball life. By 1910 there would be fourteen such deaths, not counting that of Harry Pulliam, the president of the National League, who in 1909 was *arrested* for attempted suicide even as he lay in a widening crimson circle on the floor of his Manhattan flat. We'll never know how many of the early players sought professional help, but clearly some were desperate enough to risk social stigma for a chance at relief. It was only a few years after Cobb's unexplained absence that a Wayne County sanitarium-cum-farm called

Eloise entered into a arrangement with Frank Navin to become the un-official mental facility of the Tigers. Before it closed in the late 1970s, a number of Detroit players had dropped in discreetly.

I set the likelihood of Cobb's having retreated to such a facility at about 60–40. The attendant secrecy supports that explanation, as does the likelihood that a hyper-touchy teenager will eventually crumble be-fore a star chamber of older men, even if he is at first fueled by his own defiance. So, obviously, do those several seemingly off-the-cuff references to a sanitarium in the local papers—unless, of course, that was an idea journalists were testing just to see if the Tigers management would swat it down—or unless the mental ward was a ruse perpetrated by Cobb himself in cooperation with Armour and Navin to cover another, even more po-tentially scandalous scenario.

And what might *that* be?

Allow me to float a theory.

Cobb didn't end his relationship with Charlotte (Charlie) Lombard when he left the Augusta Tourists. They were still actively courting in 1906, though not engaged because Charlie's wealthy father, Roswell, wasn't happy about her marrying a $1,500-a-year ballplayer. Suppose, for the sake of argument, that Charlie had become pregnant at around this time and experienced complications as a result of an abortion, miscar-riage, or some other difficulty that compelled Cobb to rush to her side. The record shows that's not a farfetched notion. Charlie was prone to obstetrical problems. Over the course of her life with Cobb, whom she would marry two years later, she would become pregnant thirteen times but carry only five children to term. Cobb would again without warning leave the team in midseason 1908 to travel to Augusta to marry Charlie in a small ceremony so unplanned for (or disapproved of) that several key relatives (including his mother and sister, Florence) would be missing, and a few months after that Charlie would suffer an unspecified medi-cal crisis. Does Cobb's disappearance of 1906 seem to presage his more widely acknowledged but still controversial departure of 1908? Could the operation and even the sanitarium have been cover stories to preserve a young woman's privacy and reputation?

And yet I remain, with qualms, in the "mental hospital" camp. The main reason is that if we believe Cobb left the club to be with Charlie we must also accept that he didn't stay at her side for very long, or that he came and went a couple of times during his six-week sabbatical. The *Free Press* mentioned in a small note that he was in the stands at Bennett Park for a game against the Athletics on July 31. Though he would like to "get back in the game soon," the paper said, "it will be several weeks before he is right." Also, starting in mid-August, Cobb played at least a dozen games with the crack amateur team from the Detroit Athletic Club, presumably working his way back into midseason shape. (He didn't hide his identity, but apparently posed for no photographs and the Detroit papers did not cover these appearances, a further sign that they were for the most part abetting his policy of silence.) All this wouldn't have left much time to be with the woman for whom he had temporarily dropped out of baseball. That Cobb was off being treated for a nervous disorder or "breakdown," as it was then called, is the most logical guess.

Changes were in order if the Tigers were going to win more games, fight less, and keep their manager. While Cobb was away, the team dealt with two of its biggest troublemakers: catcher Jack Warner was sold to the Senators, and Twilight Ed Killian fined $200 and suspended indefinitely for tearing up the clubhouse in a drunken fit. Armour also took off from the team, as he had the year before, to visit "parts unknown," said *Sporting Life*, and sign an unnamed outfielder for the 1907 season, probably someone intended to replace McIntyre—though what the Tigers needed most was a good-hitting first baseman. None of theses moves, however, succeeded in slowing the club's downward trajectory. As August wore on, the Tigers sank into sixth place. Rushing to the aid of team management, as sportswriters frequently did, Joe S. Jackson attempted to assure cranks that the brain trust was taking a smart, measured approach. It would not panic and make meaningless late-season moves that would leave the Tigers in poor shape for next season. It would husband its resources wisely. "The club realizes that a bag containing $5,000 cannot be put on the slab to pitch a game of ball," Jackson wrote.

The public, however, wasn't buying his line, or many tickets, either. On some days barely 1,000 people scattered themselves in the Bennett

Park stands. Rumors circulated that Ban Johnson, who as president of the American League seemed to possess powers beyond any of the magnates, once again was considering moving the strife-ridden and barely profitable club to Pittsburgh, or even recasting it as a minor league franchise. On August 28, Navin had to deny a report that he had already decided not to re-sign Armour for the following season and was talking to Hugh Jennings, the thirty-eight-year-old manager of the Baltimore Orioles, who themselves had migrated downward from the National to the Class A Eastern League several seasons back.

Cobb rejoined the Tigers on September 2, at Sportsman's Park in St. Louis. "The entry of a hero on the public scene goes unnoticed," the great A. J. Liebling wrote in *The Earl of Louisiana*, "but his *rentrée* always has an eager press." Not so in this case. No beat reporter acknowledged in print that the young star had ever been away for the heart of the season. Cobb got a single and stole a base as his team lost 1–0 to the Browns in a dull, rain-shortened contest. The next day the Tigers dropped a Labor Day doubleheader to the Browns, and Navin, who had traveled with his team, announced that, despite what he had said a few days earlier, Bill Armour would indeed be succeeded by Hughie (as most people called him) Jennings in 1907. Armour, who had agreed to finish out the season with the Tigers, wasted no time in demonstrating how awkward the next month would be by making a rambling, self-aggrandizing speech in which he blamed Ban Johnson for his firing, saying the AL president, fed up with the club's internal squabbling, had forced Navin's hand. Armour also said that he was "persona non grata" in the National League because of all the brilliant poaching he'd done from it over the years, and concluded, "Hence, I am practically out of major league ball." He was right about that—he would move on to the Toledo Mud Hens of the American Association and then out of baseball. He was managing a drugstore in Minneapolis when he died, "of a fit of apoplexy," in 1922.

Three days later, when the Tigers were in Chicago to face the first-place White Sox, many of the players effectively went on strike against their lame-duck leader, saying they were too sick or injured to take the field. Others simply got lost between their hotel and South Side Park. "Just as the game was about to be called [that is, started] today," the *Chi-*

cago Tribune reported, "Manager Armour discovered that [the announced starting pitcher George] Mullin was nowhere to be found." Except for a couple of untested late-season call-ups, the entire pitching staff was missing or unavailable for that day and the next, as were many veteran position players like Donovan, Schaefer, and McIntyre. Cobb was one of the few regulars ready for action. "As the team played today against Chicago," the *Free Press* said, "there was a pitcher in right field, a catcher in left field, an outfielder on first base and a first baseman on second." Armour was said to be "frantic" as the White Sox beat the Tigers 2–0 in the first of what were warmly remembered as "the Cripple Games." The supposedly Hitless Wonders won again the next day as well 13–5.

Peering back at those waning days of the season through the prism of old newspaper clips, it is painful to watch Armour, his pride mortally wounded, trying to put an ever-finer point on his position. In a bizarre joint interview with Navin on September 15, he told Cleveland's *Plain Dealer*, "I'm not kicking on the money matters. I'm objecting to the treatment accorded me personally. Navin and myself have always got along fairly well. [Owner Bill] Yawkey for some reason took a dislike to me in midseason last year. Yawkey and Navin are not experts at baseball. They think they have a pennant winning team here. They have not. The best manager in the world can't make a man hit. Yawkey is pleasant if you win, but he cannot stand to lose. He does not seem to consider that no one feels worse than I when a game is lost."

Then it was Navin's turn. "Personally, neither Yawkey nor myself have anything against the present manager," he said. "He is conscientious, eager to win, has unquestioned ability in developing young players. I will not question his knowledge of baseball, either. The great trouble with Armour is, he is too lenient with his players. They know it and take advantage of him in every way."

Armour said in rebuttal that he may indeed have been too easy on his players at times. "I've found it policy to be good to them," he said. "But I am not disappointed at the outcome of my policy in handling my men. Other causes have been to blame. If we could have hit, we'd won. If we had not been constantly hampered by injuries we might have had a chance."

Navin brushed aside the injury excuse, already shopworn in 1906. "A baseball leader must be recognized by his men as the leader," he said. "He must be full of dash and ginger, so that his men will be filled with the same spirit. That is why we have secured Hugh Jennings. He is what the city wants. He is a scrappy Irishman who will not take anything from anybody that he does not see fit to take. Jennings is out on the coaching lines, fighting all the time, and never lets a man forget he is the boss and that they are not running the team."

For Armour the indignities had only just begun. On September 22 the manager was "savagely attacked," said the *Plain Dealer*, by former Tiger Jack Warner under the grandstand at Bennett Park following a doubleheader that Detroit had played against the Washington Senators, the disgruntled catcher's new club. Oddly, it was Warner, wanting to put his spin on the story, who called the *Free Press* with a description of the assault, saying that it had been dark, and that Armour "had no time to ward off the first blows, which landed on his face." Spectators on their way out of the stadium separated the two. Warner, said the *Plain Dealer*, "claimed that Armour branded him falsely as a disturber" earlier that season but, worried that his former manager would swear out a warrant for his arrest, he caught a train for Chicago, where the league offices were, so he could personally give Ban Johnson his side of the story (the rest of his team moved on to St. Louis). Johnson heard him out, then took no action in the matter, saying he was barred from doing so because the fight had not happened on the field. Curiously, he had never used that logic when punishing players for their involvement in barroom brawls—but then he was no doubt secretly pleased with Warner for pummeling one of his more vocal critics.

The Tigers won nine games in a row in late September, knocking the Highlanders out of the pennant race in the process, but it was the kind of meaningless run of baseball fortune that follows mathematical elimination and offers no real hope. An atmosphere of frontier lawlessness hung over the club as it became clear that Detroit would finish in sixth place and once again draw fewer than 200,000 to Bennett Park. Often in those final weeks, no one bothered to man the coaching boxes, and "consequently," said the *Free Press*, "many runners died while making impossible tries for a bag." Players stopped caring or concentrated on settling old scores as reality returned and the team lost five of its last seven. In the first game of a doubleheader in St. Louis on October 6, the penultimate day of the season, Browns outfielder George Stone, who would lead the AL with a .358 average, hit a sharp liner off southpaw Ed Siever into left center field. "Neither Cobb nor McIntyre made a move for the sphere, which rolled all the way to the flag pole," said the *Free Press*. Thus a likely double became a two-run inside-the-park home run in what would be a 7–3 loss. Though he had just as much of a gripe with McIntyre regarding the play, Siever confronted Cobb in the clubhouse and said, in the parlance of the day, "You threw me down." The two had to be separated.

That evening at Planter's Hotel, the no longer grand hostelry where the Tigers stayed, Cobb was buying a pack of chewing gum at the lobby cigar stand when Siever abruptly abandoned a gaggle of teammates and came up to him from behind. Another Tiger—Bill Donovan—again intervened, saying, "Now don't have any trouble here, fellows."

After walking away, Cobb took up a position behind a column, hoping, he later admitted, to eavesdrop on Siever to see if he had something bad to say about him. The pitcher immediately noticed Cobb, though, and calling him what the *Augusta Chronicle* described as "a vile name," swung around the column with his left fist high in the air. Cobb was often said to be more of a brawler than a boxer, but in this case he deftly blocked the blow with his own left hand and smashed Siever's jaw with his right. Then he hit him in the face a couple of more times as the pitcher slumped to the floor. The final blows were particularly vicious, witnesses agreed, coming after the recipient was probably already unconscious. It's not as if Cobb had lost control, though. Several eyewitness accounts said that after administering the beating he "calmly" stepped over Siever and walked away from the scene.

In retrospect it's clear that something was happening at that moment, something more than just another fight. Or maybe something had already shifted, silently, inside Cobb, and the result was just then becoming manifest. He was on the verge of twenty years old now, and the fifth best hitter in the American League, with a batting average that season of .316.

If baseball meant anything, he deserved respect, if not special treatment. And yet for months he had been harassed, ostracized, and assaulted by a clique of jealous, less-talented men—of which Ed Siever was a prime example. For the most part Cobb had taken his punishment without fighting back. But at some point enough had to be enough.

Several witnesses said that he returned to the lobby a moment later and, still exhibiting a strange calmness, kicked the prone pitcher in the face.

CHAPTER THIRTEEN

IF WHAT THE TIGERS NEEDED most in the opinion of their secretary, Frank Navin, and the league president, Ban Johnson, was a stern disciplinarian, Hugh Ambrose Jennings was a most interesting selection for the manager's spot. Hughie had risen to prominence in the 1890s with the old Baltimore Orioles of the National League, a team rent by outlandish internal squabbling—mainstays John McGraw, Wee Willie Keeler, and Jack Doyle would wrestle in the shower like newlyweds while the beat reporters scuffed their soles and twirled their pencils, waiting for quotes—and famous for cheating and tricks. The Orioles hid extra balls in their conveniently tall outfield grass, "stumbled" in front of opposing catchers trying to throw out a runner at second base or tag a man coming home, and went out of their way to be seen filing their spikes, as part of their nonstop attempt at intimidation. Sometimes they were penalized, sometimes not. Jennings, a scrappy, redheaded shortstop with oversized, freckle-flecked features—he looked surprisingly like Henny Youngman whereas the Tigers scout Heinie Youngman, not surprisingly, didn't—was their resident expert at being plunked. The genial son of a Pennsylvania coal miner was hit by more pitched balls—287—than Craig Biggio (285) or any other major leaguer. On three occasions, he managed to get three free passes to first base by that means in a single game. When seeking victimization, he tried to pick his spots, looking for off-speed pitches to get in the way of, and he perfected a method of surreptitiously pinching himself to create a red welt meant to sway a skeptical ump. Still, he got stung frequently, and a fastball to the temple once left him unconscious for four days. Then there was the time, during the winter of 1900–1901, when he dove, one dark night, into the unilluminated Cornell University swimming pool, and found out the hard way that it had been drained. The accident, though not baseball-related, did the work of a thousand beanballs.

This last episode left him with a reputation. When he got in a fight with an umpire after that, he would often hear, "Well, at least I'm not dumb enough to jump into an empty swimming pool!" That was a low blow. Hughie was not stupid; he'd been at Cornell studying law. Yet for whatever reasons, his behavior, over the years, became increasingly strange.

By the time he reached the Tigers at the age of thirty-seven even his supporters—the staunchest of whom was probably Tim Carroll Hurst, the famous "Fighting Umpire," who would punch you in the gut hard if you tried to block his vision—would have to say Hughie was an unusual man. That he managed the team from the first base coaching box when his boys were up to bat was not in itself strange—a lot of nonplaying managers did that back then—but the way he behaved in that box surely was. As skipper of the Tigers, Hughie had a habit of screaming "Ee-Yah!" and pulling up grass and tossing it like confetti, to either celebrate some good turn of events or rouse his men to action. As he did this he would bicycle-pedal his legs or perform an eccentric dance. Sometimes he would blow a tin whistle, shake a rubber snake, or put down a parade of windup toys that he had bought at a five-and-dime to scoot along the ground. At least once, as part of his attempt to distract the easily distractible south-paw Rube Waddell, he briefly shared his coaching box with a dog.

He was sometimes admonished for these actions, sometimes not.

How did the fantastic "Ee-Yah Man," as he soon came to be called, get hired by the Tigers? Navin, after all, claimed to be looking for a sober, no-nonsense leader who would command the respect of his fractious club. It's true that Jennings hadn't behaved half so oddly the year before, when he was managing the latest iteration of the Orioles, who were then in the Eastern League, so Navin might not have known exactly what he was buying into. But Hughie's connection to the raucous Baltimorians of the 1890s made him anathema to Ban Johnson, who, when he found out that Navin was considering him for the job of skipper, told the secretary, "Jennings has that old Oriole stamp on him. We cleaned Oriole rowdiness out of this league, and I won't have it brought back!" Why, in the face of such strong resistance from the most powerful man in the league—Johnson wielded the same airtight authority over the AL as J. Edgar Hoover later would over the FBI—as well as his own stated objectives, did Navin persist in his pursuit of Hughie, ultimately offering him a relatively generous ($4,000) contract?

There are at least two reasons for his interest in Jennings. One was that the Orioles, for all their shenanigans, played the brand of baseball that Cobb would later be credited with inventing—"scientific" baseball. At a time when other teams were happy to swing the bat and get any kind of hit, McGraw and his boys judiciously employed the hit-and-run play, the sacrifice bunt, and, yes, the famous Baltimore chop to their enduring advantage, taking three pennants in the days before there was a World Series.

Beyond that, Hughie possessed a quality that has shortened the duration of many a courtship: he was being coveted by others—specifically the New York Highlanders (who were thinking of replacing Clark Griffith, or worried that he'd leave) and the Boston Americans (who found themselves in that awkward interval between one manager who wanders off occasionally and another who ingests carbolic acid). The interest of the more glamorous (and financially successful) East Coast teams fueled Navin's desire to make Hughie his sixth manager in seven years. His only problem was that he didn't want to pay the $5,000 that Ned Hanlon, the owner of the Orioles, was asking for Hughie's signing rights—well, that and Johnson's objections. He got around the latter by having owner Bill Yawkey not so subtly suggest to the league president that he might withdraw his investment in the team if couldn't hire the manager his secretary wanted. As for Hanlon's price, Navin simply ignored it and drafted Hughie as a player for the then standard $1,000 fee, though he had no intention of ever using him as such. Financially speaking, it was all the same to Hughie, who was just happy to be back in the major leagues, even if it was with a team he had never seen play.

Navin soon learned that his new manager was very different from his previous one, and not just because he comported himself during games like the entertainment at a rich kid's birthday party. Whereas Armour had enjoyed negotiating with and nagging his men, at least via the U.S. mail, Jennings basically abstained from dealing with the team's more difficult personalities. Cobb was at first startled and then offended by his almost utter lack of interaction with the new skipper. Why wasn't Jennings reaching out to him? Between the time he took over the club, in September, and the end of 1906, Hughie had just one conversation with Cobb—a brief chat to assure him that he wouldn't be traded, not to the White Sox or to the Naps for the talented but older (thirty) outfielder Elmer Flick, as rumor had it. (Except that rumor had it right. Hughie already had a line out to Cleveland manager Nap Lajoie about a possible Flick-for-Cobb swap.)

With no one doing the day-to-day player relations work, Navin had to step into the breach, handling the men's nonstop requests. "You never know what strange propositions ballplayers will pop at you," he said. "You have to be ready for any emergency." When Cobb wrote in early February of 1907 asking for a $300 advance on his salary (which had been raised to $2,400, but which would not start arriving until April), and offering to pay interest on the loaned amount, Navin wrote back—for the last time addressing him as "Dear Sir"; after that it would almost always be "Friend Tyrus"—assuring him that the check was being processed and that he didn't want to get into the unpleasant business of charging his players interest. When a few days later McIntyre bitterly informed the Tigers in writing that he refused to don their uniform again at any price—this was getting to be an annual ritual—the secretary responded with a dictated shrug, saying that he could not force him to play, of course, but neither would he facilitate his playing for anyone else by making a trade. The reserve clause gave the team all the leverage. "If you can afford to quit baseball," he told Matty, "we can afford to have you do so." Then the secretary wrote to Jennings to inform him of McIntyre's latest outburst, adding, "I do not think there is any question but that he will weaken when the time comes."

You have to wonder if Navin didn't experience a bit of buyer's remorse after signing Hughie in such a rush. He was suddenly working a lot harder than he had been when Armour was there, and that was no doubt cutting into his horse-playing time. Apart from dealing with the ballplayers and keeping Jennings posted about what was being said by both sides, the secretary had to buck up his new manager's spirits whenever Hughie expressed pessimism about ever getting the Tigers to stop squabbling and focus on baseball. "Don't get discouraged!" Navin urged Hughie in letters more than once that spring.

McIntyre—who, as Navin had predicted, would report to camp and sign a contract—was a constant grouser and a disruptive force, but he was also a pretty good hitter, and, like most of the other players who had no money and wanted their egos stroked, he was easy for a sharp man like Navin to manipulate. Cobb, on the other hand, was, from a managerial standpoint, chess in three dimensions: more refined than most ballplayers, and more thoughtful, but after a year in which he'd absorbed a lot of abuse and endured the shame of having his mother on trial for the death of his father—all the while becoming the best hitter on the Tigers—his identity remained a work in progress. As a Southern gentleman, he had always drawn a line in the sand that marked the leading edge of his honor. Now it seemed that line was moving further from him, closer to you (whoever you were), and the wrath unleashed by crossing it (as Ed Siever could tell you) was proving much more violent. If you were a Tiger, he wanted to be friends, but not as much as he wanted to be Ty Cobb, something he was still in the process of defining.

It's an obscure footnote to the Cobb story, but among the first people to experience the new, even less easygoing Tyrus was an unfortunate farmer's son from Royston named Charlie Putnam. He and Ty were about the same age and may have once been schoolmates. On February 18, 1907, about a month before Cobb left for training camp at Augusta, Putnam "made remarks said to have been about a near relative" of the ballplayer, most likely his mother. The quote is from a petition for Cobb's arrest filed shortly after Putnam regained consciousness. Despite Ty's growing renown, and the supposed leeway allowed in the South to a man defending his family's honor, a grand jury indicted him on the charge of assault. The case would meander through the system for more than a year without ever coming to trial. Ultimately Charley Putnam and his father, James, had a change of heart, and wrote letters requesting that the accused not be punished as long as he paid their court costs of $9.45—which, though it represented about half of what he got for playing in one major league baseball game—Cobb did.

In the scheme of things, the Putnam fight was but a tune-up for a more famous fracas that happened not quite a month later, shortly after Cobb arrived for spring training. The first thing Ty did upon reaching Augusta on March 12 (a day late; he'd managed to miss another train connection) was to sit down with Hughie for what the *Free Press* described as an hour-long "heart-to-heart." The manager wanted to make sure Cobb was generally happy and shared his optimism about the coming season. Hughie had no quarrel with "the beardless boy of 20 who is making good with a rush," as B. F. Wright of the *Sporting News* had recently called him; he liked Cobb from the start and appreciated his talents, but neither did he have a strong sentimental attachment to the kid the way Armour and Navin did. Jennings saw Cobb as an asset of great value, a superb young player who was improving every day, but also perhaps the biggest obstacle to team peace, which happened to be his highest priority. As much as he liked him, the manager would not have hesitated to trade Cobb for a highly competent but less controversial man.

In taking this position, Hughie put himself in direct opposition to the team secretary. Either the manager didn't care what Navin thought, or he simply didn't pick up on his boss's signals. Navin didn't brag about discovering Cobb, the way Armour often did, but he had a gut belief, bolstered by observation and statistics, that the kid whom the Tigers found more or less by accident in 1905 would turn out to be better than Sam Crawford, their reigning star, or maybe anybody else in the majors. He wouldn't have traded Cobb under *any* circumstances, for any number of reasons, some of which seemed to go beyond baseball. Navin, who never had children, felt close to Cobb from the day he met him, a nervous, travel-worn C-leaguer who had just lost his father under appalling circumstances. The two would excoriate (and extol) each other over the years as only a father figure and son-substitute could. The fact that a preternaturally stingy man like Navin had given Ty an unsolicited raise the year before said much about his feelings—as did his reaction a few months later when he caught the kid filching a sensitive document off his desk.

In late September of 1906 the secretary had been sitting in his office at Bennett Park with Cobb and Joe Smith, the sports editor of the *Detroit Journal*, when he turned away momentarily to take a call. While turning back he saw Cobb slip a sheet of paper into a newspaper, which he then folded beneath his arm. The page listed monthly salaries for all the men on the roster, confidential information in which Cobb and all his teammates would have a keen interest. The theft was a fireable offense, but because he didn't want to part company with Cobb or have to explain to anyone else why he wasn't, he made a snap decision to literally look the other way.

But we were talking about a fistfight.

Cobb was on his way to afternoon practice in Augusta on March 16 when Henry "Bungy" Cummings, the Warren Park groundskeeper, hove into view. He and Cobb were acquainted, if only because, as previously reported, Cobb had criticized Cummings's work when Bill Armour asked him to inspect the field for carnival-related damage a year earlier—but it seems that everyone in Augusta knew Bungy, an affable man with obvious problems. The two or three noncombatants who witnessed the early stages of the encounter agree that Cummings was, as the *Free Press* said, "partially under the influence of liquor" and garrulous as ever. As he approached Cobb, he (depending on which paper you read) either extended a hand, or put out both arms for a hug, and shouted, "Hello, Carrie!"

What did he mean by that? The salutation has befuddled Cobb scholars for more than a century. Had Cummings mistaken Ty for someone else? Had the witnesses misheard his greeting? A venerable mystery may have a simple solution. Carrie Nation, the famous temperance crusader who destroyed saloons with an ax, had been touring the South that winter and in fact had visited Augusta, giving a lecture at its Miller Walker Hall a month earlier. Cobb (who by all accounts abstained from alcohol at this time) may have told the groundsman (then or on a previous occasion) to sober up or go sleep it off, and Cummings may have sarcastically referred to him as the lady prohibitionist. It was common in those days to ask a teetotaling friend or disapproving spouse, "So, who are you? Carrie Nation?"

Anyway, what seems beyond dispute is that Cobb, rather than shake Cummings's hand, pushed him away. In modern retellings of the story, people often ascribe Cobb's actions to racism—he didn't want to be touched by a black man, they say, or he felt Cummings's display of familiarity highly impertinent. This is one of those assumptions about Cobb that is based strictly on his being born in 1886 in Georgia; if he ever said anything to or about Cummings, racist or otherwise, we don't know what it was. Meanwhile Bungy clearly was a man who, because of his alcoholism, had a tendency to violate people's personal space; he would later be arrested for wandering into someone's house, not far from the ball field, and babbling vulgarities. Cobb may simply have been trying to avoid an annoying person blocking his path to the clubhouse.

The sportswriters noticed nothing further, until a few minutes later, when Cobb and catcher Charlie Schmidt fell to the ground near Cummings's outfield shack locked in combat. Players and journalists came running. "Schmidt landed heavily with a right to the jaw," said the *Chicago Daily Tribune*, "while Cobb scratched the catcher's face badly. A number of short arm punches were landed by both, and Manager Jennings had considerable trouble parting them." Schmidt, who, as we have seen, already had fought with Cobb once, and sucker-punched him on another occasion, said he attacked his teammate yet again after he came upon Ty choking Cummings's wife, Savannah, whom he said had tried to stop Cobb from bludgeoning her husband. "I have my opinion of anyone who would strike a woman," Schmidt told the assembled press. In response, Cobb "immediately suggested to Schmidt that he should seek a climate warmer than Georgia," said the *Free Press*, and further told the writers that everything the catcher alleged was untrue. It's worth noting, I think, that he didn't claim that beating up Cummings and his wife was permissible because they were Negroes who had become too familiar or aggressive (as is sometimes alleged or suggested); what he said, rather, was that he did not beat them up. Since there were no witnesses and none of the newspapermen saw fit to ask the Cummingses for their version of events, it was his word against that of Schmidt, a man who had assaulted him now on three occasions. Indeed the catcher seemed strangely obsessed with Cobb, determined to stir up trouble with him in a way that even Matty McIntyre wasn't. Some fourteen years later the whole story would emerge when sportswriter Hugh Fullerton revealed that Hughie

Jennings had used Schmidt to engineer a "gentle frame up" of Cobb—in other words to have him associated with so much turmoil that Navin would finally come around and agree to trade him. If you know this, then you know it's possible that Schmidt may have exaggerated what happened with Cummings or, as Cobb insisted, made up the incident from scratch.

After the trouble, Cobb was "quiet as a lamb," said one paper. "I am in the right," he said, "and so long as I know that fact I don't care what is said or done." Schmidt, meanwhile, "made no secret that he is sore over the occurrence." Jennings, "who plainly is much wrought up," soon issued a statement that more or less summed up his philosophy: "Harmony in a ball team is absolutely essential to success, and I intend to prevent dissension among the players at all costs, no matter who is affected." A short time later Hughie penciled himself into that day's intra-squad game and while at bat "purposely took three pitches" to the ribs, "bringing to mind," said the *Free Press*, "the days of the past when he used to get hit at least once every game." I suppose we all have our ways of working off job-related stress.

Virtually all reports of the scuffle suggested that Cobb's departure from the Tigers was imminent. Whoever was right or wrong in this particular case, the words "Cobb" and "fight" were sharing too many newspaper paragraphs—or so the men who composed those paragraphs insisted. As good as he was on the diamond, said the beat writers, who in any discussion always assume the parental role, the kid was too much trouble and would have to go.

No one in training camp seemed more upset by Cobb's latest dustup than Jennings. Without consulting Navin, he sent a telegram that evening to the Cleveland Naps' spring headquarters in Macon, Georgia, trying to revive the Flick deal. Flick interested him both because of his batting average and because he was as dull as Cobb was charismatic. The diminutive Ohioan did have one famous fight—in 1901, with Nap Lajoie, who didn't like being kidded about his decidedly rube-ish clothing (the Frenchman broke his hand and was out for several weeks)—but Flick's name seldom appeared in the newspapers outside of game stories. Today he is one of those Hall of Famers nobody knows.

Cobb himself was all for a trade. He was tired of getting beat up every couple of weeks by the much larger Schmidt, and despite what he said about not caring what people thought of him keenly disliked the idea of being seen as a troublemaker. He wanted to go someplace different and start fresh. If Detroit couldn't or wouldn't place him on another major league team, he told friends, he might just drop out of baseball.

Navin couldn't stop Cobb from quitting, but he could and did scotch a trade. On March 18, he wrote to Jennings, expressing sympathy about the state of affairs down in Augusta, but, while keeping up the pretense that the manager had the power to make whatever personnel decisions he wanted, he advised his skipper to dispassionately think things through. "Am very sorry to hear of the trouble with Cobb," he said in a letter addressed to Hughie at the Albion Hotel. "It seems hard to think that a mere boy can make such a disturbance. On last year's form he has a chance to be one of the grandest ballplayers in the country. He has everything in his favor. It would not surprise me at all to see him lead the league this year in hitting and he has a chance to play for fifteen years yet." (Navin was right about the former prediction and off, on the conservative side, by seven years regarding Cobb's career.)

"Flick [Navin continued] is a dangerous man to bother with for the reason that he has about all the money he cares for, and is liable to quit on you at any time, besides being a great deal older than Cobb.

Do not get discouraged. Keep after [the players] and things might turn out all right yet. . . . You will find that every club manager in the American League will be after Cobb on the quiet, making him all sorts of propositions, salaries as high as $4,000 or so, and everything to make him dissatisfied with his present surroundings. . . . It was published in all the papers that you wired Lajoie and he wired you back that he would not trade. [In lieu of Flick, Lajoie offered outfielder William "Bunk" Congalton, a proposition Jennings wisely rejected.] I think it is a good scheme not to let the papers know anything about trades for players until the deal is pulled off.

Now, Hugh, don't let the Cobb business bother you too much and keep up your grand spirit and you might line them up all right yet. If we only start off winning, I think everything will be all right. You understand that I will back you up on everything you want to do, but we do not want to make any mistakes.

A week later, Navin wrote to Jennings again, reiterating how important the kid was to him personally.

*I would be sorry to let Cobb get away for the reason that he is such a
young ball player. There is no telling what kind of a ball player he might
make in the future. I had in mind that if he still continued his fresh tactics that I could get the clubs in our league to waive on him, and send him
to some minor league club for a time. It might reduce the size of his head,
and let him know where he got off at. I think I can do this if you cannot
get along with him. I would not like to part with him.*

A few days later Jennings told the press that the internecine warfare
had ceased, and that there was peace in our time. "Talk about the affair
of Saturday having caused dissension is all rot," he said. "The matter has
been entirely smoothed over and both players regret their hasty conduct.
I am sure there will be no more of it." To further ensure against trouble,
Hughie moved Cobb to right field and put Sam Crawford in center, making him a buffer between Cobb and McIntyre.

Jennings seemed sincere in his optimism—and he must have been
heartened when, a day or so later as the Tigers worked their way north,
Cobb requested permission to make a side trip to Royston to pick up
his family. Amanda and his sister, Florence, would live with him at 2384
Woodward Avenue for the entire 1907 season, and his brother, Paul, also
an outfielder, was heading for a tryout with the Kalamazoo White Sox of
the Class D Southern Michigan League (he would play in 34 games for
them, hitting .242, before moving on to a semipro team in California).
Surrounded by his closest kin, Cobb would surely be less likely to be
picked on or to provoke others. But upon rejoining the team in Columbia, South Carolina, a few days later, he was still agitating for a trade. "He
cornered the manager one night and said, in substance, that he wanted to
get away from Detroit," said an unsigned piece in the *Free Press*. Despite
Navin's several letters about the importance of keeping Cobb, Jennings
told Ty that he was in fact trying to arrange for his exit. Flick was now
signed for the season with Cleveland, but Clark Griffith of New York
had hinted that he might want to make a swap. When Hughie heard
back from the Highlanders the next day, however, they were offering only

Frank Delahanty, a .238 hitter, a proposal that was either, as Hughie said, "a humorous effort," or an indication of just how wary some people were of young Tyrus.

Why would any manager hesitate to take a kid who hit .316 the previous season? Baseball men are conservative by nature and a lot of them didn't know what to make of Cobb. He frightened them because, for one thing, he didn't *look* like the other deadball era stars. Lajoie, Honus Wagner, John McGraw, Elmer Flick—those men were all squat and thick and hammy, while he was tall and (in those early years) relatively lithe. Even stranger was the role he assigned himself as an offensive player—to be the cause of worry in the opposition. He did this not by running wild on the base paths but by *seeming* to run wild. "Some of my greatest thrills in baseball," Cobb said in his 1925 memoir, "came from taking third and home when I was expected to stop at second." What pleased Cobb, others found upsetting (which was, of course, the point). Bill Donovan, though his friend, called him "too wild," and predicted "the baseball gods" would punish him one day for disrespecting "the laws of baseball." "No one person is bigger than the pastime," the pitcher said—and Cobb probably agreed with him, just not with the limitations men like Donovan imposed upon the game.

Charlie Schmidt, meanwhile, was scary in a different way, the way a wounded beast is. This was in part because he was actually wounded and hobbling around that spring on his left ankle, which he'd broken toward the end of the previous season and never got fixed. The Tigers refused to pay for an operation, a position they took more or less automatically with any .240 hitter with so-so defensive skills. Before the players' union, teams went case by case when it came to medical bills, and Schmidt was a classic example of a man who didn't merit special consideration. He knew it, too, and that probably hurt more than the ankle. Cobb they coddled, but the only time Navin and Jennings paid attention to *him* was when he whined about wanting a raise—and then they told him to shut up and play better and something might eventually happen. Schmidt's teammates also tended to ignore him, except when he was doing his popular barroom trick of pounding a nail into a block of wood with his bare fist or retelling the story of the time he'd sparred with heavyweight contender Jack Johnson.

When Schmidt came up from the minors the year before, no one bothered to haze him, even though he was, like Cobb, a Southerner, from Coal Mountain, Arkansas. He didn't even merit their disapproval. Schmidt may have thought that beating up Cobb would make him more popular with the McIntyre clique, so he kept on doing it. It was on March 29 at Meridian, Mississippi, where the Tigers had gone to play two games against a team of all-stars from the Cotton States League, that the catcher attacked Cobb for the fourth time. Once again, there appeared to be no inciting incident, no words exchanged before the bigger man hauled off and punched the slighter man in the face. Cobb, bloody and dazed, had to be helped back to the New Southern Hotel, where he was tended to by his mother and sister.

What was happening with the Tigers was pathetic. Yet instead of playing the incident in Meridian as an example of serial bullying, the papers went with their familiar "Cobb gets belligerent" motif. It simply made for a grabbier story, the wiseass kid who got his comeuppance. "Cobb Had Enough: Lasted One Minute in Fight with Schmidt" was the headline in the *Sporting News*. The reader was meant to shake his head and emit a rueful chuckle.

Ban Johnson wasn't laughing, though. Never one to see beyond the surface of any situation and have anything other than a knee-jerk response, he immediately wrote to Cobb demanding an explanation, and to Navin, chastising him for allowing this pugnacious youngster once again to run wild. We don't have his letters, or Cobb's response, but Navin's reply to Johnson is a museum-quality con job. In it we see a man who, while no doubt exasperated with the situation, is conniving full-bore to keep Cobb on his team—by convincing Johnson that no one was angrier at the youngster than he, Frank Navin.

My dear Johnson,

> *I have your letter regarding Cobb. I thought that Cobb was getting the worst of it last year on the club, but on investigation, I found that*

a great deal of the trouble was caused by himself. He has the southern aristocracy notion in his head, and thinks he is too good to associate with ball players. He will not allow any of the older members of the team to make a suggestion to him. When a suggestion is made, he will make some impertinent answer. He has the notion that he is quite a fighter. He has been arrested at night for fighting on the street with citizens of Detroit, who had nothing to do with the ball club at all. [There is no record of such an arrest.] In fact he is what you would call a real fresh young man, with an inflated idea of his own importance. I think exaggerated ego would fit him exactly.

Donovan, Lowe, Crawford and some of the older members of the club were his friends until he absolutely refused to be friends with them. Lowe told me on the quiet that Cobb was one of the freshest young men he had ever seen, and when I told Lowe to talk with him and make suggestions to him on several occasions, he did not think he wanted any more insults.

[Cobb] does not associate with good people, and the women who are his friends are of the worst class in the city. As an illustration, he left a couple of passes one day at the box office for some women who came to get them. One of the detectives of our city happened to be standing around the office and asked what player left the passes for those women. We found out it was Cobb, and when Cobb "was called" for it, he tried to bluff the detectives though, until they agreed to show him on the register where they had been arrested for almost all the crimes on the calendar a number of times.

Not for publication, no matter whether Smith [he means Schmidt] was in the right or not, I am tickled to death that he got a good trouncing. It might do him a world of good.

> *Yours truly,*
> *Frank Navin*

Satisfied with the secretary's response, Johnson let the matter drop without disciplining the team or either of the battling players. Thus by dint of mock outrage and false umbrage, Navin created a diversion and hustled Cobb past a dangerous checkpoint.

But if Johnson was assuaged, Cobb wasn't. On March 29, he wrote to Kid Elberfeld, venting his disgust. Eleven years his senior, and a major leaguer since 1898, the fiery Highlander shortstop had become a sort of mentor to the young man whose face he had once pushed, pedagogically, into the stony ground at Bennett Park as Cobb slid headfirst into second. In the eighteen or so months since, Cobb had acknowledged receipt of the lesson by knocking Elberfeld off his feet as he slid into second at Hilltop Park ("My feet collided with his leg and he was knocked four or five feet. He got up, rubbed himself, looked at me calmly and went back to his position without saying a word. 'Well, you've learned something,' his look implied. 'You beat me to it that time, and I've got nothing to say.'") and the older man had become a sounding board for Cobb's burgeoning frustration.

The letter:

Mr. Norman Elberfeld, Atlanta, Ga.
Dear Sir & Friend:

I wired you yesterday, at least had a friend send, so could not explain fully, so I thought it best to write you. Well in the first place I had more trouble—Schmidt takes a shot at me without any provocation in the least. He called to me as I started out to warm up at the ball park and as I turned he said either he or I would get whipped so we had one. It was short. He belted me one in the eye so I left the park and met Jennings on his way down and I told him it was all up as to me staying on the team. He called a meeting last night and he said they all—McIntyre, Siever, Killian and Schmidt—was ready to make friends and the rest seemed very nice to me when they came down from the meeting. Then I saw Jennings. He wants me to stay but I told him I was not going to stay that I would put him on notice then and that I guessed I would go home from Birmingham and stay until I was traded, or I would quit the game for good—and by George I will before I play with this Detroit Club. I told him if he carried me to Detroit as he said he would have to do before he traded me so he could see Mr. Navin and Mr. Yawkey that I would not play in a single game with them. I told him I would help him out in

*exhibition games as Jones is hurt. Rossman is out so that calls Crawford
on first and then I thought it good policy to be as easy as I could and put
him on notice that I would not play.*

*Now Elberfeld, I am not going to play with these "suckers" some of
them I mean and if I make good my threat which I surely will I am
going with the club that will stand to me if I am laid off. I will want my
time made good. I mean by that if I have to quit the game for a month
before they trade me I will expect that salary to come from the club that
gets me so will [Clark] Griffith do it?*

*Now let me hear from you at once all about it at Little Rock, Ark. c/o
Marion Hotel. Now you can bank on me making good on my threat as
I see it's my chance and now is the time, and I am glad I had the scrap
because I want to go.*

*I am writing Navin this a.m. and telling him I won't play with this
club any longer. So you can see I am dead in earnest—So answer quick.*

Your friend
Tyrus R. Cobb

Whether Elberfeld wrote back to advise a bit more patience we don't
know. Maybe the act of writing the letter relieved at least some of Cobb's
stress. All the record shows is that he never acted on his threat.

They had changed managers and tinkered with their roster but the Tigers
were still not a lovable club—unless you embraced their outlandish mis-
anthropy. When they stopped in Birmingham in early April, Davy Jones,
normally one of the more even-tempered men on the squad, was arrested
for assaulting a twelve-year-old newsboy who he said had "thrust" a paper
on him and requested a nickel. Dusting off his Cornell law degree, Jennings represented the outfielder in court and won a prompt acquittal.
This allowed the team to move on to the next town with its outfield intact, but assaulting an urchin and then outmaneuvering the kid in court
were not the sort of feats that made you a must-see attraction. Back home
in Detroit, ticket sales were sluggish.

Still, Joe S. Jackson and some of the other beat reporters managed to see some bright spots. The team was healthy—"Not a cripple in the crop," one journalist said of the pitching staff. "Crawford, Cobb and McIntyre are stinging the ball," Jackson noted, and Claude Rossman, the Tigers' new, left-handed first baseman, though a man of delicate nerves, was proving to be a brilliant bunter who fit nicely into the lineup behind Ty. Rossman was Cobb's roommate that year, and together they worked out a play that demonstrated the near-telepathic levels of communication that can be attained by a Georgia Baptist and an upstate New York Jew. The strategy behind it was simple: when Rossman came to bat with Cobb on first, the latter would sometimes flash a subtle signal just before the pitcher began his windup, then take off for second. Rossman would push a shy little roller toward the left, the third baseman would rush in to field it, and by the time he did and threw to first, Cobb would have, as the scribes liked to say in those days, "achieved the penultimate sack," aka the hot corner. If the throw to first was even slightly imperfect, he came home—and the cranks went bughouse.

So there was cause for hope yet.

"If we only start off winning," Navin had written to Hughie Jennings, *"I think everything will be all right."*

— CHAPTER FOURTEEN —

THE TIGERS DIDN'T JUST WHIP the Cleveland Naps in the first game of the 1907 season—they looked like the Chicago Cubs doing it. "It was an opener to enthuse the home fans," wrote Joe S. Jackson of Detroit's 2–0 victory. "It showed the ginger that was promised in the reports from Dixie land." With gunmetal clouds scudding ominously above the Bennett Park cobbles, and temperatures hovering around 40 degrees (and a little German band getting laughs by playing "In the Good Old Summertime"), George Mullin threw a three-hit shutout, Germany Schaefer stroked two doubles, and Cobb had what every opposing club would soon fear most: a typical day. He went 2-for-4, stole a base, and scored both Tiger runs. In the fourth inning he reached first on a bad throw and went to second on Rossman's "Lone Star League base hit," said the *Free Press*. Then, wrote Jackson, "on a short passed ball Cobb hustled to third, beating the play by an eye-lash, long growth." He jogged home soon afterward when Schmidt stroked a single. In the eighth, Cobb hit a single, broke for second as soon as the ball was returned to catcher "Nig" Clarke (so called because of his swarthy complexion), then kept going when Clarke's rushed throw got by Nap Lajoie and skittered into the outfield. It was, as it often was when Cobb forced fielders to make fast decisions, a comedy of throwing errors. Center fielder Flick's peg was wildly off-line, and as soon as Cobb saw despair in the upward-rolling eyes of third baseman Bill Bradley, he bounced up from his slide and dashed home, where, in a cloud of dust, he was judged safe by another longish eyelash.

In Bennett's stands and in the next day's newspapers, joy mingled with surprise. The Tigers looked sharper than even Navin had expected. Maybe he shouldn't have canceled the ceremonial first pitch as well as the annual

opening day appearance of the Elks Club marching band—decisions that
suggested he was less than optimistic about the new season. As the Tigers
trotted off the semifrozen field the (subpar) crowd of 6,322 souls rose in
warm appreciation. The feeling was mutual. It had been ages since Detroit
players heard even something as applauselike as the muffled thump of
gloved hands clapping.

"If we only start off winning, I think everything will be all right."

True stories don't turn on a dime, though. Except for Rossman, the
Tigers, at least on paper, were essentially the same imperfect ensemble
they had been the year before, when they led the league only in dissension. Meaningful success was out of the question for 1907—or was it?
They dropped the second game of the season, won the third, lost the
fourth, and for the next few weeks seesawed their way through the schedule, teasing the public and the press. Attempting to analyze the situation
and solve the riddle of whether he should bother to get his hopes up,
Joe S. Jackson could only conclude that it was the semi-good pitching
staff that rendered the Tigers semi-bad. Hmmm. The maddening .500-
ness of it all made people fidgety, as ambiguity always will. Besides, so-so
no longer satisfied the once quaintly sylvan center of the carriage-making
trade; Detroit was picking up steam—and carbon monoxide—in the race
(with Indianapolis) to be America's Motor City. A year before the Model
T Ford arrived, and revolutionized society by allowing average Joes to
afford an automobile, the town was already starting to feel like Cobb
was feeling: feisty; ready for respect. Detroit in 1907 was a cosmopolis
shooting its cuffs. In baseball terms, the attitude adjustment meant that
Bennett denizens, no longer happy just to be part of the pack, yearned to
contend for the pennant, and maybe even win the World Series, already
a four-year-old tradition. Like Narcissus staring pond-ward, Detroiters
yearned to see their burgeoning fabulousness reflected in the ball scores.
Today we call this "being a fan," but back then hitching your mood to
the fortunes of a sports franchise was something new, and still thought to
be harmless.

For Cobb, April was the cruelest month. Suffering from what the
patent-medicine peddlers of the day called catarrh, a fancy fin de siècle
name for a cold, he was hitting .247 on May 9 and acting sluggish on

the bases. But then the fog began to lift, inside and outside his head, and everything looked brighter. In retrospect, we can see things already improving in the dark and dank area of team morale, thanks in large part to Hughie Jennings's decision to rotate certain players through the third base coaching box while he cavorted (and cajoled and *Ee-Yahed*) on the starboard side. So there was method to his sideline silliness after all. Stationing McIntyre across from him now and then meant that Matty and Ty were forced, at least in theory, to interact and behave like teammates when the latter was on base. Jennings also arranged for Cobb and McIntyre to sleep in facing Pullman berths on train trips, like Dick Powell and Joan Blondell in *Footlight Parade*. If such tactics didn't transform them into best buds, exactly, they did stall the momentum of their reciprocal hate. The pair might even have progressed to frenemy status if McIntyre hadn't shattered his ankle in early May sliding into second. That put him out for the season and effectively atomized the anti-Cobb clique. Everyone exhaled. Cobb and Ed Siever soon got beyond their Planter's Hotel fight, shook hands, and became pals. Before the year was over, Cobb even made up with Charlie Schmidt.

As the Tigers lightened up, they flew higher, and maneuvered more nimbly through the schedule. On May 24 their winning percentage hit .600. Though third in the standings behind the White Sox and Naps, they had the look of a club on the come—and were suddenly more than sports page fodder. "Under the guidance and inspiration of manager Hughie Jennings," said an editorial in the *Free Press*, "our boys have become a fighting force in baseball." These Tigers never gave up—a pleasant contrast to their 1906 counterparts, who, as we've seen, sometimes didn't even *show* up for games. On the 9th of May they beat the Highlanders in an exhausting contest despite being down a run with two out in the ninth. With the sun getting low and many cranks already slouching toward the streetcars, "Capt. Bill Coughlin spat on his hands, grabbed a handful of dust and hit the third ball pitched" (wrote Joe S. Jackson) for a double that knocked in a run to tie the score. Moments later, "Crawford fell on one for a clean single through the box, and it was all over." It was over for the Highlanders, anyway; the Tigers had only just begun.

Over and over that year, said Frederick G. Lieb in his highly regarded but only semi-dependable history of the club, the Detroiters displayed newfound courage. Ten days later, they fell behind 4–0 to the Philadelphia A's in the third inning as more than 4,000 "sat silently and groaned," according to Jackson—who apparently had superhuman hearing. In the bottom of the inning, though, "The Tigers transposed their supporters from mourners to merrymakers by what is variously described as a carnival of clouts, a batfest or a slugging bee." Call it what you want, Detroit beat Connie Mack's men that day 15–8. Cobb had four hits—two doubles and two singles—in six trips to the plate. His average had risen nearly 30 points in the previous two weeks, but more astounding was that the Tigers, essentially the same team that had finished sixth in batting the previous season, now led the AL with a .253 team batting average. "Three Pitchers Clawed by Jungleers to Please Big Crowd" ran a typical Detroit headline. The *Free Press* editorial writers felt obliged to remind their excited readers that "our boys won't win every game."

They won enough, though, so that on July 25 they moved into second place, and a week later bobbed up to first, though really there was a roundelay of teams—the Tigers, While Sox, Naps, and Athletics—taking turns at the top that summer. The anxiety associated with snapping open the sports pages each morning caused an epidemic of "dementia baseballanus," according to the *Free Press*, which noted, "If you're immune you don't belong here." Each game day hundreds if not thousands jammed the downtown bars like the Metropole, Geis's, and the Normandie, where electric news tickers delivered a bare-bones play-by-play of the Tigers game. (This was known to have happened elsewhere in America, but only during the World Series.) Detroiters who just wanted to drink their lunch in peace groused about the town's sudden obsession. "Confound baseball!" said one unidentified man. "The bootblacks were talking about the game this morning, the barber could hardly spare the time to shave me as he was arguing the relative merits of Cobb and Crawford as hitters, and then . . . one man whom you would never have suspected of insanity came in and asked them to find out how the weather was in Philadelphia. When I asked him why he replied, 'If it rains all morning and is gloomy all afternoon, Mullin'll win sure!' Can you beat it?"

No one seemed more captivating to the general public than Cobb,

who by early August was third among AL batters, with a .322 average. His steep ascent was strictly his own doing. He and Jennings were
friendly, but the manager left him alone, wisely offering him nothing but
back-pats and the freedom to turn himself into the iconoclastic player
he wanted to be. Hughie, who knew what was teachable and what was
not (and also knew a little something about hitting—he had a .312
lifetime batting average over 18 years), didn't desire, as a manager, to be
surrounded by dimwits who demanded a lot of coaching. "If that guy's
brains were made of nitro-glycerin and they exploded the bust wouldn't
muss his hair," he would say when he saw an example of bonehead baseball. "Give me a man who can think with his arms and legs, and I'll make
a ballplayer of him!" Or better yet, let him figure out how to do the job
himself. At first Ty, who had cultivated a string of father figures (Uncle
Ezra, Grandpa Johnnie, Leidy, Dad Groves, Armour, Navin, and, later,
Connie Mack) didn't understand what was going on; he felt rejected by
the new skipper in spring training and asked one of the sportswriters to
act as a go-between and ask Jennings if there was a problem. Jennings for
once was not shy about communicating with Cobb. Instead of using the
scribe as a messenger, he marched right up to his star and said, "There's
nothing I can teach you." Ty, who no doubt would have bridled at being
too closely managed, soon came to appreciate the laissez-faire approach.
Hughie "allowed me to seek my own salvation in my own way," he later
told a writer for the *Sporting News*.

Cobb's thoughts about hitting are well documented. Like Ted Williams, he liked to talk about the craft to almost any scribe who sauntered
up and asked. But unlike Williams, he wasn't big on dispensing advice,
especially during his playing days. Hitting was so personality-driven, he
believed—Nap Lajoie crowded the plate, Wagner stood as far away from
it as possible, especially small men used especially large "biffers" to a degree that surprised even him, a Napoleon buff—that there was, he felt, no
use in trying to give general one-size-fits-all directions. For the most part,
when the younger Cobb talked about hitting he focused on what worked
best for him, specifically, as a batter. One reason was that he wished to
stress that he wasn't some of freak of nature—the dreaded "natural"—
born with a rare knack for smacking a round ball with a round bat. He

had to think through everything he did at the plate (and on the bases), accepting this and rejecting that bit of conventional wisdom, as all the best baseball men did. Beyond that, he wanted it understood that the techniques he employed as a hitter were part of an overarching philosophy that came down to keeping the opposition anxious.

This was not a common way to frame one's approach to the game, but more unusual still was his desire (need?) to have strangers who knew less about baseball than he did, and who sometimes showered him with bottles and curses—the common cranks, in other words—comprehend what he was up to on the field. If they only *understood*, he felt, they would stop asking if he filed his spikes and stop calling him "the Dixie Demon" and much worse. They would appreciate the game more and have a better time at the ballpark. They would see he was not a bad guy. Cobb's worst fear, apart from going 0-for-4 on any given afternoon, was being seen as a semi-civilized, club-wielding, spike-brandishing brute. Alas, explaining himself turned out to be a lifelong endeavor. His autobiography, *My Life in Baseball*, written in his final months, was one last attempt to set the record straight, his capstone apologia—but it didn't work out. In the end it was hackwork and half-truths. The only things coauthor Al Stump explored deeply were Cobb's reserves of Scotch and bourbon.

If Stump were a better ghostwriter he might have picked up on the pugilistic strain than ran through Cobb's philosophy of the game and made something interesting of it. Cobb was like a professional fighter not because he occasionally beat up people in hotels and beneath grandstands and was beaten up in turn, but because he thought in terms of footwork, force, and feints. Start with force. Base path collisions were nothing terribly interesting in themselves but, used judiciously, they gave context to his every move as a runner by creating a constant anxiety in the opposition, a feeling that anything might happen next. "I rarely took a chance that I had not figured out carefully in advance," he said—and yet "I tried to make it appear that I was acting on sudden impulse, and relying on luck." If you were a defender who thought he was heedless, the sight of him dancing just off a sack would command a too large portion of your brain. The threat of violence was a valuable commodity, as effective as violence itself and much less dangerous, but it had to be cultivated. Cobb understood this, and it is why in the late innings of games in which the Tigers were far ahead or hopelessly trailing he would often be at his most bizarrely belligerent, wishing to convey that he was likely to sacrifice his body at arbitrary moments. It wouldn't be far off the mark to say that Cobb spent the first half of his life trying to seem unhinged, and the second half explaining he had been acting deliberately the whole time.

You might say the fancy footwork started as he strode confidently from the bench, juggling three bats. What he was doing, with a subtle swagger, was what Mike Tyson did when he stalked into the ring wearing an old ripped poncho: making it clear that you, the pitcher, were the person with the problem, and, by the way, your problem was him. Thus an opponent becomes gelatinized before the battle is joined. One must manage one's macho, though, and not just swing for the cheap seats. His pitty-pat hitting was the equivalent of wearing down an opponent gradually with stiff jabs; fighting cleverly. Getting on base was the point in those days. All of the stars of that era "choke up on their bats and use their brains," Cobb said. But getting the pitcher to choke is even better. So stride to the plate, and then stand in there confidently, like you've never heard that baseball is basically a game of failure, and the best batters make out two thirds of the time. The single most important rule of hitting, Cobb once said, is "don't let the pitcher think he has anything on you."

Once in the batter's box, Cobb's feet did double duty, as foundation and camouflage. His default position was a stance previously unseen; H. G. Salsinger called it "a freak stance." "Instead of standing with his feet far apart, flat and firm, he stood with his feet close together, on his toes, crouched over, his hands gripping the handle of the bat," Salsinger wrote in a 1951 remembrance in *Baseball Digest*. "In this position [the pedal equivalent of the split-hands grip, it sounds like] he was able to shift quickly with the pitch." Cobb would never be so predictable, though, as to always stand the same way, like, say, Ted Williams did to Cobb's oft-expressed (but fundamentally paternal) consternation. The placement of his feet was sometimes an effort at misdirection—Cobb might take a wide stance to suggest he would be trying to pull the ball to the right side of the diamond, then jump his feet together at the last second and poke the ball toward left field.

"Ty was the only lefthanded batter who could ever line an inside pitch into left field just inside the foul line," Salsinger wrote in 1951. "Curious to know how Ty did this, Jean Dubuc, a very smart pitcher, kept studying him closely in practice and discovered that when the ball left the pitcher's hand Cobb would sometimes shift around and be facing the third baseman when he hit the ball. If the opposing team had an outstanding first baseman, Cobb *never* hit in his direction." At other times he might plant his feet wide, and yank the bat back like he was trying to hit a home run—but at the last millisecond slide his left hand high up the barrel and deliver a *bunt*. We have no film, but his bunt swing and his home run swing were said to be shockingly similar. (Likewise, if he ever assumed a bunt stance during a pitcher's windup, he probably wasn't bunting.)

On still other occasions, he might plant his feet precisely where they needed to be to handle a particular pitcher's curve—and stay put. He felt you always had to respect a good curveball. "If there is a right-handed pitcher in the box I stand ahead of the plate and remove about a foot," he explained to Dudley Porter, a quote-polisher for the *Atlanta Constitution*. "If the twirler is left handed, I stand well back to get ready for the curve after it breaks. In other words, I try to catch the curve on the right-hander before it breaks, and that of the southpaw after." Cobb had been tinkering with this approach since his days with the Royston Reds, but 1907 was the year he fine-tuned it to something like perfection. Cobb actually hit *better* against left-handers that year (.378) than pitchers in general (.350). Against Rube Waddell, a much better than average southpaw for the Philadelphia Athletics, he hit .417.

To merely skim the 1907 chapter of *The Ty Cobb Scrapbook*, an invaluable, career-encompassing collection of game summaries by Marc Okkonen, is to get a sense that Cobb was playing a richer and saltier version of baseball than most of his opponents—imagine regular versus Canadian bacon, truly an unfair fight. When he wasn't drawing a walk, then scoring from first on a sacrifice bunt (August 8, at Philadelphia), he was stealing home (twice: June 29, against the Naps, and July 5, against the A's) or doubling up runners at first with pinpoint throws from right field (twice on June 18 at Philadelphia) or making a bare-handed catch of a sinking liner as he skidded along the outfield grass, "eventually doing cartwheels to regain his balance" (against the Highlanders on May 14). An equally remarkable play involved a catch he didn't quite make, at Columbia Park in Philadelphia, where, attempting to haul down a towering fly hit by A's outfielder Rube Oldring, Cobb ducked under the rope in left field, pushed his way through a sea of startled standing-room-only spectators, and managed to come within a foot or two of the ball (September 27). Cobb crashed into those reliably hotheaded Philly fans "like a football player bucking the line," said the *Free Press*.

The kid was fearless. He had no trouble hitting the great Cy Young (a double and a single on July 6) or causing the revered Highlander first baseman Hal Chase to double-clutch and make what biographer Charles Alexander saw as "maybe the most embarrassing" throw of his storied career, allowing Cobb to (once again) score from third on one of Rossman's patented squibblers (June 11). Among the great pitchers of his era only Addie Joss, who held him to an average of .266, and Waite Hoyt (.265) were able to more or less tame him. Against Walter Johnson, whom he often called the best pitcher he'd ever faced, Cobb hit his lifetime average of .366, just as he did against Hall of Famers "Chief" Bender and Herb Pennock. He hit .343 against Eddie Plank, .362 against Stan Coveleski, .335 against "Red" Faber, .341 against Ed Walsh, and .429 against Smoky Joe Wood.

And not everything was Punch-and-Judy. No one ever hit a shot farther at Cleveland's League Park than Cobb did when he smacked a rare (for the deadball era) outside-the-park home run to the opposite field on May 30. On the very best days, of course, he did it all. On July 30, 1907, at Hilltop Park in New York, Cobb got four hits, scored three runs, stole a base, and made a circus catch to save a homer as the Tigers thumped the Highlanders 6–1. Winning pitcher Twilight Ed Killian, who once turned crepuscular at the mention of Cobb's name, now brightened. "Let him get on first base and all he's got to do is keep running," he told the assembled press. "The other fellows don't know what to do with the ball when Cobb starts!"

A life of discipline and denial ran behind this larkish-looking style. As he would tell Grantland Rice years later on the radio, baseball was "all work," a 24/7 deal. Cobb didn't drink or even smoke the occasional cigar just yet. He bragged that he avoided "dissipation of any kind" including "going to parties in cafes." He swore off "picture shows" (thus missing the first, fifteen-minute version of *Ben Hur*, which came out in 1907), chewing gum, and coffee, believing they were bad for the eyes, and therefore the batting average. He wore sliding pads early in the season *because* they gave him blisters, and felt the calluses that replaced them allowed him to remove the pads and run more freely, though by the end of seasons his legs were an archipelago of open sores, his flannel uniform pants often blotted with blood. When in early September of 1907 he jumped over a rope in Cleveland to catch a fly ball and cut his hand on a broken pop bottle while landing, he stayed in the lineup, even though the bandages interfered with his batting, even after the wound became infected. (The folktales notwithstanding, not all deadball players were such dead gamers.) While his teammates went out for the evening, he usually returned to his room after his post-dinner amble to be with his books and newspapers. Reading was also bad for the eyes, he believed, but he couldn't forswear it.

In 1907 he began to make a scrapbook. "It was during the season when I first won the batting championship—my third year with Detroit—that I got my big thrills of newspaper publicity," he wrote in 1925. "I saved every clipping. Looking them over now I find the articles of praise and just criticism far outweighed the unfair ones." Then, though, the proportions seemed in reverse: "Unfortunately, it is a human trait to remember the unkind things after the nice ones are forgotten." All his life, Cobb would be a prospector of pain, a relentless finder of fists that he could jam his chin against. Although unkind articles were hard to come by after the Tigers started winning, he always maintained a mental file of real and perceived slights that he could call up and pore over whenever his mood started drifting toward the serene.

His day-to-day existence did improve, though, once fate hustled Matty McIntyre into the wings. Cobb would have tense relationships with fellow Tigers in the years to come, but he would never again battle physically with a teammate. The heat and hate now emanated mostly from the dugout of the opposition. For there lurked men who took the brunt of his talent, and learned more than they wanted to about their own limitations. A Tigers-Naps game at Bennett on June 29 of that year provides a case in point. With two out in the second inning and Crawford on first, Ty hit a triple off the scoreboard in center. "Cobb rounded third as [Joe] Birmingham's return throw was in the air, on the way to [third baseman Bill] Bradley" Jackson wrote. "Figuring that the latter would expect him to stop at third, Cobb kept going for home. [Catcher Harry] Bemis called for the ball. Bradley made a perfect throw. The ball was in Bemis' hands when Cobb was three steps from home." Ty looked like a goner. A smiling Bemis blocked off the plate, "presumably expecting Cobb to walk in and be put out. Instead, Cobb made a head-first dive. He struck Bemis with his shoulder, and the catcher was knocked off his balance, and dropped the ball. This, of course, made Cobb's run count."

From a play like this we can readily see why fans loved Cobb's brand of baseball, as well as why someone like Bemis, a lifetime .255 hitter destined to be outshined in the annals by much lesser men than Cobb, didn't: he felt, as Jackson wrote, "shown up by a player that outguessed him." Indeed, so put out was "Handsome Harry," that he began to beat Cobb on the head with the ball "as he lay across the plate, face downwards." Davy Jones was the first Tiger to rush to his teammate's rescue, and most of the others were soon at the scene, helping Jones and umpire Silk O'Loughlin, who sent Bemis to the showers and refused to listen to the Naps players' pleas that Cobb be ejected as well. As Jackson noted, "he [Cobb] at no time exchanged a blow with anybody." If Cobb was angry with Bemis on that balmy Saturday afternoon, he took it out on the ball, going 4-for-5 as the Tigers won 12–2 in another of those we've-got-to-stop-at-five-to-catch-a-train-shortened games.

It was not just Cobb's mature playing style—the emphasis on base running (as opposed to simply stealing) over batting (as freakishly good as he was as a hitter)—that came more clearly into focus in 1907. He also set the tone that year for his long-term role on the team—the resident superstar who was neither a pariah nor just one of the boys. In some ways his was an isolated existence. Cobb was virtually alone in the "celebrity ballplayer" niche, the only other resident being Christy Mathewson, the tall, handsome Giants righty who'd been class president at Bucknell (where he starred in baseball and football) and who still holds the record (along with Grover Cleveland Alexander) for most wins (373) in the National League.

"The Christian Gentleman," they called Mathewson, though he was too slick, too naturally mass-market, to act overtly religious. The other greats of that and the previous era—Lajoie, Wagner, McGraw, Anson, Willie Keeler, Walter Johnson, Cy Young—were everything you could want in a ballplayer but not superstar stuff, not camera-ready copies of swashbuckling stage actors, or the romantic heroes of boys' books, the way Cobb and Mathewson were; they were too plain and/or potty-mouthed to make anyone swoon. Cobb, by year's end, had landed his first big endorsement deal, for Coca-Cola; many more would follow. But in the first decade of the twentieth century, celebrity came with few precedents and no owner's manual. There were no back issues of *People* magazine to peruse for lifestyle tips or cautionary tales. Cobb was on his own as far as figuring out what the rules were, how to *be* in the world, where to draw the line with the would-be agents and brokers and the strangers who came up to you on the street and giddily informed you that you were Ty Cobb.

Besides his baseball skills, what put Cobb in that elevated category was his uncanny knack for being wherever the spotlight was headed. On September 30, he found himself in what the *New York Times* described as "probably the most exciting game ever played in major league baseball," and he would always call the most thrilling of his career. Allow me to set the scene. By that late point in the season, the White Sox and Naps had fallen back into the AL pack, leaving Detroit and Philadelphia alone at the top to slug, or rather small-ball, it out for the pennant. The Athletics, ahead by four games on Labor Day, lost ground after their ace righty, Chief Bender (the putative inventor of the slider and the unquestioned master of the talcum powder pitch), hurt his arm, and led the race by just 3 percentage points when the Tigers came to town for a three-game series starting on Friday, September 27. The showdown would have been tense under any circumstances, given the closeness of the standings, but the presence of Jennings in the coaching box heightened the stakes. Hughie was hated in Philadelphia for the havoc he helped wreak as a Baltimore Oriole, and upon his return to the majors as the Tigers manager he was mocked mercilessly in the local dailies for his "bellowing and monkey-shines" (Connie Mack's words) near first base. Horace Fogel, a former major league manager who'd become sports editor of the *Philadelphia*

Telegraph, called him a "lunatic" who "chased up and down the coaching lines like a hyena. Why not build a cage for him at each ballpark in the circuit?" Fogel wrote. "If he must have a policeman's whistle and toy sirens to blow why not give him bells to ring and pistols to shoot off?"

The opener was no thing of beauty, unless you were a Detroit bug (fan). Hughie's men prevailed 5–4 as Bill Donovan scattered 13 hits over nine innings. The win put the Tigers in first (by 8 percentage points) with only a handful of games to go, and left the folks back in Detroit with a strange and exhilarating feeling. No team from there had won a championship since the Western League season of 1887, when a walk took five balls, home plate was made of marble, and as Frank Navin wistfully recalled, "Less than $5,000 covered the entire salary list of the players."

More than 24,000 tickets were sold for Saturday's game, to be played in a stadium that sat fewer than 14,000, but it rained hard and the washout was rescheduled as part of a Monday doubleheader (Sunday baseball was illegal in Pennsylvania until 1933). The demand for seats now reached dangerous levels. When the A's locked the gates at 1:30 on the 30th, a half hour before game time, 25,000 or so were inside and from his perch in the press area Jackson could see a cataract of cranks pouring over the center field wall. He later learned that "there were thousands of fans outside, and they stormed the gates breaking the one to the grandstand and smashing the bleacher turnstiles." The *New York Times*, which was covering the game because of its national implications, estimated the true attendance at 40,000, and noted that "roofs of surrounding houses were crowded, the thrifty householders charging from 25 cents to a dollar for standing room." Inside the park, a sea of standees encircled and shrank the field. "All of the outfielders were crowded together towards the diamond," Jackson reported, "while the catcher and first and third basemen had no chance whatever to go after foul flies."

Donovan started for the Tigers, despite having pitched a complete game just two days before, and for a while he looked predictably weary. It was 7–1 in favor of Philadelphia going into the sixth inning, and some people back in Detroit, following the game via electric tickers in various downtown locales, were in need of a good bucking up. Fortunately, there were plenty of street urchins among the Tigers faithful and bucking up is what street urchins do. The next day's *Free Press* recounted a bit of dialogue supposedly overheard in a store on State Street, where bulletins were flashed from Columbia Field: " 'It looks bad for the Tigers, doesn't it son?' asked a man whose fortune is reckoned in six figures" of a Detroit newsboy. " 'Bad nothing!' replied the kid. 'Them Tiges is never beat 'till de last guy is out in the nint'. Cobb and Sam Crawford and Shafe will git to dat Rube in a minit and we'll make mornamilllion runs!' "

Rube was of course Rube Waddell, who had replaced starter Jimmy Dygert in the second inning after the famously skinny spitballer (five-foot-ten and 115 pounds, by some accounts) had allowed just one run. Relief pitchers were still a rarity in those days, and being pulled for one was generally taken as a reprimand from the boss, and a kind of public humiliation, but Connie Mack would have used every last twirler on his staff if necessary given the importance of the game. Mack in this way was more coolly professional than Hughie, who worried about his players' feelings, perhaps to a fault. Hughie kept Donovan, a Philly native, in for the whole game, simply because, as Mack noted ruefully, "Bill's father, brothers, and a whole host of Philadelphia relatives and friends used to come out whenever Donovan pitched against us. Jennings never would have humiliated him in his own home town."

Leaving him out there wasn't such a bad idea, though—not this time, anyway. Donovan got tired, then stronger again. All he needed was a few runs to work with. The Tigers scratched out four in the seventh, through a combination of poor Philadelphia fielding and fluky hits. The A's scored once again in their half of the seventh, and the Tigers added a run in the top of eighth, so Detroit, down to their last three outs, was still behind 8–6. The tension was palpable, at least in the crowds gathered around the tickers back in Detroit, where, one paper said, nervous men kept throwing down their cigars and lighting up new ones. "One big enthusiast chewed off one side of his drooping moustache while others made a quick lunch of their finger nails." Crawford led off the ninth inning and stroked a single on the first pitch. Cobb was up next.

Waddell said afterward he hadn't been worried about Cobb tying the game with one swing because the "the kid" hopped around too much in the batter's box to plant his spikes squarely and get any leverage on the ball. In fact, Cobb, despite his high batting average, had hit only three homers that year, a modest number even then.

His fourth came two pitches later. Waddell had thrown him an inside fastball for a called strike, and then thrown him the exact same pitch again, thinking it would be the last thing Cobb expected. It wasn't. Cobb said he figured Waddell would try to be sneaky in precisely that way, and so he, Cobb, was sitting on the pitch. It was a home run all the way. A ball thrown in the ninth inning in those days might be lopsided and squishy from almost a full game's use, and thus especially hard to knock very far, but with all the doubles and fouls hit into the overflow crowd that day, the pill Waddell dispensed to Cobb was relatively fresh and bouncy, and it sailed far over the fence in right field, tying the game. Connie Mack was so stunned, said his biographer, Norman L. Macht, that "he slid off the bench and tumbled into the bats lined up on the ground in front of him." He arose with great dignity, however—and immediately replaced Waddell with "Gettysburg Eddie" Plank. The Athletics failed to score in their half of the ninth, so the game went into extra innings.

In the 11th, Cobb doubled and Rossman singled him home, but Philadelphia retied the game when Davy Jones, trying to make a fancy one-handed catch, turned a can of corn into a double. His teammates were steamed. "When we all came to the bench we threatened to do him bodily harm if we lost," Cobb said some years later. "Jennings endeavored to smooth over the situation, but none of us was speaking to one another throughout the rest of the game." In the 14th, the Tigers came still closer to disaster. Attempting to get under a towering fly hit by first baseman Harry Davis, Sam Crawford pushed into the roped-off mob in center. As he made the catch, a Philadelphia policeman purposely jostled his arm and knocked the ball loose. Jennings jumped from the bench and screamed "Interference!" but Silk O'Loughlin, who was (of course) the home plate umpire that day, said he hadn't seen what happened and asked his (sole) colleague, Tom Connolly, who had been positioned behind second base, to make the call. Connolly ruled in favor of the Tigers and declared Davis out, a brave decision given the combustible nature of the crowd. A stampede might then have ensued, but as spectators booed and hollered and seemed ready to rush the field, Rossman and Athletics coach Monte Cross squared off near second base, and fought furiously until police arrested the Detroit player and hauled him away. This was a lucky break. Later it would be said that by engaging in a kind of single combat, Rossman and Cross provided a distraction that forestalled a full-scale riot. In any case, within fifteen or so minutes, the grandstand noise had reduced itself to an intimidating simmer and the contest continued.

Strangely, "the greatest game in baseball history" had no grand finale, no resolution whatsoever. In the 17th inning, with the ball almost impossible to see at more than a few feet's distance and the score tied 9–9, the game was called on account of darkness, and the second half of the doubleheader postponed indefinitely. No voices were raised in protest, perhaps because no one had the energy. "When the contest ended," said the *Times*, "players and spectators alike were simply exhausted by the terrific nervous strain."

The schedule, however, contained a few more games. Philadelphia faltered through its final week while the Tigers went to Washington and won four straight, with Cobb getting 13 hits in 18 plate appearances (a .722 average) and stealing four bases in the first game. It was another one of those hell-bent performances of his that hurt the opposition's feelings. One play in the last game of the series was particularly telling. Cobb singled, then stole second, seeming to hurt his knee as he slid in. He limped around for a while—then stole third, "jarring himself sliding around Bill Shipke and hooking his foot into the sack," wrote Jackson. To everyone's surprise, though, he broke for home on the next pitch, a grounder to third—and got caught in a rundown. "He danced up and down the line with the entire infield after him. Finally Jim Delahanty overtook him, chased him toward the plate and stabbed him in the back with the ball. The force of the blow, following his exertions, knocked Cobb down and took all the wind out of him. Delahanty dropped the ball and it rolled away. But though Cobb was only a yard or two from the plate, he could not get up and step on the rubber, or even crawl to it. He lay there until he was tagged out, after which he was helped to his feet and back to the bench. He fielded one more inning and batted in the eighth, getting another single, after which he was forced to quit."

Three days later in St. Louis, in his last at-bat in the last game of the regular season, Cobb hit his fifth home run of the year. But by then the Tigers had already won their first pennant.

CHAPTER FIFTEEN

MAYBE HE DIDN'T PACE HIMSELF. Maybe his inability to go those last two feet to home plate in the final game of the regular season showed that he was completely out of gas. Maybe the Tigers as a team couldn't deal with the extra hoopla, or had an inferiority complex when it came to the National League. Maybe they were the last team in history to feel intimidated by the Chicago Cubs. But for whatever reason the 1907 World Series went about as badly for Detroit as things would go for Butch Cassidy and the Sundance Kid down in Bolivia a few weeks later.

In the first game, the clubs played 12 quiet innings before the game was called on account of darkness with the score tied 3–3. The Tigers then lost the next two games, both played at Chicago's West Side Grounds, managing only one run in each. Detroiters, happy to be in their first Fall Classic, and accustomed to the underdog role, retained their buoyancy; the *Free Press* said they were, despite being behind 0–2, still "woozy" with glee. When the Series moved to Michigan for game four, "street fakirs" selling Tiger pins, buttons, canes, pennants, and "Hughie Jennings whistles" could be found on many corners in downtown Detroit. Dawn found kids lined up to buy tickets (and newspapermen there to observe them, the idea of people constructing their entire day around a sporting event still seeming novel). Sidewalks outside places that had a running news ticker became impassable.

But the yearning of the bugs was, as usual, not enough. The Cubs played as if they were still angry about losing to the Hitless Wonder White Sox the year before in what remains one of the greatest World Series upsets. The Cubs won the next two games, and the world championship, allowing the Tigers only a single run in 18 innings. They deserved the crown. Although their leading batter, first baseman/manager Frank Chance, was a notch or three behind Cobb when it came to average (he hit .294 that year), they were consistent and clutch, and their defense, led by the double play combo of Johnny Evers at second and Joe Tinker at short, was the stuff of poetry. ("Baseball's Sad Lexicon," written in 1910 by *New York Evening Mail* columnist Franklin Pierce Adams, begins, "These are the saddest of possible words, 'Tinker to Evers to Chance.' Trio of bear cubs and fleeter than birds, Tinker and Evers and Chance.") More important, they had a remarkable five-man pitching rotation, featuring the six-foot-two Orval Overall, who had 23 wins that season, and Mordecai "Three-Finger" Brown, whose farm-machine-mangled right hand proved a fine tool for fashioning curveballs. (Staff earned run average: 1.73.) "Them ain't no Cubs, them's *bars* [bears]!" advised a hideous cartoon Negro in the *Free Press*.

Cobb was flummoxed, and ultimately stymied by the Chicago pitching staff. He hit only .200 for the Series, and since he was seldom on, could work little base path magic. He managed a triple in game four, but as the *Sporting Life* said, he "too often fanned at fatal moments." In game five it was the Cubs who pulled off a flashy double steal and Cobb who got thrown out trying to "purloin" third. Jack Ryder of the *Cincinnati Enquirer* called him "the official lemon of the World Series." ("I was hurt by that remark," Cobb told a Detroit writer.) Goat horns could just as easily have adorned catcher Charlie Schmidt, who, playing with broken bones in his hand, consistently made what *Sporting Life* called "weird throws" that allowed the Cubs to run wild—but really no one on the Tigers was entirely blameless.

Fortunately, Detroit had forgiving fans. Like movie actors honored just to have been nominated, they looked at the bright side and celebrated the Tiges and "Our Ty," as he was becoming known, for bringing back a pennant. At a gala season-ending dinner for the team held at the Cadillac Hotel on October 16, 200 admirers, "nearly all men prominent in professional life or strong in the business affairs of the city," gave Jennings a five-minute ovation. Edward J. Eaton of the Michigan Military Academy read a (rather leaden) parody of the Ernest L. Thayer poem called "Ty Cobb at the Bat." The team presented Navin and owner Yawkey with "diamond cuff buttons." Deep into the evening, some Tigers gave brief, funny talks and the entire assemblage joined in a rendition of "Michigan, My Michigan." Everybody went home happy from a season that had started—a lifetime ago, it seemed—with the Bungy Cummings mess.

Better than the love, perhaps, was the extra money that even limited success brought. With Yawkey magnanimously adding his owner's share of $15,000 to the pool, each player on the Tigers realized $1,946, an amount that came close to doubling Cobb's $2,400 annual salary. This was his first experience with feeling flush and he liked it. He immediately signed up for several barnstorming games and an assignment to referee a "catch-as-catch-can, best-two-out-of-three falls, strangle-hold barred" wrestling match at Augusta's Grand Opera House. He also accepted an offer to serve as honorary editor for a "Special Ty Cobb Edition" of the *Atlanta Journal*. (Not paying much heed to the "honorary" part, he showed up for the one-day assignment with an armful of ideas, said Joe S. Jackson, including "a big layout for a 'collection of stars'" that featured Matty McIntyre and Charlie Schmidt, but not himself.) In his serialized memoir of 1914, *Busting 'Em*, Cobb would write that 1908 was a turning point for all players, not just for him—a fork in the road where they needed to decide whether they preferred to keep treating the "modern" game as a temporary "frolic" the way "bad actors" like Rube Waddell and Bugs Raymond had done, or a profession "like doctoring or lawyering" that would provide one with the wherewithal to think long term, about a wife, a house, and a family. "Baseball is a healthy business," he wrote. There was money in it for taking, though prying it from the iron fists of the deadball magnates was always going to be tough.

Up until that time Cobb had been relatively easy to negotiate with, so Frank Navin had not used much muscle when composing the letter that accompanied the one-year $3,000 contract he sent Cobb on January 9, 1908. "Friend Ty," he started out, "I know you would expect and are entitled to considerably more than you received last year, and for that reason made the increase [$600] as large as possible." Then he dropped in the boilerplate "times are tough all over" passage that all players got in the letter that accompanied their contracts ("Prospects in this country are not very bright for next year. There are thousands of men out of employment in this city") before returning to the curious way that he usually addressed Cobb in salary letters, i.e., with a careful mixture of flattery and deflation.

Of course you know the stringency of the money market as well as I. . . . I would like to give you everything you deserve, as you are entitled to every consideration, still I know that you are level headed enough to know that maybe next year everything will not break so well for us, and for you, and you know everyone loves the winner. Do not pay too much attention to what people say to you about yourself and the club, because you know that with a little bad luck we would not have won the pennant. I only wish we could get another crack at the Cubs, to see if our boys could even up our very bad defeat of last year.

But things had changed from the days when Cobb was grateful just to have made the club, and he promptly sent back the contract, unsigned. If he included a letter, it has been lost, but he told reporters he wanted a three-year deal totaling $15,000. Further, he wanted his salary guaranteed, so if he got injured he would still be paid. If this sounded greedy (and to some people it did), Cobb said that the public must consider that

the best part of my life is being spent in playing the game, and it is impossible to study and learn any other profession without giving up professional baseball entirely. In summer I find that I cannot read without injury to my eyes and corresponding injury to my batting average. Last spring I started on the road with novels and other literature but had to give them up. I even cannot read much in the newspapers without feeling its effect on my sight. So you can readily see that I am justified in asking for $5,000 [a year]. The best years of my life are being devoted to the game, and if I don't make my maximum salary right now, I never will get above the sum offered me.

Cobb was no doubt the first and last baseball player to argue that he should be compensated for having to forgo Henry James and Wilkie Collins.

Cobb as yet had no formal ties to the nascent labor movement involving the players (in 1912 he would serve as a vice president of a new organization called the Baseball Players' Fraternity), but he obviously had considered the need for major leaguers to improve their bargaining position in light of the baseball boom. He told *Sporting Life* that he believed all contracts should be guaranteed, and the reserve clause limited to five years, after which a man could become a free agent, selling his services to the highest bidder. Right now, he observed, "the league has a man just where it wants him." This was radical thinking, generally resisted by the sporting press, which reflexively supported the status quo, though some papers in the South were sympathetic to Cobb's stance, if not the larger notion of unionization. Cobb felt he was arguing from a position of strength, since attendance at Bennett had jumped to nearly 300,000 from 175,000 the year before, and he was surely responsible in large part for the increase. Walter Taylor of the *Atlanta Journal* figured that "about one fifth the attendance in the American League could be credited to Ty Cobb's popularity," so he was actually worth much more than he was asking for, and the *Augusta Chronicle* noted that "Cobb takes more desperate chances on the base paths than any man in the world today," and thus deserved to have his medical expenses guaranteed.

Within organized baseball, Cobb's demands were viewed as unrealistic, a pointless disturbance of the rites of spring. Hughie Jennings called Cobb's request for a multiyear deal (never mind the other demands) "absurd on its face." The *Free Press* said that Cobb's holdout was driving Detroit sportswriters "to a liquid if not a watery grave." Navin, who in fact had already given Davy Jones a three-year contract on the condition that he keep the terms secret, wanted to keep his favorite player happy, but because he thought Cobb was sure to crow about a multiyear deal, he feared setting a precedent. To give Cobb what he wanted would "lead to a hold up on the part of every other player," he said in a letter to Jennings. Still, in March he invited Cobb to come up from Royston for a discussion to see what they might be able to work out. "If the Detroit club wants me as much as I want to play for the Tigers we ought to be able to get together quickly," Cobb told the *Free Press*, and Navin added that he expected no difficulty "now that Ty has agreed to talk to me directly."

The meeting in Navin's office, which lasted three hours, did not go as smoothly as anticipated and when Cobb left, calm but unsmiling, "nearly everyone had abandoned hope." If negotiations failed to resume, Cobb did have some options. He could play in some kind of outlaw league, beyond the boundaries of organized baseball (like the new Union League, which was offering him $10,000 to join its Philadelphia franchise); he could coach (he had an offer from the University of Georgia, albeit for just $800 per season); he could take the Spalding Company up on an invitation to work for them as a glorified bat salesman; or he could cobble together some combination of the above. The *Chicago Tribune* dismissed these as "not even original bluffs" and Cobb himself said that the options did not appeal to him. Realizing that someone had to break the stalemate, former Detroit mayor George P. Codd volunteered his services, and after a few conversations with him Cobb said he'd accept a one-year contract for $4,000, with $800 to be added if he batted .300, and a deal was struck. "WE-E-AH! COBB SIGNS CONTRACT!" said the headline in the *Free Press*.

Although Cobb had hardly won a clear-cut victory over Navin, he would ultimately realize more than 50 percent more than he was originally offered, and more important established himself as a new kind of "serious" player who considered baseball a profession and was open to pursuing business opportunities as they arose. In financial terms, 1908 was a breakthrough year for Cobb, and a prelude to negotiations two years hence, which would result in a three-year contract at $9,000 per season, a deal that made him, along with Christy Mathewson, Nap Lajoie, and John McGraw, one of the highest-paid men in baseball. He was starting to become involved in myriad sideline schemes. He would soon own a Hupmobile dealership in Augusta ("I can easily see why people fall for the gas carts," he said in an ad. "No happy home is complete without one!"), he became perhaps the first athlete ever to trademark and license his signature (initially to a company that made athletic shoes, including spikes), he purchased stock in the *Augusta Chronicle*, and endorsed Post Toasties ("Old Michigan's wonderful batter/Eats TOASTIES 'tis said once a day. For he knows they are healthful and wholesome/and furnish him strength for the fray"). At twenty-two, Cobb was the key figure in what was quickly becoming a cultural and commercial juggernaut.

Of course, all the success hinged on how well he hit a baseball, and

ran the bases; there were no guarantees. To the outside world, his great-
ness seemed to follow naturally and serenely from the fact that he was
Ty Cobb, the greatest. Charles Comiskey called him that and so did Cy
Young and Ring Lardner. Dear old Georgia exhibited him—and Nap
Rucker—at the state fair that year, like blue-ribbon bulls. The city of
Chicago presented him with a trophy for being its Most Popular Visiting Player. When Cobb came to town, Chicago's best and smartest
sportswriter, Ring Lardner, would buy cheap seats in right field in South
Side Park, within shouting distance of Cobb, so he could banter with his
favorite player for nine innings. Cobb never disappointed him, with his
quips or with his play. On opening day of 1908 in the White Sox park,
he hit a single, double, and home run, made two breathtaking catches
(one a fence climber, the other a full-body slider)—and when a disgusted
crank threw a lemon at him, "he accepted it with a bow of thanks," baseball historian Marc Okkonen tells us, "and proceeded to suck it dry with
pleasure."

Cobb was playing with panache now. Trying to explain why such a
fierce opponent could have followers in rival cities, Heywood Broun of
the *New York Morning Telegraph* said it was "because he gave them more
for their hard-earned ticket than any man alive or dead." In Detroit he
was as big a celebrity as Henry Ford, and much more exciting. At home
against St. Louis in late April, he stretched a single into a double with
a pretty fadeaway slide—then when second baseman Jimmy Williams
bounced the ball hard in frustration for missing the tag, he scampered on
to third, where he again slid in safely, and drew a standing ovation. By
mid-May he was hitting .365.

Owing to some alchemy that defies explanation, the confidence Cobb
exuded was achieved by means of constant worry. (This may be why
he wanted the wind in his face.) It was as if he doubted himself to the
point where his only option was to have faith in himself—the tortured
"wearing, tearing," insomnia-inducing thought process he looked back
on and shook his head sadly at in retirement. He still kept notes—some
on paper, some in his head—on every pitcher and catcher in the league,
delineating their tendencies, weaknesses, and talents. He was sensitive to
statistics and felt he had to work hard to keep his numbers high. He slept

fitfully during the season and by his own admission could be bad company. Abusive fans found it increasingly easier to get under his skin. And if he slumped a bit forget it; he would explode at the clubhouse man for hanging his towel on a different peg than it had been on in the last game in which he got three hits.

"He fought for every point and fought his fellows if they did not battle as hard for victory as he had," recalled sportswriter Hugh Fullerton. "I sat behind Cobb on the clubhouse porch once with Germany Schaefer, watching him instead of the game. He moved before each pitch, and leaped in one or another direction each time a ball was thrown, never still for an instant and always tensely observant of every move made on the field." Cobb received his first major league ejection (from Silk O'Loughlin) on May 2 at Bennett, after trying unsuccessfully to stretch a triple into a home run; he simply couldn't stop arguing. More eruptions would follow. On long train trips, he would sit by himself looking out the window, morosely cataloging things he could have done better in the last game, and plotting surprises for the next. "I would think, 'I haven't tried to score from second base on a bunt in a while—maybe they think I've given up trying'—and I would try that the next day."

Is it any wonder that a sleep-deprived perfectionist, prone to such zone-outs and an abject failure at fool-suffering, would get into so many fistfights? No; what's surprising is the vehemence with which he insisted he was no brawler. The late W. H. Cobb had told him in the letter he wrote when Ty was fifteen to "*Conquer your anger and wild passions that would degrade your dignity and belittle your manhood*," and Cobb liked to think he had fulfilled his father's wishes. He bridled when described as chesty, pugnacious, a temperamental Southerner who drew his sword too quickly. He insisted that the amount of fighting that he and other ballplayers engaged in was wildly exaggerated by the press and fans—"Loads of people I've never met think of me almost as a barroom gladiator," he said. "I wouldn't intentionally hurt another player for twice my salary"— even as his list of scuffles lengthened.

While it is true that he seldom if ever threw the first punch in a brawl—"I don't believe Cobb ever picked a fight just for the sake of a row," said Walter Johnson, "but start something unfair and you'll get a fight whether you're a ballplayer or a taxi driver"—he did have an exqui-sitely short fuse. Today he is often tsk-tsked for the quality, yet many in his day found his explosiveness entertaining. To a degree it humanized a virtuoso who played baseball spookily well, and because he provided such a dizzying array of examples to choose from—fights with complete strangers, fights with teammates, fights with rival players, fights with hotel employees, shopkeepers, and rowdy cranks and such—it also made him, as the expression goes, larger than life. He was like a protagonist in a penny dreadful or a silent movie: Ty Cobb took even less guff than the most take-no-guff guy on your Christmas list. True, some, when they read about his latest misadventure, gleefully hoped he had come out on the short end, but others liked that he had not lost touch with his inner wild-child, the way they, as they had gotten older, somehow had, *sigh*. He was a crash test dummy for the average Joe, an object lesson in what would happen if you didn't always wait for the other guy to say the proverbial "just one more thing."

But I'm making fighting sound like something it's not. In the event, most spontaneous fights are ugly and stupid. Consider Cobb's assault on a man named Fred Collins, which shows how his next battle was sometimes only a faux pas away. Or maybe not even that far, since Collins almost certainly did nothing wrong. The incident occurred on June 6 of the year under discussion, 1908, as Cobb and roommate Claude Rossman exited the Pontchartrain Hotel to board a bus that would take the Tigers on the short ride to Bennett Park for a game against Boston. Collins, a twenty-nine-year-old, Canadian-born black man who worked for the Detroit United Railway, the transport company that provided the city's trolley service, was pouring asphalt on Woodward Avenue, in front of the year-old "Pontch," when he held up his hand to head off approaching foot and auto traffic "which would have cut into the newly laid asphalt," said the *Free Press*. "You can't cross here," he told Cobb and others. Collins was a solid citizen, long on the job. Five years before, while pouring asphalt for a different Detroit company, he'd spotted a runaway horse dragging a carriage; he chased it down and saved the white woman huddled on the vehicle's floor. He hadn't received so much as a "thank-you" from the lady's husband for his trouble, he had told the newspaper at the time, and his experience with Cobb would be even less pleasant. Cobb hadn't liked his order to stop, Collins said, even though "I didn't tell him anything more than I tell hundreds of people every day, and in fact I wasn't talking to him." The two exchanged "hot words," and in a moment they were throwing punches. Describing it, the *Free Press* writer fell into Pierce Egan mode: "Cobb rushed the negro and both exchanged lefts and rights to the head and face in rapid fire order. Cobb's blows had great force and truer aim and simply rained on the negro's face. The negro landed half a dozen times fully on Cobb's face, but his blows lacked steam, as the ballplayer had him working on the retreat." And so on. Soon five other black men on the work crew "advanced towards the fighters with upraised irons, weighing 75 pounds each, and a sixth negro flourished a rake." White men intervened and pushed the black men away. "An instant later the fighters grappled [again] and both rolled into the dust against the curb, Cobb on top."

It was Rossman who "rushed through the crowd" and finally got between the combatants and stopped the fighting. The lines he is given by the *Free Press* sound like something Jimmy Stewart would utter on screen a couple of generations later. "What do you mean by getting into mixups like this?" he supposedly demanded of Cobb. "Do you want to break up the ball club and get killed?" As the first baseman posed these well-crafted queries, Collins went looking for a policeman to arrest Cobb for "striking him while he was wearing eyeglasses," then considered an especially heinous offense.

The Collins episode is one of the cornerstones of the often advanced argument that Cobb was a full-throttle racist (though the word didn't exist then; the closest thing was "racialist," which suggested someone with formal theories about white supremacy based on genetics or some other branch of pseudoscience). It is easy to see why. Unlike the Bungy Cummings dustup (which devolved into a he said/he said debate), Cobb versus Collins was a clear-cut confrontation between a black and a white man, taking place in broad daylight outside a downtown hotel before some 200 witnesses. That Cobb overreacted seems beyond question. "If he wants to settle the negro problem, let him settle it," said the *Chicago Tribune*, somewhat perplexingly. "But this is neither the time nor the

place." The *Free Press*, which chanced to have a reporter at the scene, definitely saw race as the flint in Cobb's flare-up. "What the ___ have you got
to say about it, nigger," the newspaper says he asked Collins when he was
being advised to not cross the street. Cobb was angered, the anonymous
reporter speculated, because "the negro evidently did not treat him with
the deference the colored brother extends to the white man down in dear
old Georgia."

Once again Cobb's alleged racism can be attributed to a presumption
about his attitudes based on the date and location of his birth. Royston,
Georgia? 1886? The problem with newspaper reports about bigoted behavior in early-twentieth-century America is that the papers were often
as racist as anyone else, if not more so. Northern dailies loved the idea of
Southerners acting like stereotypical Southerners, and Detroit newspapers
enjoyed Ty (as they defined him) being Ty. Shame, shame, and all that.
But a wink came with every finger wag. In fact the *Free Press*, history's
main source about the Collins incident, was, like many other newspapers
in matters regarding race, utterly without standards or scruples. In its
gleeful account of the Collins incident (headline: "Ty Cobb Increases His
Batting Average by Battering Up a Negro Wearing Spectacles") Collins is
called "the negro" or the "shiny Ethiopian" more often than he is called by
his own name. (Cobb, meanwhile, is either referred to by name or called
"the ballplayer" throughout.) Much more disturbing is the cartoon illustration that ran with the story, showing a chimplike being in overalls trading punches with a man in a checked suit, as other chimp-things scurry
to the scene. At the lower right of the panel, a policeman holds one dark-
skinned and one battle-stained white individual and asks, "Which one of
youse is Ty Cobb?" Clearly, the *Free Press* thought its readers would enjoy
an account of Cobb going off (again) like an overwound alarm clock and
slugging a Negro. And since no one will ever know how much Collins's
skin color mattered to Cobb at the moment he erupted—he had the same
reaction in similar situations with several white men, as we shall see—the
paper chose to impute an attitude to Cobb that matched its editorial
wishes or perhaps its cartoonist's whims.

To its credit, the local court was less amused with Cobb's actions
than the *Free Press* was. The ballplayer received a summons and had to
appear (with his face still swollen) before a Justice Jeffries the next day.

"If you are guilty, you'll have to pay a fine," said the judge. "Your batting average won't save you. We pay when we go to see you and you ought to pay when you come here." Then "the court consulted its pocket [Tigers] schedule, found that the team would be home next Monday, and set the hearing for that date." Ultimately, on the advice of his attorney, Cobb settled privately with Collins for $75. "When a man is insulted it is worth $75 to get satisfaction," Cobb said when asked later. "I settled not because I thought I was the offending party, but because I did not want to be inconvenienced later on. *I would have done the same thing to any man.* [Italics mine.] I would act again in a similar manner under the same conditions."

One reason we can't make assumptions about Cobb's attitude about race based simply on the year and location of his birth is that his immediate family is, as we've seen, rife with exceptions to the rule about Southern attitudes. Cobb himself left very little evidence of his feelings on the issue prior to the advent of Jackie Robinson—but he did leave some.

On a road trip to Chicago that happened a couple of weeks after Cobb settled the Collins case, Germany Schaefer came upon a sixteen-year-old black boy hanging around South Side Park, and invited him to come along with the Tigers and be their mascot. "The Tigers have a pickaninny batboy with hair full of corkscrew kinks," noted the *Detroit News* a few days later. It was not unusual in those days for major league clubs to go about with one or more urchins in tow as a combination talisman/gofer, and more often than not those children were black. They got their expenses paid, and maybe a few pennies more, but job security was negligible; if a team went on a bad streak the mascot might get the blame, and a kid who got picked up in Chicago might get cut loose in Boston or St. Louis. Like the other youngsters adrift in organized baseball back then, the teenager Schaefer found got paid no regular salary and took his chances in return for food and shelter. It is frequently said in the Cobb literature that his name was "lost to history," but his name was Ulysses Simon Harrison, one of at least ten children born to Robert and Maudie Harrison of Paragould, Arkansas. No one called him that, though, not after Schaefer, or one of the scribes, rechristened him Rastus, after the happy black chef on the Cream of Wheat box.

Even for a boy who'd probably seen a lot already, it was a bizarre interlude. Bill Donovan touched him with his pitching hand before each start for good luck. Third baseman Bill Coughlin, the team captain, constantly rubbed his head. Schaefer rubbed his bat in the boy's hair before each plate appearance. Cobb, though one of the most superstitious men on the team, did not treat Ulysses as a talisman. Instead, "he was the Ethiopian's main defender and patron," H. G. Salsinger wrote. He made sure Harrison was fed and had a place to sleep, even if it was a corner of the Bennett Park clubhouse. Road trips brought them closer still. On segregated trains, Cobb stowed Harrison beneath his berth, sometimes obscuring him with luggage, and he even let the kid share his hotel room, secretly, so as not to rile the other white guests. "Rastus" seemed to have come and gone from the Tigers at various times for no discernible reason, but after both the 1908 and 1909 seasons Cobb took the boy back to Georgia with him and employed him as a domestic and later as a helper in his Hupmobile showroom in downtown Augusta. (Harrison also spent time at the Indianapolis home of shortstop Donie Bush in early 1910.) By 1916 the erstwhile mascot, by then twenty-four and married, was working steadily as a chauffeur for Detroit construction magnate F. H. Hubbard, a job Cobb may well have helped him procure.

Cobb got people agitated and stirred controversies almost everywhere he went but it's interesting how in certain seasons those episodes would group themselves in a particular city. One year it might be Philadelphia where he had a lot of problems with rivals or fans or the authorities, another year New York or Cleveland. In 1908 Boston was his bête noire. His troubles there started in mid-July, when he got into a dispute with Amos H. Whipple, the manager of the Copley Square Hotel, the "High Class Modern House, Suitable for Ladies Traveling Alone," over room service charges. Cobb refused to pay extra for meals brought up to him from the kitchen; according to the *Chicago Tribune*, this was "not something expected by Southern gentlemen when they were home." Besides those checks, Whipple said he was also owed for a cuspidor—this was a very Edwardian-era argument—"which Cobb broke showing his friend how he made four hits in one game." In consequence of the debt, Whipple was refusing to return the "shining badge" that Cobb had received for winning the previous year's batting title, and which he upon checking in had consigned to the Copley's safe. The dispute dragged on for two months before a settlement was reached. It was, in one sense, just another in a series of scuffles (and worse) that Cobb had with people in the hospitality business, but it also shows how boyishly proud he was of his baseball accomplishments—proud enough to take his prize along on road trips, to show to people along the way. (The truly dazzling diamond-studded medal is now on display at the Ty Cobb Museum in Royston.)

Cobb had additional problems that year at the Huntington Avenue Grounds, the park that preceded Fenway as the Red Sox' home base, owing mostly to his playing his normal game and the Boston players feeling that in doing so he was singling them out for a spanking. On July 13 he preyed upon Red Sox pitching for two singles, a triple, and a game-winning 10th-inning home run. He also, in the fourth inning, got into a halfhearted shoving match with shortstop Heinie Wagner after he, Cobb, was thrown out trying to steal second. Players from both teams trotted out and separated the two before anything happened, but some Hub fans felt compelled to bid the Detroit kid something stronger than adieu. Cobb responded verbally and cheekily gestured for them to sit back down. On July 30, with the Boston cranks still sore at him, he went 3-for-4 against the forty-one-year-old Cy Young and, with the nimbleness of an infielder, threw out catcher Lou Criger at first base on a one-hopper to right. Later he made a putout at second as part of a double play. Afterward some Boston players grumbled that Cobb was always trying to show them up.

The situation festered until a mid-August game at Huntington when Red Sox righty Cy Morgan struck out Cobb twice with the bases loaded. As they passed each other on the field following the second whiff, Cobb said something Morgan didn't like, and the pitcher threw down his glove and charged him. Once again, others intervened before punches were thrown, but some bleacher fans were now riding Cobb hard and vowing vengeance—or so said Red Sox owner John I. Taylor, who wanted Cobb banned in Boston for using "vile and abusive language." Taylor claimed he was making the request for Cobb's own good, since according to *Sporting Life* "a half dozen bugs had threatened to kill him." American League president Ban Johnson said he could issue no edict, since no formal complaint had been filed, but he did send Cobb a letter advising him to mind his manners. It was much ado about little, but it added spice to a long, dull Red Sox season, which may have been Taylor's intention. *Boston Herald* scribe J. C. Morse put the alleged feud in perspective when he termed it "pure rubbish." Calling Cobb "one of the biggest cards to appear in this city," he noted "there were people here that hissed and hooted at Cobb for some of his actions, but the very next moment they were howling themselves hoarse for some brilliant play he had made."

IS IT SUPERFLUOUS TO SAY that Ty Cobb never did things the easy way? Even his wedding was tangled in controversy—not about the fact of it, or the bride he took, but about the timing. I mean, it is fine to get married in the middle of a pennant race, just so long as you, the groom, are not probably *the* key figure in that race's outcome.

The first hint of imminent I-dos for Cobb came in late 1907, when he sent *Detroit News* writer Paul Bruske "a peppery message" giddily confirming his engagement to Charlie Lombard, but denying a rumor (possibly made up by him for the occasion) that he was getting married in the spring. After that, he said nothing of nuptials until he suddenly took off in early August of 1908, with his lucky black bat, for what seemed like a hastily planned ceremony in Augusta. Arriving late because of the inevitable transportation glitches, he barely had time to duck into a rooming house to change his shirt before proceeding on to the Oaks, the elegant Lombard family estate where his seventeen-year-old bride-to-be nervously waited, in a room full of "palms, ferns and cut flowers," along with about twenty-five guests (but not his mother, sister, or brother). Why Cobb's uncle Clifford Ginn was his only relative there is unknown, but in the end it was a joyous occasion and they seemed the perfect couple: the dashing young athlete and the hazel-eyed daughter of an old-fashioned industrialist said to be worth as much as one million dollars. The timing of the event is what bothered some fans; since ballplayers have off most of the year, why was he was getting married on August 6, at a moment when the Tigers were battling for the AL lead with the suddenly dangerous St. Louis Browns? It was a delicate question, as questions about impromptu weddings tend to be. Bruske, in his *Sporting Life* column, felt compelled to broach it—but concluded (rather improbably) that it was ultimately a matter of Cobb, the pampered team pet, throwing his weight around, just because he could.

"To the out-of-town fan, his absence must seem remarkable," Bruske wrote, "but it is merely one of those characteristic idiosyncrasies for which he is noted. . . . But what can you do about it? The player is there with the goods on the diamond." (No child was born to Charlie in the next nine months, but she did suffer an unidentified "illness" in November that forced the couple to cancel a combination honeymoon/barnstorming trip to Japan.) Bruske further suggested that the star had taken off for Augusta without informing manager Hughie Jennings, but considering that when he rejoined the Tigers on August 9, Navin gave him a set of cut glass bowls as a wedding present and paid for Charlie to travel with the team for a few weeks, that does not seem likely. Whatever the reason for his sudden departure, he had the club's blessing. Nor did most of his hometown fans hold a grudge. They welcomed him back to Bennett Park with a warm ovation as the local press crowded around Charlie Cobb's field-level box seat (where she sat, "heavily veiled," with her new mother-in-law, Amanda) and, in the next day's paper, gushed over her looks, generously calling her one of the great Southern beauties.

Boston, which would finish fifth in the AL that year, wasn't the real problem for Cobb or the Tigers in 1908. Nor ultimately were the Browns. Cleveland and Chicago were. As August became September, Detroit, which had been in first place in the standings since mid-July, got knocked off the summit by Lajoie's surging Cleveland Naps, with the White Sox only a game or so behind in third place. The last two weeks of the season were a scramble the likes of which the AL had never before seen—the closest pennant race in its seven-year history.

On the final day of the season, October 6, the Tigers were in front with the White Sox and Naps tied for second, a half game behind. Cleveland played, and beat, the Browns in St. Louis. Meanwhile, Detroit and Chicago faced off at South Side Park. Cobb's performance in that closing game counters the assertion, sometimes made in the days when people still talked about his spotty World Series play, that he wilted in the clutch. With the season on the line he smacked a first-inning triple that knocked in two runs, soon scored himself, and before the day was over added two more singles, another run batted in—and drew a pickoff throw from pitcher Ed Walsh that eluded first baseman Frank "the Bald Eagle" Isbell and allowed Crawford to come home. Meanwhile, Bill Donovan tossed a two-hit shutout, giving the Tigers a 7–0 victory and their second consecutive flag. "Mad Crowds Fill Streets Shouting Praises of Tigers" screamed the *Free Press* headline. "The bray of cornets punctured the general uproar and now and then a cannon-like explosion shook the pavement. Bonfires were a common thing. Burning wagons were hauled swiftly up and down Woodward Avenue. Roman candles and skyrockets shot from the sides and fronts and roofs of buildings." A "jubilee" broke out in the lobby of the Pontch. As the evening wore on, though, the energy in the streets turned ugly. Several policemen were attacked by the crowd and seriously injured and someone threw a block of concrete through the just installed plate glass window of the J. L. Hudson department store. "The broken glass was valued at $500," said the *Free Press*. "Store management says it is worth it." Nobody seemed to care that the 1908 pennant came with an asterisk, because the Tigers had played one fewer game—153—than Cleveland. Today Detroit would be compelled to make up the canceled contest (which if they had lost would have resulted in a tie with Cleveland, and forced a one-game playoff), but in those days the rule book contained no such provision and the standings stood.

Matters had come to an even wilder—and less legitimate—conclusion in the National League, thanks in part to the famous Merkle Boner. Poor Fred Merkle of the New York Giants was a nineteen-year-old rookie first baseman, the youngest player in the NL. On September 23, with the Giants, Cubs, and Pirates still locked in a season-long struggle, he started his first major league game, against the Cubs. In the bottom of the ninth, with one out, a man on first, and the score tied 1–1, right fielder Harry McCormick came to bat. "The Moose" had a knack for being involved in what one biographer calls "quirky baseball events." Once he got a pinch single that the umpire said didn't count because he hadn't finished announcing his name to the crowd (once formally introduced, McCormick struck out). On another occasion, while waiting in the on-deck circle, he swung at an errant throw from the outfield and hit the ball out of the park. If you asked him for an autograph he would rubber-stamp your paper with a little image of a moose. Anyway, on this occasion he hit a sharp grounder to second and reached safely on a fielder's choice, thus inserting himself into yet another memorable baseball moment. For it then became Merkle's turn to bat, and he used it admirably, hitting a single off Cubs righty Jack "The Giant Killer" Pfiester. Moose scooted to third.

This brought up Al Bridwell, the Giants shortstop, who hit the first pitch he saw into center for a single that sent home McCormick with what should have been the winning run. The hundreds of fans who ran onto the field certainly thought it was, and Merkle, seeing his way impeded by swarming spectators, made a right turn and began jogging toward the Giants clubhouse, out in dead center. By rule he was supposed to step on second base for the run to be officially tallied but this was a technicality rarely observed—unless you were Cubs second baseman Johnny Evers, who was known as a constant conniver. "Gimme the ball!" Evers shouted to center fielder Solly Hofman, who managed to come up with it, or something very similar, and threw it in Evers's direction. His toss was intercepted—and heaved into the crowd—by a Giants pitcher named Joe McGinnity, who was serving as first base coach that day. Cubs pitcher Rube Kroh then retrieved the ball or something very similar from the stands and threw it back to Evers, who fought his way through the mob to second base, and touched it for the force-out. Obviously men who were not in the game (Kroh and McGinnity) could not be involved in a play that, in any case, should have been declared dead as soon as a fan touched the ball. Yet the two umpires on duty that day, Bob Emslie and Hank O'Day, ruled Merkle out and voided the run he'd knocked in. With the cranks refusing to return to their seats, the game was then called on account of darkness and went into the books as a tie. This was patently ridiculous—umpire Bill Klem, a future Hall of Famer, called it "the rottenest decision in the history of baseball"—but a week later the Giants' appeal was denied by the National League president, Harry Pulliam, and the decision stood.

Immediately after the "boner" game, the *New York Times* found Merkle guilty of "censurable stupidity," but his misery had only begun. Ten days later, on October 3, the Cubs were 97–55 on the season and the Pirates were 98–55. Because the National League insisted on makeup games, they played one in Chicago, which the Cubs won 5–2, eliminating Honus Wagner and his boys from the race, and forcing a one-game playoff with the Giants, who also had finished with a record of 98–55. Before a Polo Grounds crowed estimated at more than 40,000, the Cubs breezed past the Giants to win their third consecutive pennant. Now it was by general consensus Merkle's fault that the Giants weren't in the World Series, and the New York fans got angry at him all over again. He was doomed to hear himself booed and called "Bonehead" and "Leather Skull" until his retirement in 1926, and to afterward get the occasional visit, at his fishing lure company in Florida, from a writer asking him to relive the moment one more time.

This has not really been a digression because it helps put into perspective what came next: a strange deflation in the prevailing mood. Start with Cobb. As happy as he was to be getting another shot at the World Series, he was displeased with his overall performance, and by having to fend off criticism from those who said that having his own schedule—Jennings let him practice when and where he wanted to and show up for games at the last minute—and a new bride were hurting his performance. When you look at the numbers the charge sounds almost funny. In a season dominated by pitching—Ed Walsh of the White Sox was 40–15 with a 1.42 ERA; Addie Joss of the Naps allowed just 1.16 runs per nine innings while going 24–11; and so on—Cobb hit .324. This was, indeed, 26 points below his average of the year before. (The editor of *Sporting Life*, Frank C. Richter, was so upset by the baseball-wide decline in averages that year that he proposed making outfielders play without gloves as a way of giving hitters a break.) At the same time, Cobb did lead the league in hitting for the second straight season and was the only man to crack three figures in the RBI department (108), numbers that to a degree perhaps offset his disappointment.

But it wasn't just Cobb who felt down. The year's tense, emotionally exhausting pennant races seemed to leave both league-leading cities limp. The World Series, for all its pomp, felt anticlimactic, and the smallest number of people ever showed up to watch it played. Admittedly, there were extenuating circumstances. In Detroit—where the Tigers had sold a record number of tickets during the regular season (436,199)—it rained steadily the day of the first game, keeping the attendance at 10,812 instead of the expected 25,000 or so. (Navin could have forgone the giant white sheet he put up to block the view from the wildcat grandstand.) Some Cubs fans meanwhile were staging an ad hoc boycott of the Series in response to owner Charles Murphy, who raised prices for the Series and then, it was said, sold a huge block of tickets to scalpers for his personal gain. (Murphy never admitted guilt, but he did agree to pay back the team for several hundred reserve seats.)

On top of this, the men most responsible for hyping the Series to potential customers—the sportswriters—felt badly treated that fall by the major leagues, whom they accused of giving away their press seats to "actors, politicians and barbers." According to Tigers historian Fred Lieb, Chicago scribe Huge Fullerton complained that at the Giants-Cubs playoff game at the Polo Grounds he had to "dictate 5,000 words while sitting in the lap of Louis Mann, the well-known character actor." The journalists' outrage led to them to stifle their usual boosterish instincts and not say quite so often in print that fans really ought to come out and support the home club.

Sifting through a sheaf of old clips from the 1908 Series, one thinks of the slightly less old joke: it's not a complex—you really are inferior. In more ways than one, the Tigers weren't in the same league with the Cubs, owing largely to Chicago's superior pitching. At least Cobb put up Cobb-like numbers—"He was anything but a lemon this time" said *Sporting Life*—to a chronological point. In the first game, which was frequently interrupted by groundskeepers who shoveled sawdust into the wet batter's box and onto the pitcher's mound, he knocked in a run in the first inning with a sharp single, giving the Tigers an early lead, and then, after Detroit fell behind 5–1, beat out an infield hit in the seventh, starting a rally that brought the score to 5–4. An inning later he bunted safely and finessed his way around the bases to score a run that put the Tigers ahead going into the ninth. Alas, Tigers righty "Kickapoo Ed" Summers couldn't hold the lead, and the Cubs won 10–6.

Game two, played in Chicago before 17,760, was a scoreless tie until the Cubs broke it wide open with six runs in the eighth against Bill Donovan. Cobb had one hit, a single, in the ninth that knocked in the Tigers' run in their 6–1 defeat. Righty starter Orvie Overall, who pitched an inning of relief in the previous game, had given Chicago its sixth consecutive World Series win over Detroit. Said the *Free Press*: "It begins to look as if the local Nationals have something on the Tiges."

Still at the West Side Grounds for game three, on Monday, October 12, Cobb and pitcher George Mullin combined to help the Tigers win their first World Series game. Cobb had three singles, a double, knocked in two runs, and stole two bases. Detroit sportswriter Will B. Wreford noted that when Cobb was on first he shouted out to the catcher that he was going on the next pitch—and did, successfully, "spoiling a chance for a play on him by dumping Tinker as he slid." A few pitches later he "tipped [catcher Johnny] Kling off again that he was about to steal third and he did, Kling's rather low throw getting away from Harry Steinfeldt." Some would say that since the Tigers were far ahead at that point he was merely showing up the opposition. Cobb would say he was sending a message—You never know what the hell I'm going to do—that would lodge someplace in the opposition's subconscious.

In that case it was more or less a moot point, though. Cobb got on base only once again in the Series, via a walk (in game five), as the Tigers were shut out twice, 3–0 in game four by "Three-Finger" Brown and 2–0 by Overall in the finale, both times before veritable coffee klatches of cranks at Bennett. (Only 6,210 turned out for game five, still the smallest crowd in World Series history.) Thanks to his strong start, Cobb hit .368 over the five games, but the Tigers as a team batted a sorry .209. "It is all over," wrote Jackson, "and the players may go home to hibernate." Except that it wasn't all over. First the melon had to be sliced, as the players used to say. The spoils were a lot smaller than the year before, when owner Yawkey had dumped his share back into the pot. Yawkey in the interim had sold most of his shares in the club to Navin, who had much less generous instincts, and kept the owner's share—just under $20,000—for himself. Each Tiger got only $870 that year, each Cub $1,318. After the accounting was done the teams played two exhibition games, one in Chicago, the second in Terre Haute, Indiana—that were nearly as well attended as some of the Series games in Detroit, and which reaped the players an additional $300 or so per man. The Chicago game featured "field events"—foot races and throwing contests—open to any of the players who felt like entering. Ostensibly these were just for fun, though side bets were likely. Ty participated in four of the five events, and won three of them: the 100-yard dash (10⅖ seconds), the circling-the-bases race (13⅘ seconds), and the bunt-and-run-to-first (3⅕ seconds), failing only in the long-distance throw.

Cobb in 1908 had a good year by anyone's standards but his own, and he sounded apologetic as he gave his last interviews for the season to the baseball press. He promised he would keep himself in shape by hunting and hiking in the off-season and report to spring training—it would be in San Antonio, Texas—early "as I want to make a batting and base-running record next year that I always will be able to point to with pride." He couldn't wait to blot out the memory of that league-leading but disappointing .324. Feeling chastened, he declined to ask for a raise for 1909, and signed his one-year contract for $4,000 as soon as it arrived in the mail.

— CHAPTER SEVENTEEN —

TYRUS RAYMOND COBB WAS THE greatest hitter of them all, his
.366 lifetime average over twenty-three and a half seasons still the highest
ever recorded. This achievement is not traceable simply to superior hand-
eye coordination; what it shows most vividly is that Cobb understood how
to hit in his particular baseball moment, just as Adrian Constantine Anson
and George Herman Ruth, the offensive stars who bracketed him histori-
cally, understood (or intuited) how best to approach the discouraging art
in theirs. Pop (b. 1852) and the Babe (1895) both generally tried to teach
the ball a lesson. Anson, a huge man, drove stinging line drives and had
21 home runs in 1884 for the National League Chicago White Stockings
(who played in a bandbox, but still). Then came Wee Willie Keeler in the
John the Baptist or if you prefer Christopher Marlowe role, presaging
Cobb, who though built to be a slugger—built rather like Ted Williams,
whom he in some ways resembled temperamentally as well—understood
that muscle wasn't the point. "I never take a good healthy swing at the ball
any more," Cobb told the *New York Times* in May of 1910. "*I like to do
that*, but you can't get anything in the big leagues swinging the willow. The
spitball pitchers would make a dunce of you in short order, to say nothing
of the boxmen who have mastered a good change of pace." (The *Times*
obviously got an insider's price on quote polish, and lavished it on.) The
men of Anson's age "swung onto the ball with the force of a trip-hammer,"
Cobb continued, but "*the great hitters of our time grab their batting sticks
a foot or more from the handle and, instead of swinging, aim to meet the ball
flush*. It's just like the short-arm punch in the prize ring. The long swingers
with their terrible haymakers seldom get the money nowadays. *I stick to
the sure system of just meeting the ball with a half-way grip.*"

Italics mine. Willingness to accept the things about the deadball era that he could not change—the deadness of the ball, for example—his.

And yet hitting wasn't quite half of his game. It was his base running that put him not just on top of the heap but up there in the penthouse somewhere (pretty much by himself, for better and worse) and made him—though he didn't have much of a sense of humor himself when it came to baseball—the locus of joy. "I'll tell you why fans go out and see Cobb above any man in the game," Grantland Rice's dentist said to him, according to a piece the writer published in *McClure's Magazine* in 1915. "I went out to see him play the Yankees. He was in a batting slump, didn't get a hit, but broke up the game. How?"

Rice, in the chair, responded with "a weird gurgling, thrumming sound."

"I'll tell you," the dentist continued. "With the score tied and one out in the eighth he got a base on balls. He trotted slowly and carelessly two thirds of the way to first and then, thirty feet away, he suddenly started at top speed, rounded the bag, and whirled on to second. The pitcher, rattled by such a wild move, threw badly to second; and, before the ball was back, Ty was dusting the dirt from his uniform at third, waiting to score ten seconds later on a short outfield fly. Great stuff?"

The patient "gagged again, and blinked."

"It beat all the home runs in the book! It was just a Cobb play—the kind of play that only Ty Cobb would try and get away with!"

Rice's dentist may have been apocryphal but the emotion he displayed when discussing Cobb was typical early-twentieth-century fan stuff. Although the modern era of two leagues had started only in 1901, the game had been around long enough for people to realize how intensely boring it could often be, despite its beauty, like a young Brigitte Bardot telling you about the dream she had the other night, and the Georgia Peach was the tangy antidote to that. He was always up to something, or someone else was in a dither because of what he'd just done. True stories about Cobb sounded like one-reel silent movie plots. Consider a game in Cleveland in which Cobb's perfectly timed base running turned a tap-back to the box into an inside-the-park home run. Davy Jones had been on third, and when Cobb made contact Jones unwisely got caught in a rundown while

Cobb flew around the bases at top speed. The second Jones was tagged out by catcher Steve O'Neill, "a foot from third," said ex-umpire (and ex-Tiger) Babe Pinelli, who dined out on the story for years, Cobb passed him, kept on going for home—and, without sliding, scored the game-winning run, first baseman Doc Johnston being "too awed by what he was witnessing," said Pinelli, to cover home plate, as the textbook suggests.

Rice's dentist, however, was probably referring to a game on June 4, 1915, at Hilltop Park when Cobb singled off Slim Caldwell, then stole second, third, and home, "his lithe body swerving away from [catcher Les] Nunamaker's reach," said the *Times*, "and clouds of dirt kicked up by his spikes blinding the eyes of Nunamaker, Caldwell and [home plate umpire] Silk O'Loughlin" (natch). Pitcher Caldwell was so frustrated by the result that "he threw his glove high in the air" and was "put out of the game for being mad because Cobb had outwitted him."

"The winged-footed wonder," they called him but of course his pure speed was hardly the reason opponents skied their gloves or (remember Jimmy Williams?) slammed the ball into the dirt after Cobb had wangled an extra base or two. His bag of tricks contained actual tricks. Cobb sometimes slid into second, howled in pain, asked for time, limped around, winced, howled some more—and then lit out for third on the very next pitch. More central to his maddening running style, though, were his powers of observation, which could be employed from a stationary position. Like other base stealers, then and now, he focused mostly on pitchers and how their habits differed immediately preceding a pickoff attempt, particularly in regard to hands and feet. Cy Young, in his dotage by the time Cobb faced him, had a reputation for holding runners close—the hulking six-foot-two righty would basically stare them back to whatever bag they might have managed to achieve—but Cobb noticed that he held the ball away from his chest and up close to his chin, as opposed to right on the breastbone, when he planned to attempt a pickoff at first. Once he made the discovery, Cobb said, he watched the great man do the same thing at least eight times before acting on it—but after that he could usually steal second on "good old Cy" without even sliding.

Cobb wasn't always so methodical; other observations had to be made, and exploited, in the moment. Fred Mitchell, an American League catcher and later manager of the Cubs, recalled that one day at Hilltop in 1910, Cobb was on third base with two out, and Mitchell whipped a peg down there, just to keep him close. After taking the throw, third baseman Frank LaPorte "sauntered" to the mound to discuss Cobb strategies with the Highlanders pitcher, "tossing the ball up in his glove about a foot or so, as players unthinkingly do" as he went. The reader can probably sense where this is going. Cobb, said Mitchell, stood "carelessly" on the sack, seeming to stare into the middle distance. One toss, another toss—"and then Cobb broke for the plate at top speed," Mitchell recalled. "I've never seen anything sprung more suddenly. Instantly there was shouting and confusion. I yelled for the ball, and LaPorte, startled, failed to see Cobb and didn't know where the play should be made. By the time the ball finally reached me Cobb had slid in."

Cobb stole home so often—a record 54 times in his career, 21 more times than the man in second place, old-time Pirates outfielder Max Carey—that some people thought he could pull off what is perhaps the most exciting play in baseball at will. This was an impression he happily reinforced on April 20, 1912, when he scored the first Tigers run ever at Navin Field, the iron-and-concrete park that replaced Bennett, by dashing in from third, hook-sliding around catcher Ted Easterly, and stealing home in the first inning of the first game ever played in the new stadium. (Five days later he hit the first home run ever struck at Navin.)

Some of Cobb's contemporaries said his sliding technique was a thing of beauty—and we'll have to take their word for it, since there is almost no moving footage of him on the bases, just a relatively few semi-helpful stills. "Cobb has developed a slide into the bag which no modern player can equal," said Hughie Jennings.

It is more than a fall away slide, although it is generally called that. He throws himself away from the baseman and around him, catching the bag with his toe or his hand. This is a stunt for a contortionist. It has caused endless arguments in the stand when Cobb has seemed to be out at second or third while the umpire insisted on calling him safe. Most of the time, at least, he was safe. Other players would have been out, but not Cobb. He had eluded the baseman's groping hand and wriggled back to the bag like an eel. It is certainly a masterpiece, that slippery, baffling slide of Ty's.

Burt Shotton, a longtime St. Louis Browns outfielder (and later manager of the Dodgers), saw Cobb's slides from a different angle. "One time, I had the ball in my hand behind third, backing up a throw there," he recalled. "I positively had Ty trapped half way to the plate. I said to myself, 'Ty you old so-and-so, I got you this time.' I threw home in plenty of time to get him. Then I saw Cobb slide. Nobody slides today the way he did. The ball went in one direction, the catcher's glove in another and our catcher, Paul Krichell, in still another. Of course, Cobb was safe."

In a semi-famous photograph of that incident Cobb appears to be flying foot-first into Krichell's crotch while the catcher squints like the just shot Lee Harvey Oswald. By Krichell's own testimony, though, the image is deceiving. The only ball Cobb was aiming for was the one in his opponent's hand, and he struck it with force and precision. "Cobb came tearing into me, and when you talk about explosions that was one," Krichell recalled in the early 1950s, by which time he was better known as the Yankees scout who had discovered Lou Gehrig. "He must have been loaded with TNT!"

"The ball hit the grandstand on the fly," Krichell said. "I was mad and stunned. He was mad and shaken. I started cussing him and he had a few dirty words that he shouted at me. The next thing I knew we were fighting, but it was one of those baseball fights where more words than blows are exchanged. Billy Evans was the umpire and he had us both fined."

Cobb had nine styles of slides in his repertoire: the hook, the fade away, the straight-ahead, the short (or "swoop") slide ("which I invented because of my small ankles"), the headfirst (which he never completely abandoned), the Chicago slide (referred to by him but never explained), the first base slide, the home plate slide, even one called the cuttlefish slide, so named because he purposely sprayed dirt with his spikes the way that cunning squidlike creature squirts ink. Coming in, he would always watch the infielder's eyes to see which side of the bag the ball was headed toward, and then try to slide the other way. A lot of his energy went into avoiding contact, which could of course facilitate a tag. Contact could not be avoided, though, in one of his biggest (but now largely forgotten) innovations, the slide into first, which he liked because as often as he employed it, it somehow managed to retain the element of surprise.

To some infielders, Cobb was like a shape-shifter who didn't approach but mysteriously *appeared* at the base they were charged with defending. Umpire Billy Evans said that Cobb was the only runner he ever saw who didn't slow up even slightly while transitioning from a flat-out run to a slide. Cobb said that the key was to slide with a kind of glee, or at least the appearance of glee—"like you enjoyed the act of sliding." This was, he admitted, particularly hard to do in the early part of the season, when each slide scraped a swatch of skin from his legs—skin that would grow back tougher, he believed, and make sliding in the home stretch of the season less painful. Yes, sliding pads existed in Cobb's day but whenever a reporter recoiled at the sight of his bloodstained uniform pants, and asked the inevitable question, he would say, "I do wear pads sometimes, when the pain becomes too much, but I try to do without them because the blame things retard my speed." Speed of course translated into force. "It was no fun putting the ball on Cobb when he came slashing into the plate," said Wally Schang, who caught for almost every American League club. "But he never cut me up. He was too pretty a slider to hurt anyone who put the ball on him right."

All the pretty slides and steals—897 lifetime, a record that stood for almost fifty years before it was surpassed by Lou Brock, then Rickey Henderson—all the crazy dancing off the bags and even crazier shouts to catchers that he was going on the next pitch . . . *"I'm going, I'm going, watch me, oh, yes, I'm going!"* (and then in fact did)—all that spoke to his core mission of, as he said many times, "creating a mental hazard for my opponents." He preferred, if possible, to defeat you without touching you, to puncture hopes, not hides, and in that way score runs (like the four he scored in Philadelphia on July 12, 1911, without getting a single hit). "I don't know how many times I tagged Ty out at second base," said Roger Peckinpaugh, a shortstop for several AL clubs, "yet he never so much as spiked me. On his slide to second, he'd usually throw his feet out toward center field, and try to grab the base with his hand. I'll never forget the feeling, though—just knowing that guy was taking that big lead off first and would be coming at me any second."

This brings us to the subject of intimidation. To watch Cobb for just a few innings was to see that making opponents worry—about pain, embarrassment, or baseball setbacks: the possibility of a run scoring or a man advancing—was the most important part of his game. Intimidation doesn't much sweeten the atmosphere on the diamond, it is true, but as a tactic it does have the advantage of working. Said Steve O'Neill, a longtime catcher for the Naps: "Our infielders didn't want any part of those spikes and they gave Cobb too much of the base." Exactly. "When a player steals a base he immediately unsettles the other side, the pitcher especially," Cobb said. "He gives his club a psychological advantage." Boston southpaw Ben Hunt agreed. "You have to watch the bases awful close on Cobb, and when a pitcher does that he is less effective. On an infield out Cobb makes his two bases right along. Even if you get a throw to the bag ahead of him, you aren't sure of putting him out, for he dodges the basemen and slides around or under in a majority of cases."

While it is relatively easy to find examples of men who, in the heat of battle, cried out that they were spiked by Cobb and demanded his expulsion or suspension, rare to the point of nonexistence are the more reflective quotes from peers who describe him as sadistic or a "near psychopath," as Bill Bryson called Cobb in his recent book *One Summer: America 1927* without the slightest bit of supporting evidence. Bryson should have dipped into the archives, which, over and over, yield attempts by less-renowned opponents to draw a distinction between tactics and terrorism. "Cobb was the roughest, toughest player I ever saw, a terror on the base paths," said Shotton. "He was not dirty, though. I never saw him spike a player deliberately. But if you ever got in the way of his flying spikes, brother, you were a dead turkey."

"As long as I watched him play, no one can convince me that he went out of his way to hurt anybody," said Urban "Red" Faber, who pitched for the White Sox from 1914 through 1933. "He wanted an open shot at that bag and if you were in his path, that was your hard luck, and if you had the ball he'd try to knock it out of your mitts. I don't see how you can argue against that kind of base-running method, especially if you had the desire to win that Cobb had."

Yet people did argue against it, even in Cobb's day, calling him the "Dixie Demon" and "dangerous to the point of dementia." Which at first was fine with Cobb. "I liked it when my opponents thought I was a little crazy," he admitted. Then he realized he couldn't turn off the criticism, or slow its momentum. Until the end of his days he felt dogged by the label "dirty player." Why was the reputation so hard to shake?

For two reasons, I think.

First, the public and the press of Cobb's era displayed a giddy fascination with spikes that wasn't shared by the men who laced up their six-pronged, kangaroo-leather booties every day and went, as it were, to the office. Spikes were generally afforded a far too important role in the daily business of baseball by that first generation of modern followers, most of whom had come of age in a time before they might have encountered them personally—in a time, that is, before scholastic sports—and thus viewed them with excessive wonder. "That baseball will soon be the most dangerous of games unless a means is found to do away with spikes is the opinion of many experts," said the *Newark Evening News* in 1909—a year when twenty-six men *died* playing organized football. Hard-bitten rank-and-file deadball men, men like "Rawmeat" Bill Rodgers and Pearce "What's the Use" Chiles, didn't see spikes as intrinsically evil—at once vaguely Jules Verne–ish and menacingly medieval—the way many civilians did. To professional players, cleated shoes were pretty much just another piece of locker room jock-junk, a tool that had the potential to be misused, but ultimately no scarier than a ball or bat, either of which, after all, could kill you.

Among major leaguers, only wide-eyed yannigans, having heard the (true) tales of Honus Wagner coming in high and hard, and Nap Lajoie spiking three men in one inning, ever fretted over how frequently spikes were deployed as weapons in the bigs. Which is why in 1908 a bunch of Tiger benchwarmers, led by starting second baseman Germany Schaefer, were able to get a rise out of some Highlander rookies by pretending to file their spikes on the top step of the Detroit dugout—a fairly common prank, first pulled by the Baltimore Orioles of Hughie Jennings's day, and later by John McGraw's New York Giants (Fred Snodgrass tells us in *The Glory of Their Times*), that was to live on in infamy (once a couple of credulous reporters wrote about it) and become attached to Cobb as the story in retelling got stretched and embellished. Cobb didn't sharpen his spikes that day or at other time, and didn't jokingly pretend to, as he would still be explaining fifty years later on television. In 1910, in fact, already starting to get tired of being smeared as a dirty player, he wrote a letter to Ban Johnson (which the Tigers subsequently released to the public) suggesting that major leaguers be required to *dull* their sharp new spikes with a file, and that every man's spikes be checked for excessive sharpness before each game by an umpire. "This would be a good way," he told Johnson, "to eliminate the accidents caused by spikes."

The letter had roughly the same effect on Cobb's reputation as the testimony of the ballplayers who came forward over the years to weave variations on Germany Schaefer's seminal statement: *"Cobb is a game square fellow who never cut a man with his spikes intentionally in his life, and anyone who gets by with his spikes knows it."* In other words, it didn't help him. Nothing could, not even the testimony of the most renowned umpire of the day, Silk O'Loughlin, who said, "I've been on top of many plays in which Cobb was the runner and I never saw him cut anyone intentionally." For besides the excitement engendered by spiked shoes, and the obvious appeal of an alleged nutcase who ran amuck within the cozy confines of the organized baseball terrarium, there was the vivid—and inconvenient—spectacle of people getting spiked. We don't know how many there were exactly, but Cobb surely speared at least a dozen or so along the way—and I'm not talking here about accidents. He drew blood from his boyhood idol, third baseman Bill Bradley, and helped knock the A's from the 1909 pennant race by spiking their promising young shortstop, Jack Barry, so badly that he missed a couple of crucial weeks. Ossie Bluege, a third baseman for the Washington Senators, remembered a time when he and his shortstop had Cobb hopelessly trapped between second and third: "I walked up the line toward shortstop with the ball in my hand, in a little bit of a crouch to tag him and he just threw himself at me with spikes in the air. He didn't slide. He just took off and came at me in midair, spikes first, about four or five feet off the ground, so help me just like a rocket. He hit me in the upper part of my arm, and cut my shirt sleeve."

Bluege made the play nevertheless. "I tagged him out, but I was so mad I was going to konk him with the ball while he was lying on the ground. Billy Evans was the umpire and I started to step on Cobb's toes and Evans pushed me away and said, 'Cobb you're out, and out of the ballgame.' The next day I was standing around the batting cage waiting my turn to hit when up walks Mr. Tyrus Raymond. Just as sweet as apple pie. He's apologizing."

"Son," he said, "I hope I didn't hurt you."

"I'm alright," I said.

"Good," he said. Then the look in his eyes changed just a little, his face got mean, and he said, "But remember—never come up the line for me."

The distinction was often too subtle to discern from a seat in the grandstand or a stool at a tavern where one might peruse an account of the previous day's game, but Cobb's spikings almost always came in the course of a larger and more philosophical dispute over right-of-way. "The base path belongs to the runner," he steadfastly maintained, sending notice that anyone who stood in "my little patch" in front of the bag was liable to be run into or upended and in the process hurt in any number of ways, spiking included.

"Cobb never spiked anybody," said Sam Crawford in *The Glory of Their Times*. "If the infielders get in the way, that's their lookout." Many—including infielders—agreed with him. "Ty was misunderstood," said the well-traveled AL first baseman "Tioga" George Burns, a few years after Cobb had retired. "People always thought he was going out of his way to spike people, but when the infield doesn't give the runner a piece of the bag to get into, he deserves to be spiked." Forty years later, contemplating the photo of their violent home plate encounter that has so often been used to indict Cobb, Krichell would say, "In a way, it was really my fault. I was standing in front of the plate, instead of on the side, where I could tag Ty as he slid in. But out of that mix-up I learned one thing: never stand directly in front of the plate when Cobb was roaring for home. If you did, it was at your own risk."

Cubs shortstop Joe Tinker said in 1910 that he was tired of hearing about Cobb "cutting down infielders while getting around the bases." "Why didn't he spike me when he had a chance in the world championship series? Simply because I know a base-runner's rights and stay in my place."

"Cobb slides hard," Tinker went on, "and a baseman ought to know enough to give him room. In some of the games of our World Series with

Detroit, Cobb slid into first and second so hard that he tore the bags out of place, and we didn't give him any more room than was coming to him, either."

That was the thing about Cobb that earned him the respect of the men whom he was barreling into: he didn't ask for anything special on the base path, just what was his, and he, like his victims, would accept the consequences of an ensuing collision. "I didn't get these marks riding elevators or sliding down banisters," Cobb said, "with a chuckle," in 1958 as he rolled up his pants cuffs for a *New York Times* reporter. "Even though I was referred to as a terror on the baselines, these scars proved the boys of my day gave as good as they received."

"Cobb could take it," said Charley O'Leary, the Tigers shortstop from 1904 to 1912. "When a fielder would give him an elbow or a knee, or knock him a half dozen yards, he didn't come up crying or appealing to an umpire. No sir. Whenever they'd spike him, and they cut him many times, he didn't get out of the game for a week or so. Nothing like that for him. He'd rush to the clubhouse between innings, doctor his injury himself [often with a wad of chewing tobacco, of which he had begun to occasionally partake], and then come dashing out on the field."

Steve O'Neill of the Naps once favored Cobb with the greatest compliment a catcher can give. "He came home on a base hit and I was blocking the plate. I got him in the kidneys and knocked him out. When he came to he didn't say a word. He just got up and limped out to his position."

If you asked Cobb if he'd ever spiked anyone on purpose he would usually say no, definitely not, and that he was deeply proud of the fact. "I-am-not-a-spiker!" he said, emphasizing each word, in an interview he gave as an old man, wearing a ratty red bathrobe. Every once in a while, though, when he was in a more expansive mood, he would say yes, in fact, he had indeed spiked some men intentionally "but only three." Then he would tick off the names. The strange thing was that each time he recited his list it was a little different. Over the years it included Hobe Ferris, Lou Criger, Cy Morgan, Billy Sullivan, Frank Isbell, Jack Warner, and Dutch Leonard—but *only* those three, understand?

At no time did he ever put John Franklin "Home Run" Baker among the men he had intentionally spiked.

CHAPTER EIGHTEEN

THE FAMOUS BAKER SPIKING INCIDENT, as it quickly came to be called, happened on Tuesday, August 24, 1909, a day of 90 degree heat, in a game between the Tigers and the Athletics at Detroit's Bennett Park. It tends to verify everything said in the previous chapter about Cobb and the early-twentieth-century cranks in regard to base running, with the exception of the notion about him being a player people loved to hate. At some point in the story, the action shifts to Philadelphia, where you didn't have to be a visiting opponent to experience vitriol. They just hated you there, without necessarily loving to do so. This is the town where people later threw D-cell batteries at Phillies outfielder Dick Allen and snowballs at Santa Claus. In Philadelphia, a small but vocal minority of the fans hated Cobb plain and simple. They threatened to kill him for what he had done to Frank Baker, even though he hadn't done very much. In the end their anger helped the story spill out of the sports pages and into the general conversation.

Connie Mack's Athletics were one game up on the Tigers in the AL standings when they pulled into steamy Detroit in late August of '09, though the Tiges were on a five-game winning streak during which Cobb was batting over .600. Navin and Jennings had recently revamped their team, sending Claude Rossman to St. Louis for first baseman Tom Jones and Germany Schaefer to Washington for Jim Delahanty—the infield that had brought the Tigers to their first World Series in 1907 was now completely gone. The Tigers were a less quirky, more businesslike team now, and it was going to be a crucial three-game series—all of which makes it hard to explain the home club's behavior in the first inning of the first game, for which an above-average-size crowd of 9,700 had gathered.

Judging by bemused contemporary accounts, neither Cobb nor his team-mates seemed to be concentrating very intently. Davy Jones led off with a single, moved to second on a sacrifice bunt—then, with Cobb taking a pitch, inexplicably broke for third where he was, said Joe S. Jackson, "snared easily" by a peg from catcher Paddy Livingston to Frank Baker. Then Cobb walked, stole second—and just as inexplicably lit out for third as Crawford took ball four. Livingston's throw had him out easily, but as Cobb slid in, twisting away from Baker, he scraped the fielder's exposed right forearm with his right spike. Baker, who had a reputation for being "spikes shy," had been standing a foot or so off the base, toward left field, keeping the running lane open, but then he leaned back awkwardly into Cobb's "little patch" and wound up tagging him ahead of the base, on the shoe or ankle, as he simultaneously incurred the deadball era's most controversial wound.

It was decidedly small and superficial, as controversial wounds go. Though the call had gone their way, Baker and Mack complained to the umpires about Cobb's method of sliding, the former stomping around to relieve—or perhaps dramatize—the pain. No one was ejected, or even admonished; the A's trainer trotted out and treated Baker's cut and the game resumed a few minutes later with him seeming fine despite his ban-dage. In the end it was an exciting contest in which the Tigers came from behind in the seventh inning—with Cobb knocking in the tying run and scoring the go-ahead one—to win 7–6. (Baker was 0-for-4 for the day.) Jackson's *Free Press* account led with the happy news that the Tigers and A's were now tied atop the standings. He didn't even mention the little brouhaha between Cobb and Baker at third.

That was hardly the end of it, though. Most Philadelphians, in those days before radio, didn't hear about what happened until the next day, but when the reports trickled in the A's cranks ran the gamut from annoyed to downright murderous. Baker, who like Cobb turned twenty-three that year, was a sweet dull farm boy from Trappe, Maryland, whom Connie Mack had found swinging for the fences of the Class B Reading Pretzels. Although he didn't get the nickname "Home Run" until he hit two in the World Series of 1911, a year in which he led the league with 11, he was a Pop Anson–style power hitter who seemed well suited to help the improving AL franchise for years to come. Operating with a paucity of good information about the "spiking," some A's rooters became convinced that Cobb had practically disemboweled Baker with his "armored shoes," as the outraged *Chicago Tribune* called them, thereby dimming their hopes for a third pennant. That was hitting a Philadelphian where it hurt.

No one was madder, or fake-madder, than Connie Mack, who the next day made a long, fiery speech to the papers about Cobb and how it was his "second nature to act mean on the ball field." "I would not have him on my team for nothing," said the man who had once overseen a raucous Pittsburgh Pirates club and would one day pay Cobb a sweet sum to play for him. "He boasted before the game that he would get some of the Athletics," Mack went on, disingenuously. "He made good by spiking Baker and all but cutting the legs off [second baseman Eddie] Collins [whom Cobb had upended while stretching a single into a double in the seventh inning. Jackson had written that afterward "Collins was game and made no kick"]. I think he gets up in the morning with a grouch on and it sticks on him all day. Then when the game is on he gives vent to his feeling by making trouble. He may be a great player, but he is a pinhead in this respect." After hearing Mack's side of the story, and only Mack's, AL president Ban Johnson dashed off a letter to Cobb saying he "must stop this sort of playing or you will have to quit the game." The *Chicago Tribune* denounced Cobb on its editorial page, saying, "Everyone likes a winner, but there are ethics to be considered besides mere victory, and no action on the ball field can be more contemptible than the willingness to injure an opponent." The venerable *Boston Globe* sportswriter Tim Murnane called Cobb "a butcher."

Predictably, the Detroit press rushed to Cobb's defense. Jackson said the A's were "crybabies" and added, "the real players don't run to the bench and tell their managers about the naughty boys every time they get mussed in a mix up." Paul Bruske said that "Connie Mack made a tactical error—he put it into his players' minds that they are in danger of bodily injury in the heat of such a series." Jennings called Mack "a squealer" and noted he had a history of blaming others whenever his pennant hopes started collapsing. In 1902 he had accused St. Louis of using a "buzzer" (a signal for conveying stolen catcher's signs from the scoreboard to the batter) when his team lost four straight to the Browns, and five years later he charged umpire Silk O'Loughlin with "crookedness" after the A's lost a large lead in the famous 17-inning game that ended in a tie. "Now he makes one more holler by accusing Cobb of injuring one of his players," Jennings said. As for Ban Johnson, "He ought to find enough to do looking after the basic league business. He has no right to criticize Cobb in the manner he has without first getting a statement from the player."

The public was left to imagine what would happen when the Tigers next stopped in Philadelphia, about three weeks later, on September 16. In the meantime, Cobb's statement came. "It was most ungentlemanly of Mack to go to the newspapers knocking me," he said in an open letter published in a number of dailies and weeklies.

> He goes around with the salve in one hand and a pile driver in the other and expects to get away with everything. Mack knows I have never spiked a man deliberately. And he also knows that the runner is entitled to the line. If the baseman gets in the way he is taking his own chances. When I slid I made for the bag. If the man with the ball is in the way he is apt to get hurt. But that is his lookout. He has no business on the line. It is a plain case of squeal with Mack. In Philadelphia [the 17-inning game] when they were seven runs to the good and we had no chance to win, both [Jack] Barry and Collins dove into Schaefer and tried to put him out. And Collins did get [Oscar] Stanage and put him out for a week. But we didn't holler. That is baseball. If we get hurt, we take our medicine and don't go around crying over it. Collins is all right. He tried to block me off Tuesday but I dumped him. He didn't say a word because he knew that I was right. He goes into the bases the same way I do and he's hurt as many men as I have.

Collins was notably silent as the controversy swirled, and some years later he admitted he didn't support Mack's sentiments. ("I want to correct the erroneous impression that Cobb deliberately went out of his way to spike opposing players," said the second baseman. "It just wasn't so. His spikes left their marks on countless players, but that was because he was such an aggressive, victory-hungry player. If anyone blocked his way a collision was inevitable. He was an elusive slider who frequently slid away from a tag rather than adopt football tactics.") Even Baker lay low and issued no statements as Cobb drew ardent endorsements from the *Cincinnati Enquirer* and Chicago Cubs owner Charles Murphy, who told a Pittsburgh reporter,

> *Connie Mack is sore, and you know what a sore man will say. Ty Cobb is not a dirty baseball player. No one ever observed his playing closer than I did during the last two world championship series, and if there had been anything of the "dirty" ballplayer in his makeup he surely would have brought it to the front then, when there was so much at stake. I never saw Cobb make a move that would lead one to believe that he even contemplated an act that wasn't clean baseball. True, Cobb slides feet first, but that is one of the points of the game. He is not the only player who slides feet first and does it aggressively.*

In the wake of those supportive words, the *Detroit Daily News* produced the ultimate defense of the city's favorite son: a photograph of the disputed play taken just a few feet from Bennett Park's third base. Action photos were relatively rare in those days, and seldom preserved a particularly auspicious situation, but this one showed Cobb's unthreatening fade-away slide in crisp detail, and it exonerated him completely. Frank Navin sent it to Ban Johnson with a testy letter:

> *All this talk about Cobb spiking base runners is "rot." If you can tell me a player who has been put out of the game by Cobb during the time he has been with our Club, with the one exception of [Ed] Bradley, I will be glad to have you do so. . . . Fortunately, we have a picture of the game he made the wail about, and I am enclosing it. You will notice that Cobb is trying to get away from the base-runner [sic], and not sliding for him. Cobb is on the inside of the bag. Any of the players will tell you that Cobb makes a fall-away slide and does not slide directly into the bag at all, while if he had any intention of getting any player he would drive directly for him. I think a great injustice has been done to Cobb in this matter.*

Dozens of newspapers across America, including the *Sporting News* and *Sporting Life*, splashed the picture across several columns. Still, some Philadelphians remained unimpressed. Over the next few days, Cobb received several threats including a "black hand letter" advising him that he would be shot by a sniper if he ever dared take his position again at Shibe Park in Philadelphia.

The Baker incident helps us understand that the modern myth about Cobb being universally reviled in his day isn't true. Connie Mack's statement triggered more expressions of support than I can include here without redundancy. But the events of that season also yield clues about Cobb's inner self. The wad of tobacco he took out of his mouth to use as a poultice, the curses he flung back at cranks who taunted him, the firmness he showed in his response to Mack, a man whom he like almost everyone else in baseball held in childlike awe—all of these things suggest that Cobb, at twenty-three, was losing his innocence.

Certainly, it would have been impossible just a season or so earlier to imagine Cobb walking somewhat unsteadily into the Euclid Hotel in Cleveland at about 2:15 a.m. after a dinner with a bunch of show business types, as he did nine days after the Baker incident, on Friday, September 3, 1909. The events of that dark morning are frequently presented as further evidence of Cobb's racism—but they shouldn't be because no one involved in the story was black. But more about that in a moment. Let us first sketch the agreed-upon facts.

On the afternoon of the previous day, the (pennant-contending) Tigers and the (thoroughly mediocre) Naps played to a rain-abbreviated tie. Detroit's 14-game winning streak was still intact, though, the club was still in first place by a few games, and Cobb, who had averaged more than one stolen base per game during the streak, was hitting a league-leading .362—so on balance he couldn't have felt too despondent. That evening he and several of his teammates went together to the Euclid Avenue Opera House to see George M. Cohan's latest musical, *The Man Who Owns Broadway*, then working its way to New York City. After the show Cobb dined at the luxurious Hollenden Hotel with Vaughan Glaser, an actor and producer who had approached him about the possibility of doing a stage show in the off-season, and an actress from Glaser's theater company named Fay Courteney, a soignée San Francisco brunette. (It's likely that Cohan, who liked to hang around with ballplayers—and who bet heavily on baseball—joined the group, but that Cobb chose to keep him out of what became a messy situation. Cohan later said he had met Cobb and other Tigers that day, and that he considered him "a real Yankee Doodle boy of the only Yankee Doodle game and better than anyone they have around the red, white and blue ball lots.") Cobb left the Hollenden at 1:30 a.m. he said, and went straight to the plainer Euclid.

There was considerable disagreement over what happened next. The Euclid's manager, Fred Avery, said that Cobb was "roaring drunk" when he arrived, and couldn't find his room. While admitting that he had begun to take a beer now and then, Cobb denied being intoxicated, and said he found a note at the front desk informing him that some teammates were playing poker and shooting craps in a room on the second floor, should he care to join them. He said he asked the bellhop to take him up on the elevator, but the kid said that considering the hour he could take Cobb only to his own room, on the third floor, and not to anyone else's. They argued about this for a bit, and then the bellboy stalked off, or tried to. "As he turned away," Cobb later told the *Sporting News*, "I seized his coat sleeve and said, 'Hold on here. I'm a guest at this hotel and it's your business to do what I ask you.'"

This tense exchange was merely the curtain-raiser. At that moment, Cobb said, "the watchman or house detective came up, and wanted to know what I was doing. An argument started between us which ended with the watchman striking me behind the ear. We grappled and fell to the floor of the lobby. The other fellow had his finger in my left eye and I could not get away. I was afraid he was going to ruin my eye. I had one hand free, and finally got out my silver penknife and raked him across the back of the hand with it. Then I got loose." In an interview given separately to the *Chicago Tribune*, Cobb added, "as he backed toward the grill room entrance he drew a gun and covered me. Holding the gun in one hand, he walked up and struck me several times with his billy. He asked the clerk who I was and the clerk said he didn't know."

The forty-seven-year-old watchman, George Stanfield, told a tale even more Grand Guignol:

When I came to the elevator I found that Cobb had struck the elevator boy. He began calling me vile names. I struck him. We sparred, and then my foot slipped and I fell, striking my head against the elevator grating. Cobb was on me in an instant saying, "I'll kill you now." I felt the sting of the knife. The blood welled up from under my collar from a deep cut on my shoulder. It dripped down into my eyes from a gash in the scalp. Through the blood I saw his hand descending to my face, and I threw up my left hand to shield my face. The knife blade passed clear through it. I threw him off and started backing away, flourishing a gun. I seized my club from the hotel desk and struck a blow that brought him to his knees. I struck him again and he raised his hands above his head and begged me not to kill him.

In the game he played about twelve hours later, Cobb, swollen and barely scabbed over, was 3-for-4 against the Naps' journeyman righty Cy Falkenberg—but that is a mere fun fact. The more important question is, Did the Euclid Hotel incident have racial overtones? Do those fights reveal Cobb's virulent bigotry, as has long been alleged?

In Charles Alexander's 1984 *Ty Cobb* and Al Stump's 1992 *Cobb: A Biography*, as well as virtually every other book, article, Internet posting, or doctoral thesis about racism in sports of fairly recent vintage, the Euclid bellboy and George Stanfield are described as black or, when a white author wants to drive home his sensitivity, African American. But how do we know their race? In none of the several hundred accounts that appeared in newspapers across the country in the days following the incident is the bellboy's full name given, and not once is he referred to as a Negro. Can we assume that all bellboys of that day were black? Common sense, old photographs, and federal census records tell us no, we cannot. Sifting through the latter I found a white teenager who lived a few blocks from the Euclid and gave his occupation (in 1910) as bellboy. Even if George H. Skelly, as he was called, is not the kid that Cobb argued with, his existence confirms that there were white people in the trade. That the Euclid's bellboy wasn't black, though, we can be all but certain because no one at the time said he was.

Anyone familiar with early-twentieth-century journalism knows that the word "Negro" was then considered a flavor-enhancer beyond compare, a semantic spice stirred into stories and headlines at every opportunity. NEGRO ASSAULTS WOMAN beat WOMAN ASSAULTED six ways from Sunday. TRAIN KILLS NEGRO was inarguably better than even the not-bad DEATH ON THE RAILS. In secondary references the black person might become a "coon," "pick" (or "pickaninny"), "darkie," or "Ethiopian," even in the mainstream press. When Cobb had his run-ins with groundskeeper Henry Cummings and street worker Fred Collins, the papers could not stop reminding readers that those fellows were not Caucasian. But in the sea of clippings that mention the bellboy at the Euclid there is, as I've said, nary a "Negro."

But what of George Stanfield? If we can be 98 percent certain about the junior member of the night staff, the watchman is a sure thing. Not only was Stanfield never referred to as a Negro by the newspapers, his race on the federal census report of 1910 is given as white.

Yet Charles Alexander's Cobb biography, published seventy-five years after the incident says that both the bellhop and the night watchman were black. I asked Alexander via email where he got his information about the Euclid pair and he said simply that it was in the contemporary accounts. But it isn't. (He also in his book calls Stanfield "Stansfield.") Worse yet, you will hear, as I have quite a few times (though not from Alexander), that Cobb stabbed to death a young black waiter in Cleveland for "being uppity." This is merely the original Euclid Hotel tale distorted almost beyond recogniton after numerous retellings.

Once news of the assault broke, midway through a doubleheader on September 4, reporters mobbed the clubhouse at Cleveland's League Park in pursuit of Cobb, but after the Naps beat the Tigers in both ends of the twin bill, Hughie snuck him out a side door, and he and his teammates boarded a train for St. Louis. There once again we see Cobb thriving on— or at least in the midst of—adversity. On September 5, he was indicted by a Cleveland grand jury on the not insignificant charge of assault with intent to murder and Stanfield announced he was suing him for $5,000. That same afternoon, in the third inning of the first game against the Browns, Cobb, though still bandaged heavily, walked, stole second and third, and came home on a bobbled infield grounder; five innings later he scooped up a sinking liner and without breaking stride drilled the ball home to nail the sliding runner as the Tigers beat St. Louis 5–1.

• • •

Before he could get back to Cleveland to face the justice system, Cobb had Philadelphia, and Frank Baker, to deal with. The first people to enter Shibe Park on Thursday, September 16, for the Tigers' first game there since the Incident were 400 policemen, sent by the city to provide extra security. No one was being casual about the threats to Cobb. Visiting teams usually put on their uniforms in their hotels in those days, and rode to ballparks in open wagons or buses known as "tally-hos" as a way of publicizing the game, circus-train style. Feeling that practice was too dangerous under the circumstances, Jennings had his men dress in mufti and travel in taxis and cars to the A's new stadium, where Connie Mack was letting them share his locker room. (Cobb's car had a motorcycle escort.) The Tigers manager asked the players to assemble at noon (the game was scheduled for 3:30) in the lobby of the Aldine, but when he came downstairs he found them in the hotel's music room, pluckily practicing what Jackson called "a little ragtime chorus" to keep their spirits up. Hughie made a brief speech about "the seriousness of the situation" and told them that they should be on their guard, even though their hosts had banned the sale of soft drinks (beer was never available) to minimize the number of flying bottles.

To almost everyone's surprise, loud applause greeted Cobb when he stepped on the field for pregame practice. It came not from the lowlifes in the 50-cent grandstand seats, the *Detroit Free Press* assured its readers, but from the people of obvious breeding in the dollar-a-seat upper tier. Overall, the mood remained tense, though. Before the game started, Davy Jones got into a shoving match with A's outfielder Danny Murphy, and the two had to be separated. Feeling the stares of the more than 27,000 who turned out despite a steady drizzle, Cobb looked jumpy and was, leaping a foot or two in the air when a car on the street backfired while he was standing in right field, trying to seem nonchalant. He went hitless in four trips to the plate that day, striking out twice—once, in the third inning, with the bases full. Jackson attributed his bad game to his "high nervous tension. No ballplayer who had read so much and heard so much about what was to be done to him on a certain day, who had received in his mail a dozen threatening letters, and who could look around a ball field and see several hundred extra policemen there to protect him, could be expected to go up to the plate and concentrate his entire attention upon the game." Referring to the final outcome—a 2–1 victory by the A's that brought them within three games of the league-leading Tigers—he concluded, "the trouble Connie Mack started cost today's game."

The Philadelphians couldn't come to a consensus on how to treat Cobb. That evening, hundreds of them gathered outside the Aldine Hotel and did their best to look like an angry mob, but when at twilight Cobb sauntered out for his evening constitutional, cigar in hand, the crowd parted and allowed him to walk through unmolested. He himself once said, "I always find that I have less trouble with people when I'm in street clothes."

The next day even the sight of the old-school Tigers uniform—they were the last club to abandon the chippy-looking standup collars—failed to set the locals on edge. The audience of almost 28,000 was cheerful, even silly. In the bleachers, men engaged in the boyish fad of gleefully demolishing each other's straw hats. Some 200 boaters were destroyed, said one paper. Down on the field, Cobb seemed to exhale. He bunted for two hits and knocked in a run with a sacrifice fly. After he stole third in the first inning, Baker shook his hand to show that he had no lingering resentment, and Shibe Park shook with cheers. In the fourth inning, Cobb made a spectacular fielding play on a "line fly" hit by Harry Davis. "He could not locate the ball until it was just about to pass over his head," Jackson wrote. "Then he jumped into the air, grabbed the ball with one hand and came down against the crowd, clinging to the sphere," and saving a "sure double." After that, not even the Tiger's 5–3 win could sour the mood. When the game was over, hundreds charged onto the field to pat Cobb's back and shake his hand. Baker told the reporters that his injury had been exaggerated and that he never really had a problem with the Tigers star.

Cobb would manage only two hits over the next two games, both of which the A's won. The crowd at the first of them, played on a Saturday, was given as 35,000, which if true made it one of the largest ever in Philadelphia. No one misbehaved and nothing especially interesting happened that day, or until the fourth inning of the Monday finale, when Cobb, in the process of stealing second, slid hard into shortstop Jack Barry and badly sliced his left leg. There was a moment of silence. Then as Barry limped off the field to get stitches—he would be out for the rest of the season—he gestured to show that he held no grudge against Cobb, and that he considered the injury an accident. The crowd erupted and Cobb stood sheepishly, receiving their ovation. Their attitude toward him would change, and change again, over the years, but in the meantime Cobb must have felt whipsawed after a long weekend that he had started out as a marked man.

Christy Mathewson was probably as popular as Cobb at the time, but no one was simultaneously as popular and unpopular as young Tyrus. In every American League city except Detroit he was at once the dreaded enemy and the biggest draw. He created both internal conflict—should I boo this fellow or appreciate him?—as well as arguments between two separate cranks sharing the same stadium armrest. Ultimately, though, you had to give Cobb his due. In 1909, making good on his pledge to improve on his league-leading batting average of .323 the season before, he had not only his best year to date, but the best year anyone ever had in the history of organized baseball. He topped both leagues with a .377 average, and led the AL in hits (216), runs (116), runs batted in (107), stolen bases (76), home runs (9), and total bases (296). He was also— along with Sam Crawford (.314) and pitchers George Mullin (29–8, with a 2.22 era), Ed Willett (21–10; 2.34), and Ed Summers (19–9; 2.24)— a piston in the engine that kept the Tigers in first place for all but a few days of the 1909 season, and powered them to their third consecutive pennant.

The Tigers played the Pirates that year in the kind of World Series that sets up well for hungover sportswriters because of its obvious parallels. You didn't have think too hard to see that Pittsburgh was, if anything, even more dominant in the National League than Detroit was in theirs, winning 110 games that year to the Tigers' 98. In Honus Wagner it had a marquee star who had almost all of Cobb's ability (and none of his charisma). It even had a resident bad boy in outfielder-manager Fred Clarke, who got arrested a few days after Cobb's Euclid Hotel fight for running into the stands at Forbes Field and pushing a fifty-two-year-old heckler down a flight of concrete stairs. (The papers referred to it as "another Cobb case.") The scribes hyped the Cobb-Wagner showdown as if it were the Jack Johnson–Jim Jeffries fight that everyone wanted to happen. If you believed the advance stories, this series wouldn't merely decide the world championship, it would settle the question of who was the game's best player.

In the end, the most interesting thing the public learned was that seven games do not necessarily a memorable Fall Classic make. The Tigers somehow pushed the Series to the limit without ever seeming like they believed they could win it, constantly clunking up from behind, like a horse cart trailing behind a car in heavy traffic. Crowds of diminishing size sat in 30 degree dampness watching games played out with the inevitability of the Oberammergau passion play, or so it seems in retrospect, the vantage point from which baseball can best be tortured into something like narrative coherence. Almost nobody was at his best. The Pirates made 12 errors along the way, the Tigers 17. The umpires made bad calls and, even though there were four of them on the field simultaneously for the first time, at least once had to seek the testimony of spectators about where a ball landed.

Detroit's real problem turned out not to be Wagner, though he batted .333, but a rookie right-hander named Charles Benjamin "Babe" Adams, whom Fred Clarke named as the surprise game one starter. ("It was expected Clarke would use his number-one pitcher Howard Camnitz," Fred Lieb wrote, "but the Kentucky Rosebud was just recovering from an attack of quinsy.") In the first inning of the opener the Missouri farm boy—who'd gone 12–3 that year, with an ERA of 1.11—appeared nervous, walking Davy Jones and Cobb—but he got a grip and held Detroit to six hits in a complete game 4–1 victory. With Bill Donovan pitching in game two, the Tigers won by a score of 7–2 as Cobb stole home to cap a three-run rally in the third inning and later singled. In game three Cobb had a single, a double, and two RBI, but Wagner had three hits, three RBI, and three stolen bases as the Pirates retook the lead in the Series with an 8–6 win. George Mullin evened things up again in game four by throwing a five-hit shutout in which Cobb had a double that knocked in two runs (final score: 5–0). In game five Adams threw another six-hitter and, aided by Clarke's three-run seventh-inning homer, again beat Detroit, this time 8–4.

Game six had the fewest witness—just 10,535 came to freezing Bennett Park—but the most suspense; after getting roughed up for three runs in the first inning Mullin settled down and pitched the Tigers to a tense 5–4 win. Cobb hit a double in that game that knocked in Davy Jones, but it was his last hit in the series. He was 0-for-4 in the final as Adams scattered his by now signature six hits and tossed a shutout, while the Pirates scored eight. Maybe Cobb's ability to feed off adversity finally failed him. Perhaps that still festering mess in Cleveland weighed too heavily on his mind. Maybe he was worn out by the extra-long railroad route he and his wife Charlie had to take every time the scene shifted from Detroit to Pittsburgh and back, to avoid Ohio, where there was a warrant out for his arrest. But for whatever reason, it was another weak World Series performance for the game's best hitter, who batted just .231.

Did these annual fall fizzles bother Cobb? They must have, though because teams scatter as soon as the Series ends, and the scribes were probably hesitant to broach the subject in the first place, there are virtually no statements from him on the subject. The one disappointment about the 1909 series that he *did* discuss regarded a story that started circulating the following spring. In the first inning of the first game, it was said, Cobb, after being walked by Adams, shouted down toward Wagner, "Hey, Krauthead, I'm coming in on the next pitch!" And when he did slide in as promised, an angry Wagner supposedly tagged him hard on the face, dislodging several teeth. The story was fiction based on an incident that occurred four innings later, when Cobb, without verbal warning, stole second with a fade away slide and Wagner accidentally brushed his face with his glove, causing a split lip that had to be attended to by the team trainer (Cobb stayed in the game). Cobb and Wagner became friends during that Series and made the first of several off-season hunting trips soon afterward. Both denied that any taunting, or dental damage, had occurred that day in Pittsburgh, but for a certain kind of fan it was a feel-good story about a jerk who gets his comeuppance and thus was very hard to discredit. Indeed the tale was still being repeated in 1958, when an exasperated Cobb told the *New York Times*, "That story about me and

Hans Wagner simply never happened. Yet only recently I met Wagner's daughter and she looked at me like I was some kind of ogre."

If things you *don't* do in the Series stay with you for decades, imagine the import of the things you do. Babe Adams's postseason performance in 1909 was why, when he died in 1968, the town of Mount Moriah, Missouri, put a large black granite monument on his grave. He didn't just beat the Tigers that fall, he broke their hearts. They came away feeling not like they had gotten closer than ever to being world champions but also like they could never surpass the best NL club. They'd lost their *joie de guerre*. Instead of praising Hughie for getting the team as far as he had, Navin groused about his manager to the press, saying (as owners do when they don't know what else to say) that he hadn't been enough of a disciplinarian.

Cobb couldn't settle in for the off-season back home in Georgia until he dealt with the Cleveland case. When the news of it had first broken, Navin had told him to relax and focus on baseball, that the Tigers would take care of everything, including legal fees—and Cobb promptly sank back into the warm bath of special benefits that has been obligingly drawn for elite athletes ever since. (Edmund S. Burke, a former director of the Federal Reserve Bank of Cleveland and a prominent polo player, came forward to pay Cobb's $500 bond.) Since the day he was charged in early September, his team of lawyers had labored to make the problem go away, but only partially succeeded. In return for $115, George Stanfield agreed to withdraw his civil suit and stop pressing criminal charges. The paltriness of the settlement, though, disgusted and enraged Ohio authorities, who vowed to prosecute Cobb with or without help from Stanfield.

On October 20, Cobb returned to Cleveland for the first time since the incident—the Tigers had no games scheduled there after September 4—and pleaded not guilty to a charge of felonious assault. While maintaining his innocence, and telling the press that he had hurt himself more with his knife than he'd hurt Stanfield, he seemed something between exasperated and frightened about the effect the case could have on his on- and off-field lives. He thought his reputation as a heedless brawler was feeding off itself and taking on a life of its own. "The accidental spiking of Baker this summer was taken to make me out as a reckless, rowdy ballplayer, going around with a chip on my shoulder," he told the *Sporting News*. "That spiking was accidental and nobody worried over it more than I did. Then this trouble came along and I'm upset. I wanted to go into the automobile business in Augusta this winter but now I'm so worried I don't know what I'll do."

At his sentencing a few weeks later, though, his mood appeared to have shifted. Now he seemed cocky, perhaps because a deal had been struck for him to plead guilty to a (much) lesser charge of simple assault. To the chagrin of his lawyers, Cobb, while on the stand, pulled out the silver penknife that he had used in his fight with the night watchman—he'd been allowed to keep it, rules about evidence being somewhat looser then—and, while extolling its virtues, proudly held it aloft for all to admire. When the judge gaveled down a $100 fine, Cobb patted his pockets and said he didn't have that much money on him, but (should one assume a wink here?) he would surely drop by and make good on the debt the next time the Tigers came through Cleveland the following season. His lead lawyer then jumped up and begged the court's permission to send a check by messenger in a few hours.

In an interview with the *Detroit Times*, Navin tried to frame the Euclid incident as an educational experience. "Cobb has a hot temper and, when provoked as he was, he simply let it run away with him as a whole lot of people would, when discretion would have been the better part of valor. He's learning right along now how to master himself and I don't think he will get mixed up in another affair of this kind." (At another time, though, the owner said, "If Cobb were less impetuous, he would be less valuable to the club.") Cobb, continuing to make light of things, said, with a smile, that he was through battling. "The next man that wants to fight me will have to be able to run faster than I!"

Something was happening with Cobb at the end of his fourth full season. He seemed to be trying on different personalities to see how they felt—the old question of how to *be* in the world as a famous ballplayer—and for those around him it was hard at any point to gauge how much he was pretending. Maybe this was just a function of his getting older, and losing his innocence as he did. Or maybe the praise of lordly types like

Charles Comiskey was starting to have an effect. Comiskey, the founding president of the White Sox, had recently written an article for the *New York Times* declaring Cobb the greatest player in history. "He plays ball with his whole anatomy—with his head, his arms, his hands, his legs, his feet—and he plays ball all the time for all that it is to him." Cobb, sounding modest, called Comiskey's piece "the greatest compliment I ever received in my life," but it was difficult to shrug off such rhapsodies, if even you wanted to. Once he'd had a conscious desire to appear humble—if not to opposing pitchers, then to the public. "Many was the time," he said, "that I would walk out to my position in the outfield with my head down and my shoulders hunched to show people in the stands that I didn't have a swelled head." Now maybe not so much.

CHAPTER NINETEEN

LITTLE DAVID SILVER AND HIS pal little Lester Elliott didn't think Cobb was so difficult to deal with.

When the Augusta, Georgia, YMCA held a dinner to honor Cobb in January of 1910, those two boys, both age eleven and sons of local merchants, proposed to work for free, as servers, so they could get close to their hometown hero. They got their wish and Cobb wound up shaking their hands, and when he found out how they'd finagled their way in, he insisted that they sit down and eat, and before the evening ended, said the *Augusta Chronicle*, he came by and "visited" with David and Lester for a while, in the relaxed Southern way, pulling up a chair and chatting with them at their table. Afterward, the boys were said to be "as happy as happy can be."

Cobb liked children, as most people do. This needs to be said because in his 1994 *Cobb,* Al Stump portrays his subject as a cackling skinflint who ignored kids' letters and steamed the one- and two-penny stamps off the self-addressed return envelopes they had enclosed in the vain hope of a reply. Stump was heavy-handed and melodramatic with his imaginary details, but he had an almost unerring sense of what some readers would thrill to—namely, a monster in superstar's clothing. It is, I must admit, a compelling idea, and a reputation for being a kind of seriously unfunny W. C. Fields has become a part of the Cobb myth ever since. The truth is less fascinating. The real Cobb treated young fans as they should be treated, often talking at length to the ones he met in person, and answering virtually every piece of fan mail, even if it sometimes took him a couple of months to get to a particular question or request. Photographs show him bobbing in a sea of children, pen in hand, smiling—a familiar

sports hero pose that has been struck over the years by many. His standard speech to high school students contained these lines: "Whatever
you undertake, do with all your might. Work hard, play hard. There is
no discredit to being beaten by a stronger opponent, but you should see
that there are none stronger than you, if that be possible." When he was
appearing in Atlanta with *The College Widow* in late 1911, and he heard
about a local boy who wanted to see the show but couldn't because he was
seriously ill, Cobb went to the home of nine-year-old George Weyman,
sat at his bedside, posed for family photographs and "promised to send
him three balls which he has played in the big league games," said the
Chronicle. (Little Georgie bounced back and became a bond trader.)

We know from letters sold at auction that when a child asked for his
autograph, he would sometimes provide it (in his trademark green ink)
along with a picture or brochure containing hitting tips, and a note of
apology for including the unsolicited stuff. He would always say he was
honored by the request. Letters Cobb sent in response to kids' questions
run as long as five pages. "I would not advise any boy to play big league
ball unless he is sure of himself," he would sometimes say, "and can with-
stand the temptations offered him every day." To a boy named Tyrus Dahl
he once wrote, "I am honored you have the same name as I and my only
hope is that you will be able to live up under the handicap." In 1953,
while serving as a guest instructor at a baseball camp in the Ozarks, he
struck up a mentoring relationship with a Canadian boy named Koosma
Tarasoff, who he thought might have major league potential. Over the
course of three years, Cobb sent him long, thoughtful letters about life
and baseball and paid his way to his home in Menlo Park, California,
to give him personal instruction. He eventually got the teenager a tryout with the Pittsburgh Pirates. It didn't go well, and Cobb was "disappointed," Tarasoff recalled in 2004, but his failure didn't end their
closeness. "Sure, I heard Cobb had a bad Irish temper, but he was a good
human being and I think his actions show things."

Cobb's interactions with adults were without question more complicated
and less consistently pleasant. Someone whose golden rule is "put up a
mental hazard for the other fellow" is by definition not always going to

be easy to be around. I suspect that if we were able to put the question to Tigers president Frank Navin of whether he was difficult he would say, "Definitely, no." Then he would get back to us a short time later to say, "Actually, yes."

Navin was Cobb's boss, the man who negotiated the Tigers contracts, and in their day (and beyond) Cobb had a reputation as a hard bargainer that was not entirely deserved. His salary holdouts raised eyebrows and made headlines, and his prolonged negotiation of 1913 would be characterized by decidedly harsh language on both sides, but the record shows that those things didn't happen very often. We have already seen how, feeling contrite about hitting a mere .324 in 1908, he became an easy mark for a shrewd businessman like Navin and reupped without comment for what he had been paid the previous season. Most Januarys, salary talks between Cobb and the club were simply not necessary, and not just because the Dixie Demon could be surprisingly nonconfrontational. As stingy as he was, Navin understood that Cobb was by far the biggest draw in baseball, a man who had singlehandedly made the Tigers—still very much a small-market team—third in attendance in the American League. (Largely because of Cobb, he added 3,000 seats to Bennett Park in 1910, and would soon afterward build the new stadium.) Thus Cobb's happiness was tied directly to Navin's wealth.

But the team president also had a sentimental side, as he'd shown when Hughie wanted to trade his favorite player and Ban Johnson wanted to exile him. He saw Cobb as a kind of surrogate son, a once raw recruit who had blossomed under his care into something special, and for that reason, too, Navin didn't want to lose him. If Sam Crawford, the Tigers' second best player, groused about Cobb getting special treatment at contract time, and lots of other times, well, there was not much Navin could do about that. (Crawford was still grousing fifty years later, even after Cobb pulled strings to get him into the Hall of Fame.) Navin cared less about offending others on the team than about keeping Cobb happy. (Batting away Charlie Schmidt's complaints in 1909 he wrote, "Cobb drew more money than anyone on the team last year. He made a wonderful record and was entitled to what he got.")

"Ty Cobb Does as He Pleases, and Detroit Club Owner Grins" said one headline. The brief salary talks of January 1910 told the whole story. On that occasion, the boss, as an opening gambit, offered a three-year deal at $9,000 per, and the star reached for his fountain pen. The amount was more than ten times what the average government worker earned that year, and it made Cobb, at age twenty-four, the fourth-highest-paid player in baseball behind Nap Lajoie, a fourteen-year veteran who received $12,000, but had only a one-year contract, Christy Mathewson ($10,000), and Honus Wagner ($10,000). "I don't know how long I'm going to be in baseball," Navin told the *Pittsburgh Press*, "but I never expect to be lucky enough to pick up another Cobb. I am going to cling to him for as long as he stays in the game."

He would change his mind eventually, but not for quite a while.

Not that Cobb didn't try the boss's patience. What could make him most maddening, in fact, was his base path habit of refusing to follow the script. In March of 1910, two months after he and Navin had their frictionless accord, something any reasonable observer would have thought was the start of a new era of harmony and cooperation, he dragged and then dug in his heels about spring training, telling the owner, through the press, that he had better things to do than go to San Antonio (to which the Tigers in 1908 had moved their preseason headquarters, because Navin was able to secure a nightly rate at the Menger Hotel of $3 per man). Cobb was philosophically opposed to spring training. "Training trips are useless for the baseball player who takes care of himself," he said.

> For a man who is prone to taking on flesh or for players who do not keep themselves in condition over the winter, a training trip is all right, but there are any number of players in the big leagues to whom it is a detriment. They go south, and they take off more flesh than they really should. They work under a boiling sun, and they get tired out. When the time for the opening of the season comes, they are stale. For my part, I believe in doing light work throughout the winter and when spring comes a week with the team puts me in midseason form.

Topping the list of preferable pursuits for him in 1910 was tending to his first child, Ty Jr., born on January 30 of that year. Such a priority was difficult for the team president to publicly dispute, but Cobb also said that he couldn't leave his brand-new Hupmobile dealership in the hands of a subordinate, and would fine-tune his body—he'd been hunting and hiking in weighted boots the whole off-season as usual—by working out with his old team, the Augusta Tourists, and some "college boys" who were playing semi-organized games around town. That wasn't good enough for Jennings, who told the press that he was upset by Cobb's absence. Privately he told Cobb that, too, saying in a letter that "in justice to the club" he ought to do his best to reach San Antonio by April 1 (by which date he would be two weeks late). Cobb reluctantly agreed to the new deadline, then missed it. He didn't catch up with the club until about a week later, by which time it had reached Indianapolis on its barnstorming tour north. His punishment for missing training camp? Don't be silly. Navin had only just finished writing a check for $1,200 to cover legal fees in the Euclid Hotel case. Cobb had carte blanche.

Some of his teammates resented this, of course, but they felt outnumbered. The whole world loved Ty Cobb, it seemed, except for fans in rival cities who loved to hate him, and some of those loved him best of all. Rare was the copy of *Baseball* magazine that didn't have at least one story about the Georgia Peach. In the pages of *Sporting Life*, the sainted Nap Lajoie, a player's player and a simple man who said, "I just wait for the ball I want and then hit it," marveled at "the different method Ty uses in hitting against right- and left-handed pitchers, stepping into the delivery of one before the curve breaks, and waiting for the curve to show itself in the case of the other." The first child ever born in the hamlet of Erin, Tennessee, to a couple called Dan and Dossie Cobb, was christened Ty Raymond; a Thoroughbred racehorse was named after him, as was a pretty fair trotter; a Jewish featherweight boxer born Samuel Kolb changed his name to Young Ty Cobb. It wasn't until Elvis that another Southerner so captivated the entire nation.

In late May of 1910, while the Tigers were in Washington for a series against the Senators, Cobb was feted at a White House dinner by President William Howard Taft's top aide, the Georgia-born Archie Butt. (Cobb brought as his guest Tigers third baseman George Moriarity, who during the 1935 World Series as an umpire would distinguish himself by stalking over to the Chicago Cubs dugout and threatening to eject the entire team after some players had made anti-Semitic remarks to Tigers star Hank Greenberg.) The next day Cobb broke his rule about forgoing the midday meal to lunch at the Capitol with Vice President James S. Sherman. "If I don't do well this afternoon it will be chargeable to this delicious strawberry shortcake!" he joked, and one can imagine his teammates rolling their eyes and pretending to gag as they read the quote in the next day's paper. But unless a fellow Tiger made peace with Cobb's special status and Cobb's willingness to reap the benefits of it, it could be a very long season. Following the luncheon, President Taft sat in a steady rain to watch Detroit beat his hometown club 5–1. All of the players lined up to shake Taft's hand after the game, but only Cobb got a back-pat and a "Warm congratulations, Ty" from the president.

Of course, only Cobb, who got two hits that day, was hitting .370 something at the time.

Cobb's role on the team started changing in 1910, as the Tigers dropped back in the standings and it became increasingly clear that the dream of a fourth consecutive pennant was slipping away. It would be an overstatement to say that he began to usurp Hughie Jennings's duties, but he did begin to lose faith in the manager and, without discussing it with anybody, he assumed responsibility for giving signals for the hit-and-run play and the bunt when he was at the plate. If this bothered Jennings he as usual avoided direct discussion. We do know that it bothered Davy Jones, by now the Tigers regular left fielder and leadoff batter, who grumbled at the idea of taking orders from someone who was ostensibly a peer while the manager stood off in the coaching box, mindlessly yelling "Ee-Yah!" Matters came to a head at Bennett Park on August 2, 1910, as Jones told Lawrence Ritter when the author interviewed him for *The Glory of Their Times* more than fifty years later:

> *We were playing Boston this day, and Ray Collins was pitching against us. Cobb never did hit Collins too well, so the idea of being in a slump and batting against Collins too didn't go down very well with Ty. He'd just as soon sit this one out.*
>
> *In about the third or fourth inning of this game I got on base and Ty came up to bat. I watched him for the hit-and-run sign, like I always did,*

but he didn't flash any. Then suddenly, after the first pitch, he stepped out of the box and hollered down to me, "Don't you know what a hit-and-run sign is?" Yelled it right out to me.

Jake Stahl was the Boston first baseman and he said to me, "Boy, any guy would holler down here like that is nothing but a rotten skunk."

But I knew Cobb, so I just ignored him. Those were his ways, that's all. Well, the second pitch came in and curved over for strike two. And was Cobb ever mad then! He went over and sat down on the bench and yelled, "Anybody can't see a hit-and-run sign, by God, I'm not going to play with him." Meaning me.

He just sat there and wouldn't play. They had to put in another batter. All he wanted, of course, was to get out of the game because he couldn't hit that pitcher. That's all it was, and I was the fall guy. He put the blame on me.

The true story is not quite as good as the way the nearly eighty-year-old Jones remembered it. A dispute about signals did occur, along with some yelling, but newspaper accounts show that Cobb did not walk off the field but played until the end of the game, going 0-for-4 as the fourth-place Tigers lost to Boston 4–3. Immediately afterward, however, he did announce that he would no longer take the field for the Tigers if Jones was in the lineup and, following an off day, he failed to suit up for the next game (which the Tigers won 4–2). Officially he had "stomach troubles" just as officially he had suffered from a toothache a few weeks earlier, when for reasons unknown he didn't arrive at Shibe Park until the third inning of a game against the A's. Jennings said he was angry about Cobb's behavior, but as usual he said it to the press, and not Cobb—which only reinforced Cobb's impression of him as a weak leader.

It again fell to Navin to mediate the situation, which was more complicated than it may have seemed, since Davy Jones himself was a grouch and "not the most popular man on the team by any means," according to writer E. A. Batchelor. Navin and Cobb met at the team office, perhaps as the game of August 4 was being played, and talked at length about a situation that besides Jennings and Jones, also involved Sam Crawford and shortstop Donie Bush, both of whom Cobb had been riding hard, in the manner of an overbearing manager, as the team struggled to find its old form. Navin later told Jones that he gave Cobb a stern lecture about getting back on the field or facing a suspension, and that Cobb immediately fell in line. That's probably not what really happened behind the closed door of his office, but it was, as Navin knew, the story Jones wanted to hear. What Navin actually said to Cobb that day we'll never know, but we can deduce from hints he dropped that he shared his star's disenchantment with Jennings, as eventually would several other players on the squad. Most likely he and Cobb bonded over their feelings, and agreed that for appearances' sake, Cobb would say that in his desire to win he had overacted, and would henceforth get along better with his manager and teammates. That in any case is what Cobb did tell the reporters on his way out of Bennett on August 4.

Once again, though, Jennings didn't seem able to take a hint from Navin about the way he wanted Cobb to be handled. When the petulant star showed up on Friday, August 5, just minutes before the first pitch was to be thrown, and dispatched the trainer, Harry Tuthill, to tell Jennings that he was available to play, Jennings sent Tuthill back with the message that Cobb's services were not required that day—"whereat many Tigers chuckled with glee" said the *Boston Globe*. Whatever side you were on, it was a silly argument that was going to be settled sooner rather than later—and was the next day with Cobb going back into the lineup and issuing an odd "open letter" to the newspapers. In part it read: "I realize I am not above making mistakes. If some of my critics who have been roasting me in the paper [for causing dissension] would work as hard and as honestly as I do they would find out the real facts connected with the recent trouble on the team and would not be misguiding the public. As for dissension in the club, I can only point to our recent victories, and when the end comes the fans will find the Detroit team there."

The truce was uneasy, but uneasy was Cobb's default mode. The day he returned to the lineup following his blowup with Jones he had two hits and a sacrifice fly and stole a base. Cobb would always thrive in situations where serenity was scarce and tension palpable. Stress seemed to help him focus. He loved coming to bat with the bases full, he told the *New York Times* in 1910, because "the pitcher is worried, the infielders are guessing, and when you hit the ball the flying base runners rattle and disconcert the men who are trying to handle it." In his early memoir *Busting 'Em*, he said it was easier to work out of a batting slump on the road "because I like opposition, and I can get myself straightened out with the crowd hooting me for failing to hit." By that standard, he must have enjoyed 1910 immensely, because he and almost everyone around him seemed out of sorts all season. Near the end of May he told J. Ed. Grillo of the *Washington Star* that because of key injuries and odd bounces it did not feel like the Tigers' year—and predicted the A's would take the pennant. "Fate seems to have decreed that no team should win four pennants in a row," he said morosely.

But just because Cobb felt more comfortable leaning into a figurative headwind didn't mean that the stress wasn't also wearing on his body and mind. As the season wore on, he complained of malaria symptoms, "a slight attack of liver trouble," and "a generally run-down condition," all which, said the *Free Press*, was contributing to a weakness of his eyes. By late August the problem was fairly severe. Told by an eye specialist to rest, he missed a four-game road trip to Cleveland in early September, and when the Tigers returned they found him wearing smoked glasses (though not while playing) for an inflammation of the nerve in his left eye. He also suffered, he was told, from significant nearsightedness in the right eye. Despite these problems—or, knowing Cobb, perhaps because of them—he was at that juncture hitting around .380.

And yet with Nap Lajoie having one of his better years, .380 wasn't enough to put Cobb in the lead for the major league batting title, and the Chalmers Trophy—a $1,500 Chalmers-Detroit 30 sedan—that, for the first time, went with it. For most of the 1910 campaign, Lajoie, who at thirty-five still had his fluid swing and liquid stride, had been hovering at around .400. Since the Frenchman (who was actually born in Woonsocket, Rhode Island) had, in 1901, hit .426, any kind of freakish number seemed possible for him, and Cobb (who already owned a Chalmers car, a present from the company for driving it in a "Good Roads" promotion the previous autumn) intimated that he had resigned himself to finishing second and breaking his string of three consecutive batting titles. It would have been no shame in losing to Lajoie, who had hit above .300 all but once since he started with the Phillies in 1896, and who was such an outstanding all-around player that the team had changed its name from the Bronchos to the Naps. In the final weeks, though, things got exciting. Lajoie started to fade, Cobb, who was twelve years younger, surged, and, with only one game left in the season, he led Lajoie .383 to .376. (Or at least those were the numbers everyone was working with. Statistics in those days were kept by the sportswriters, who would then run them by the league offices for certification, with a sometimes weeks-long wait before they became official. Changes in the initial numbers, based on errors of mathematics or observation, were not uncommon.)

With the newspapers focusing on the dramatic Chalmers race, and pressure mounting on the leaders, both Cobb and Lajoie acted ignobly, to varying degrees. The former sat out the last two games of the season; although several different reasons for his early retirement were proffered by him and Navin, it was presumably a way of preserving his lead. Lajoie, meanwhile, participated in perhaps the most blatantly dishonest double-header in the history of major league baseball.

The Naps played the final two games of the season against the Browns on Sunday, October 9, at Sportsman's Park in St. Louis. Normally, it would have been a meaningless twin bill—Cleveland was in fifth place, the Browns last in the eight-team league—but because of public interest in the contest for the Chalmers car, instead of about 1,200 people the games attracted more than 10,000. St. Louis must have contained a good number of optimists because if the local bugs expected to see Lajoie overtake Cobb, they were hoping for a near-miracle. By the lights of the press box mathematicians, he would need at least seven hits to win the batting title.

In his first time up that day, Lajoie hit "a screaming three-bagger" over the head of center fielder Hub Northen, said Red Nelson, the Browns' rookie who had served up the pitch. Few noticed it at the time, but third baseman Red Corriden, another rookie, had been playing so far back against the right-handed-hitting Lajoie that he seemed more like a second left fielder. He said later that his manager, Jack "Peach Pie" O'Connor, had told him that the Frenchman would "tear your head off with the line drives" if he stayed any closer to the bag.

It was a dubious strategy to stick with, though, for while Lajoie was

certainly no pitty-pat hitter, when he came up again and saw where Corriden was standing, he promptly pushed a bunt toward the left side of
the infield and easily beat the throw to first by the oddly slow-moving
Bobby Wallace, probably the league's best defensive shortstop. Again no
one thought too much of the play, which could have been seen as just
Lajoie being a smart hitter. But thereafter things got strange. On his third
trip to the plate, Lajoie, and everyone else, saw Corriden playing in that
same distant spot, and this time the Frenchman dropped another bunt
along the third base line, and reached first without Wallace even making
a throw. His fourth time up he looked out at the same defensive forma-
tion, laid down another bunt and yet again had a single. It wasn't just the
way the fielders were lining up; the pitches he was getting seemed curiously easy to hit. Had Nelson even been trying to throw the ball by him?
"I used some curves when Lajoie was a bat," the pitcher said later. "But he
hit them easier than the straight ones."

Nap went 4-for-4 in that game, though the Browns won it 5–4.

The second game was more of the same thing. Lajoie got up five times
and reached base safely on every single occasion by pushing or tapping
the ball in the direction of Corriden, who never once crept in from the
outfield grass. In his next-to-last at-bat, Lajoie drove in a run with his
"hit" and so under the scoring system then in place he was credited with a
sacrifice and not charged with an official at-bat. For the day, then, he was
8-for-8, raising his average to .384, .001 higher than Cobb's. After the
game, won by Cleveland 3–0, Browns players slapped Lajoie's back and
fans poured from the stands and tried to carry him away. A quick press
box check of the records revealed that no one had previously gotten more
than seven hits in a doubleheader—and seven of Lajoie's eight hits were
bunts! As Jon Wertheim wrote in a *Sports Illustrated* piece commemorat-
ing the 100th anniversary of the bizarre incident, "Then as now players
might go an entire season without logging seven bunt singles. Lajoie had
seven in one afternoon."

Lajoie later said that he received a telegram of congratulations that
evening signed by eight members of the Tigers. He never revealed their
names, but presumably none was Ty Cobb. The story of the 1910 batting
race has often been used to make the point that Cobb was widely disliked,

and that many of his own teammates, as well as the St. Louis Browns, were pulling for Lajoie. But is that true? Cobb certainly was not as widely beloved among ballplayers as Lajoie, who, though he had a temper—I've already mentioned the famous fight with Flick, and he once spit tobacco juice into an umpire's eye—also had the decency to be not quite so out-landishly good as Cobb, and therefore to not attract so much attention, which he could in turn be resented for. Sports in 1910 still bore traces of nineteenth-century notions about honor and manliness and team play that, for some people, made standing out as an individual problematic— it was a little like standing out in Garrison Keillor's not-so-imaginary version of small-town Minnesota. The president of Harvard University from 1869 to 1909, Charles William Eliot, thought that ball-carriers in football ought not search for holes in the line that could lead to gaudy breakaway runs, but should do the modest, gentlemanly thing and plow headfirst into the nearest man-pile. (Eliot also didn't like baseball because he believed curveballs and other deceptive pitches to be unsportsmanlike.) Cobb stood out on purpose—it was an essential part of his "psychologi-cal" approach. Meanwhile the Frenchman was by all accounts avuncular and unpretentious—he wanted you to call him Larry; he carried a needle and thread to repair his (and other people's) clothes, and if you sat next to him on the bench, he might talk to you about his chicken farm. Probably even Cobb would have conceded that Larry was more likable than he.

But, Cobb aside for a moment, it was almost certainly not a universal outpouring of love for Nap Lajoie that led to the spectacle at Sports-man's Park. One must also consider that many people, including players, gambled on baseball in those days, and that the Chalmers race was a hot proposition with bookmakers from coast to coast. (Peach Pie O'Connor told the press he was leaving town soon to attend—and bet on—the World Series.) Many thousands likely wagered on who would win the car. Given how far behind he was, one could probably have gotten excellent odds on Lajoie on the morning of the doubleheader, and as the Browns would demonstrate, if rather ham-handedly, they had great influence over the outcome of the race. It would be naive to assume that money didn't play a larger role in the Chalmers scandal than anyone's pro-Lajoie, or anti-Cobb, feelings.

The wonder was that the Browns were so obvious in their cheating. First to complain were the St. Louis reporters who witnessed the game. Ernest Lanigan, a writer for the *Sporting News* (and the leading baseball historian of the day), said, "If President [Ban] Johnson does not order an investigation of the way Napoleon Lajoie secured eight hits in eight times at bat, it will only be because . . . the big monarch believes that the Browns had a right to do whatever they desired fair or foul to deprive the king of batsmen of his just deserts." The Missouri racetracks, he noted, had been closed for less crooked behavior. Billy Murphy, sports editor of the *St. Louis Star*, said he was sure that Browns manager O'Connor was aware of the frame-up "and winked at it." The chief umpire on duty that day, Billy Evans, said that he had picked up on rumors in the previous weeks "that Lajoie was being helped to win the batting prize. I have heard that the pitchers of various clubs were out to get the auto for Larry, that they would put the ball in the groove for him, with nothing on it, whereas Cobb would be asked to swing against the best stuff they had in stock. It sounded plausible, but I can truthfully say that not until yesterday have I seen Lajoie helped out." One of St. Louis's many shoe companies, Hamilton Brown, thought the home club's offenses so egregious that it offered to contribute "a large portion of the cost of an automobile to be presented to Cobb."

O'Connor's explanation was surpassingly lame. "Lajoie outguessed us," he said. "We figured he did not have the nerve to bunt every time. He beat us at our own game." Proclaiming his innocence, Lajoie got off a telegram to the *St. Louis Post-Dispatch*: "After I made my first hit, a clean drive to center for three bases, the St. Louis men played deep, expecting me to pound the ball out every time. I fooled them right along. The pitchers did their best to deceive me, I am certain." He also said that his "sacrifice" at-bat should in all fairness have been scored as a base hit, giving him a total of nine for the day.

In Detroit, Navin called the incident "a raw deal" and the papers weighed in strongly in Cobb's defense. While conceding that "some followers of the game feel that Cobb needs a warning against excessive self-esteem," the *Free Press*, on its editorial page, said their hometown hero was "robbed of a hard-won prize by trickery" and called "the intentional poor fielding" "the worst blow ever dealt to organized baseball." Should Cobb have played the last two games to underscore his superior sportsmanship? In an ideal world, yes, definitely, said E. A. Batchelor, who had taken over as the lead sportswriter on the paper after Joe S. Jackson's move to the *Washington Post*. Batchelor explained that "the Peach had planned a motor trip to New York with friends" during those last two days of the long-long season, "and probably was as glad to get away from the diamond as is the ordinary man to leave his work after he had been sticking to it for a long time." Whether he was "quitting" to preserve his lead in the contest was a question "nobody but his own conscience can answer." And yet "whatever Cobb's sins . . . all of this does not in the least mitigate the contemptible actions of the Browns in making it possible for Larry to fatten his average."

Lajoie, not the most agile of arguers, seemed to grow testy under the strain. "So it looked suspicious to Navin, did it?" he said. "Well, he knows what he can do. He can take it before the league."

A formal investigation did seem like a good idea, especially after the official scorer of the October 9 games, *St. Louis Republic* sportswriter E. V. Parrish, came forward to say that there was an attempt to pressure him into helping Lajoie.

> *In the first game, in which I gave Lajoie four hits for as many attempts [he wrote in the October 13 paper] the scoring was attended without incident, save that there was a continual procession to the press box for information regarding scoring which was given.*
>
> *Harry Howell, former pitcher of the Browns, and now scout for the club, came to the pressbox. "How did you score that play?" asked he after Lajoie had batted [for the eighth of nine times that day].*
>
> *"A sacrifice hit and an error," I replied.*
>
> *"Can you stretch it a point and make it a hit?" he asked.*
>
> *"I could, but I won't."*
>
> *Howell attempted to argue the correctness of the scoring.*
>
> *A few minutes after he left, the bat-boy of the Browns came to the press box and handed me this unsigned note: "Mr. Parrish—If you can see where Lajoie gets a base hit instead of a sacrifice, I will give you an order for a $40 suit of clothes for sure. Answer by boy."*

1

2

ABOVE: Young Ty (*front left*) was at first rejected by his hometown team, the Royston (Georgia) Rompers.

LEFT: Matty McIntyre led the hazing that may have brought on Cobb's nervous breakdown in 1906.

3

Home Run Baker later admitted that Cobb was sliding *away* from him during their famous 1909 "incident," but Ty's reputation as a spiker was set.

4

The Pittsburgh Pirates shortstop Honus Wagner was in Cobb's class as a ballplayer, but lacked charisma.

ABOVE LEFT: Team comedian Germany Schaefer once played second base in a rain slicker to convince the umpire to call the game. During the off-season he performed a recitation called "Why Does Tyrus Tire Us?"

ABOVE RIGHT: Napoleon Lajoie was a bit of a rube, but he was such a great all-around player that the Cleveland franchise changed its name to the Naps.

Tris Speaker, another superstar of the Deadball Era, was a frequent houseguest of Cobb's in Augusta. After they were exonerated in a game-fixing scandal, they finished their careers together, playing for Connie Mack on the 1928 Philadelphia A's.

After Cobb's father was shot and killed, American League President Ban Johnson (*standing right*) became one of the two main authority figures in his life, along with Detroit Tigers owner Frank Navin.

No one in the Deadball Era threw harder than Walter Johnson. Cobb crowded the plate on him, knowing that the Big Train worried about hitting batters with his heat.

Although this 1912 picture is often used to indict Cobb, catcher Paul Krichell said it was misleading: Ty wasn't spiking him, just knocking the ball out of his hand. After the collision, the two fought fiercely, if briefly, and both were fined.

Cobb (*left*) got along better with his fellow Southerner Shoeless Joe Jackson (*center*), whom he called "the best natural hitter I've ever seen," than he did with teammate Wahoo Sam Crawford (*right*), but in the 1950s he campaigned successfully to get Crawford into the Hall of Fame.

LEFT: The all-time leader at getting hit by pitched balls, Hughie Jennings often managed the Tigers from the coaching box, where he behaved rather bizarrely, ripping up grass and throwing it like confetti, shaking rubber snakes and constantly shouting "Ee-yah!"

BELOW: Cobb's fans were fascinated by his split-hands grip, which allowed him to make adjustments to his swing at the last second. Although the hitting manuals advise against the technique, it worked brilliantly for Cobb.

RIGHT: Cobb employed Alex Rivers as his personal bat man for more than ten years.

BELOW: Cobb's well-deserved reputation as a bibliophile (he couldn't resist biographies of Napoleon) sometimes resulted in him receiving books instead of trophies or flowers.

14

15

In 1926, Giants manager John McGraw tried to pluck the Peach from the American League. "Lay off Cobb!" Commissioner Kenesaw Mountain Landis said.

17   The great George Sisler (*left*) was an admirer of Cobb's, but from a distance. Ty and Babe Ruth had a more complicated relationship, if only because he had dated Ruth's wife.

18   When Joe DiMaggio was in the minors, Cobb sent him letters of advice and even helped him negotiate his first contract with the Yankees.

After I arrived home from the ball game that evening my telephone rang.

"This is Mr. Lajoie," the voice said. "I understand that you are having some trouble regarding my hits in today's game."

I replied that I was having no trouble. That it was other parties who were having the troubles.

"How many hits did you give me?"

"Eight hits in eight trips to the plate."

"Don't you think I should have had nine in nine times at bat?" was the answer.

My reply was that had I thought so I would have scored them as such.

"There is no chance for you to see nine hits?" came over the phone.

"Absolutely no," I retorted.

After refusing an invitation to go to a hotel the conversation was cut off.

(Lajoie later admitted making the call.)

Cobb steered a careful course in his initial comments about the affair. "I was surprised when I read of the result of the games in the papers," he said, "and I am sorry that either Lajoie or myself did not win the prize for the highest average without anything occurring which could cause unfavorable comment. I am not prepared to make any charges against either Lajoie or any member of the St. Louis team." He added, though, that if Nap was awarded the car "under the current circumstances" he would "not be able to congratulate him."

For the following six days the matter was in the hands of the American League. Ban Johnson summoned O'Connor and Corriden to his office for an interview. They showed up a day late, and only after the AL president had issued an ultimatum—and then, when interviewed separately, simply stuck to their story about Lajoie "outguessing" them. Soon afterward, the American League secretary, Rob McRoy, who was charged with double-checking the stats, delivered his report—and Johnson, on October 15, announced his verdict. Not surprisingly, he found that nothing untoward or illegal had happened in his well-run league. "A thorough investigation has satisfied me that there is no substantial ground for questioning the accuracy of any of the eight base hits credited to Player

Lajoie of the Cleveland club by the official scorer in the double header on Sunday, October 9 at St. Louis," he said. Furthermore, he said he was counting Lajoie's so-called sacrifice as a ninth hit, for the rather specious reason that veteran *St. Louis Times* sportswriter H. W. Lanigan (Ernie's younger brother) reported it as such in his paper that day.

So that meant O'Connor was vindicated and Lajoie had won the automobile, right? Actually, no and no. Behind the scenes, Johnson pressured Browns owner Robert Lee Hedges to fire the manager—who, tainted by the scandal that officially hadn't happened, would never work in major league baseball again. Moreover the league president also announced that his man McRoy had miraculously found in the annals a game that had not been counted for Cobb: the second half of a doubleheader on September 24 in which he had gone 2-for-3. Thus, said Johnson, "their respective batting averages are a follows: Cobb, 509 times at bat, 196 hits, percentage .384944; Lajoie, 591 times at bat, 227 hits, percentage .3840948. [As the *Chicago Tribune* noted, Johnson got the math wrong; Cobb's number should have been .385069.] Cobb thus had a clear title to the leadership of the American League batsmen for 1910 and is therefore entitled to the Chalmers trophy." Matter settled, then? Not quite. Johnson's declaration about a "clear title" was immediately followed by a request for company president Hugh Chalmers to provide cars for both Cobb and Lajoie.

This soon was done, and the rules were altered so that when Cobb won the car again in 1911 it was for being "the most important and useful player to the club and to the league" in the opinion of a panel of sportswriters, and not for simply having the highest batting average. Still, "looking at it from any angle," Batchelor wrote, in 1910, "it is a nasty mess." He didn't know how right he was. In the late 1970s researchers Pete Palmer and Leonard Gettelson discovered that the September 24 game had *not* been overlooked after all, just entered mistakenly for the next day, but baseball commissioner Bowie Kuhn declined to make a correction, which would have put Lajoie in the lead—assuming his numerous phony hits were also preserved in the record.

Cobb spent his twenty-fifth birthday, December 18, 1911, in Havana, Cuba, where he was touring with a barnstorming team of Tigers led by pitcher George Mullin. He had joined the group a couple of weeks late—he wanted to stick around in the States to see the auto races at Atlanta and Savannah—but once he got there (with his wife, baby son, and in-laws) he seemed to enjoy himself. He clowned in the outfield, pretending to bobble easy fly balls, and gratefully accepted a diamond-studded watch fob presented to him by awe-struck Cuban fans. The games he played in sound exciting. He was thrown out trying to steal second a few times by Bruce Petway, one of several black players from the American Negro Leagues who were rounding out the Cuban team that winter. Petway's superb defensive feats led to stories about Cobb angrily vowing that he would never play against black players again, but those are unsupported by any contemporary news accounts and clash tonally with Cobb's other quotes from the time, which, while not particularly diplomatic, praised the local weather and extolled his teammates for demonstrating the superiority of American baseball. The Tigers did go 7–4–1 while Cobb hit .370 in the five games he played. He had no reason to be angry and there is no evidence that he was.

— CHAPTER TWENTY —

ONE EARLY NOVEMBER DAY IN 1911, Ty Cobb was driving through New York Central Park in the luxurious, open-topped Chalmers Model 30 sedan he had received for, among other things, hitting .420 that year, when something strange happened. Strange things happened frequently to Cobb, so it was probably with something like a world-weary sigh, or maybe a grunt of annoyance, that he pulled off the scenic speed-way and onto a flat stretch of grass as a policeman who had swept along-side him on a motorcycle was indicating that he urgently must. What could be the problem? He had been traveling well below the posted speed limit, or so he thought. And yet as soon as he got out of the car he heard the cop say, "You're under arrest!"

Did this Johnny Law know who he was talking to? He should have; Cobb was a true celebrity at that point. Although the Tigers had tailed off since they last won the pennant in 1909—they had finished second in the AL that year, but 13½ games behind the Athletics—he had won the batting title every season since 1907. And since, like most ballplayers of his day, he looked seriously at whatever moneymaking opportunities came along, weighing each for the potential damage to his dignity, he seemed omnipresent, even in the off-season, thanks to all his projects and endorsements. Just a few days earlier he had "managed" the "Ty Cobb All-Stars" (basically a bunch of amateurs, semipros, and Germany Schae-fer) in an exhibition game played against another fake team at the Polo Grounds, and now he was passing through Manhattan on his way to a performance of *The College Widow* that evening in Newark.

If the cop recognized him he was clearly not a fan. From the moment he dismounted his motorcycle, the man seemed to be spoiling for a fight.

Cobb himself was not in a pacific mood that afternoon. During the run of his play, he got very little sleep and felt constantly irritable. "The theatrical life is too nerve-wracking for me," he had told Batchelor when the *Widow* came to Detroit. "My health is suffering. I need to take a rest." With him in this condition, any encounter with a provocateur was not going to end well.

A year is a long time in baseball. For both the Tigers as a team and Ty Cobb as an individual, 1911 had gotten off to an almost scarily good start. On an opening day that would have otherwise been remembered for a relentless, freezing drizzle, Cobb clouted an opposite field home run and his team beat the White Sox 4–2, the first of six consecutive victories. For the month of April, Detroit would go 13–2. "Tigers Perpetrate Another Massacre," was a typical headline. Weirdly for the Tigers, things had been going smoothly since spring training, when, after another beseeching letter from Navin—"your failure to [attend] creates a feeling on the club, which was brought out in the papers last year"—Cobb actually made it to the new preseason site in Monroe, Louisiana, if a couple of weeks late. In the relaxed atmosphere there, he and Davy Jones talked things out and patched up most of their differences, though according to Navin, *Detroit Daily News* writer Paul Bruske almost ruined everything when he wrote that Cobb "ate humble pie" to effect the peace. "This will put [Cobb] right back on edge again," the owner said in a testy letter to Bruske. "You know Cobb's disposition as well as I do, and when he reads an article like that, he is 'up in the air.'" Many were nervous when dealing with Cobb—but not Sam Crawford, who only grudgingly went along with Navin's exhortations that he, Jones, Donie Bush, and Cobb should all play nicely together. Crawford was often shockingly frank with the press about Cobb, saying for the record that he was the cause of dissension on the team and that he cared only about his own personal glory and statistics. It was mostly a one-way feud, though; Cobb never seemed terribly bothered by him. It may have been Crawford's status as the perennially second-best Tiger that fueled his anger. Even when he achieved his all-time-high batting average of .378 that year, Cobb's .420 put him deeply in the shade.

• • •

To at least some degree, the ridiculously high numbers posted by Cobb, Joe Jackson (who hit .408 that year), and Crawford could be attributed to a new livelier ball that had been introduced, with purposely little fanfare, during the World Series of the previous autumn. Created for the American League by Benjamin Franklin Shibe, a sporting goods manufacturer and part-owner of the Athletics who was born in Philadelphia just forty-eight years after the death of the Founding Father, it had a rubber-coated-cork instead of a pure rubber core and it came off a bat like a jackrabbit, which is exactly what many people called it. (The Spalding Company quickly began making a similar model for the National League.) As Bill James notes in his *Historical Baseball Abstract*, run production in the AL in 1911 rose to 4.6 per game, up from 3.6 the previous season, and Cobb and Joe Jackson both had .400-plus seasons, the only time that barrier was broken (except for Cobb's .409 in 1912) between 1901 and 1920. League officials and owners, who wanted to make the game more exciting, but without giving the impression they were resorting to artificial means, denied that the new ball was any bouncier, but Cobb complained that it was so souped up that it changed the game fundamentally—by hampering his ability to bunt. He could no longer deaden the ball enough, in his artful way, to beat it to first base, he said, genuinely concerned that the cork-centered sphere would put a serious crimp in his career. Somehow he adjusted, though, because on May 1, he was hitting .379, with four game-winning RBI and three homers—which except for the homers for him was typical.

The Tigers that spring seemed unstoppable, going 19–9 in May. On its editorial page the *Free Press* said they were "some baseball team" and, serving up the spicy synonyms like a Bennett Park wiener vendor, noted that "swats, bingles and wallops are as common in the jungaleers camp as dandelions in a shiftless neighbor's front lawn." As for winning their fourth "rag," or pennant, that was no problem. Though "the season was still in swaddling clothes," the editors said, "ginger and sand and heady ball playing will bring the Tigers to the tape [so surely] that second place won't be worth fighting for."

Cobb himself inspired a good deal of the giddiness. His fielding alone brought fans to their feet. At home against the Browns on April 23, wrote Batchelor, "he made two shoestring catches by diving headlong at the ball, each time rolling along on his ear after accomplishing the theft; he went back a mile to pull down one of Frank LaPorte's welts and covered a lot of ground in snaring another drive by [Jim] Murray. Altogether it was the most sensational fielding performance that any one player would be likely to furnish in many weeks." And yet despite such glove-work it was his batting and especially base running that made Cobb worth $100,000 a year to the Tigers, in the opinion of *Sporting Life* and others. In the same game in which he'd made those acrobatic catches, Cobb singled, went all the way to third on Crawford's routine infield groundout, "easily beating [Pat] Newman's hurried and inaccurate throw," then trotted home on Jim Delahanty's sacrifice fly. Two innings later, he turned a badly handled infield roller into a double, went to third on a fielder's choice, and scored the tying run on a Delahanty single. (The Tigers would win in the 10th.) The following week at Bennett, Cobb and company made the Naps look, said Batchelor, "like the steamfitter's Married Men's nine." Final score: 14–5. Cobb had three steals, including a swipe of home that succeeded despite the four Clevelanders who had him trapped in a rundown—until he spun away and slid across the plate, looking more like the Thief of Baghdad than the Georgia Peach. Against the White Sox on June 18, he led a Tigers comeback in a game in which they had been trailing 13–1, getting five hits in six at-bats including a triple and one of his slide-into-first-base singles that allowed the tying run to score. At the time he was in the midst of what would stretch into a record 40-game hitting streak—and batting .443.

Another game, another two or three hits, another Tigers victory: it happened with such regularity in the first part of 1911 that it almost sounds rote. Yet Cobb always managed to keep things interesting by mixing in a controversy or two. Even if he wasn't the instigator, he seemed constitutionally unable to ignore a challenge, and thus a few pointed words could escalate into a tense situation in a few innings.

The Tigers' visit to Shibe Park on June 8 was just such an occasion. Trouble started brewing in the first inning when Cobb and A's southpaw "Gettysburg" Eddie Plank (who had been born in that Pennsylvania town a dozen years after the battle) got involved in some serious jawing. (What they were arguing about remains obscure, but Plank was a notorious dilly-dallier, and Cobb may have been telling him to hurry the hell up.) When Cobb trotted to his spot in right field in the bottom of the inning, the cranks took up their pitcher's cause, whatever it was, and soon began to underscore their remarks by hurling discarded lemonade-stand lemons at him. Cobb, perhaps remembering that he had once stood in the same outfield and worried about being killed by a sniper's bullet, took even more than his usual umbrage at this, and began to hurl the lemons back, applying a dollop of metaphorical mustard to each, so that they struck seats and spectators with an angry splat. Umpire Jack Sheridan, who was an undertaker in the off-season, and looked the part, calmly walked from behind home plate to the outer edge of the infield to express in sepulchral tones his sincere hope that the outfielder would return his attention to the national pastime. But Cobb kept slinging the citrus and by the end of the third inning, said the *Washington Post*, he "had to be grabbed by Sheridan and shoved to the bench before he would stop. This added to the crowd's excitement, and to Cobb's temper."

The bad feelings festered until the sixth inning when Cobb, after getting his third hit in three attempts, stole second, then tried, a pitch or two later, to steal third. He was called out, but in the process briefly got his spikes snared in the blousy sleeve of his old friend Frank Baker. A gasp went up from the crowd and an angry—but unscratched—Baker, said the *Washington Post*, "grabbed Cobb by the legs and swung him around with much force." Cobb, meanwhile, "naturally resented this and jabbed at Baker with his cleats." For defending himself in this manner, said the *Detroit Free Press*, "Cobb was hissed and booed in the delightful manner Philadelphia has of showing its disapproval of anything that goes against the Athletics."

Almost miraculously, nothing else happened just then, but two innings later, with Cobb on third, he and Baker started "accidentally" stepping on each other's toes, then shouldering each other, until coaches and teammates rushed over to pull them apart.

By then it was a foregone conclusion that the crowd was fixing to erupt, and in the ninth inning, as Cobb caught the soft fly ball that ended the game with the Tigers up 8–3, "the bleachers on both side of the field belched forth a torrent of humanity," the *Free Press* said, and the cranks, said the *Post*, "swarmed on the field and headed straight for Cobb, who came walking in slowly, and deliberately tossing the ball up in the air. The rest of the Detroit players ran out on the field and surrounded Cobb, and, aided by an escort of police, pushed and shoved the Southerner to the bench. It required some pretty rough work to keep some of the hotheaded fans back"—the *Free Press* said several Tigers were swinging their bats to carve a swath for Cobb—"and as Cobb was being taken through the gates a wild rush was made to get him. His bodyguard, however, was equal to the occasion, and no harm came to the Tigers' demon outfielder." The Detroit paper said it was only the cowardice of the Philly fans—who kept urging each other to strike Cobb, but who didn't have the nerve to throw the first punch themselves—that kept the riot contained. "For lack of a match to start the conflagration, general disaster was averted," Batchelor wrote. "Had one of the Tigers been struck there would have been standing room only in the Philadelphia hospitals tonight."

Tigers fans, who had been reading so much that summer about dissension in the ranks, must have been pleased by reports of their boys brandishing bats like swashbuckling swordsmen to get the star into a waiting cab. If there was anti-Cobb sentiment on the club, it could not be running too wide or too deep. Could the newspapers have been exaggerating the dissension supposedly wracking the Tigers? For the cranks it was a heartening thought.

And yet baseball is a game that, even as it intrigues and inspires you, will find a way to break your heart. As the 1911 season wore on, things fell apart. The pitching came back to earth and the Tigers' rookie phenom, first baseman Del Gainer, could not stay healthy. Neither could Cobb, but while Gainer missed a long stretch of the season with a sprained wrist (an absence that corresponded with the start of the Tigers' steep decline), the normally "gorgeous Georgian," as the *Atlanta Constitution* called Cobb, muddled through with unshakable symptoms of bronchitis including a "hacking cough"—the prelude, he and some sportswriters believed, to typhoid fever. "He feels pretty punk every day," said one paper.

Cobb did miss a few games here and there, and was constantly in the care of doctors, some of whom he didn't listen to when they advised taking an extended leave. On most days he was in the lineup, haggard-looking but a handful, still. "Though on the verge of an ambulance call, T. Cobb figured in the day's doings," wrote Atlanta scribe Fuzzy Woodruff on August 2. "He went to the plate three times, rapped out three hits, one of them being a home run, another a three-sacker, scored three runs, swiped two bases and having decided he had earned his pay, called for the doctor and went back to the hospital." He told Gordon McKay of the *Philadelphia Times* that he could "hit the old pill all right, but when he got on the sacks he lacked the old steam and stamina." This caused Woodruff to wonder in print, "what would have happened if Cobb didn't have a few ailments tucked away in his southern system."

The statistics failed to bear out Cobb's claim that he was sluggish on the base paths. In a scholarly article in SABR's *Baseball Research Journal* in 1991, Larry Amman noted that while 1911 was not Ty's best year by some definitions of the term—"His 1910 batting average of .385 was actually higher relative to the whole league, and the year of his greatest run production was 1917"—it "ranks as his best for hitting, fielding, and base-running combined. In the field he exceeded [Cleveland's] Tris Speaker in total chances per game and in fielding average. On the bases this was Cobb's most successfully daring campaign. His youthful energy combined with a mature baseball wisdom to produce a quality of play never seen before."

Yet Cobb alone could not pull the Tigers out of their tailspin. After starting the season 21–2, they won only 24 of the 40 games that constituted his hitting streak (which ended, without ever being noted by the local papers, on July 4, five games short of the major league record set by Wee Willie Keeler in 1897). Between July 20 and the end of August, Detroit went 15–24, a record that locked them securely into second place behind the eventual league-champion Philadelphia A's.

With the season over, Cobb turned to making money. His family was growing—his second child, Shirley Marion, had been born on June 2— and though he had no agent or manager to guide him, it seemed only natural that his .420 average and the acclaim that came with it ought to somehow be, as we would say today, monetized in some way beyond mere salary. He had a knack for making money: a $1,000 investment in cotton futures during a trip to New York City in September of 1910 had blossomed in only ten days time to $7,500. Nor was it difficult for him to find opportunities; people came to him. In short order, he signed up to "cover" the 1911 Athletics-Giants World Series with a series of partially ghostwritten articles for the Wheeler Syndicate of New York; lent his name to the J. K. Orr Company of Atlanta for their Ty Cobb model of high-button dress shoe; and he agreed to join the touring cast of *The College Widow*. As all these things show, though, it was still difficult to find special, classier projects—things more worthy of the man whom *Sporting Life* had recently proclaimed "King Tyrus the First." That same year he had chatted (again) with President Taft, met the labor leader Samuel Gompers at a New York dinner staged in his (Cobb's) honor, and had a post-theater get-together with New Jersey governor (and Augusta native) Woodrow Wilson, even managing to get off a little joke. (When a press member asked, "Why don't you run for sheriff of Detroit?" Cobb said, "Can't. I've stolen too many bases. They'd use that against me.")

No other ballplayers traveled in such rarefied circles—yet plenty of others dabbled in the same not terribly exalted off-season ventures as he was pursuing, and Cobb was left to wonder if, for him, anyway, the act of exhibiting himself upon the stage and all the rest wasn't a bit unseemly. Every night before the footlights was not a triumph, the reviewers not always kind. When the sports editor of the *Birmingham News*, Allen G. Johnson, filled in for the paper's theater critic and mocked his acting in the next day's paper, Cobb got apoplectic. Giving in to an impulse that many performers have felt, and wisely suppressed, he fired off a letter to Johnson that seemed to presage the bluster of Donald Trump: "I am a better actor than you are, a better sports editor than you are, a better dramatic critic than you are, I make more money than you do, and I know I am a better ball player—so why should inferiors criticize superiors?"

Though most of the write-ups he received for his acting were positive— if sometimes tinged with a slightly demeaning whiff of surprise—Johnson's was the only one Ty responded to. More than most people, he focused on the negative, and in doing so could, in his darker moments, perceive anything short of a rave as a put-down.

This was his problem with the cop who stopped him that day in

Central Park, or rather it was the cop's problem. We don't know who said what first, but Cobb and the peace officer were soon trading blows— fighting so heatedly, in fact, that Cobb didn't notice the man who popped from the bushes to snap their picture. It was only when the photographer told the combatants that they could stop, and the policeman suddenly begged for mercy, that the situation revealed itself for what it actually was: a publicity stunt, arranged by the producers of *The College Widow*, meant to capitalize on Cobb's reputation as a brawler. The cop had been an actor, the photographer a press agent who planned to distribute the picture of Cobb battling a policeman to New York City area newspapers.

The photo was never published, or even developed, it seems. No one knows why, but I suspect that the camera, rather than staying a camera, ended its life as a hat.

"Don't get Cobb mad," Connie Mack said.

If only a man named Claudius Northrup Lucker had heeded that advice.

CHAPTER TWENTY-ONE

OF MEDIUM HEIGHT AND MEDIUM weight with brown hair and brown eyes—according to his World War I draft registration card—Claude Lucker, as he was most commonly known, did not exactly cut an impressive figure. His most striking feature was his hands, which lacked the usual number of fingers. He had three on one hand and none on the other, a rather seriously mutilated extremity. He had lost the fingers and more while employed, circa 1910, as a pressman at the *New York Times*, and later, in an arbitration case, his representative blamed the accident on "the exacting and depressing nature of the work required of him." Inexperience may have also been a factor; he hadn't been in the printing trade very long. Previously Lucker (often spelled incorrectly as Lueker) had labored on the East River docks, steps from the boardinghouse where he lived on James Slip, within wafting distance of the Fulton Fish Market. Since the accident, though, he'd been handling miscellaneous assignments for a man named Thomas F. "Big Tom" Foley, a lawyer who held the title of sheriff of New York County.

Foley was a Tammany Hall power broker who hired a lot of people to do a lot of politically expedient things. Whatever tasks the thirty-one-year-old Lucker did for Foley, he clearly made enough to survive and even splurge a little on extras, like a smartly cut suit, a rakish derby (judging from the one extant photo of him), and an alpaca coat, lightweight enough for early-season ballgames. That in fact is how Ty Cobb first came to think of him—as the loudmouth in left field with the alpaca coat.

On May 11, 1912, the Yankees' biggest crowd of the young season, announced at 20,000 (or 5,000 above the official capacity) came out to Hilltop Park in upper Manhattan to see Cobb's first appearance in

Gotham that year. (It was in 1912 that the scale tipped and "Yankees" overtook "Highlanders" as the sporting press's preferred name for the franchise.) That Cobb was the main draw may be stated with confidence. While the Tigers were playing poorly—stuck in sixth place with a record of 10–13—he was as usual somewhere up in the stratosphere, leading the league with an average of about .370 and running as wild as ever on the bases. He'd been in an especially good mood since he quit *The College Widow* that winter several weeks before the scheduled end of the run—talking at length to interviewers and even pulling some pranks. One day in late April, when the Tigers were arrayed shoulder to shoulder for a team photo at the new Navin Field, a picture that was to be taken with a slowly rotating panoramic camera, he got the notion to scoot around the photographer while the lens panned, so that he would appear, looking perfectly composed, on both the left and right sides of the shot.

Now, during a pregame ceremony during which he received his fourth Honey Boy Evans "World's Champion Batsman" trophy from the minstrel Honey Boy Evans himself, he smiled wide, taking the rousing cheers as a sign that one of his big fears—that the public would be disappointed in him for leaving the sold-out *Widow* early—was for naught. It was hard to gauge the mood of the Hilltop crowd, though. About fifteen minutes later, when he was tagged out on the front end of a double steal, and exchanged heated words with Yankee third baseman Albert "Cozy" Dolan, Cobb was booed until the rafters shook. A few innings after that, when umpire Silk O'Loughlin simultaneously ejected Yankees manager Harry Wolverton, pitcher Jack Quinn, and catcher Gabby Street for repeated complaints about his calls of balls and strikes, the "wild-eyed hoodlums" in the crowd, said the *New York Times*, began to shower the umpire with "bottles and glasses." The *Detroit News* said that Cobb "stood between [O'Loughlin] and the stands to spoil the aim of the throwers." Nevertheless, two bottles barely missed O'Loughlin's head and another struck him on the foot. Said the *Times*: "The game stopped and the umpire and ballplayers gathered around the plate and looked into the stand to see where the fusillade was coming from."

The best answer may have been "a place of despair." The Tigers and Yankees were a dreary duo of second-tier clubs that season, destined to finish sixth and eighth respectively, and they looked it from the start. A mere 242,000 would come to Hilltop Park in 1912—only the St. Louis Browns would do worse at the gate—and far too many of those who did show up spent the day hurling missiles and insults in the general direction of the bad baseball, and otherwise demonstrating their dystopian angst. The ugliness of May 11 was just business as usual.

Abusive fans were a hot topic in 1912. Players and spectators alike complained about a rise in rowdyism. You couldn't bring women or children to the ballpark, many said, even in the supposedly family-friendly American League, without fear of their ears being singed by horrible language. Jack Fournier, a star with the National League Brooklyn Robins, came close to quitting the game because of the "ugly epithets" he had to endure. "Ballplayers should be protected from insult," said Jim Callahan, manager of the White Sox, expressing a growing sentiment. "The gambling element is the one which usually indulges in this sort of abuse. Oftentimes a player has to exercise all his self-control to keep from going after his tormentors."

What exactly did the "mockers" and "knockers" holler? No doubt the usual four-letter words came up, along with bespoke disses fashioned from odd gossip scraps gleaned from the dailies. ("I hear your sister's in town—guess I'll be seeing her tonight!") The *Detroit News* that year, curious to find the most common baseball catcalls, came up with these: "Hang crepe on your nose, your brain's dead!" "Butter fingers!" "Bonehead!" "Solid ivory!" "Ice wagon!" "You're a big swell-head!" "Stay out of them saloons and get some sleep!" and the ever-popular "You're a dub!" (No, not dud, *dub*.)

As quaint as these things sound today, they made grown men froth with anger. I've already mentioned how Pirates manager Fred Clarke pushed a heckler down a flight of stairs in midgame, and that Tigers skipper Ed Barrow once emptied a cuspidor on mouthy cranks. Such things happened often. It didn't even make headlines when Phillies coach Kid Gleason, while on his way to the clubhouse after being tossed for fighting, chased down and assaulted a fan who had hit him on the head with a pop bottle. The usually mild-mannered Cy Young charged into the stands to challenge a crank who called him a quitter, and Giants third baseman

Art Devlin beat up someone whom he (wrongly) thought had referred to him as a yellow dog. In his wonderful book *Baseball: The Golden Age*, Harold Seymour notes that Phillies pitcher Sherry Magee "knocked out a drunk who, after abusing him from the bleachers, followed him to the clubhouse to continue his insults" and reminds us that Rube Waddell also once hopped into the bleachers to beat up a "fan." (Waddell, a strange, childlike man, was frequently bedeviled by spectators who, as he got set to throw a pitch, held aloft mirrors and puppies, both of which could purportedly mesmerize him.) Cobb himself had some experience in this area, having once, in 1910, gotten partway into the stands to confront a black spectator who had heckled him for several innings, saying what we don't know, before police intervened and got him back on the field.

Lucker was more persistent and more vulgar than the average heckler. No "You're a big swell-head!" for him. The Tigers played the Yankees four times during that May series, and he was there for every game, apparently by himself, riding Cobb hard, using language that witnesses described as bigoted and obscene. Unlike some of Cobb's other taunters, Lucker never focused on his Southern background, no doubt because he himself was a Southerner, born in South Carolina and raised partly in Georgia, as he said later, in his own defense, not far from Cobb's hometown of Royston. At the same time, though, he attempted to pander to what he assumed were Cobb's regional prejudices; a good number of his ugly assertions involved Cobb's mother being a "nigger lover" and Cobb himself being "half black." When Cobb responded, as he sometimes did, by shouting from the field for him to shut up and "Go back to your waiter's job," Lucker would say, "Go out and play ball, you coon!" As soon as the Tigers trotted out for batting practice each day during their New York stay, the taunts would begin anew, and Cobb would steal a glance into the left field bleachers and see the alpaca coat (only somewhat unseasonable; the temperature hovered around 60 during the series) and sigh. As professional ballplayers knew, there were churls in every port, but Lucker was the loudest and the worst.

By the fourth game, May 15, Cobb's patience, a fine filament under the best of circumstances, was wearing thin. When he muffed a fly ball during fielding practice, and someone—"Not me!" Lucker later swore in an interview with the *New York Sun*—yelled "Hey, are you on dope?" Cobb, who usually "took the joshing good naturedly enough," said Lucker, instead "got peevish right away." No doubt, but if the star was out of sorts that day, it wasn't because of his hitting. He had five singles in 12 at-bats during the series, an average of .417. The Tigers had won two of the previous three games. It was much more likely Lucker's incessant nagging that had him on the verge of eruption.

On his way out to right field in the third inning, Cobb stopped at the Yankees dugout and asked if Frank Farrell, the team's co-owner, was around. He wanted to point out Lucker and request that he be removed from the park. But Farrell couldn't be located, Cobb apparently preferred not to deal with lesser functionaries, and the game continued. As the fourth inning started, and the stream of invective continued, one of Cobb's teammates, it may have been Davy Jones but we don't know for certain, approached him and said something to the effect of "You can't let that guy get away with this." That bit of peer pressure, combined with whatever Lucker was shouting at the moment, was all the extra incentive Cobb needed. He ran down the third base line, hopped the low railing, ran up the stairs, and began punching and kicking his tormentor. It wouldn't have been a fair fight under normal circumstances, with Cobb, at six feet and about 190 pounds, so much bigger than Lucker and a trained athlete at that, but considering Lucker's disability, it was a pathetic spectacle for which there could be no excuse. Even if Cobb, in his fury, had failed to notice Lucker's deformity, people in the surrounding seats yelled "He's a cripple!" and "He has no hands!" Cobb's oft-quoted response was "I don't care if he has no feet!" The remark made no sense but did show that he heard what they were saying and was in control enough to, in a manner of speaking, converse. What strikes the modern reader is how small a role Lucker's disability played in the subsequent discussion of the beating. *No one* seemed to give it much weight. Cobb continued to flail away. This wasn't just a one- or two-punch affair. Lucker told the *Sun* that Cobb struck him "first on the forehead, then on the side of the head, then kicked [me] in the legs. He cut me with his spikes, tore a big hole behind my ear and cut my face in several places."

When Cobb was finally pulled off his victim and escorted back to the field by teammates, the crowd cheered—not for the handicapped patron, but for *him*, a member of the enemy camp. And even though Silk O'Loughlin promptly threw Cobb out of the game, as he knew he must, the ump seemed sympathetic and let him stay on the bench in violation of the rules for a few innings. No other fan seems to have come to Lucker's aid, or in any way consoled him. Lucker himself said that the first person to arrive at his seat was a man from Ban Johnson's office, who urged Lucker not to have Cobb arrested. Johnson happened to be at Hilltop Park that day and when the ruckus broke out, he immediately dispatched a minion named O'Neill to make it clear to the spectator that his supposedly family-friendly league wanted to take care of things without involving the authorities. What, if anything, Lucker was promised for not pursuing criminal charges, we don't know, but O'Neill soon escorted him from the stadium. "I was told that Johnson planned to take immediate action [against Cobb]," Lucker said later, "and I thought it best to let it go at that." The victim, though he "looked like he should be taken to a dressmakers to be sewn up" in the opinion of the *Philadelphia Herald*, was composed enough "to give a sketchy history of Cobb's ancestry" to anyone within hearing distance on his way out.

The game resumed and the Tigers won 5–1.

That hardly ended the matter, though. As with previous Cobb controversies, the Lucker incident became table talk and tavern talk for much of the nation. In the newspapers, Tom Foley defended his employee, saying he had always been a "quiet fan." Lucker kept changing his story, at first agreeing with Foley, then saying to the *New York Sun* that he routinely "kidded the ballplayers from his accustomed seat in the leftfield bleachers" but "had always gotten along with Cobb"—and then amending that statement to note that ever since they were boys together down Georgia way he and Cobb had "never harmonized." Cobb told the *Sporting News* that he had known and been abused by Lucker since the previous season.

Last summer I remonstrated with him and advised him to pass me up— that I was only human and trying to earn my living out there and I could see no justice in his attacking me. His remarks then were insulting but not obscene. As soon as the man got into the park yesterday, he went after me.

He did not wait for the game to begin but he started as soon as we started batting practice. I walked to the other side of the field and tried not to hear him. [Donie] Bush asked him to stop, but it did no good. Finally I went to him and asked him to lay off me and when I spoke to him he cut loose with a flow of the worst talk I have ever heard. Then I lost my temper, jumped into the stands and let him have it. I am sorry for the effect such an incident had on the game and because of my family. A ball player, however, should not be expected to take everything, as we have some self-respect, and cannot endure more than human nature will stand for. When a ballplayer can't take it, how can they expect women to do so, who attended the game by themselves or with their husbands?

Johnson did move quickly (if somewhat vaguely), announcing the following day that he was suspending Cobb for an indefinite number of games and fining him an amount to be determined. Cobb said the penalties, whatever they were, were unfair—"A great injustice has been done to me and I should have been given an opportunity to state my case." (Again, the matter of Lucker's handicap seemed moot to everyone.) Quite a few people agreed with him, especially in his home state and adopted city, but beyond those places, too. On May 16 he received a telegram signed by both of Georgia's U.S. senators and all of its congressmen: "As Georgians, we commend your action in resenting an uncalled for insult." In Detroit, Cobb's latest troubles were the top story of the day. Mayor William Barlum Thompson said, "Cobb was perfectly right in resenting with his fists insulting remarks made from the stands." William F. Connolly, a well-known Detroit political figure, called Ban Johnson "un-American" for denying Cobb his paycheck without a hearing, while Judge James Phelan dismissed the league president as a "swell-head." One of Cobb's most impressive defenses came from Hugh Fullerton, an influential sportswriter then with the *Chicago Tribune*: "Ty Cobb goes around the circuit year after year, singled out as the special mark by every violent fan, and he has learned to endure almost any kind of abuse possible. If the epithets and accusations made by the Highlander fan toward Cobb was half as bad as the Detroit players claim, it was a cause for violence. The wonder to me is that other spectators could sit and listen without taking a hand in it and beating up and throwing out the person using such language."

From other quarters, though, came sentiments much less Cobb-friendly. Preachers and teachers and newspaper editorial writers denounced him, sometimes vehemently, for his impulsive reaction. One could tell, by listening to this side of the argument—the "parental" point of view, let's call it—that the role of the baseball player in society had changed. Over the past decade they had stopped being perceived as carnies and lowlifes from whom little was expected—*Don't lay around the house like a ballplayer*, Eddie Cantor's grandmother had told him—and were now thought of as role models, honor-bound to set an example for their youthful admirers by doing the right thing: in this case, turning the other cheek. Ironically, Cobb himself had more than once welcomed the "higher class of men" he saw streaming into the major leagues and pushing out the less serious player of his youth. Now the *New York Times* and other arbiters of public morality were condemning him—the man who led the league in presidential back-pats—for being no better than baseball's vanishing Neanderthals. The *Times* was especially tough on Cobb in the wake of the Lucker affair. "When he hears the cheers from the multitude in the bleachers he is not offended," its editorial said, "but when a few call him unpleasant names he takes the law into his own hands, because the league does not employ uniformed men to whip the offenders or shoot them." The paper called Ban Johnson "brave" for banning Cobb and said "cordial praise is due him."

Leave it to a Goody Two-shoes like Christy Mathewson to come down somewhere in the middle, stating a balanced, conventionally wise position that might have gotten him elected commissioner of baseball (if such an office had existed) or governor of Pennsylvania (his home state) but did not necessarily contain much true wisdom. "Of course Cobb is a high-strung individual, who is more likely to resent remarks made to him from the stands than most players," the Giants pitcher said, "but still the epithets that are applied to some of the fellows in some cities, especially those where no regular police are stationed, should be stopped. I, personally, think it is rather foolish to strike a spectator; not that some of them don't have it coming to them, but the player invariably is the sufferer."

With all the hemming and hawing he had to do, it must have slipped Mathewson's mind that in 1905 *he'd* punched a smart-alecky "lemonade boy" at Philadelphia's National League Park, splitting the lad's lip.

Still, without knowing it, he was, in this statement, articulating a policy that would be invoked down through the decades every time a player and a spectator tussled. What happened in 1922, for example, when Babe Ruth chased a heckler through the aisles of the Polo Grounds and then, failing to catch him, stood on the dugout roof and challenged any fan in the stadium to a fight? Or when Ted Williams, on several occasions in 1956, spit at Boston fans? There was no hearing. Nobody asked what had gotten those famous men so angry, and over how long a period of time the provocation had dragged on. No, Ruth and Williams were simply and summarily punished. The customer is always right; the ballplayer, already overly favored by fortune, should have known better, always.

Cobb's Tigers teammates, however, were having none of that nice-sounding, politic stuff. In 1912 the ballpark was still a bit like the Wild West, with a code of conduct to govern relations between spectators and players very much a work in progress. The latter, believing they were evolving faster than the former, wanted owners to increase police presence in stadiums to control the behavior of the sometimes barely civilized cranks. Since they rarely initiated the harassment, they considered themselves the aggrieved parties and saw no reason to settle for the magnates' feeble attempts at crowd control, which usually amounted to scheduling an occasional Ladies Day in hopes of diluting the testosterone. Ballplayers of that day were rallying around the issue of rowdyism more readily than even the hated reserve clause. There was no way Cobb's teammates would stand for his being punished while Lucker thumbed (or somethinged) his nose at them. They were behind him from the moment he hopped the rail.

Before that, actually.

The story that Cobb was hated by his fellow Tigers, even long after the hazing stopped, has continued into the present, but in fact by 1912 his teammates had more or less learned to live with the idea of a resident superstar and with the reality of Ty in particular. They had come to realize that for their own mental health, they just had to accept that he'd always be drawing lines in the sand, overreacting and generally making things more complicated. His saving grace was that what he wanted for himself—the chance to opt out of spring training, for example—he wanted for everybody. A month before the Lucker incident, the team had checked into the Chicago Beach Hotel and he had promptly announced that he did not like his room, on account of its being too close to the railroad tracks out back. The noise, he said "upset my nerves—I am almost sick." The management offered to make a change, but said a quieter room would not come open for seven hours or so—which only displeased Cobb further. Hughie Jennings offered to put him up, by himself, in any other hotel of his choosing, but Cobb rejected that solution, saying he wanted the whole team to pull out of the Chicago Beach so they could be together and at a quieter place. When Jennings declined to do that, Cobb stormed off and did not show up for the next day's game against the White Sox, which the Tigers lost 12–7. Such bouts of brattiness were unprofessional and inexcusable, but they came packaged with a league-leading batting average and a style of base running like nothing previously seen, and if you didn't excuse them what could you do? Besides, a good many of the less jealous players actively liked Cobb.

In December of the previous year, about ten teammates had gone as a group to see him perform in *The College Widow* in Detroit, and after his curtain calls, while the rest of the audience was still present, they presented him with a "handsome traveling bag" as a token of their admiration for his mind-boggling 1911 season. All of those present and a few others, back home for the winter from various far-flung states—a group that, significantly, included Davy Jones and Sam Crawford—had contributed to the gift's purchase. Pitcher Bill Donovan, the designated speaker, told a sheepish-looking Cobb that he hoped the suitcase "contained a lot of hits" and added "if Ty only runs the bases and cracks the old baseball in 1912 as well as he wins the college widow the American League pennant will float over the new Bennett Park next fall!"

The possibility that the team as a whole would sit out in support of Cobb came up among the players as soon as Ban Johnson's suspension came down, and they discussed it openly with the press. "The stand of the Detroit players has put to rout all talk of dissention in the ranks of the Tigers on account of the jealousy of Cobb," said *Sporting Life*. Navin let his players know he agreed with them in principle, but he pleaded with them not to interrupt the season, saying that because he had just built a new half-million-dollar stadium he was in precarious financial straits. He needed the cash flow, and wanted desperately to avoid the $1,000-per-game fine that the league would impose on the club if it failed to follow the schedule. The Tigers took the train to Philadelphia, where on Friday, May 17, they played and beat the A's 6–3 without Cobb in the lineup. Navin tried to assure the press that the moment of crisis had passed and that the problem could be solved via calm discussion. But even as he articulated this position, speaking to reporters, one paper noted, with a "very broad grin," he and Jennings, with some help from A's manager Connie Mack, were scouring the vicinity for sandlot and schoolboy players who might serve as strikebreakers if the Tigers walked out. The likelihood of that happening only became greater as the hours passed. On Friday night, the players, following another meeting, sent Ban Johnson this telegram:

> *Feeling Mr. Cobb is being done an injustice by your action in suspending him we, the undersigned, refuse to play another game after today until such action is adjusted to our satisfaction. He was fully justified in his action as no one could take such personal abuse from anyone. We want him reinstated for tomorrow's game, or there will be no game. If players cannot have protection, we must protect ourselves.*

Beneath this were the names of Crawford, Jones, and sixteen others— more than twice as many, by the way, as had signed the telegram of congratulations to Nap Lajoie for winning the "Chalmers Trophy" two years earlier. "We will stick together and win out," Cobb told the papers.

More than 20,000 came out to Shibe Park the next day, Saturday, May 18, to see what would happen. The Tigers, including Cobb, trotted out for batting practice. After a few moments, their first baseman Jim Delahanty asked the umpires, Ed Perrine and Bill Dinneen, if Cobb's suspension had been lifted. When they replied that it had not, Delahanty waved his teammates off the field. Some went back to the hotel, some into the stands to watch the game between the Philadelphia Athletics and the "Detroit Tigers." The first player strike in the history of major league baseball had begun.

By virtue of their very appearance, the squad of substitutes, or if you prefer, scabs, that emerged from the Athletics' clubhouse moments later struck a strong blow for organized labor. As noted by the future sportswriter Arthur "Bugs" Baer, who was among the twenty or so who suited up for the subs, "Any ballplayer who could stop a grapefruit from rolling uphill or hit a bull in the pants with a bass fiddle was given a chance of going direct from the semipros to the Detroits with no questions asked." The ace of the ersatz Tigers was twenty-year-old Aloysius Travers, a seminarian who was not even the best pitcher on the St. Joseph's College nine. Also on board was a thirty-one-year-old grifter who called himself Billy Maharg (a backward spelling of his real name, Graham) who in 1919 would become implicated in the Black Sox Scandal. It was, in other words, a crew of misfits worthy of a latter-day Hollywood sports comedy—and a Bad-News-Bearish film might have been made of the episode if only there had been the even slightest hint of something resembling a plot twist. But no, the fake Tigers didn't score one for underdogs everywhere by beating the big bad big leaguers from Philadelphia. Nor did they, by dint of either wacky stunts, belief in their dreams, or old-fashioned self-reliance, come surprisingly close to carrying the day. Instead the future priest got shelled and found himself behind 8–0 after four innings, by which point a large portion of the crowd had requested a refund—and the man who wore Cobb's (numberless) uniform, a future Philadelphia policeman named Bill Leinhauser, went 0-for-4 and had a fly ball bounce off his head. The final score was Athletics 24, "Tigers" 2.

The game only added fuel to the debate. The editorial board of the *Detroit Free Press* thought the idea of the players banding together to protect themselves was just fine. "The Tigers were perfectly right in doing as they did in Philadelphia," the paper said. "Ban Johnson has been inviting rebellion on the part of the ball players. Now he has it. . . . Only good can come from the affair." The *Sporting News* came down forcefully on the side of the owners and blamed Cobb for the trouble. It called him "a natural insurrectionist, pre-disposed to take the law into his own hands." The

New York Times also weighed in angrily on behalf of management. Comparing the players strike to a mutiny of soldiers and then, somewhat less stirringly, to a mutiny of bank clerks, it said "The sole underlying cause of [the Tigers' action] is the growing resentment of all authority and discipline throughout the world."

There was no Sunday baseball in Pennsylvania, but Ban Johnson called off the Monday game, then came to Philadelphia, where he assembled the Tiger players in his apparently spacious hotel room and told them they would each be fined $100 per game if they continued to strike. They remained resolute—until, later that day, Cobb, saying he was concerned about their financial hardship, urged them to go back to work. On Tuesday, in Washington, they returned to the field and beat Walter Johnson and the Senators, as they were now called, 2–0. As part of the settlement negotiations, their fine was reduced to $50 per man for the Philadelphia game they had boycotted. Cobb accepted a ten-day suspension and a $50 fine and the league said it would "take measures" to protect the players. (Not happy with Johnson's penchant for vagueness, an American Leaguer–turned–lawyer named Dave Fultz started the Baseball Players' Fraternity later that year. Cobb agreed to serve as one of four vice presidents, a mostly honorary title that showed he backed the organization's modest goals of increased security and more favorable waiver rules for those whose teams no longer wanted them. Partly because it failed to focus on the reserve clause, the biggest obstacle to a player ever earning his true market value, the BPT never gained traction and within a few years had disbanded.)

The next time the Tigers came through New York, in July, many predicted that Yankee fans would try to seek retribution on Lucker's behalf. They needn't have fretted. Nothing ugly occurred, but thriving in the uneasy atmosphere, as usual, Cobb reached first via a single in the first inning, then came all the way in to score when Crawford singled behind him—it was the first of Cobb's four hits that day. A week later, returning to the scene of the strike in Philadelphia, he had seven consecutive hits over the course of a doubleheader, and left town batting .430 for the season.

• • •

From a financial standpoint, at least, Cobb was now becoming comfortable. That autumn, he would ask for $15,000 a year, and then, after holding out until the second week of the 1913 season, sign for $12,000, which still made him the highest-paid player in the game (Lajoie's salary had dropped to $9,000). Feeling himself to be beyond grin-and-grip appearances at state fairs, and touring theater companies, he became instead, for the most part, an investor. He would still do a little barnstorming under the right circumstances, and lend his name to products such as a tonic called Nuxated Iron, but basically his off-season "activities" now centered around owning stock—in the *Augusta Chronicle* and Coca-Cola, and, before long, on the recommendation of the important men he was meeting in Detroit, General Motors as well, investments that over the decades made him rich. At twenty-six, he was a director of the First National Bank of Lavonia, Georgia, and a partner in a sporting goods retailer, W. B. Jarvis, that had stores in Detroit and Grand Rapids. He was also acquiring farmland in south Georgia and residential real estate.

His mother, Amanda, considered him a success, and said as much. "I am not so proud of Ty for the name he made for himself," she told a reporter from the *Los Angeles Times* in July of 1912, "as I am that he grew up, left home, made hundreds of new friends and always remembered me. Every opportunity he gets he likes to send me some little greeting and he likes to run home whenever he gets a vacation." In April of 1913, Ty and Charlie would buy a two-story house just off Walton Way, near what is now the main entrance to Augusta State University. Out back it had a stable for a horse or two and kennels for his beloved hunting dogs. It was not palatial, but it was handsome and airy, a sign to himself and the world that he was more than just another ballplayer. From certain angles, his life there looked idyllic. "He hunts, he shoots, he plays poker and he reads, all very much after the style that he plays baseball," said a profile of him that ran in the *Boston Globe*. "His wife is a Georgia girl and they have two children, a boy and a girl." On a typical off-season morning, Ty would linger over the morning paper, smoking a cigar, preferring not to be disturbed, then spend a couple of hours playing with his and the neighbor's kids. (When I visited the house in 2011 with Don Rhodes, author of *Ty Cobb: Safe at Home*, an Augusta-centric biography, the current owner showed me the termite-scarred remains of a child-size baseball bat dating back to Cobb's time that she had found behind the furnace.) Yet the externals of Cobb's life could be misleading, especially if they suggested true and deep contentment. He was always at least a bit anxious about one thing or another and no wonder. Newsworthy stuff kept happening to him.

On August 11, 1912, as he and Charlie were rushing from their home in Detroit at 103 Commonwealth to Michigan Central Station to catch a train for an exhibition game in Syracuse, New York, their open Chalmers was set upon by three hoodlums. The men were, Cobb said, "partly under the influence of liquor" and carried knives. As the car was traveling down a quiet side street, the men hopped on the running board and in some hard-to-place foreign accent, Cobb later said, demanded money. A struggle ensued and Cobb was stabbed on the shoulder. His wound wasn't serious but somehow the *Detroit News* got wind of the incident and blew it up into something worthy of a special edition. For an hour or so that evening, newsboys were standing on Detroit street corners hollering "Extra! Extra! Ty Cobb Is Dying!" "The murder of a president or a report that an alderman had refused a bribe scarcely could have upset things more," said the rival *Free Press*.

Laughing about it on the phone from Syracuse, Cobb told the *Free Press* that the men had quickly realized who he was, got scared, and ran away. Was it really as simple as that, though? Some speculated that the men were goons hired by Tom Foley to punish if not kill Cobb for what he'd done to Lucker. Others said it had something to do with a dispute between Cobb and a clubhouse attendant known as Scabby over a craps game. Cobb himself confused the issue by telling the *Syracuse Post-Dispatch* a much more self-aggrandizing tale than the one he'd told the *Free Press*, one in which he had his three attackers subdued and begging for mercy.

Nor do the accounts of the mugging end there. Decades later Cobb's ghostwriter and biographer, Al Stump, came up with two more, one for each of his Cobb books. In the latter one, written when Cobb was no longer around to dispute things, he claims that Cobb told him that he chased down the ringleader of the trio and pistol-whipped him with the Belgian Luger that he always carried. Cobb "slashed away until the man's face was faceless. Left him there, not breathing, in his own rotten blood," Stump wrote in his inimitable style. "Cobb believed he killed this mugger. A few days later a press report told of an unidentified body found off Trumbull in an alley." In 1996, two years after Stump's book came out, however, an ex-Syracuse prosecutor and forensics expert named Doug Roberts investigated Stump's claim of an unidentified body being found, and wrote, in an exhaustive piece published in the *National Baseball Research Journal*, that there had been no such "press reports" nor did the Wayne County coroner during this period process a corpse that could by any stretch have been one of Cobb's attackers.

Perhaps the most interesting thing about the attempted carjacking, or whatever it was, was that Cobb got off the train in Syracuse, went directly to the stadium, had his wound cleaned and dressed, and then got three hits in a Detroit victory over a team from the New York State League. From there the Tigers traveled to Manhattan for a game against the Yankees. Their luggage was lost, though, and they had to make do with borrowed New York road uniforms and, said the *Free Press*, "ill-fitting, unbroken footwear" hurriedly bought for the occasion or perhaps supplied by the Yanks. Playing in those cruel shoes, Cobb had two of the club's three hits that day and in the field "killed off a couple of triples by the most remarkable catches seen in a decade."

Faced with adversity, he produced gems. Was he the Peach or the Oyster?

PART THREE

STANDING ON TOP OF THE dugout, Cobb faced the cheering fans and—though he would need to say a few words to them, and at the age of almost thirty-two, still hated public speaking—smiled. His manager for the last eleven years, Hughie Jennings, stood, or rather, danced next to him, in his celebratory "Ee-Yah Man" style, his increasingly shaky hold on the team not a issue just then, his complexion, in actuality somewhere between "florid" and "jaundiced," today striking one sportswriter swept up in the happy moment as a fine "healthy tan." It was that rare thing for a team whose fate it had been for almost ten years to help form the pack behind the annual pennant winner: a feel-good moment. People cheered and applauded the two Tigers, even though this was the Polo Grounds, in those days after Hilltop but before the stadium, New York Yankees turf.

It was a strange time in baseball. The date was August 24, 1918, smack in the middle of both the influenza pandemic that would kill more than 50 million people around the globe, and America's involvement in World War I, and for that summer at least the championship season seemed to many a trifling matter. "I don't believe people care to see a lot of big, healthy young men on the field playing ball," Cobb had said two months earlier, "while their sons and brothers are abroad risking their lives to conquer the Huns." The U.S. government had two months earlier declared baseball a "nonessential industry" for the duration of the war, and the magnates were preparing to shut down the season early, by Labor Day, a move that they portrayed as patriotic, but which in fact had more to do with sagging attendance and a scarcity of good men as players signed up (or were drafted) for service and several minor leagues went bust.

The Tigers' season would end (symbolically if not literally; there were actually two more games) with a squadron of military "aeroplanes" flying acrobatically over Sportsman's Park in St. Louis and Cobb and George Sisler, the phenomenal young second baseman for the Browns, pitching. But that surreal finale was still a week away. On this hot and humid Saturday afternoon in New York there was a speech to be made, and between halves of a doubleheader against the Yankees, Cobb clambered atop what is every ballpark's natural podium to say his piece. At the sight of him and his manager the crowd first stood and gave a prolonged ovation, then, sensing he was not a commanding speaker, quieted itself. "We all have to help the war effort!" Cobb said in his high-pitched voice. "We should all buy war savings stamps—I've just bought $250 worth myself!" Then, once their cheers subsided, he gave them even bigger news: he had enlisted in the Army, he said. He would have not just some show job like coaching the baseball team, but would work in the "hazardous gas and chemical division," an outfit more dangerous than the infantry. He expected to be in France by the end of October. There was a very good chance, he added, that whatever happened to him Over There, fighting Fritz, they might never see him in a baseball uniform again.

One imagines a moment of silence—this was a surprise that needed a second to sink in—followed by a lusty roar, not just for his bravery but for the spectators' own good fortune. Baseball fans are always delighted to stumble upon a historic moment, like Merkle's Boner or Ruth's Called Shot. Now the 8,000 in attendance that afternoon could someday proudly say, along with five or six million other baseball fanatics, "I was there when Cobb retired."

Apart from being a rare joyous interval for the jungaleers, it was for Cobb an even odder juncture, a time when he faced no opposition—not from his fellow players, a front-office father figure, a stodgy league president, a perfidious press: not even from a grandstand full of Yankee cranks. "The crowd cheered and yelled as lustily as it ever did for one of Ty's long drives," said the *Milwaukee Sentinel*. It was not, as things turned out, the end of an era—it was not even the interruption of a career—but it made perfect emotional sense to think that it might have been. There was a certain logic to the idea of him exiting the stage now, after thirteen seasons.

He was, as much as anyone ever is, a fully formed man, and a baseball player with nothing left to prove, as well as a wee bit past his prime. In the six seasons since Cobb had charged into the stands at Hilltop Park to beat up an obnoxious disabled man much had happened in his life, but little had changed fundamentally.

As Fred Lieb, the Herodotus of the Detroit Baseball and Amusement Co., writes in *The Detroit Tigers*, "The season of 1913 was pretty much a duplicate of 1912, another sixth-placer, with the percentage dipping from .451 to .431. . . . Cobb again provided such artistic success as there was. He won the batting crown for the seventh successive season. Again it was a tussle with Joe Jackson, and at the finish Ty led by the usual margin. . . . Cobb wound up with .390 to the shoeless one's .373." (Jackson would be his main rival for the batting crown from 1911 to 1920.) A more telling stat, however, was that Cobb finished third in stolen bases that year (with 51), behind Clyde Milan of Washington (75) and Philadelphia's Eddie Collins (55). The decline can be explained in part by leg injuries. He jammed his right knee while running the bases in late June at League Park in Cleveland, and soon afterward in Chicago shortstop Buck Weaver came down on the same swollen joint with his spikes, putting Cobb on the sidelines except for pinch hitting duties for the next week. (Trying to ease himself back into the lineup, he convinced Jennings to let him play second base, but after one game, in which he made three errors on five easy chances in a loss to the Athletics, the experiment was abandoned.)

Another factor in the steals decline was that his season didn't begin that year until April 30, owing to a months-long salary squabble marked by bitter public statements. Navin, knowing that Cobb hated being depicted as a troublemaker, told the press in mid-April that the dispute was over discipline, not money.

> *Mr. Cobb did not make baseball; baseball made him. A player cannot be bigger than the game which creates him. To give in to Mr. Cobb now in his present attitude would be to concede that he is greater than the game itself, for he has set all its laws at defiance.*
>
> *If Mr. Cobb doesn't like a room a hotel clerk gives him he quits the club for a week. If he doesn't like what a silly man in the grandstand yells*

*at him he punches his face and is again out of the game. . . . If he doesn't
feel like practicing he stays away from the park. He believes that his
greatness precludes his being subject to club discipline. I think Mr. Cobb
eventually will recognize his fault—until he does there can be no understanding between us.*

At first Cobb said "I shall make no comment" about Navin's accusations, "which were meant to mold public opinion against me." And for
a few days he stayed mum and kept up his regular schedule, which that
spring had included a bit of barnstorming in the South with a team of
"All-Stars," and community-service events like a dinner for the Animal
Welfare Committee of the Twentieth Century Club, and an appearance at
the state prison in Atlanta with opera singer Enrico Caruso. He must have
been brooding about Navin's characterization of him, though, because
before long he issued a lengthy, signed statement that accused the owner
of "blackening my name as a ballplayer." In it Cobb claimed that he was
hardly the only Tiger who missed an occasional practice and asked why
if his alleged offenses had been so disruptive to the team's spirit was he
not punished at the time they occurred. Cobb got support in his position
from members of the U.S. Congress, particularly Representative Thomas
Hardwick of the Augusta area, who criticized the Tigers for not showing
the Georgia Peach the proper respect, and, more significant to Navin and
his fellow magnates, vowed to revive dormant antitrust legislation that
could, if passed, lead to a radical restructuring of major league baseball.
Not long after Hardwick made that threat, Navin broke the stalemate by
inviting Cobb to meet with him in Detroit to settle the matter, just as he
had done five years earlier. Sitting face-to-face, the two took only a couple
of hours to come to terms, and when Cobb signed his contract for 1913
he said, "This will be my last holdout."

It turned out to be a dreary year for Cobb, one in which he frequently
despaired over the mediocrity of the club, and fantasized about being
traded to New York, Boston, or Philadelphia—and did a lot of sighing.
On a rainy June afternoon in Syracuse, where the Tigers had gone for
their annual exhibition game against a team from the New York State
League, he was described by the *Free Press* as holed up in his hotel and

"spending most of the day writing letters in the seclusion of his boudoir." Yet by the end of the season he had worked his way through the gloom and he and Navin were as solid as they had ever been. When one day Navin opened a letter from Washington manager Clark Griffith and found a check for $100,000 and a note saying, in effect, All I want for this is Ty Cobb, Navin wrote back to say his star was not for sale. After Cobb signed a $15,000 contract for 1914 that December, he wrote Navin something that sounds a little like a love note:

> Since our talk in New York [where they both went to watch the A's-Giants World Series], where we came to understand each other so well, I have only one thought in mind, how foolish I think I have been ever to think of leaving Detroit to play on some other team. I am entirely satisfied with the conditions under which I am playing in Detroit, due to your generous treatment, and I hope that I shall remain with the Tigers as long as I am able to play the game. I am absolutely satisfied with Detroit. I like the city, the fans and the management of the club. My treatment by the owners of the club has been of the very best and I want the fans to know that I am loyal to them and to you. You undoubtedly have seen several stories in the papers recently about trouble between me and the club, but I don't know how they originated. The offer you made me in New York has greatly pleased me and I want to take this opportunity of thanking you. Please give the letter, or any part of it to the press. Go as strong as you want with it and I'll stand back of every word.

Was this a sign of a kinder, gentler Cobb? Was he finally mellowing? Not yet. For the duration of his career, he never stopped getting into scuffles (or worse), unable as he often was to ignore even the slightest hint of provocation. In late August of 1914, for example, he barged into the Senators' clubhouse after a game at National Park, and a few moments later found himself in a furious "grappling contest" with Washington pitcher Joe Engel. The Tigers tried to pass it off as "friendly" roughhousing, but Engel needed five stitches after Cobb "forced him heavily against one of the doors of a locker," said the *Washington Post*, and neither combatant would subsequently comment on the affair. It was probably over something that had happened that day on the field, though; most of Cobb's spats fit with the tit-for-tat testiness that marked those deadball days. Two weeks after the Engel episode, back at Navin Field, he slid so hard into White Sox third baseman Jim Breton that he almost knocked him unconscious—a payback for the day before, when Breton, an ex–football player according to the *Pittsburgh Press*, tackled and held him down while he was trying to round the bag and run home. That was the way the game was played. No hard feelings. Most of the time.

Cobb never hazed youngsters in the aggressive, quasi-formal way that he himself had been hazed, but, like a lot of veterans he demanded that players know their place in the pecking order. Yannigans had better tread carefully around him, and anything less than outright reverence from a busher would be punished. Rutledge Osborne, a second baseman for the Wofford College nine, learned this lesson the hard way. When in early 1913, Cobb's "Georgia All-Stars" crossed paths with the Wofford Terriers in Spartanburg, South Carolina, during a brief barnstorming tour, the cocky Osborne used the occasion to taunt and tease Cobb, in what seemed like an attempt to impress the hometown crowd. Cobb said little that day, but shortly thereafter, when Wofford and the "Stars" met up again in Greenville for a second game, he noticed Osborne on the hotel elevator—and dragged him off and into his room, where, the student later said, "he demanded an apology." Instead, Osborne drew a pistol and in the ensuing melee he was beaten up rather badly, both by Cobb and some of Cobb's teammates, who had come running when they heard the commotion.

"The Hotel as Battlefield" could be the title of a chapter in a history of those days. Although ballplayers, because they fought and caroused more or less constantly, were usually limited to the second- or third-best place in town, one of Cobb's most famous battles occurred at the luxurious Oriental Hotel in Dallas. It was in March of 1917, when the Tigers and Giants were playing a series of exhibition games in Fort Worth. The trouble started when Charlie "Buck" Herzog, the New York utility infielder, rode Cobb hard during batting practice for spending the morning on the golf course and showing up late. That night at the Oriental, where both clubs were staying, Cobb told Herzog "that he would do well to stay off me." But the next day Herzog, who had a reputation for being irritating, resumed the goading, and in the third inning, after Cobb had singled, he attempted to steal second and "came in a little high" and spiked Herzog (who had been blocking the base path) in the quadriceps. The two rolled in the dirt a while, too close to each other to throw meaningful punches, until they were separated by teammates and dragged to their respective dugouts. But that wasn't the end of it. A few hours later, while Cobb was having dinner at the hotel, Herzog, said the *New York Times,* "went over to Cobb's table and notified the Detroit star that he would call on him in his room, and they would settle their differences." The affair had the trappings of a duel. Both men even agreed to bring seconds—Giants infielder Heinie Zimmerman for Herzog; Detroit trainer Harry Tuthill for Cobb.

The *Times* report is written so assuredly, and with such detail, as to suggest its (uncredited) reporter had a bedside seat:

> *After a few words the belligerents threw off their coats and proceeded to dust off the furniture with each other. The result was a foregone conclusion, as Herzog weighs only 147 pounds while Cobb weighs not far from 200 pounds. Herzog was worsted in the encounter, Cobb knocking him down two or three times, cutting him up about the face, and dislodging a couple of teeth. Tuthill and Zimmerman watched the scrap, and when it had gone what they considered far enough they separated the combatants, who then shook hands and declared a truce.*

A few moments later, in the lobby, Cobb ran into Giants manager John McGraw, who "proceeded to give him a tongue lashing," presumably about his behavior on the field that day. After listening for a few moments, "Cobb kept his temper and walked away" from the already legendary skipper without saying a word. Before he retired for the evening he told a group of reporters that he would not play against the Giants again that spring "because I don't want to be the goat." The next morning, with Jennings's approval, he left to work out with the Reds in Cincinnati. "He is too valuable a piece of property to be brawling around with men who have less to risk," said the manager, "and I am glad he is going to be removed from this atmosphere."

The Reds that year were being managed by the retired Christy Mathewson, who was writing a syndicated newspaper column on the side. As soon as Cobb arrived he interviewed him about the Herzog incident. Cobb said he was "extremely sorry" about what had happened. "I did not want to get in a jam with him and I didn't want to hurt Herzog. I shouldn't have minded but he got my goat and I lost my temper, and I realize I have a bad one, especially on the ball field."

Reading the accounts of a famous fight Cobb had with a Detroit grocer in 1914, one gets a sense of how close to the boiling point he always was. This drama unfolded on the evening of June 20, a Saturday, after a game in which Cobb had walked twice in four times up as the Tigers beat the visiting Senators 1–0. Arriving home from Navin Field with Washington manager Clark Griffith, Walter Johnson (by then a close friend of Cobb's), and several other Senator players—who said opponents did not fraternize so much in those days?—he found his wife, Charlie, upset over an argument she'd had with one William Carpenter, proprietor of the Progressive Market, on nearby Hamilton Boulevard. She had called the merchant to say that a small piece of fish she had bought from his shop appeared spoiled. We don't know how he responded initially, but his tone was not friendly, and when she replied that owing to his attitude she would not be shopping with him again he said, "I'm glad of it, because I don't want your trade." It was only a few minutes after Charlie told him this story that Cobb was standing in the Progressive Market with a .32 automatic revolver.

Pointing to the telephone with his gun, he told Carpenter that he should call Mrs. Cobb and apologize. This much was done, but just as he was hanging up, and Cobb was calming down, one of the store's butchers, Carpenter's twenty-year-old brother-in-law, Howard Harding, walked in, saw what was happening, grabbed a meat cleaver, and ordered Cobb to leave. It is not clear whether he recognized his famous customer, but Cobb said, "he seemed to want trouble and I gave him what he was looking for." After handing his firearm to a bystander, a teenage boy who worked in a neighboring store, he went outside with Harding and began trading blows. Cobb soon had Harding down on the sidewalk and was about to hit him again when Carpenter intervened, closely followed by the police, who led both combatants into a paddy wagon for transportation to the Bethune Avenue station. They were released later that evening. In an interview with the *Free Press* the next day, Carpenter could barely contain his outrage at the special treatment he thought Cobb was receiving. "If no criminal action is taken against him I'll institute a civil suit, for slander, based upon the epithets that Cobb hurled at me," Carpenter said. "I think it is my duty to the public to have Cobb suppressed, and I'm willing to do all I can to suppress him. He's dangerous when he gets mad. I think he's unsafe. He gets mad just like a child and he is just as easily soothed. He quieted right down when I apologized."

Many who know something about Cobb, but don't know quite enough, file this incident under "hate crime" or "bigotry." For this we can blame biographer Charles Alexander, who, just as he did with the Euclid Hotel brawl, gives the incident unwarranted racial overtones by describing one of the principals—in this case, Howard Harding (whom he calls Harold Harding)—as "a young black man." How he came to think Harding was not white is difficult to say. The young man is never referred to as a Negro in contemporary accounts, and his race is noted with a legible W on federal census forms. Alexander's errors have found many willing ears. We should not be surprised. Monsters intrigue us.

At the police station Cobb was "released," said the *Free Press*, "on the personal bond of W. G. Chittenden, one of the proprietors of the Pontchartrain Hotel." Carpenter it seems was on to something when he spoke of favoritism. Detroit police commissioner John Gillespie said that while Cobb perhaps did not strictly speaking have a permit to carry the revolver he brought to the Progressive Market, he had the informal permission of the city to own the gun, based on his status and tendency of some people to pick on celebrities. It was that kind of thinking that caused Carpenter to press charges. On June 24, a warrant was issued for Cobb for disturbing the peace. The next day he pled guilty in Justice Court and paid a $50 fine, the maximum. The laws of physics were harsher on him still: he had fractured his precious right thumb on Harding's working-class head and would be out of the lineup for nearly two months. He said, as he usually did in such situations, that he felt "keenly disgraced" by his actions, and he apologized to his family.

He might have also apologized to the club. During his absence, the Tigers, who had been in first place in late May, went 17–25 and dropped far out of the pennant race. Not everything had gone so badly in 1914 for Detroit. Thanks to Navin's expert negotiating the team had repelled most advances from the Federal League, a rival outfit that was begun the year before, and before it went out of business in 1915 had succeeded in jacking up player salaries across the board while siphoning off 20 percent of the American League's attendance. Not only did the Tigers not lose anyone valuable to "the Feds," they acquired during this time two excellent Harrys, one an outfielder, the other a pitcher. Harry Coveleski, a tall southpaw from the coal-mining hamlet of Shamokin, Pennsylvania, had a meteoric rise with the Phillies in 1908, then developed arm problems that put him back in the minors. A complicated fellow, he was said to have a crippling aversion to the song "Sweet Adeline," which when hummed by his opponents in a way that mimicked a trombone, the historian Fred Lieb tells us, caused him to come apart emotionally, the way Rube Waddell did when you showed him a puppy. By the time a Tigers scout spotted Coveleski playing for Chattanooga of the Southern Association in 1913 he had reinvented himself: now he was a rubber-limbed workhorse (he'd pitched 32 complete games for the Lookouts, winning 28 of them) with a crippling aversion to the song "Silver Threads Among the Gold." Go figure. Before his arm went bad again, and all the mean tromboning overwhelmed him, he went 65–36 with a 2.30 ERA for the Tigers over the following three years.

The other Harry, Heilmann, would last longer and prove to be a key figure in Tigers history. Navin heard about the nineteen-year-old San Francisco kid when he was hitting .300 for the Portland Beavers of the Pacific Coast League, and signed him for $1,500 (the Beavers had signed him for a spaghetti dinner, so that was a step up). The plan was to have him replace Sam Crawford, who turned thirty-four that year and was getting slow and expensive, in right field. Heilmann, still an awkward adolescent, wasn't ready to do that in 1914, but after a year or so of seasoning back in the PCL with the San Francisco Seals, he returned and became a pretty fair hitter for the Tigers—and then, over the next three years, he became a great one. "Slug," as he was known, more for his lack of foot speed than for his home run production, hit above .390 four times for Detroit, including 1923, when he hit .403. Some said he had a tense relationship with Cobb, the only Tiger to exceed his .342 lifetime batting average. But in what amounted to a deathbed interview, given in 1951, shortly after Cobb had written him to leak the news that he had been elected to the Hall of Fame, Heilmann said it was Cobb's coaching that transformed him from a .280 hitter into a star. "Cobb was a great teacher of batting," he told H. G. Salsinger. "He taught me everything I knew. There was never anyone like him and there will never be another." In time Heilmann, Cobb, and Bobby Veach would form one of baseball's best all-time outfields, but not even the three of them could save the Tigers from finishing fourth in 1914.

The enduring mediocrity of the Tigers did not tarnish Cobb, who was by then baseball royalty. "Ty Cobb is Henry Ford's assistant in the job of keeping Detroit in the headlines," wrote the syndicated columnist George Fitch. "Caruso couldn't fill Detroit's ballpark once in a lifetime, but Ty Cobb has been doing it for years." He had come into the big leagues almost a decade earlier with what seemed like a shockingly naive—or maybe it was insane—style of play and in spite of peer pressure and direct advice to do things more conventionally he had modified his methods only sparingly—and achieved thrilling and unprecedented results. Special exceptions were for him the rule; he could get away with almost anything. Ban Johnson declared that his meager total of 345 at-bats that year was enough for him to qualify for the batting title, which he won, with an average of .368, for the seventh straight time. Nor was he done putting up big numbers. The next season, 1915, was arguably his overall best: he hit .369, knocked in 99 runs, and stole 96 bases. "I always regretted that I didn't make it a hundred steals," Cobb said. Such were his regrets.

The only player who came close to overshadowing him (now that Honus Wagner, in his late thirties, had slowed drastically) was Tris Speaker, the center fielder for the Boston Red Sox. Speaker, who played a very short center, close behind the second baseman, was generally considered a better fielder than Cobb and was almost as good a hitter. He was a proven winner, too, having helped lead Boston to the world championship in 1912. What the pride of Hubbard, Texas, lacked was charisma. St. Louis Browns manager George Stallings once told *Sporting Life* that Speaker was "a greater baseball player than Ty Cobb overall— but not a star. In my opinion, a star is a player who makes his individual work stand out. Ty Cobb is a star." Indeed in 1916 Cobb became the first ballplayer to be offered the lead role in a feature film. Lost to history now, *Somewhere in Georgia*, with a script by Grantland Rice, was a silent six-reeler that told the story of a Detroit Tigers rookie who gets kidnapped by a crooked bank clerk. Shot in a few weeks on Staten Island, it was not a blockbuster, but the film did demonstrate that Cobb had transcended baseball.

Everyone in America knew who he was, and to prove it a newspaper in Syracuse, New York, asked its editorial cartoonist to draw a picture of a necktie and another of a corncob on the face of an envelope. The piece, with no other markings on it, was dropped in the mail and a few days later it reached the home of Ty Cobb in Augusta.

CHAPTER TWENTY-THREE

EARLY IN THE YEAR NOW under discussion—1915—a Detroit resident on trial for prostitution was asked by the judge if she could name the governor of Michigan, and when she lit up and hollered "Ty Cobb!" he banged his gavel and let her go. I mention this only because I wonder if Hughie Jennings, the manager of the Tigers, had a picture of this woman, or someone like her, leaving the Pontchartrain Hotel through a side door with team owner Frank Navin. How else to explain Hughie's continuing employment? The club hadn't won a pennant since 1909, his players groused about his dubious leadership skills (a problem tied to his drinking), and as far back as 1911 Navin could be heard making what sounded like pre-firing grumbles. "I'm not at all satisfied with the way things are going," he told the sportswriters. "Jennings appears to have lost hold on his men. They seem to have no confidence in his judgment. Our pitchers have been handled poorly and the team has shown little science. In fact, under Jennings we have always won on the abilities of our players, rather than by strategy." The only thing more ominous would have been the dreaded "vote of confidence" each skipper receives while his replacement is being fitted for his uniform. And yet five disappointing finishes later, Jennings was not only still around but making about $10,000. He was also, along with Cobb, partners with Navin in the ownership of the Providence Grays, a minor league club to which a nineteen-year-old pitcher named Babe Ruth had been sent the previous season after a few less than satisfactory games with the Boston Red Sox.

What kept Hughie in the owner's good graces? If we can rule out blackmail, then it likely had something to do with the fact that he was a salt-of-the-earth sort, a lovable leftover from the riotous old Orioles who was much esteemed around the league. Navin's fellow magnates were always saying things like "I'd snatch up ol' Hughie in a moment if the Tigers ever let him go." Whether they meant this or not, it may have convinced Navin that his manager was more valuable than he sometimes seemed, dancing around the coaching box, punctuating his incessant patter (*Atta boy, Ty; Way to go, Ty; Way to hit the ball, Tyrus*) with strange little *Ee-Yah* yelps. Or perhaps it was Hughie's ability to always win *just enough* games that kept him in his job. It was indeed the rare season when the Tigers weren't at or close to the top for at least a little while, fanning the flame of hope.

For a considerable stretch of 1915, it looked as if Navin's patience was finally paying off. As Fred Lieb wrote, the Tigers that season appeared to have coalesced into pennant contenders again. "The outfield was really a punishing affair—Bobby Veach came fast that year, hit .313 and bombarded the fences with 40 doubles and 10 triples. And Crawford still had plenty of dynamite in his cudgel; he just missed .300, finishing with .299, and was second to Ty (.369) in number of hits [183 as compared to 208]." Hughie meanwhile packed the infield with the baseball equivalent of Styrofoam peanuts—necessary but interchangeable utility men like Ralph "Pep" Young and Ossie Vitt—and for pitchers he had not just Coveleski but the righties George "Hooks" Dauss and Jean Dubuc, a long-forgotten trio who that year combined to win 63 games. It is no wonder the team went 18–7 at the start and spent most of the season either in first place or, as Lieb put it, "a short mashie pitch from the top" behind the Boston Red Sox.

The revitalized Tigers and Cobb seemed to inspire each other. Although he had said in spring training (he was there from the start for a change) that he planned to take it easy on the base paths in 1915, in order to give his battle-scarred legs a break, he wound up running more often, and more successfully, than ever before. In June alone he stole home five times. "Look, there he goes!" said the supposedly stodgy *New York Times* on the fifth steal:

Ty Cobb is loose again on a base-galloping spree. He romps to first on a single. Slim Caldwell pitches to Nunamaker, and the ball nestles in his

*big mitt. Cobb, a few feet off first suddenly bolts into action and races
to second. Nunamaker, amazed at the Georgian's daring, stands dumbfounded.*

*He throws the ball to Dan Boone just as the Southern Flyer jumps
into second base. The steel spikes flash in the waning sun and Cobb is lost
in a cloud of dust. Nunamaker's nervous toss rolls into center field, and
the Georgia Gem bounds to his feet and tears to third. He's as safe as the
Bank of England. Cobb's sarcastic smile angers his hoodwinked opponents.*

*Now the speed-crazed comet dashes up and down the third-base line,
trying to rattle Caldwell. Will Cobb have the nerve to try to steal home?
You said it; he will. Caldwell doesn't think so. No one thinks so, but Cobb.
The Yanks' lanky pitcher hurls the ball at the batsman like a rifle ball. As
the ball left his hand Cobb bounded over the ground like a startled deer.*

*At the plate crouched Nunamaker. He was so surprised that he didn't
know his own name. Cobb dashed through the air toward the scoring
pan. His lithe body swerved away from Nunamaker's reach and clouds of
dirt kicked up by his spikes blinded the eyes of Nunamaker, Caldwell and
Silk O'Loughlin.*

*The umpire ruled that the catcher didn't touch Cobb. He also ruled
that Cobb hadn't touched the plate. While the Yankee players were protest-
ing, Cobb sneaked around the bunch and touched the plate.*

*A smart young feller, this same Cobb. Caldwell threw his glove high
in the air in derision at O'Loughlin's decision. Cobb pulled the wool over
their eyes like a "sharper" unloading mining stock on a Rube. Caldwell
was put out of the game for being mad that Cobb had outwitted him.*

And so on.

But if the Tigers were really headed back to the World Series that year,
they had to go through the Red Sox. Boston had finished second the
previous year, when the Athletics won the pennant, but now that Connie
Mack had been forced—by the financial constraints caused by the Federal League, he said—to sell off his star players, the Red Sox were widely
considered the team to beat in the AL, and they played to expectations,
holding down first place in the standings from the middle of May onward. It doesn't always work this way in baseball, but the most successful

team in the league also had the most talent: future Hall of Famers Tris Speaker, Babe Ruth, and Herb Pennock; might-have-been Hall members Smoky Joe Wood and Carl Mays; and in Bill Carrigan a manager whom Ruth said was "the best I ever played for." Besides being good they were a colorful (if not always lovable) bunch. Ruth, a left-handed pitcher then, less than two years out of a Baltimore orphanage, was already becoming famous for his Falstaffian appetites and guileless charm. Mays, a right-handed "submariner" who scraped his knuckles on the mound when he threw his exaggerated signature pitch, was a "strange, cynical figure," wrote F. C. Lane, the editor of *Baseball Magazine*, who "aroused more ill-will, more positive resentment, than any other ballplayer on record" due to his "sarcastic" attitude with teammates, and his tendency to throw at opponents' heads. Hubert "Dutch" Leonard, another headhunter, was described by historian David Jones as "a hard-throwing, spectacularly talented left-hander" who was "regarded as a selfish, cowardly player by many of his contemporaries." And Tris Speaker, a veritable riot of biases, brawled constantly with the Roman Catholics on the club and confided to Lieb that he was a proud Ku Klux Klansman.

The Red Sox and Tigers played six series during the 1915 season, a total of 22 games, and while some were pitchers' duels and some were slugfests, some one-sided floggings and some nail-biters, all were bench-clearing brawls waiting to happen. Players trash-talked trashier than usual. Batters, especially Detroit batters, constantly complained to umpires that balls were being tampered with, and demanded that they be replaced. Fans, or to be more precise Boston fans, showered the field with bottles and what the sportswriters described as "hard wads of paper," most of them aimed at Cobb. Both managers, but especially Jennings, used an extraordinary number of pitchers. Clearly something extra was at stake, and something had to give. Both teams expected to win the pennant, Boston because it inherited the leadership position abdicated by the Athletics, the Tigers because they had the best player in baseball, they felt overdue—and they had gotten off to such a swell start. And yet in each home city decidedly different emotions hung in the balance. If the Red Sox failed to make it to the Series they would be disappointed by their second straight second-place finish, but they would most likely regard it as a very frustrating delay. The Tigers, meanwhile, were older, their self-image easier to shatter. For them, no pennant meant starting over and even those on the team who had the time lacked the psychological energy to rebuild practically from scratch.

The first time the teams faced each other that year, on May 11 at Navin Field, the starting pitcher for Boston was twenty-year-old George Herman Ruth. "Built like a bale of cotton," as the *New York Times* said, the Babe (as he was already known) was not quite a phenom yet. When he had come up to the bigs a year earlier, after a couple of months with the minor league Baltimore Orioles, he had looked promising but raw, and manager Carrigan had used him in only four games (he went 2–1) before shipping him to the Providence Grays for seasoning. His Boston teammates didn't know what to make of a lunky kid who seemed so new to the world of trains, hotels, and restaurants (but sported a dandy-ish haircut that involved a pompadour "roaching" over his forehead), who showed such promise as a pitcher yet was also so interested in honing his hitting skills that he, a mere yannigan, had the temerity to take batting practice with the regulars, or at least try to. (The older Red Sox told him he couldn't and when he shrugged and took his cuts anyway, they sawed the handles off his bats. His hazing was in some ways like Cobb's, but less fierce and more contracted.)

Cobb had missed his chance to see the Babe in action the year before, when on a sweltering mid-July day at Fenway, while he was still recovering from the thumb injury he incurred while pummeling the not-black butcher, the Tigers knocked Ruth out of the box in the seventh inning, and went on to win 5–2. In the meantime he had no doubt asked around about the young pitcher and learned that while he had a tendency to wilt in the home stretch, he was (given his personal habits) a surprisingly disciplined performer who could keep batters guessing and hold runners on base. For his part, Ruth would have known Cobb by his reputation, but unless he was taken aside by Carrigan, or one of the other Boston players, and given unsolicited advice about the Peach, that would have been it. Homework would never be Ruth's thing.

What could he have learned in any case? There was no good way to pitch to Cobb, who hit lefties as consistently as righties. You could try to surprise him with a curve when he was expecting a fastball, or try to trick him outright and see how that worked. In the seventh inning of a game on August 22, 1909, at Navin Field, Walter Johnson started off Cobb with three intentional balls and then suddenly zipped the next one in, waist high and tight. Perhaps the Big Train thought Cobb would be caught off guard and proffer a feeble swing resulting in a feeble grounder; instead he stroked a triple and knocked in two runs. So scratch that. Some thought the best way to pitch to Cobb was to constantly push him off the plate or knock him down. Cobb was no Hughie Jennings, willing to let balls bounce off his noggin until the sunset. He absolutely hated the brushback pitch and felt it should be barred from baseball—which made him extra susceptible to it. It was a slim thread for a pitcher to cling to, but there it was.

We don't know if Ruth felt intimidated in that initial encounter but he was certainly overmatched. Cobb batted against him twice and calmly bopped two singles into right field. By Cobb's third trip to the plate, the Babe was already "in the showerbath," said E. A. Batchelor, having walked eight and given up five runs in five and two-thirds innings. But if the Tigers' 5–1 win felt like the start of something big for Detroit, it wasn't. The next day Ernie Shore flummoxed them with a dancing, diving pitch that looked too good to be legal. Hughie kept running from the dugout and yelling "Emory ball!" and imploring umpire Bill Dinneen to check what sportswriters liked to call "the pill" for signs of intentional scuffing. The manager's histrionics—which didn't end until Dinneen pressed a ball into his hands and told him to please send it to Ban Johnson for a more thorough examination—made the Detroit crowd chuckle, even in the midst of a 4–1 defeat. Dark clouds returned the next day, though, Thursday, May 13, when Dutch Leonard took the mound.

Leonard—and not Cobb or Carl Mays—may have actually been the least-beloved man in baseball. He continually moaned about his teammates not giving him run support, complained about his salary, criticized the owner, Joseph J. Lannin, for undermining the manager, and impressed umpire Billy Evans as the whiniest man he'd ever met, in terms of balls and strikes calls. A few weeks after the May series against the Tigers, Lannin would suspend Leonard indefinitely and send him home to California, not for any particular offense, like drinking or breaking curfew, but "just for the way he acts." From the first inning of the May 15 game

Leonard showed he was less interested in throwing strikes than throwing at Cobb's head. The two argued heatedly across the sixty feet, six inches all afternoon, as Leonard, who had pinpoint control that day, continually pitched Cobb high and tight. Cobb drew the only two walks Leonard issued, and in the sixth inning was hit (on the shoulder) by a pitch. Trying to make Leonard pay, he twice stole his way around the bases, scoring the Tigers' only runs, but the Red Sox scored four and took the series.

As he made the circuit that summer around the American League cities, Cobb was celebrated on the occasion of the tenth anniversary of his arrival in the major leagues. Before a game in Philadelphia, the town where overzealous fans once threatened to shoot him, he was presented with a custom-made double-barreled shotgun. The Boston chapter of the Shriners gave him a diamond-encrusted Ancient Arabic Order of the Nobles of the Mystic Shrine badge. On the exact date of his anniversary, August 26, before a game against the Red Sox at Navin Field, the fans presented him with two armfuls of flowers and prolonged applause. The *New York Times* on its editorial page said that even with a war raging in Europe "and the fate of empires trembling in the balance" he remained "a personality of national importance."

As its way of celebrating the anniversary, the *New Orleans Times-Picayune* had the doubly odd notion of having Hughie Jennings interview Cobb on a number of nonbaseball topics. The result didn't run as a written-through piece, but the paper did feature, in bare-bones form, a batch of Cobb's responses:

"Mrs. Cobb is not a suffragist or an anti-suffragist. She finds her interest in other problems."

"Women's dress should be utilitarian instead of ornamental. A woman should attract because of herself and not her dress."

"The tango—I guess it's all right. I never saw anything improper on the dance floor, but then you know I don't dance much."

"Parents are growing too confident. They don't give enough consideration to the character or personality of the men with whom they allow their daughters to associate."

"Votes for women. There are arguments on both sides. It's a question."

Only the Boston fans, it seems, stood apart from this groundswell of appreciation. There was more than a whiff of danger in the atmosphere at Fenway that year, and the potential for violence got increasingly palpable, as a number of commentators noticed. "Boston crowds have always been very polite and seemed anxious to applaud good plays by the visitors," said *Sporting Life* in September. "But the recent games there have been marked by fierce rooting by the populace." What was causing the upsurge in cursing, spitting, cowbell ringing, and garbage flinging? The *Chicago Tribune* thought "the transformation dates back to last season," and blamed George Stallings, manager of the National League Boston Braves—known that year as the "Miracle Braves" for going from last place to the pennant in two months, then sweeping the Athletics in the World Series—for inciting the masses with his explosive displays of anger toward umpires and opposing players. Another only marginally more plausible theory had it that the once patient citizens of Beantown were finally punishing visiting players for the bad reception *their* boys had long had to endure at various stops along the road.

It was much more likely, though, that the rowdies were incited by Boston sportswriters, like Tim Murnane of the *Globe*, who repeatedly told his readers that the Red Sox deeply appreciated and were materially aided by their boos and screams. Just before the Tigers arrived for the final set of games against the Red Sox that year, starting on September 16, Murnane added fuel by saying—truthfully or not; it's hard to determine—that during the previous series, in Detroit in late August, Cobb, while standing in the on-deck circle, was seen urging fans to make noise so as to rattle the Boston pitcher—"a cheap line of work," Murnane wrote, "especially for a clever ball player. Chances are," he said, "that the Georgia Peach will receive a little of his own medicine when he comes to town this trip."

By September, Red Sox fans didn't need much more encouragement than that. Both teams had been trying to outfox each other all summer. In their previous series, played about three weeks earlier in Detroit, Hughie had starter Harry Coveleski warm up in a secret location, somewhere in the bowels of the stadium, so the Red Sox wouldn't know whom they were facing until the last minute. A cadre of displaced Boston cranks, resplendent in red caps, turned up in the Navin Field grandstand and tried to distract Detroit hitters by "blowing horns and shaking police-men's rattles." And on a day when he went 1-for-5, a bad day for him, Cobb paid a midgame visit to the Red Sox dugout—to talk to manager Carrigan, calmly, about his continuing concerns about emery-boarding, he insisted, although Silk O'Loughlin dispatched a few Tigers to get him out of there before the conversation could get heated. Boston had won 11 of the first 19 games against the Tigers that year, but the two teams were still close enough in the standings—Detroit was in second place, two and a half back—that those four September games would make all the differ-ence. If one team swept, or even took three, the other team would be not mathematically but spiritually eliminated, its season in veritable ruins. Or so everyone felt. No wonder the papers were calling it the Little World Series.

It was over 100 degrees on the field for game one, a condition that made the single male cheerleader cavorting along the foul lines seem es-pecially incongruous. The 22,000 who came out on a Thursday afternoon were cheering despite the heat, and singing along with a band that played the Red Sox theme song, "Tessie," as well as hits of the moment such as "I Love a Piano" and "Belgium Put the Kibosh on the Kaiser." It would be wrong to imagine them as a particularly happy lot, however, especially as the game dragged into the seventh inning with the score 5–1 Detroit. They were probably wondering what to do with all the wads of paper they were stockpiling under their seats, when Carrigan switched pitchers, pull-ing out starter George Foster and replacing him with Carl Mays. As good as Foster was, Mays was the sort of player who made things happen.

The first batter he faced, in the top of the eighth, was Cobb. A few years later, Mays would say that Cobb annoyed him by standing with his right foot in front of home plate, a technically illegal move that umpires usually abided, but which left the pitcher with very little room to work. Mays started him with a fastball very near his face. Cobb said nothing. But when the next pitch came just as close, Cobb yelled "Yellow dog!" and flung his bat, which flew over Mays and came down near second base. You'd expect a fight to break out at this point; both men must have been fuming. But the newspaper accounts say that Mays retrieved the bat and handed it to Cobb, who resumed his turn at the plate. With the count now 0–2, Mays whizzed another fastball high and inside. This time Cobb instinctively put up a hand to protect himself, and the ball hit him on the wrist. What happened next was also odd: Cobb simply trotted to first. In 1920, when Mays delivered the fatal fastball that killed Cleveland shortstop Ray Chapman, sportswriters were quick to cite his plunking of Cobb in 1915 and make much of the lingering bad feeling between the two men, but at the time that it happened, the reaction of both players appears to have been muted. Cobb did take revenge, but within the rules and in his signature fashion by stealing second, going to third on a fielder's choice, and coming home, somehow, on a routine infield grounder. The run was superfluous to the final score, which was 6–1 Tigers, and therefore, perhaps, minimally inflammatory.

Sooner or later the stands were going to erupt, though, and they did in the next inning. The riot unfolded in a way that was almost a replay of events in Philadelphia in 1911, when Cobb and Frank Baker briefly renewed their animosity over the infamous 1909 "spiking." Cobb caught a soft fly ball for the final out, and thousands of fans rushed the field as he stood in place, tossing the ball lightly into the air. "Prudence would have dictated that Ty take to his heels and make for the shelter of the dugout," Batchelor wrote. "But the greatest of ball players isn't made of that sort of stuff. He waited until his would-be assailants were upon him, then began to walk deliberately in. Somebody tossed a pop bottle that hit Ty lightly, but before he could locate the man who had done so a couple of Irish policemen arrived on the scene and the hoodlums were driven back. One cur made a rush for the Tiger and a copper caught him a beautiful punch in the jaw and knocked him sprawling 20 feet away." Also as in Philadelphia, his teammates ran to his rescue. "The whole Tiger squad, some of them clutching bats, went out to meet Cobb and formed a body guard ready to give the mob the busiest few minutes of its life if anybody had started a real fight." Miraculously no one did.

One last echo of Philadelphia: at the next game, played two days later, Cobb got a lengthy ovation when he first came to the plate. Was this an apology? A way for more proper Bostonians to say "Those rowdies are not us"? Whatever the answer, the more civilized reception didn't help the Detroits. Boston's pitching was too much for them, for everybody.

Dutch Leonard beat them cleanly on Friday (despite a two-run homer from Cobb); Ernie Shore out-dueled Coveleski in a beautiful 12-inning, 1–0 game played before 35,000 on Saturday, and in the Monday finale Babe Ruth and George Foster teamed up for the 3–2 win. "I'll admit it looks now as if the Tigers have blown the championship," Cobb wrote in a syndicated newspaper article a few days later. "We had worked hard to win it, but if we would have to win by the tactics used in Boston, I am just as well satisfied we lost. I myself don't mind playing before hostile, hollering crowds. It makes any man go harder. But when a fellow has to dodge pitched balls aimed at his head and pop bottles aimed at his head, too, it is too much of a handicap." The piece ended on an elegiac note, suggesting he was conceding more than just the season. "It is a big disappointment to me not to be in the World Series again before I get through in baseball. I acknowledge that. This was a good chance this year. It may not come again in my time. That last Boston series has left a bad taste in my mouth."

He was not alone in feeling lousy at the end of a season in which the Tigers had won 100 games—more than they'd ever won before—but not the pennant. Hughie Jennings called the campaign "my biggest disappointment in Detroit."

Imagine a ball bouncing, lower and slower, until it rolls to a stop. Over the next three years the Tigers would play out their 154-game schedule, looking—except for Cobb—to writer H. G. Salsinger "like a team that did not care where it finished." It was not an interesting interval in Tigers history. A summing up should suffice: In 1916 the Tigers, despite a September surge that brought them briefly to within a half game of the lead, wound up third in the American League, behind Boston and Chicago. Cobb hit .371, a few ticks above the previous season, but not better than the .386 posted by Tris Speaker, now of the Cleveland Indians. Speaker, who would hit .345 over the course of his 22-year career, thus stopped Cobb's streak of batting titles at a record nine. The Georgian wasn't done, by any means, but here was the first hint of autumn. It certainly bothered him and it may have scared him, too, because in 1917 he picked up his game, hitting .383, knocking in 102 runs (34 more than the year before), and reclaiming the batting title.

His team, however, was heading in a southerly direction, despite Navin's and Jennings's best efforts to acquire the necessary personnel. Little went untried. The Tigers that spring returned, said the *Free Press*, "to the style of uniform in which they won three pennants. The shirt and trousers are of plain white flannel. Black caps and stockings are worn. The old English D is used on shirtfront and caps instead of the block letter that was in vogue last year." (That "D" is the oldest major league logo still in use.) Alas the throwback togs made no difference. The team started slowly, losing 14 of its first 22 games, and spent most of that year in the second division, lucking into fourth thanks only to the Yankees' late-season swan dive.

Sam Crawford, at age thirty-seven, ended his career a few days short of the end of the season, and on a bitter note, using his final interviews to say yet again that Cobb caused dissension and was primarily concerned with his personal statistics. Crawford was never able to get beyond the resentment he felt about the relatively huge salary—$20,000 at this point, as opposed to his $7,500—and special treatment Cobb received; he, too, would have liked to have been excused from spring training, to have been able to travel during the season without a roommate (as Cobb did from about 1912 onward), to miss with impunity the first few innings of a meaningless late-season game against the Yankees in 1915 because, as Cobb explained to a New York scribe who asked why, "I was attending an organ concert at Aeolian Hall." Crawford and Cobb never came to blows, but until Cobb effected a semi-successful rapprochement late in their lives, they were cool to each other at best. At a "tribute" game played for Crawford late in the 1917 season, Cobb and Jennings declined to participate in the ceremonies, staying in the dugout rather than standing in the receiving line at home plate. The Tigers, winning only three more games than they lost, finished 21½ games behind the pennant-winning White Sox in the AL standings. And things would get worse.

Crawford's comments aside, Cobb, at age thirty-one, was being talked about more like an elder statesman or a venerable font of baseball wisdom, and less like the key to a championship. "I preach Ty Cobb to my ballplayers day in and day out," said Fielder Jones, a groundbreaking strategist from an earlier generation, then managing the St. Louis Browns. "Every time we have a meeting I hold him up as an example of what quick thinking and intelligence will do for a man. One of these days I hope to get Ty Cobb in a room for a good talk on baseball. It will be a treat for me." Howard "Kid" Ehmke, a twenty-year-old pitcher, had the good luck to have the locker next to Cobb in the Navin Field clubhouse. "In the fall, he used to sit down and talk baseball with me before and after the games. The opening of every series he'd take a half hour and point out the weakness and strength of the opposing batters. Cobb knew just what kind of stuff to serve every batter." Sometimes Cobb worried about what might come next for him. "I have often wished I could become a composer," he told F. C. Lane, the editor of *Baseball Magazine*, as they wandered together through a music store in Augusta while the resident pianist played.

> But I don't suppose I have any talent in that line. Every man to his trade, and I guess mine is cut out for me. I know enough of fame on the diamond to realize that it lasts just as long as the ability to win it. I shall have my day like all the rest, and whatever I've done will be forgotten just as other records have been forgotten before. I was always ambitious, I guess. I used to think that if I were ever able to make a record on the diamond I would be satisfied. But people have been good enough to claim I have done no less and I am not satisfied.

During the season, though, there was as yet no outward change in him; he did not *act* venerable; he looked, from the grandstand, like the wild child of 1905. For starters, there was the fight he had with Buck Herzog, described in the previous chapter. Also, in July of 1916, angered by a called third strike, he threw his bat into an unoccupied section of the stands at Comiskey Park, and received another admonishment from Ban Johnson to add to his impressive collection, followed by a three-day suspension. In May of that year he flung a handful of dirt into the face of Washington's Joe Boehling (after, he said, the pitcher cursed at him while tagging him out during a rundown), and a few weeks later he had to be pulled out of the stands in St. Louis by teammates and police before he could pummel another heckler. He also continued to display the kind of base running flair—the trash talking, explosive takeoffs, swift slides, and violent crash landings—that was often mistaken for rage. "I never saw anybody like him," Rube Bressler, a pitcher for the A's, told Lawrence Ritter nearly fifty years later. "It was *his* base. It was *his* game. Everything was his. The most feared man in the history of baseball."

And yet, in his day, also the most widely admired. Cobb simply refused to be part of the Tigers' decline, which in 1918 saw them, as Lieb says, "back to where they were in 1904 under Barrow and Lowe." In a July 4 doubleheader that was swept by the White Sox, Cobb went 5-for-6 in the opener and, playing first base in the nightcap (following the ejection of Harry Heilmann), he used the hidden ball trick to pick off starting pitcher Joe Benz. Four days later he was 4-for-5 in a losing effort against Philadelphia, and by the beginning of August his batting average was .393. He would wind up leading the league with .382, though his stolen base total dropped sharply to 34. The Tigers? They finished in seventh place, four games out of last. When the war cut short the season it was a relief for everyone associated with the club. Looking sharp in his doughboy uniform, Cobb addressed the reporters who had come to the dock to see him depart for Europe, saying more explicitly what he had suggested atop the dugout at Navin Field: "I am tired of baseball."

ON A FINE OCTOBER DAY in 1918, Captain Tyrus Raymond Cobb, "resplendent in his new uniform, with his puttees and shoulder bars glistening in the sunlight," or so the Philadelphia sportswriter Robert W. Maxwell assures us, "leaned wearily against the fence of the White House in Washington" and talked about his eagerness to get to the battlegrounds of France. Mustered into the Army a week or so earlier, he was supposed to have gone first to Camp Humphreys (now Fort Belvoir) in Virginia, but "basic training" sounded to him suspiciously like "spring training," and so he asked for and received permission to skip it and join what the *Free Press* called "the chase for Huns" ASAP. As with annual preseason baseball preparations, his intolerance pertained to the tedious, not the tough. Lest he be assigned "some sort of soft snap," as he called it, Cobb had volunteered for what was known as "chemical warfare service work." According to the Army manual of the day, this was easily the most dangerous job in the service. Chemical warfare or "flame" men, the book says, "usually go into action ahead of the attacking waves of infantry, carrying tanks on their backs, and advance under cover of artillery barrage squirting flames of liquid fire from the tanks. Gas men advancing carry a sack of gas-filled bombs, which they hurl into trenches and dugouts, like grenades." It sounds borderline suicidal, yet Cobb told interviewer Maxwell—when he was not snapping to attention to return the salutes of other soldiers, Boy Scouts, police officers, and "a couple of icemen" parading down Pennsylvania Avenue in the midst of their chat—that "it's very interesting work and I enjoy it."

In theory, that is, of course. Through no fault of his own, he never got a chance to squirt liquid fire on fleeing Huns. The Allied counteroffensive, begun in early August of 1918, had quickly decimated the German army and made the Central Powers realize it was best to start hatching an exit plan—and so by the time Frank Navin received a plain, buff-colored postcard from Cobb saying, with spy-conscious sparseness, "The ship I sailed on arrived safely overseas," and nothing more, the Armistice was just weeks away. Cobb did manage to almost get killed, however, while teaching gas mask technique to a bunch of hapless enlisted men who would almost certainly never need a gas mask, at an airbase near Claumont, France, along with Christy Mathewson. The situation was a recipe for disaster. On the one hand you had soldiers distracted by the sight of two of the biggest stars in baseball—*Look, the Georgia Peach and the Christian Gentleman!*—staring back at them through creepy yellow goggles and speaking through long black hoses (there are few things more nightmarish than a World War I gas mask). On the other hand, you had two celebrity teachers who had themselves received only a one-week crash course in their subject.

The day's lesson plan involved the release of actual deadly fumes into the sealed chamber where the class was taught, and the men putting on their masks and making their way calmly to the exits. Someone, however, made a mistake of timing, which no one realized until doughboys started dropping like Huns. Then the door got stuck. Al Stump's Cobb "autobiography," *My Life in Baseball*, says that eight men died as a result of the accident, but there is nothing to corroborate that. We do know that several soldiers became ill. Cobb himself was laid up for about a week, Mathewson somewhat longer, and when the ex-pitcher died of tuberculosis seven years later at the age of forty-five, it was widely assumed that his susceptibility to lung disease could be traced to the toxic classrooms of Claumont.

Cobb came back to America on a ship called the *Leviathan*, arriving at Hoboken on December 16, two days before his thirty-second birthday. "I'm going down to my home in Augusta, Georgia, and rest up for several months," he told the assembled press. "I intend to break away from baseball. I am tired of it. I've had 15 years of it and I want to quit while I'm still good." The words sounded similar to those he had used on the way over—except now they were but a smoke screen. Just twenty-four hours before, during a shipboard minstrel show, he had mounted the stage and announced that everyone present would receive free admission to his first game back (the "password," he said, would be "I heard Ty Cobb try to make a speech"). That wasn't just the champagne talking; he fully intended to return. On the pier in New Jersey, addressing men with notebooks, he was more cagey, first refusing to directly contradict his position of two months earlier, but then, as he went along, introducing a hint of doubt about retirement, saying, rather melodramatically, "There is a danger that the terrible fascination of the game has its hold on me, but I shall make every effort to tear away from it and not sign with any club again." Finally as a kind of afterthought he added, "I naturally presume that the release that the managers gave us last fall is binding and that they have no legal strings on me now. I hope so, at least."

For those who followed the business side of baseball, those last words were a kind of wink—a signal that rather than merely musing on his future, he was negotiating, and not just on his own behalf. When the 1918 season ended early, and 227 major league players went off to war, the team owners "to avoid paying the players the balance of their salaries [for early September through early October]," says Harold Seymour in his *Baseball: The Golden Age,* employed "the subtle subterfuge of 'releasing' them with ten days notice, as provided in their contracts." As a result, all of the players, the soldiers and the civilians alike, lost a full month's pay, but were technically liberated from the reserve clause and able to sell their services to the highest bidder once the American and National Leagues resumed play. Except that the poor chumps weren't free agents, really. As Seymour tells us, "the magnates entered into a gentlemen's agreement not to tamper with each other's men. Thus the owners had it both ways," saving $200,000 in payroll but keeping their "monopsony control" over the players. Navin actually offered Cobb a contract of $19,000, or $1,000 *less* than he'd received the year before, when he batted .382 (64 points above the next best hitter in the AL, Tris Speaker), led the league in on-base percentage (.440), and was as usual the club's only real draw.

It seemed slightly bizarre to be nickel-and-diming a man who not only personified the franchise but was by then a full-fledged member of the Tigers family. Cobb was a partner with Navin in several outside business ventures, he regularly passed along his Aunt Norah's preserves to his boss, and he was at the bedside of Bill Yawkey when the former majority share-holder of the club died suddenly of the flu in Augusta in early March of 1919 at age forty-three. Wanting neither to quibble about $1,000 or take a pay cut, Cobb kept silent until Navin finally came to his senses and sent him a contract for $20,000 around March 30, as everyone knew he even-tually would. It was his fifth consecutive contract for that amount, and he signed it promptly in his trademark green.

At any point along its continuum, as we have seen, Cobb's career was a mixture of controversy and personal success, played out against a back-drop of the up-and-down, generally close-but-no-cigar Detroit Tigers. The season of 1919 would follow a similar pattern, with the exception of one outlying event, a perplexing and potentially criminal incident that occurred away from the ballpark on April 25, 1919, opening day. An eighteen-year-old black woman named Ada Morris would later claim in court papers that Cobb, while she was working as a chambermaid at the Pontchartrain Hotel, pushed her out of his room, where she had been delivering linen, and into the hallway, kicked her in the stomach, and knocked her down a flight of stairs, causing a broken rib and other inju-ries that left her hospitalized for several weeks. Cobb had no comment on the accusation, not that he was ever asked for one by either the press or the police. He was never arrested, or, as far as can be determined, ques-tioned by authorities, and mainstream newspapers did not say anything about the incident until late May, when an identical short item appeared in the *Free Press*, the *Atlanta Constitution*, and several other dailies around the United States, often with a headline like "Negress Sues Cobb."

The news was that Morris had filed a $10,000 suit against the Tigers star, that he had refused to accept the summons when a server approached him on April 26 at Navin Field, and that a judge had since signed an order of default, meaning that the case could proceed without his partic-ipation. The three-sentence squib raised serious questions, such as, who *was* Tyrus Raymond Cobb, anyway: the family man who urged the public to buy war savings stamps, who read voraciously, chatted with presidents, and was always eager to explain that his wildly aggressive playing style was a well-considered baseball strategy, not a symptom of inner turmoil—or a sociopath who could (in a drunken state, perhaps) put a woman's life in jeopardy by kicking her down a flight of stairs? Or maybe he was a bit of both, a hero with an extremely dark side? (In a memorable face-to-face conversation undertaken in about 1850, Charles Dickens explained to Fyodor Dostoyevsky that the protagonists and villains of his novels both came from the same place, a place deep within him. "I am, you see, two men," Dickens said—to which the Russian writer replied, "Only two?") Not another word about Ada Morris would ever appear in the regular press. Yet in its brevity and singularity that item had great power to tell both a story and a story *about* a story. Clearly, this business was something a concerned group of people were struggling to contain.

For any further details on the matter one had to rely on the *Chicago Defender,* a lively if sometimes hyperbolic African American weekly. Calling the alleged attack "one of the most brutal incidents ever reported" in Detroit, the *Defender* said in its May 3 edition that the trouble had started when Cobb asked the woman what state she was from and she said Pennsylvania. "There never was a nigger like you from Pennsylvania," he is said to have responded. "Mrs. Morris objected to this remark," wrote the anonymous *Defender* scribe. "Cobb forthwith plunged into the woman, showering blows upon her head and body. She attempted to fight back, but was overpowered." The story suggests that the assault took place at night, after the game against Cleveland in which Cobb went 2-for-4 and doubled in the winning run—and goes on to say that when Morris's family went to police court the following morning to obtain an arrest warrant, "the bailiff stated that it was 'impossible' for Cobb to have committed such an act and that a warrant could not be obtained at that hour." Outraged by the brush-off, a committee of black clergymen and lawyers had met at the Biltmore Hotel to collect money for an attorney and "see that Cobb was brought before the bar of justice."

A week later, though, the situation had changed. In its May 10 issue the *Defender* reported, with obvious disappointment, that Cobb would not be prosecuted on criminal charges because some "mit [*sic*] greasing" had occurred and "the Morris family, hypnotized by the sight of a few silver dollars scorned all help and absolutely refused to file criminal charges against Cobb." The reason given by "the Morris woman" for not going forward is that "too much publicity and a court trial might hurt Cobb's good reputation." That account certainly does make it sound like Cobb, or Cobb and Navin, arranged to pay for Morris's silence, just as they had ten years earlier when the night watchman from the Euclid Hotel in Cleveland was given money to abandon his case. But then, days later the *Free Press* and other papers reported her prosecuting Cobb after all, albeit in civil court. What was going on?

Without explaining this second reversal, the *Defender* on June 7 picked up the story line about the lawsuit and proffered a few more details, some accurate (the names of Cobb's and Morris's lawyers), some not (Cobb is said to come from "a family of scrappers in the backwoods"). On June 21, the paper further reports that "people higher up on the ball club have endeavored to use their influence to smother the [civil] case by the payment of a small sum outside of court," but, much to the *Defender*'s delight, Morris's attorney, one R. Nicholson, is "pitching good ball" and "has fanned away all offers" to protect the reputation of the man "known by his confederates as 'Rough-House Cobb.'" After this, though, nothing; silence, forever. The story, like the case itself, simply disappears.

The *Defender* started the same year Cobb came to the majors, 1905. A graph depicting its coverage of him over the decades would show a single angry spike in the spring of 1919, set off by peaceful prairies of positive prose. Upon Cobb's death in 1961 the *Defender* eulogized him as "the greatest," called him "a daring and impulsive base runner," and, just as significantly in a paper that viewed the world through the prism of race and wasn't too polite to point a finger, even in an obituary, had nothing to say about alleged character flaws.

In truth, it would have been bizarre to attack Cobb as a bigot in 1961. By then he had for years been publicly applauding the integration of organized baseball, cheering it louder than virtually any old-time star. "The Negro should be accepted and not grudgingly but wholeheartedly," he told the *Sporting News* in 1952, on one of the many occasions he spoke out on what was in some quarters still a controversial topic. "The Negro has the right to compete in sports and who's to say they have not? They have been competing notably in football, track and baseball and I think they are to be complimented for their gentle conduct both on the field and, as far as I know, off the field." Cobb praised the Dodgers' Roy Campanella as a "great" catcher who "had the good sense to play up close to the plate, so he could catch the ball before it broke away, and get his pitcher more strikes." He called Willie Mays "the only player I'd pay money to see," and after Campanella was permanently paralyzed in a car accident in 1958, and Walter O'Malley staged a tribute game for him at which tens of thousands held lit matches aloft to show their appreciation, Cobb wrote privately to the Dodgers owner to thank him "for what you did for this fine man."

Did Cobb, then on the verge of his dotage and embracing religion, brim with the convert's zeal, as some insist who can't get over the fact that he was, for Chrissakes, born in *Georgia*, in *1886*, and therefore *must* at some point have been severely prejudiced? It will always be impossible to say, but it is not difficult to find stories of him in the 1920s and 1930s treating Negro League players and black trainers with the decency they deserved. Detroit Stars infielder Bobby Robinson recalled a game in 1929 when a rumor circulated that Cobb was in the house—and then an inning or so later he found him in the dugout, sitting next to him and seeming eager to talk baseball. "Robinson recalled that there wasn't a hint of prejudice in Cobb's attitude," wrote Nick Wilson, author of an oral history of black and Cuban League players. "They were just two ballplayers sharing stories." How much this tells of Cobb's attitude is hard to say, but black people were a constant in his life, more so than with other ballplayers, if only because most other ballplayers didn't have a household staff, like he did. He employed at least two black domestics at his home in Augusta, and starting in about 1914 went about Detroit and elsewhere with a black valet, as successful men of that era sometimes did (the comedian Jack Benny and his sidekick Eddie "Rochester" Anderson were perhaps the last surviving example of this phenomenon).

One of Cobb's batmen, a former New Orleans chauffeur named Alex Rivers, stayed with him for at least seven years, or until oil was discovered on land he owned in Mississippi and he was reported to have become a millionaire (the tale may be apocryphal; he was also said to have become a preacher). Rivers named his first son, born in 1921, Alexander Ty, saying "it would have been Alexandra Ty if it'd been a girl," and when Cobb retired, declared "I love the man." When they had a brief reunion in the mid-1930s in California, he and Cobb fell into each other's arms and sobbed. Not that any of this was a consolation to Ada Morris, who in the 1930 federal census turns up as a domestic employed by a private family in Detroit, but whose full story we shall apparently never know.

If Cobb experienced a crisis of conscience over what happened in a stairwell of the Pontchartrain on opening day of 1919, he apparently used it the way he had used similar potential disturbances: as a threat to his serenity that helped him focus his thoughts on the daily business of base-ball. Shrugging off not just legal problems, but a boil on his leg that kept him out of the lineup for nearly two weeks, as well as an increasing tight-ness in his calves, quads, hamstrings, and hips, he picked up where he left off before the war and was hitting about .365 by the first day of summer. If he stole fewer bases than he once did—and his production in that area was down by about 50 percent from his best seasons—he still excelled at "worrying" his opponents into making mistakes that allowed him to dart and dodge his way around the diamond. "Cobb worried [catcher Sam] Agnew so much before he stole in the third," said a note in the May 20 *Free Press*, "that when Ty did go down Sam threw the ball into centerfield, which gave the Peach a chance to skid on his way to third." This was a trademark trick that, for him and the fans, never got old. But he was not at age thirty-two all fake-outs and finesse. In the same game, a 6–0 victory over the Washington Senators at Navin Field, he got "a pair of safeties, the first one nearly tearing [shortstop Howie] Shanks' gloved hand off as it sped on its way to center field, the other a roller to [third baseman Joe] Leonard that Ty beat out by a great sprint."

In the first game of a morning-afternoon Memorial Day doubleheader in Detroit, Cobb reached base only once, on an error, but managed to score the winning run against the Browns. In the "matinee game," he had two doubles and a triple in four at-bats and scored three runs, whereas St. Louis, as a team, scored only two. On July 21, he scratched out three infield hits and stole a base against Babe Ruth (who took the loss but also hit the first home run ever to disappear over the right field wall at Navin Field and, said the *Free Press*, "take flight across Trumbull Avenue"). Ruth was explosive, but Cobb—who had a .381 lifetime batting average against

Ruth the pitcher—was stunningly consistent. He had won the American League batting title by hitting .383 and .382 in 1917 and '18, and he would win it again this year, for a twelfth (and final) time, by hitting .384. He would even get in another fight with a spectator, this time an able-bodied heckler who came out of the stands in Detroit to curse and challenge Cobb as he was trotting in from the outfield at the end of a game. Cobb, who had told the man twice that day to be quiet, grabbed him by the scruff of the neck, kneed him in the groin, and then kept on walking as the fellow, the *Sporting News* said, "took a few steps and fell in a heap." Cobb was still the greatest baseball player around, and the most exciting. What he wasn't anymore was the game's biggest story.

If you counted the new livelier ball they started playing with that year, more tightly wound with string made of stronger and springier Australian wool, he was the fourth biggest story in sports in 1919 behind 3) said ball; 2) heavyweight champion Jack Dempsey, who won the title by whipping the much bigger Jess Willard in a historic three-round battle in Toledo on July 4; and 1) Babe Ruth. Numbers one and three are intimately related, of course. Ruth by then was playing the outfield for Boston on most days when he wasn't pitching, in order to get his bat in the lineup as much as possible. He held that bat very differently than Cobb gripped his much thicker club—all the way down at the knob end—and swung it differently, too, with a decisive uppercut motion, and with such force that if his spikes stuck in the clay around home plate he could, and sometimes did, wrench his back. When he made contact with what everyone but the Spalding Company (which insisted it was turning out a perfectly uniform product year after year) called the "jackrabbit ball," the results were electrifying. After leading the league with 11 home runs in the war-shortened 1918 season, and helping the Red Sox win the world championship, he hit 29 homers in 1919, breaking the modern major league record of 24 set by Gavvy Cravath of the Phillies in 1915, and the all-time record of 27 posted by Nagle Williamson of the Chicago Colts in 1884—and became a national phenomenon.

Cobb got all those pitty-pat hits, and struck out only 3.1 percent of the time, but now it hardly mattered. Even at Navin Field, as H. G. Salsinger wrote, Ruth received "the welcome due a conquering hero. He got the applause, the shrieking adoration of the multitude, in Cobb's own city. Cobb, standing aside, could feel deeply how fickle the adoration of the sport-loving public is. He saw before him a new king acclaimed." (The following year Ruth would hit 54, and after that, 59, then down the road 60.) "Cobb represents the mauve decades in baseball," said the *Sporting News*. "Ruth represents the hot cha-cha, and hey nonny, nonny period." In the Ruthian Age, dozens of once shameful strikeouts could be atoned with the occasional fence-clearing clout. Like one's sister, the plate, in the Roaring Twenties, no longer required fierce protection. This was of course exactly the opposite of the way the deadball era greats, who choked up on the bat and mostly tried to poke the ball over the infielders' heads, approached batting. After initially saying it was simply the wrong way to play the game, Cobb—whose split-hands grip now suddenly struck Washington Nationals manager Clark Griffith as "awkward" and old-fashioned, and who never hit more than 12 homers in a season—grudgingly came around to saying in public (probably with his fingers crossed behind his back) that it was a legitimate alternative style of play, a crowd-pleasing trendy thing that ought to be, uh, encouraged—but he could never bring himself to describe Ruth as the Father of Modern Baseball, or anything other than one lucky son of a bitch.

"I do not vie for prominence," he wrote in 1953 to Ruth's agent, Christy Walsh, "but I do know of all the efforts in every way possible that have been put forth by New York scribes, etc., to always play up Ruth. . . . Remember, Christy, I know who was voted in *first* [italics his] to the Baseball Hall of Fame (Cooperstown)." For Cobb, the idea that Ruth had come into the pastime as a pitcher was key to his somewhat unearned success. As a pitcher, he said years later, "he could experiment at the plate" at first. "He didn't have to get a piece of the ball. He didn't have to protect the plate the way a regular batter was expected to. No one cares much if the pitcher strikes out or looks bad at bat, so Ruth could take that big swing. If he missed, it didn't matter. And when he didn't miss, the ball went a long way. As time went on, he learned more and more about how to control that big swing and put the wood on the ball. By the time he became a fulltime outfielder, he was ready."

Cobb could see that there was no use standing in the way of the juggernaut. By 1922, home run production in the the American League more than tripled from what it was in 1918, jumping from 96 to 369, and people were coming out in unprecedented numbers to see the pyrotechnics. Not everyone favored the bombastic new way, and a decade or so later, some grew nostalgic for the more chesslike game played by Cobb and his contemporaries. Asked in 1933 if he would take Ruth or Cobb in their respective primes, Red Sox owner Tom Yawkey, just thirty at the time, said, "I'm still a fan. I would take Cobb. I like to see Ruth hit the long ones, but nothing has thrilled me more than the sight of Ty Cobb dashing around the bases, taking chances, outwitting the other side. You could never tell what he was going to do, and it was fine fun trying to figure out what he might do next. You don't get that with Ruth."

But what you did get with Ruth was more money. The lively ball, the advent of Sunday baseball in New York, and the general postwar exhilaration combined to send attendance soaring in 1919, making for what Charles Alexander rightly calls "the beginning of a sustained surge that would last for a decade." Ruth, just twenty-four when he for all practical purposes completed the transition to position player, would flare and dim like they all do, but the game people like to insist has never changed was morphing fundamentally and fast. Though Cobb would finish with the highest batting average and the most hits (191) that year playing the old way, there was no going back.

For all the individual success they enjoyed in 1919, neither Ruth nor Cobb could propel his club to the top. In baseball, it takes a village, and a deep bench. The Tigers overcame a 5–14 start after Navin bought Dutch Leonard from the Yankees in mid-May, and wound up finishing fourth in the AL, a half game behind Boston, who by securing third qualified for World Series money that figured to be $550 per player. No one could stop the White Sox that season—no one, that is, except Arnold Rothstein and his fellow professional gamblers, who, it would be revealed in the coming months, paid off seven Chicago players to ensure that the Cincinnati Reds would win the championship. Like a lot of people, Cobb had heard rumors that something was fishy with the best-five-out-of-nine series, but he said he didn't believe the stories, theorizing instead that the men who became known as the Black Sox played poorly because of "overconfidence." The truth is, though, he wasn't paying much attention. He had a new daughter, Beverly, his fourth child (his first daughter, Shirley, had been born in 1911) to attend to, and, up in the Georgia hills, far from the world that weighed so heavily upon him, plenty of birds to shoot. It would be just as well if he missed the *New York Times* piece that said "Ruth was such a sensation last season that he supplanted the great Ty Cobb as baseball's greatest attraction."

— CHAPTER TWENTY-FIVE —

AFTER THE FIRST FEW WEEKS of the 1920 season, Hughie Jennings would do his *Ee-Yah* act no more. The last little bits of his sometimes weird enthusiasm expired as he watched his Tigers lose their first 13 games, and look bad doing it. "The Tigers are not tigers," Harry Bullion wrote in the *Free Press* after a loss to the St. Louis Browns on May 7. In the field that day, Bullion added, Detroit "put on an exhibition that could rank with the worst they ever have presented to the gaze of paid spectators." They lost "without so much as a snarl." What they needed, said shortstop Donie Bush, was just "a few breaks to put the confidence back into us." He thought those breaks would be coming soon. He was mistaken. By the end of May, Cobb was batting in the low .200s. Following a game in which he went 0-for-4, a Detroit headline read "Jungaleers Drop Final Game of Yankee Series; Ruth Gets Daily Homer." (Ruth had been sold to New York that January for $125,000.) Jennings stayed in the dugout, or sometimes, claiming stomach troubles, back at his hotel, often sending Cobb to man the coaching box since he was not on base all that much in those days, and the Peach did a fair job of coaching in the classic, rubber-snake-less manner—which only helped the rumors that he was being groomed to be the team's next manager.

Meanwhile, Cobb by that point was one of the few Tigers who had a relatively easy relationship with Jennings. That April, after the manager had once again allowed his star to spend spring training working out at home in Augusta (with the Washington Senators) instead of joining the club in Macon and slogging north with a tedious but profitable barnstorming tour, they had gone together to a Mercer University alumni dinner, and since then attended events in support of James M. Cox, the

Ohio governor who, on a ticket with Franklin Delano Roosevelt, was running for president against the Republican team of Warren G. Harding and Calvin Coolidge.

Cobb, as we have seen, had once thought Jennings unfit for the job of manager because of his poor people skills—he combined an extreme aversion to confrontation with a tendency to bully and be sarcastic toward the younger or more insecure men on the team—but he had since realized the benefits of having a boss whom you can play like a ukulele. Cobb's acceptance of Jennings, however, put up a wall between him and pitchers Hooks Dauss, Howard Ehmke, and Red Oldham, who were particularly peeved at the manager, and also worsened his relationship with Dutch Leonard, who despised Hughie most of all. As the decade of the 1920s dawned, and the players sank into a premutinous state, the manager desperately needed to mend fences—but instead he announced, not to the players but to the press (as always), that the rules on the Tigers would be stricter than ever before. "I'm not going to tolerate any more alibis!" he said, as if alibis and not offense were the team's biggest problem. And so when a particularly naive minor leaguer came back to the bench after dropping a fly in a spring training game and told Hughie that he thought it had "been carried off course by a trade wind," the manager was "driven almost wild" with anger, reported Bullion, and said, "Yes and that's the same trade wind that's going to carry you back to New Orleans!" The skipper, alas, was losing his grip.

After his poor start Cobb's problems only seemed to worsen. Chasing a fly ball at Comiskey Park on June 6, he collided with right fielder Ira Flagstead and tore ligaments in his knee. It was the worst injury of his career, and he would hobble around back home in Augusta, and on the sidelines of various ballparks, for almost a month. In all it was a miserable season for him, the Tigers, and in many ways for major league baseball as a whole. Topic A was the slowly unfolding drama concerning the Black Sox scandal, and before that could be resolved (with the expulsion from baseball of Shoeless Joe Jackson, Cobb's old Tourist teammate Eddie Cicotte, and six other Chicago players), on August 16 at the Polo Grounds Carl Mays served up the underhand pitch that hit the popular Cleveland shortstop Ray Chapman in the left temple and fractured his skull.

The accident happened in the fifth inning, when the sun was getting low and the shadows long. Chapman never saw the pitch, or so it is assumed, but the sound it made led Mays to think the ball had struck his bat, and he picked up the roller and tossed it to first base as the batter pitched forward in the box, blood gushing from his ear. Chapman died twelve hours later. To all but the New York scribes, who rallied around the supposedly distraught Mays, it seemed like a clear case of good versus evil: Mays was a known brushback artist and hothead who in separate incidents in recent times had thrown a bat and a ball at hecklers; Chapman was a salt-of-the-earth type and a blushing newlywed whose last words, it was said, were a request for the wedding band that he'd left with the clubhouse man to be put back on his finger. Nor did it help Mays's case that he initially seemed to be trying to lay blame on the umpires, who he said allowed a ball with a rough spot to remain in the game, creating a situation in which he was forced to make pitches that he could not control. (The umpires who worked the game angrily retorted that Mays had a habit of roughing up balls himself, despite their admonitions.)

As word spread of Chapman's death, people in and out of baseball called for Mays's permanent banishment and some newspapers reported that the Tigers—and Cobb in particular—were requesting "immediate summary measures" against the pitcher. Was this true? It's not hard to believe that he felt no sympathy for Mays, a man with whom he'd had a long running battle, but whether he actually said something about the incident is another matter. Cobb vehemently denied that he had, but the Yankee writers whipped up sentiment against him anyway. When the Tigers next came to town, on August 21, he was hissed and booed by a crowd that had usually been surprisingly kind. The reaction bothered him, and on his first trip to the plate that afternoon, he felt compelled to make a statement. Bowing deeply to the jeering throng, he swept his right arm up toward the Polo Grounds press box, as if to say "Blame those guys." If his frustration affected his performance, though, it was only for the good. Cobb got just one hit that day, but it allowed him to put on an exciting display of base running and score a run in the Tigers 10–3 victory. The next afternoon he had four singles and a double as the Tigers beat the Yankees again. On the day after that he was 2-for-4 against Mays on the (unpunished) pitcher's first day back. The two men never resolved their differences, but forty-odd years later Mays would say of Cobb, "I'd want him over Ruth on my team. Ruth would fill your stadium. Cobb would beat you in it."

The Yankees series—three Tiger wins in four games—gave a misleading impression of a seriously flawed and dispirited team, which left New York in seventh place, with a record of 46–71. Cobb would regain his batting eye and pull his average up to .334 for the season (10th on a list topped by the Browns' George Sisler at .407), but many newspapers were declaring that his best days were behind him. "Ty is hitting like a man who hasn't had enough practice," wrote William Hanna of the *New York Sun*. "His timing of pitched balls is poor. He is off balance when he hits and he is meeting the ball thinly." Detroit would still be sulking in seventh place at season's end, ahead of only Philadelphia, which finished last for the sixth year in a row.

The awfulness of the Tigers brought a shift in the conversation. Instead of speculating about if and when Hughie Jennings might get fired, people wondered who would replace him. Cobb's name came up constantly in such discourse, especially after Cleveland, led by player-manager Tris Speaker, won the World Series that year. The cranky Sam Crawford had said as far back as 1917, after all, that Cobb was already running the club. But he always denied any interest, saying things like "Just playing the game is challenging enough" and "If I had that extra responsibility I'd worry myself to death." He may have half meant it, too, and yet Cobb did feel competitive with Speaker and did want—someday—to see what it felt like to manage and to draw a manager's pay. Partly to that end, he had signed up for an off-season job playing for and managing the San Francisco franchise in a four-team West Coast league that operated in October and November. It was while on the train to California that he received a telegram from Navin telling him Jennings had resigned and would be returning to the practice of law in his native Pennsylvania.

Navin wanted Cobb to take the skipper's job, as did the men to whom he had sold Bill Yawkey's shares in the club: Walter Briggs and John Kelsey. Those quintessential Motor City hotshots—Kelsey was in wheels, Briggs auto bodies—had paid $500,000 for a 25 percent interest in the team, after having already spent many a night bonding with Cobb at the Pontchartrain bar. Cobb continued to play hard-to-get, though, until the sportswriter E. A. Batchelor took him aside one early December day in New Orleans, where Cobb was hunting ducks and Batchelor was covering a Baylor–University of Detroit football game, and reminded him that if he declined the job it would most likely go to Clarence Rowland. "Pants," as he was known for the time when his fell off as he slid into home plate during a minor league game, was a Tigers scout who had once managed the White Sox to the world championship, but who had a reputation as a lightweight, a "cajoler and a jollier" who might keep a good thing going for a while but couldn't turn a bad thing around. It was the prospect of playing for Rowland that sent Ty, just a few days later, to the Vanderbilt Hotel in New York City, where Navin was on off-season baseball business, to talk seriously about managing the club.

The conventional wisdom about Cobb as a possible skipper was that he had plenty of baseball smarts but not enough restraint. "The commentators of the land are most suspicious of Cobb's famous temperament," wrote Damon Runyon, "the same which has led him into matches with his brother ballplayers, to leaping into the grandstand after critical spectators and into passages with butcher boys." Could Ty keep cool when umpires erred, when sportswriters criticized, and, most crucially, when the men in his care failed to replicate his feats? Once in 1917 when Cobb was filling in as coach, he grabbed his teammate George Burns, then lumbering around third base, and pushed him hard in the direction of home plate. Was that the indication of an overly hands-on management style? Runyon admitted he couldn't say for certain how it would work out but urged his readers to remember that "other men just as temperamental as Tyrus have taken over a club and proved to be successful mangers." As examples, he mentioned John McGraw of the Giants and Buck Herzog of the Reds and he might also have tossed in Ed Barrow, who as Red Sox pilot nearly came to blows on several occasions with Ruth. The only name that mattered, however, was that of Pants Rowland, for whom Cobb simply could not imagine playing. His choice then was quite stark: either quit or take a sweet jump in salary—from $20,000 to $35,000—to become the Tigers' star/field boss. The only mystery was why a second meeting with Navin was necessary. At a kind of press conference to announce his new job on December 18, his thirty-fourth birthday, he vowed not to terrorize his men—to "give credit where credit is due," said the *Free Press*, "and to correct through mild criticism."

Who said he had no sense of humor?

CHAPTER TWENTY-SIX

IF A FILMMAKER WERE EVER to make a first-rate movie of Ty Cobb's life, he or she might employ the time-tested montage technique to show how spring training changed under the Cobb administration. If so, we might see ballplayers fast asleep in their bunks while a rooster crowed and the clocks on their nightstands spun round and round—an indication of how the new manager had done away with morning workouts at the training grounds in San Antonio. Panning around, the camera would show a bed here and there that seemed un-slept-in, to signal that Cobb had also dispensed with the nightly curfew. (Maybe an actor in an adjoining cot would turn over and wink!) Then cut to our Detroit boys brunching heartily before sinking into their hotel lobby armchairs to read the paper, shoot the breeze, or just suck their teeth prior to practice time, still several hours distant. If we didn't mind conflating a couple of years, the way Hollywood biopics often do, we might set these March scenes in the two lavishly appointed Greek Revival mansions that Cobb in 1922 rented for his players just across the state line from his hometown, in North Augusta, South Carolina, so they might be more comfortable and he could sleep in his own bed.

"I've planned my whole campaign on the theory that ballplayers are human," he told Robert Edgren of the *Chicago Tribune*. "Managers always clutter up a training camp with rules and regulations. Up on time, to bed on time, diet, general conduct and all that. It's a case of threats and penalties. Well, I have studied out a new way to handle a ball team. This is one club going through spring training with no rules!" Of course, if you abused the policy and failed to put up proper numbers once the season started because you hadn't trained hard, you would soon be playing for the Columbus Redbirds or the Omaha Omahogs. Yet Cobb was serious about the freedom he was according his men, and perhaps to drive home the point he arrived two days late for his own first spring training without so much as a tiresome excuse about missed train connections.

Yes, by acting this way and saying these things, Cobb was trying to win the support of his downtrodden and no doubt, in some cases, wary Tigers—to get them behind him the way all of Detroit seemed to be on February 1, when, in celebration of his new position, it gave him the keys to the city and a testimonial dinner at which 600 people paid the astounding sum of $10 to attend. After ten vaudeville acts and speeches by Mayor John C. Lodge, Frank Navin, Ban Johnson, Hugh Chalmers, and even Hughie Jennings, Cobb called the affair "the greatest honor of my life," and, according to the *Free Press*, once or twice had to choke back sobs—but he still managed to put in a plug for his players, saying how hard they were trying, despite the recent poor results, and how sensitive they were to criticism. (As a manager he tended, for better and worse, to project his own personality onto his charges.) To ease the pressure on them, and himself, he told the assembled citizenry to expect nothing better than a sixth-place finish in 1921, one notch up from the previous year, and still in the second division—a tepid prediction that triggered a mighty avalanche of cheers. From a public- and player-relations stand-point, the modesty was a genius move.

Cobb said and did all the right things in the spring of 1921 and al-most all of the players responded positively to their new boss. Really, what was there *not* to like, at least about his attitude toward spring training and daily practice? Apart from the niceties already mentioned, the men got Sunday off, all the home-style cooking they could handle, and free passes to golf at Augusta National, arranged by Cobb himself (unless you were a pitcher; Cobb felt that pitchers shouldn't play golf because it tightened their shoulders). Along with torn hamstrings and sore arms, Cobb wor-ried about bruised feelings. "Ballplayers are full of sentiment," he said. "They have no camouflage. They come nearer being natural [meaning their true, naked selves] than men who grew up in business." One of his more innovative moves in this regard was to have relief pitchers warm up out of the sight of the starter, so as not to discourage a man already struggling. "If it were left to a vote to determine the popularity of Cobb and Hughie," wrote Harry Bullion, "the Peach would unquestionably win."

And yet spring training under Cobb did involve actual training. The afternoon workouts at San Antonio, and then Augusta, began promptly at 1:00 and consisted of three and a half to four hours of hard work, some of it outside and physical, some involving indoor "skull sessions" to talk strategy. Bunting, the hit-and-run, double steals—these nuts-and-bolts-y maneuvers were practiced endlessly, whereas under Jennings such fundamentals had lately come to be ignored. Daily sliding sessions were also part of the regimen, the men in sheepskin culottes. Cobb might not have been able to run much anymore—he had only 15 stolen bases the previous season—but he could still teach. "When I was fast . . ." he said to a writer named Prosper Buranelli who paid him a visit in San Antonio. Buranelli noted that Cobb seemed struck by his own words, and paused to weigh them before continuing. "When I was fast I used constantly to go to second base on a single. I stretched hits so regularly that I made people think I was faster than I truly was. They laid the extra bases entirely to my speed, when half of my method was psychological. I used my speed to confound the nerves and brains of the opposition."

This was a variation on his lecture about always being a "mental hazard" for the other guy, and it's nice to have it. "It is an unfortunate human thing that we do not perform as well in the emergency as out of it," Cobb went on. "We do not pinch hit well." *He* certainly didn't; his lifetime batting average in that role was only .217. Few other managers could be so thoughtful and articulate. But sometimes—too often—Cobb's teaching amounted to him describing the way *he* did things with the understanding that he wanted his players to replicate him. The problem, of course, was that not everyone could do what he did—nor, especially in the Ruthian era, did everyone want to.

The mature but still athletic Cobb of the very early 1920s was a man confident in his ideas and comfortable with himself. "His features are good," Buranelli wrote, "nose slightly beaked, and his face has a smoothness and firmness of fibre that makes you think of a carefully cut sculpture. His blue-gray eyes are roundish and you can fancy them perfectly circular with anger. His lips are full, but colorless. His chin is round and does not thrust forward in pugnacity. His forehead curves and is capacious, head domed somewhat, with neutral colored hair thinned to baldness to almost the top of the skull." For a man who read a lot—people who knew him noted that if you came upon him in his living room in Augusta he always had a book in his hand and at least one other tented on the arm of his chair or the floor—he, thanks to baseball and off-season bird hunting, had the look of an outdoorsman, an appealing mens-sana-in-corpore-sano aura that not even his burgeoning cigarette habit could dim. He seemed to love the life he had constructed for himself in Augusta, the dogs, the guns, the dinners at which some combination of Tris Speaker, Eddie Collins, Moe Berg, Joe Tinker, and Grantland Rice would mingle with his neighbors. Jimmy Lanier, for most of the '20s his personal batboy, and the son of one of those neighbors, recalled that when Cobb was asked by civilian guests on such occasions if it was true that he sharpened his spikes, the way some newspapermen said, he would chuckle and say no, he never had—and then he would ask "Jimmy, m'boy," who during the season was in charge of cleaning, polishing, and putting away those same spikes, to say whether or not he was being accurate. And Jimmy would pipe he had never known Mr. Cobb to keep a file as part of his baseball kit, and for his honesty and/or loyalty he would be given a Ty Cobb candy bar.

If Cobb wasn't a millionaire yet he was close to it in 1921, thanks to his endorsement deals with candy, clothing, and sporting goods companies, the probably useless patent medicine Nuxated Iron, a tire store, the Hupmobile dealership, the Augusta Tourists (which he now owned in partnership with several local businessmen), and his stock. One of his hunting buddies was Robert W. Woodruff, who would succeed his father as head of the Atlanta-based Coca-Cola Company in 1923, and who urged Cobb to buy and hold on to as many shares as he could afford. He did, and passed along the tip to a number of sportswriters, who, in keeping with a sacred press box tradition regarding the accumulation of wealth, almost universally didn't. "Had we taken his well-intended advice, we each could have made between $250,000 and $300,00," said Henry P. Edwards, a baseball beat man for Cleveland's *Plain Dealer*. (The business journalist Adam J. Wiederman has calculated that one share of

Coca-Cola, purchased for $40 in 1919, would be worth $9.8 million today.)

When a reporter visited the Cobb family in mid-October 1921 he found an archetypical American man of leisure, cheerfully overseeing a household full of fresh-faced baseball buffs. Ten-year-old Shirley waited at the front door for the newspaper to arrive so she could keep track of the Giants-Yankees "subway" World Series then ongoing. Eleven-year-old Ty Jr. expounded on his theory that Babe Ruth should return to pitching despite his hot bat. Dad listened and chuckled. "Yes, we're all fans in this house," said the "lovely, raven-haired" Charlie Cobb, in one of the very rare moments when she is quoted directly. "And in between times I suppose I'm the biggest fan of all!" Unless this was a charade put on for a visiting reporter, Cobb owned all of the items on the standard checklist for happiness: a loving spouse (with family money of her own), a brood of five healthy kids (Jimmy was born in July of 1921), a more than healthy income, well-recognized success. It was probably the happiest time of his life.

Indeed it was only baseball that ruined a good thing. The team he'd inherited had many frustrating flaws. Despite his prediction in April of 1921 that "Detroit will have the best pitching staff in the American League by July 1!" it actually had possibly the worst; four of its five starters—Leonard, Dauss, Howard Ehmke, and Red Oldham—would finish the season with a losing record. The middle of his infield had become so porous that he put shortstop Donie Bush, a fan favorite, on waivers in midseason and brought in center fielder Ira Flagstead to do the best he could at second base.

Left fielder Bobby Veach was a different kind of problem. The skinny, handsome Kentuckian was a consistent .300 hitter and superior RBI man, if you just considered the numbers, but he was not particularly smart; he lacked intensity (he often failed in the clutch) and thought nothing of fraternizing with opponents on and off the field—"snuggling up to them like a Labrador pup" is the way Fred Lieb put it—characteristics that drove Cobb crazy (even though he had players for other teams as dinner guests). After hounding him for a while himself—Cobb's image as what Bullion had called "the perfect manager" was already starting to crack—

he ordered Harry Heilmann, who followed Veach in the batting order, to ride him from the on-deck circle, to call him yellow and a busher, so that he would bear down harder when at bat. Heilmann was at first reluctant to go along with the scheme, saying that he liked Veach and didn't want to ruin their friendship (*"Ballplayers are full of sentiment . . ."*), but, Fred Lieb wrote, "Cobb reassured him," saying, " 'Don't worry, when the season ends I'll explain to Bobbie that I put you up to it and for his own good.' " So Heilmann did what he was told, and Veach both improved as a clutch hitter and stopped talking to him. Unfortunately, Cobb took off for Georgia after the final game of the season without making the promised explanation. By next spring, things were better between Cobb's fellow outfielders, but they were never quite the same.

Cobb would forever be a mystery to Heilmann, a large, lumbering sort—his nicknames, "Slug" and "the Horse," were both double entendres—but the second best hitter the Tigers ever had. In the 1940s, Heilmann told Shirley Povich of the *Washington Post* that he and Cobb seldom spoke to each other in the first few years after he first came to the Tigers in 1914. Cobb was cool to him, the Horse believed, because he was such a good hitter, and "Ty was always very competitive." But then when Cobb became manager, the younger man felt, "he needed me, so we talked a lot." The conversations did pick up at that point, yet there are problems with Heilmann's version of events. One is that before 1921 he was a promising but sub-.300 hitter on average who posed no imminent threat to the team's star. Also, rather than needing him so desperately when he became manager, Cobb at first benched Heilmann, then platooned him with a left-handed batter named Chick Shorten. Another thing Heilmann misremembers is that when Cobb did start talking to him it was to give him hitting tips. He got the self-taught youngster, as Charles Alexander tells us, "to stand back in the box, put his feet closer together and hold his hands away from his body." Heilmann would win the batting title that year, finishing at .394, five points ahead of Cobb. The next year he would hit .356 and the year after that .403. "Cobb taught me more about hitting than I ever knew," Harry later had to admit.

It was a difficult interlude for both Heilmann and Cobb. On the not rare days when the former reported for duty with a serious hangover,

Cobb, as was his custom in such situations, insisted that he play. Once when Heilmann went from first to third on a single and then threw up all over the bag, Cobb kept him in the game to teach him a lesson. On another occasion, Cobb changed the batting order without telling Heilmann, who wound up hitting out of turn a two-run homer that didn't count. "Harry didn't think too much of Cobb," said a pitcher named Bill Moore. But the two eventually got over their differences, more or less, and Cobb was there at Heilmann's bedside shortly before he died in 1951 to tell him that he'd made the Hall of Fame (it was a white lie; he wouldn't be elected until a year later, but he'd be gone by then).

One thing we learn from Cobb's years as manager is that dealing with people is a privilege that frays the nerves. He simply could not go for very long as the placid, perfect player-manager without, as they say in the theater, breaking character and letting his real self show through. This was not necessarily a bad thing, considering the lackadaisical way that many of the Tigers played, yet it resulted in hurt feelings. Cobb practically wore a path between center field and the pitcher's mound, walking—but more often stalking—in to give instructions to his miffed twirlers before he gave up and just started shouting his orders and suggestions. The idea of being especially considerate of his pitchers' feelings soon went by the boards as the team, after getting off to a fine start in 1921—they were in third place, two games over .500 on Memorial Day—began giving up runs by the barrel.

"The manager is permitting reverses to prey on his mind," Bullion observed. Moore remembered that once, after walking three men consecutively and going 1–0 on a fourth, he heard a high-pitched Southern-accented voice behind him yell, "You're out of the game!" Cobb was especially hard on Dutch Leonard, whom he never liked and whose performance no longer offset the pitcher's sour and snappish ways. Cobb once pulled him from a game two strikes into a batting turn because he was appalled by his inept attempts to lay down a bunt. Leonard took this quite understandably as a public humiliation. Meanwhile, forgetting about his no-rules policy, he told Cole to quit staying out all night and Dauss to "leave the beer alone." But it was not just pitchers who felt his wrath—a wrath that, by the way, was not unlike that dispensed by John

McGraw and other famously cranky managers. Cobb ran onto the field at Fenway and raged at Veach for missing the plate on a slide home and getting tagged out.

A few years into his tenure, he more or less permanently cut off communication with Charlie Gehringer after the great young second baseman, a future Hall of Famer, spoke to him disrespectfully one day during a spring training game at which Cobb had been urging his tired-seeming players to "Go out there and make some noise!" Until then, said Gehringer, who came into the league as a shy Michigan farm boy, "Golly, he was like a father to me. He took care of me, coached me, rode with me on the train and all that. He even made me use his own bat, which was kind of a little thin thing. [Like a lot of players, Cobb switched to a lighter and lighter bat as he aged.] I said, gee, I'd like a little more batting space, but I didn't dare use another one. He would have shipped me to Siberia. But he was super for the first couple of years I was up."

"That must have been one hell of a fresh remark" you might say of the response that soured Cobb on "The Mechanical Man" (as they called the consistent Gehringer). But not necessarily. Gehringer might have just given some mild back talk. Cobb, it must be remembered, was extremely sensitive to anything that might contravene the social order. Even after he became a star, he called the principal owner of the Tigers "Mr. Navin" and demanded similar deference from young ballplayers, hotel clerks, chambermaids, train conductors, store workers, and wait staff of any color or either sex. Indeed, his reaction, when such a person regarded too casually the distinction between him and them, could seem borderline batty even under normal circumstances, as we have seen. But the years 1921 through 1926, his managerial era, were far from normal. The play of the Tigers kept him in an almost constant state of agitation. It was easier than ever to set him off.

The thing is, "the Cobbmen," as the scribes started calling them, weren't all that bad, especially as batters. On offense, in fact, they were sensational. Thanks largely to Cobb's hitting clinics, pretty much the same bunch that had finished sixth in hitting the year before now had an aggregate average of .316, the highest of any team in the previous twenty-four major league seasons. Overall, because they gave up far too many runs and made a lot of errors, they finished sixth in the standings with a record of 71 wins and 82 losses. But at least that was in line with Cobb's loudly applauded preseason prediction and a step up from the year before. Navin, the scribes, the fans—all had hope. And the next season turned out even better. Once again hitting above .300 as a team, the Tigers finished at 79–75, which put them in third place behind the Yankees and Browns—their best record in six years.

In 1923 they made a serious run at the pennant. Another future Hall of Famer, outfielder Heinie Manush, whom Navin had found playing for the Omaha Omahogs of the Western League, gave the team even more punch at the plate, especially after Cobb convinced him to choke up on the bat and "poke hit" more instead of always pulling the ball to right field. (Manush hit .334 his rookie season.) After a furious final push— they won 11 of their last 14 games—the Tigers wound up in second place behind the Yankees. To Navin's delight, the league's attendance figures worked out the same way. The Tigers drew more than 900,000, the most ever, justifying the owner's expansion of Navin Field that year, from 23,000 to 29,000. After a few years of avoiding the racetrack for the sake of his financial health, he was once again a regular at the Windsor Jockey Club, across the river from Detroit. "It was now his habit to stuff seven or eight $1,000 bills in his pocket, depending on the number of races," Fred Lieb tells us. "He would bet one on each race."

Cobb was more of a half-empty guy. When he looked at the standings he saw the yawning 16-game gap between his team and the Yankees; instead of second place he saw second-rate-ness. He felt embarrassed that he had not been able to effect a more dramatic transformation in the club. As a mere ballplayer, he now realized, he'd had greater control of his destiny. "When I went into baseball," he told Prosper Buranelli in the revealing interview that ran in the *Free Press* on September 25, 1921, "I said to myself that baseball was a business and that, like any other business, it was a matter of push and fight every instant. I must get ahead of the others and keep ahead of the others." And he had done that, he had managed to become—unless Ruth knocked him off the mountaintop—the greatest ballplayer of all time.

As a manager he tried as hard as possible to be an influence. He never sat still. The *New York Times* called him "the busiest manager in six states" and said he "paced up and down the coaching lines like a caged animal, raged at the umpires, yelled at the bench for 'more pep,' turned his head to exchange quips with the crowd and patted his players on the back when they made a good play. He had a hand in everything, did Ty, and he kept the Tigers fighting." He made so many pitching changes that opposing managers complained to Ban Johnson that he was delaying games. Not infrequently, he would pull his ostensible starting pitcher after one batter and replace him with a man who threw from the other side, forcing his counterpart to remake his lineup or suffer the consequences. Many of these maneuvers succeeded to some degree, just not well or often enough to suit his standards. What he needed was a clubhouse full of Ty Cobbs, wrote Sam Greene of the *Detroit News*, "and since there was only one Cobb, his ideas obviously wouldn't work." The results he got, while an improvement on his predecessor and never worse than mediocre, seemed dreary to him. Cobb didn't want to be just another manager, at the mercy of luck and cycles and fallible players. He rued his lack of a Midas touch.

Of course, as we've seen, whenever the going was especially tough Cobb ramped up his hitting. Even biographer Charles Alexander, not always the most sensitive observer of his subject's personality, noticed the phenomenon: "Cobb's performance on the field suggested that the pressures of managing actually heightened his playing skills." In 1921, Cobb hit .389 and the following year .401, though the batting title went to George Sisler (who hit .420). In 1923 Cobb fell off considerably—to .340—but he still had more magic in his bat, as he demonstrated over the course of two games in St. Louis, on May 5 and 6, 1925. On the first of those dates, Sid Keener recalled in a *Sporting News* article in 1961, he came upon Cobb telling his sportswriter friend H. G. Salsinger that he was tired of "reading stories that say I get my base hits on infield grounders and little bunts. The big guy, oh, you know, Babe Ruth, he socks those home runs! Well, I'll show you something today," Cobb said. "I'm going for home runs for the first time in my career!" That afternoon at Sportsman's Park, Cobb in six trips to the plate had three homers, two singles, and a double as the Tigers beat the Browns 14–8. The way Keener remembered it, he missed by only a few inches having four home runs for the day. The following afternoon, though, he did hit two more homers and a single in an 11–4 Detroit win. In the clubhouse after the second game, the old scribe wrote, Cobb was "jabbering all over the place" and practically hornpiping with glee. "What will the Babe say about this trick by Ty, five in two games?" (The feat has been equaled by several players since but has never been surpassed.)

Watching Cobb and Ruth fail to get along sweetly was one of joys of the early live ball era. Cobb was perennially the more aggrieved party because he paid more attention to what was being said and took offense quicker. It pained him to see the stands at Navin Field packed to near-capacity when Boston, and then the Yankees, came to town and, at a time when he himself was slowing down and getting injured a lot, to read a quote from the Tigers' own team physician, Dr. William Keane, saying, "There are plenty of ballplayers who are as strong physically, but they cannot do the things Ruth does for the reason that their eyes and their muscles are not in such perfect accord." To Cobb, in those days the Babe was just a big lummox who would eventually eat his way out of the major leagues—or so he said, probably without really believing it was true. "Ruth is good for the game," he kept hearing. "Cobb cannot be fully appreciated unless you are a student of baseball," said Yankees manager Miller Huggins. "Ruth appeals to everybody"—but the only way Ruth was good for Cobb, it seems, was as another piece of grit that he could impearl, a negative he could transform into a plus. Besides hitting 18 points above his lifetime average when Ruth pitched, Cobb had, as Tom Stanton tells us in his book *Ty and the Babe*, a consistently higher average when Ruth was anywhere on the same field. In 1920, for example, when he hit .334 against all opponents, he averaged .420 against the Yanks. When it came to Cobb's managing, however, Ruth had the opposite effect, bringing out Ty's overly prideful side. The Tigers were the only team in the American League that chose not to pitch around Ruth, a decision, on Cobb's part, that yielded disastrous results. In 1921, for example, Ruth had the game-winning hit in three of the Yanks' first four encounters with Detroit, and he also twice hit game-winning homers in a four-game sweep of the Tigers in mid-June.

In the second game of that series, played in New York on Sunday, June 12, single combat between Cobb and Ruth was narrowly avoided, but their respective armies clashed. Wrote Harry Bullion of the *Free Press*: "Close to 32,000 people were undecided whether to weep out of shame for the athletes, give vent to joy or feel insulted at the spectacle." The trouble began during batting practice, when Ruth, put off by something Cobb had said to him during the previous day's game, refused a photographer's request to take a picture with his rival. The Babe, no idiot, was hardly insensitive to the slurs that came his way. Biographer Robert W. Creamer tells us that teammates and opponents alike "made pointed insults about his round, flat-nosed, heavily tanned face; they called him monkey, baboon, ape, gorilla." Upon hearing that Ruth wouldn't pose, Cobb chose the gorilla option and did his best impression of one in front of the Yankees dugout. Ruth, "taking it as a challenge," according to one paper, charged Cobb, and would have fought with him right there had not umpires intervened. Once the game began, the two stars exchanged words every time they passed on the field, and in the fifth inning, said the *Bridgeport Telegram*, "struck the pose Dempsey and Carpentier will assume July 2" and glared at each other until umpire Bill Dinneen broke the tension.

Dinneen was a sort of Neville Chamberlain figure. Earlier in the game he had been slugged in the stomach and jaw by Donie Bush following a disputed call but he did not eject the Tigers shortstop until, when the inning ended, Bush tried to hit him with a thrown ball. All eyes remained on Cobb and the Babe, though—until in the eighth another fight erupted between Tigers first baseman Lu Blue and Yankees catcher Wally Schang following a collision at the plate, which in turn caused both teams, said Bullion, "to pour off the benches like smoke out of the funnels of a trans-Atlantic liner." Ruth and Cobb found each other in the fracas and were again about to mix it up when Miller Huggins tackled his star to keep him out of trouble. Bullion wrote that it was "humorous" to see the manager, "half as big as Ruth, trying to budge the Babe. But while that was going on Ainsmith rushed to the plate to challenge somebody and 'Ping' Bodie challenged Eddie," and so on. The melee didn't end "until Blue arranged to fight [Yankees coach] Charley O'Leary under the stands after the game." The results of that contest went unrecorded.

Ruth and Cobb were at the center of a very similar battle royal that took place three years later almost to the day, but at Navin Field. That time the inciting event was a pitch that drilled Yankees outfielder Bob Meusel in the ribs, causing him to crumple. Ruth yelled that he'd seen Cobb signal pitcher Bert Cole to plunk Meusel, and ran out of the dugout toward the mound. Cobb scurried to defend his man but Huggins once again played referee, now with the help of umpire Emmett "Red" Ormsby. Thousands of Detroit fans soon engulfed the principals and, with all in chaos, and people somehow pulling up seats and tossing them onto the field, Ormsby declared the Yankees winners by forfeit. Curiously, with that climactic catharsis the feud seemed to run out of steam. The 100 or so extra policemen that Navin arranged to be brought in for the next day's game proved unnecessary, nor were such precautions ever needed again.

It's likely Cobb finally figured out that it looked bad for him to be bothered by the man whom fate had so obviously sent to be his replacement. "I've always liked Ruth," Cobb began saying, with a straight face. Batboy Jimmy Lanier remembered only the friendly last days of the rivalry: "One time when Ruth hit a tremendous home run he was coming around third base and he yelled at Mr. Cobb, in the dugout, '*Now* do you want to tell me how to hit?'" After Cobb's retirement the two greats often golfed together and spent long evenings drinking whiskey and swapping tales, the way ex-ballplayers do. Maybe they weren't such an odd couple after all. Besides having baseball and success in common they also had Claire Merritt Hodgson, a Georgia native and a *Ziegfeld Follies* girl who was Ruth's second wife. In her autobiography, *The Babe and I*, Mrs. Ruth said she had known Cobb "very well" as a teenager back in Athens, before he married Charlie, and for what it may be worth, Al Stump, in his second book on Cobb, suggests they were young lovers.

Since he couldn't lavish it on Ruth without looking like a sore loser, and could take it out on the Tigers only so much before it became counterproductive, what did Cobb do with the rage that obviously rose within him as things went less than grandly during his managerial years? He appeared during this stretch of a half dozen seasons to exist in a state of low-grade fury, with occasional flare-ups, stomping around in center, strutting the sidelines, "bullying and goat-getting," said John E. Wray of the *St. Louis Post-Dispatch*, and spouting "rough-riding stuff." This obviously wasn't relieving the tension. So to whom did he vent? How did he cope?

This brings us to the topic of umpires. On September 24, 1921, Cobb and Billy Evans, a close personal friend who had called him out at second base earlier that day on an attempted steal, engaged in a bloody half-boxing, half-wrestling match after a game under the stands at Griffith Stadium in Washington. You could tell by the way he threw punches and cursed that Cobb believed he had been safe on the play. He "inflicted a hard blow on Evans' mouth that caused an abrasion," according to a reporter who witnessed the scene. Then the two "went into a clinch, fell into the cinders and rolled around" until "park officials succeeded in separating the battlers," who shook hands and apologized, friends again.

Evans was probably not surprised to hear Cobb suggest, immediately after the play, that they meet postgame to settle things with their fists. He had been baiting and battling umpires with odd enthusiasm since he took the skipper's job. The behavior actually started in late 1920, when he had first tried his hand at managing, in San Francisco; he had that December incurred the largest fine ever levied in the Pacific Coast League—$150— for stalking out of a game in the sixth inning after an umpire refused to remove a ball Cobb said was being scuffed by the pitcher. In March of 1921 he announced, "in strident tones," said the *New York Times*, but without explanation, that he refused to play an exhibition game against the Giants because the umpire was to be the apparently onerous NL veteran Bill Brennan. After that, amid many minor run-ins, he had the fight with Evans and then, in St. Louis, a screaming match with umpire Frank Wilson, whose toes he purposely stepped on with his spikes. He may have also worked to get him fired; when Wilson was relegated to the minors two weeks later he blamed Cobb. Pants Rowland, putting in a stint as an umpire, also got a serious tongue-lashing from the man who'd beaten him out for the Detroit managing job.

Cobb had been rough on umps when he first came up, but never to this degree. Back then, when big league baseball was still relatively new, everybody in the game seemed to see umpires as villains working if not for the other side then specifically against them. Whether the attitude stemmed from a widespread innocence about how things worked down on the field, or the fact that so many people were betting on the games, is hard to say, but players routinely struck umpires, fans threw bottles and rotten vegetables at them, and team owners threatened to take them to court. A week before Cobb came to the majors, Tigers supporters, outraged by a call, mobbed umpire Jack Sheridan and chased him into the clubhouse—where he declared the Washington Senators the winner by forfeit. Umps in those days were everybody's punching bag. The drama critic George Jean Nathan, an avid baseball fan, counted 355 physical assaults on umpires by players and fans during the 1909 season alone. Abe Pollock, who had been a boxing referee before becoming a professional ump, said that players had often spiked his feet, bumped him, and kicked him in the shins; he didn't quit, though, until the day when a fan "dropped a bull terrier on the field, pointed to me and said, 'Sic 'em!'"

Cobb, like most other people who played or followed or ran the game, in time came to realize that while umpires may make mistakes, instances of them favoring one team were exceedingly rare. He also saw that there was little to be gained by being a constant bother to the men in blue. "Once I showed him who was in charge," said Silk O'Loughlin, "I never had any problem with him." According to the *Chicago Tribune*, Cobb promised in April of 1910 that he would "not sass an umpire, no matter what the umpire may do to provoke him." It was a vow he broke frequently, before and after he wrote in his 1914 memoir, *Busting 'Em*, "umpires are the bravest men in baseball" and "I have long since seen the folly" of being rough on them—but never with the lack of restraint he showed after he became a manager. Some of his fellow skippers, especially Clark Griffith of the Senators, thought his behavior downright unseemly, and told Ban Johnson that all of his griping (as well as his pitcher switching) was slowing down games to the point where they were getting tedious.

Cobb's ever-loyal batboy, Jimmy Lanier, said that the only time his boss ever disappointed him came during this period, when Cobb abused two umpires in a spring training game against the Cardinals at Warren Park in Augusta in early April of 1923. After being called out by Harry Pfirman when he attempted to steal second base, he threw a handful of dirt in Pfirman's face, then refused the order of crew chief "Steamboat" Johnson to get to the showers. They argued for at least five minutes before Johnson declared the game over, and then the crowd surged onto the field, jostled the umps and demanded refunds. Cobb, who as a part-owner of Warren Park had employed the umpires for the exhibition series, sought out Johnson in the mob and told him he was fired. Later that night, starting to regret his behavior, he went to Johnson's hotel and gruffly rehired him—"but," said Lanier, "he made a fool of himself, I thought."

Cobb often felt ashamed of his angry outbursts; he was, after all, a true *personage* who played poker and sipped bootleg whiskey with the president of the United States, Warren Harding, at a private all-men's club outside Augusta, not to mention a Southern gentleman. On some days he could be the most considerate man you ever met, slipping $20 to a raggedy-looking child he saw along the road or going into the stands to check on a woman who'd been struck by a foul ball, and telling her that if she had any resulting medical expenses, she should send them to the Detroit Tigers. "The King," as some Detroit sportswriters called him, shouldn't be throwing dirt in some poor umpire's face or holding up a game by acting like a stubborn child. "I rode home with him," Lanier went on, "and he went in and told Mrs. Cobb what had happened [with the umpires]. He said that he had made the biggest mistake of his life."

The end of the affair is always a sad thing, and Cobb and Detroit were starting to drift apart, not dramatically but perceptibly, even a year before the city threw him another big shindig, this time to celebrate his twentieth year as a Tiger. The city was a booming, more modern, younger place than it had been when he first put his bags down at Michigan Central Station. He was fitting in less comfortably, to the game and to the era. He was now the oldest player in the American League, railing at the kids on his lawn. He could still poke the ball over the infielders' heads—he batted .338, .378, and .339 over the next three years, 1924, '25, and '26—but in 1925 and '26 he was managing from the bench with increasing frequency, and because he was heavier and chronically leg-sore, he could no longer play his signature game, the mad dance around the bases to a tune only he could hear. Since there was no film of him to watch, newcomers to Detroit—and there were a lot of newcomers to Detroit in those days—may have wondered what all the fuss was about. Or what caused him to get in so many scrapes with service workers. In February of 1925 he "attained new heights of dignity," said the *Atlanta Constitution*, with uncharacteristic sarcasm, after "he engaged in heated and profane repartee with a comely waitress over the size of a lunch check" in a Union Station restaurant. The woman alleged that she had to hit him on the head with a glass plate to get him to simmer down. He was booked on a charge of disorderly conduct and released after posting $11 bail. It wasn't serious—he denied that she'd ever plunked him—but it was silly and more than a little embarrassing. Not long afterward, as the team was stumbling out of the starting gate, a columnist for the *Washington Post* reported that he'd heard a rumor that some fans were circulating a petition calling for Cobb's removal.

The root problem was what it always is in sports: too much losing. Cobb could have delayed games and played his quaint brand of throwback baseball all he wanted if the Tigers had come closer to winning a pennant—but they didn't. In 1924, the year before Cobb's physical decline began in earnest—he made 625 plate appearances, the most of his career—the Tigers put up a record of 86–68, and passed the one million mark in attendance, but still finished in third place, 10 games behind the Senators and eight behind the Yankees. In 1925, they regressed, and got booed from the (4–14) start. "This city has soured on the Tigers," a *New York Times* reporter wrote when he came to Detroit. Cobb himself, said the *Washington Post*, was frequently the inspiration for "the raspberry chorus," even though his pitchers, which as a group had an ERA of 4.61, probably deserved it more.

No one was more of a problem to him than the once great Dutch Leonard, who had left the team in 1921 after a salary dispute with Navin and returned in late 1924 following a few seasons in an outlaw West Coast league. Leonard pitched not at all badly the following year, going 11–4, but he accused Cobb of overusing him as a means of punishing him for his outspokenness. He said that Cobb wanted to permanently ruin his arm so as to put him out of the business. Whether it was true or not, it was a very Dutch Leonard–ish thing to say. Cobb, for his part, called it ridiculous, but it may have given him an idea because on July 14 he left Leonard in a game in which the Athletics were walloping him for 12 runs and 20 hits, forcing him to go the full nine innings. In September of that year, he put the pitcher on waivers and, as the Dutchman told it, made a few phone calls to other front offices to assure he would not be picked up. Leonard's enforced return to his farm in Fresno turned out to be fruitful for him in more ways than one—he became, by his death in 1952, a kind of raisin king—but he left the game vowing revenge on Cobb and, as we shall see in the next chapter, no one can say he didn't give it his best shot.

The 1925 Tigers finished at 81–73, good enough only for fourth place, 16½ games behind Washington. While this may not have seemed like the kind of campaign that ought to be interrupted for a special Ty Cobb Day, it *was* the twentieth anniversary of his joining the club in mid-season as an unheralded yannigan, and so following pregame ceremonies on August 29, Cobb stood bareheaded at home plate in Navin Field and shook the hands of thousands of fans as they filed past. At the new Book Cadillac Hotel that evening, 600—including Connie Mack, Mayor John W. Smith, and umpire Billy Evans, who was rumored to be Cobb's replacement as manager—gathered to make speeches and present him with a grandfather clock said to be worth $1,000. The spirit of this banquet wasn't the same as the one four years previous, though. For one thing, Cobb was miffed at the *Detroit News* for its plan to publish, without his permission, the first book-length biography of him, really a collection of fifty-eight H. G. Salsinger sketches that had already run in the paper and which the *News* had advertised under the title of *Our Ty*. In deference to him, no copies were printed but the incident strained relations between Cobb and his oldest friend in the press box. What annoyed the guest of honor even more, however, was the point in the evening when Navin presented him with a $10,000 check, said to be an extra sign of the club's appreciation. Cobb contended that the "bonus" was nothing more than what the Tigers owed him anyway by the terms of his contract, and that Navin was using him to buff his own public image. The cord that had bound those two for so long was fraying—yet not quite ready to break. That fall, the owner offered Cobb a new contract that raised his salary to $50,000, and Cobb promptly accepted it. Clearly, Navin, who had stuck with Hughie Jennings through 11 pennantless seasons, found it difficult to fire managers, and even harder to separate from surrogate sons. As for Cobb, he wanted one more chance to clear up the muddle that was his managerial tenure.

No such luck. Things stayed inconclusive. Nineteen twenty-six, Fred Lieb tells us, was "another one of those might-have-been seasons," somewhere between crummy and Cobbian, thanks again to superb hitting undercut by lackluster arms. Cobb kept himself out of the lineup for most of the second half; he'd started the year by having surgery to remove benign growths caused by excessive exposure to sunlight from both eyes, and then he'd strained his back, but his critics said he was simply tired of hearing so much booing. The Tigers, close to the top all summer, with Bob "Fats" Fothergill filling in at center field when Cobb rested, were sixth in the end, with a kissing-your-sister record of 79–75. Even worse, though, was that attendance had dropped by about 300,000 from just a few years before. "Ty Cobb has lost his popularity," wrote Henry Edwards of Cleveland's *Plain Dealer*, and while that was an exaggeration, fewer and fewer wanted to watch him run the ball club. When asked about rumors that he was retiring, Cobb said, "I guess some of the fans hope it's true."

After the final game of the 1926 season—the second half of a doubleheader against Boston in which he ground out in his one at-bat as a pinch hitter—he got out of town quickly, and far from baseball. Instead of going to the World Series (in which the Cardinals, led by second baseman–manager Rogers Hornsby, beat the Yankees in seven games), he went with Tris Speaker and others to hunt bear and moose in the Grand Tetons. When he returned to Detroit, on Wednesday, November 3, he was carrying his letter of resignation, which he left with Frank Navin's secretary.

CHAPTER TWENTY-SEVEN

BECAUSE THE ANSWER SEEMS A lot less obvious now than it did in late 1926, let us pose the question anew: Was Ty Cobb a success as a manager? The answer I think depends on how you define "Ty Cobb." If you see him as a man who would not be content unless any endeavor he undertook absolutely reeked of excellence, then no, he certainly was not. His record in his half dozen seasons as the Tigers' skipper was an odorless 479–444, good for a pleasant-enough .519 win percentage. This was slightly below the .523 that Hughie Jennings had earned in the six years prior to Cobb's ascension, but securely ahead of the .469 that two successive managers produced over an equal span immediately after Cobb. So tough call, the thumbs-up-or-down thing, no? A reasonable person, removed from the zeitgeist and looking at just these numbers, could go either way. Cobb himself seemed to recognize this when he discussed the issue with Fred Lieb a few years after his retirement. His pertinent quote, which appears in Lieb's history of the Tigers, has, it is true, a certain air-brushed quality, and yet it compactly states the case for him not being an out-and-out bust:

"Maybe I was not a managerial success, but just as surely I was not a managerial failure," Cobb allegedly told the Tigers historian over dinner in a San Francisco restaurant.

I took over a seventh-place club in 1921, and with the exception of that year, all of my clubs won more games than they lost. Four were in the first division. We played interesting, exciting ball, drew well at home, and next to the Yankees were the best attraction on the road. I was continually handicapped by inadequate pitching, but Earl Whitehill and several other

good prospects were developed. Heilmann developed into a full-fledged
star under my management; he was a natural hitter, and I taught him
everything I had learned in my long career. We always had hitting clubs,
so I must have imparted some of my own hitting knowledge to my players.

That may sound reasonable now, but in late 1926 the speaker of
those words would have been pilloried. Cobb was still widely revered as
the greatest ballplayer who ever lived, no mere jock but a philosopher of
the pastime, an innovator and sage. The second most popular synonym
for him in the Detroit press, after "the Peach," was "the King." Not long
before, attempting to convey what it meant to be Ty Cobb, E. A. Batchelor had written of an eerie encounter he had on a rainy evening in Mississippi, when the train carrying the Tigers north from spring training
ground to a halt at a water tank station. A score of "countrymen" who'd
heard that "Mistah Ty Cobb" was coming through, and who "dun druv
10 miles" to see him (it's hard to tell from the lamely rendered dialect
and other description if the rubes were black or white) emerged from the
crepuscular mist and pressed their weathered faces against the Pullman
windows. "I jest wanted to shake yo' hand," said their leader. "Glad to see
you; very glad indeed," says Cobb. "Won't you all sit down?" Then, in the
ten minutes before the train began to move on, he "talked about everything but himself" and "made every man there feel that his hero had lived
especially for this moment."

People loved Cobb so much they asked for his autograph on balls and
bats and shirts—a relatively new thing—and they named their children
after him, boys especially. They just didn't want him to manage anymore,
and within the confines of Navin Field, when he was in his uniform and
they were wearing their fan-faces, they weren't afraid to make their disapproval manifest. The consensus, articulated by the scribes, was that he had
made a mockery of his once promising "no rules" policy, and disheartened
the team by becoming a classic martinet. Even those who didn't think he
managed badly thought he managed far too much. "That man makes me
so nervous I don't know if I'm here or in Pekin [Peking]!" one of his players supposedly said. In the wake of his resignation, his presumed friend
H. G. Salsinger—who may have still been angry with Cobb for blocking

the publication of his book a year earlier—wrote a stingingly negative review of his performance in the *Sporting News*, saying "As a player he was without peer; as a manager he became a man with a number of superiors." Cobb's "natural nervousness" did him in, Salsinger said. "It caused his varying moods. He never moved at an even keel. He was either too generous in his praise or too biting in his criticisms. He left wounds that never healed."

Many harsh things were said at this time, by people on both sides; it was, after all, a divorce. Cobb claimed he was victim of a conspiracy involving Navin, Ban Johnson, and Kenesaw Mountain Landis, the flamboyant, capricious commissioner of baseball. He said those men wanted him out of the league, and in fact they may have, for reasons that hadn't yet surfaced publicly but soon would. Still, the Tigers' owner swatted down the contention, saying "I don't know what he means when he talks about conspiracy. He was on a player's contract. That contract had expired; therefore it was unnecessary to engage in any conspiracy to drop him." As for Cobb's charge that the Tigers undermined his efforts with their penny-pinching ways, Navin had an answer for that, too, which he gave in a very blunt interview with the *Detroit News*. He said that he and his partners, Briggs and Kelsey, had let Cobb know that they were willing to go into their own wallets to "buy and present to the ball club" any player that the Tigers as a corporation could not afford—but that Cobb had failed to identify such a player who was actually on the market. He also said that of the players they *had* acquired on their manager's recommendation, "some were satisfactory but most were not." He then mentioned Rip Collins, Del Pratt, Wilbur Cooper, and "a player named Goebel"—names he knew would land like Dempsey combinations on Tigers fans' collective solar plexus, rendering them nauseated. (Goebel, for whom the Tigers gave up the .290 lifetime hitter Ira Flagstead at Cobb's urging, never even reported to Detroit.)

Navin also knocked his former manager for failing to develop young players the way Joe McCarthy of the Chicago Cubs routinely did, and for causing unhappiness in the ranks. "It is true that I intended dropping Cobb at the end of the 1925 season because 11 or 12 players on the Detroit club demanded that I sell or trade them," he said. "They did not want to work under him. I explained this to Cobb so he would be able to handle the situation, and I had Harry Heilmann promise me that he would help me remedy the condition."

Navin had cried the blues before about Cobb, but never in this particular key. Whatever he did or said publicly or privately, his goal until this point had always been to keep Cobb close (and Cobb's enemies closer). When Hughie Jennings tried to frame young Ty as a troublemaker so that he'd be traded, and Ban Johnson wanted to bounce him out of the league for continually fighting, Navin employed a brand of psychological jujitsu that made it sound like he sympathized—like he was madder, in fact, than either of them at his problem child, even as he hustled Cobb safely behind his skirts. When Cobb was accused of spiking Home Run Baker, it was Navin who sent the exonerating photograph to every sports editor on his list. The old nickel nurser had given the unheralded rookie from Royston, Georgia, an unsolicited raise and twenty years later made him the highest-paid player-manager in the game, at $50,000 a season. He had put the Peach into good investments and paid lawyers to extract him from some very sticky jams. He'd met a boy reeling from the death of his father at the hand of his mother and helped mold him into a man—but a man whom he was now estranged from, done with forever, it seemed. Navin's anger, when it flared, had always been fundamentally paternal, never just a disciplinary technique or a negotiating pose, and so sometimes it seemed especially fierce. But this wasn't anger. This was the end of the road.

What was really fueling the public argument between Cobb and Navin did not begin to surface until November 29, 1926, when Tris Speaker unexpectedly resigned as player-manager of the Cleveland Indians. Spoke was thirty-eight years old then, his legs had begun to go, his average had dropped to .304, and his departure came amid numerous managerial denouements—but in other important ways the leave-taking confounded logic. His Indians, blissfully unaware that they were, man for man, a second-division club, had hung close to the Yankees all season and finished just three games behind the Ruth-Gehrig combine in second place. The *Plain Dealer* called their showing "something a little short of a baseball miracle." Speaker was the club's biggest, as well as its only, drawing card (though Homer Summa, Garland Buckeye, Ike Eichrodt, and By Speece were name players in their own way). Surely team president Ernest Barnard would have happily reupped the local hero at his $30,000 annual salary—and yet Speaker said he was, in effect, leaving baseball to pursue his love of geometric metal stamping with the Geometric Stamping Company of Cleveland. Huh? The *Plain Dealer* editorial writers said they were "bewildered" by Speaker's exit. So were a lot of others. The *New York Times* called the move "a profound mystery."

Speaker's and Cobb's resignations made perfect sense, though, separately and together, to a small group of baseball insiders aware of a drama that had been unfolding behind the scenes all that summer. It was still late May, in fact, when Dutch Leonard, who had been stewing among the prunes and figs on his California fruit farm, came to Ban Johnson's office in Chicago with an unsettling story to tell about Cobb and Speaker and two letters to prove that what he had to say was not pure spite. Johnson, who probably realized the pitcher had a grudge against Cobb for canning him in 1925, and also resented his former friend Speaker for not picking him up off the waiver wire, at first tried to stymie Leonard by refusing to meet with him. Always a bit lily-livered, and now in the later stages of alcoholism, Johnson struggled to summon the energy and gumption to solve even routine problems. All Leonard did, though, was peddle his potential bombshell elsewhere—namely to Frank Navin, one of the more influential owners in the American League as well as the immediate boss of a man he was ratting on. Navin, too, at first said he was too busy to talk to Leonard, but when he finally did he was impressed enough by what he heard and saw to call Johnson and tell him that he must sit down with the wounded and therefore dangerous Dutchman. This the league president did, and a short time later, with the help of Johnson's lawyer, Henry Killilea, Navin had arranged to buy Leonard's letters, as well as his silence, for $20,000.

What could be worth so much? The story Leonard told was more than a few years old, but it involved gambling and was set, if only by coincidence, in the significant season of 1919, when the White Sox lay down in the World Series and let the Reds win, after accepting bribes from professional gamblers. It was precisely the kind of story that Johnson wished the public not to hear, a tale that, whatever its particular merits, was sure to reinforce the idea that baseball, and his American League in particular, was riddled with corruption. Leonard set his opening scene, in melodramatic fashion, under the Navin Field stands. He said that on September 23, he, Indians manager Speaker, Cobb, and Smoky Joe Wood, a former pitcher but by then an outfielder for Cleveland, had gathered there and got around to discussing the next day's game. The Tigers had beaten the Indians earlier that afternoon, wiping out the very slim chance they'd had of winning the pennant. Cleveland now was guaranteed to finish second, but the Detroits were still battling the Yankees for third place, the last remaining spot that came with a share of World Series money.

According to Leonard, Speaker told the group that the Indians, since it was all the same to them, would let the Tigers win—and then someone pointed out that as long as the outcome was certain, it made sense to get down a bet. Cobb allegedly said he was in for $2,000 and suggested that a Navin Field worker named Fred West would be able to place the wager. Leonard said he'd bet $1,500 while Speaker and Wood promised to put up $1,000 each. The transaction didn't go smoothly, though. West's bookmaker got nervous about taking so much action, and wanted to get an okay from his boss in Chicago. It also appears that Cobb changed his mind about his participation. Speaker also may have dropped out and been replaced in the little syndicate by a never identified friend of Wood's, a "man from Cleveland." In any case, West, according to Leonard, was able to get down only $600 each for the three men at odds of 10–7.

The letters the pitcher had saved—one from Wood, the other from Cobb—did not back him on every single aspect of his story but they generally supported the idea that a bet had been discussed and attempted by at least some of the men he mentioned. Wood, in his note, left no doubt about his involvement:

Cleveland, Ohio, Friday

Dear Friend Dutch:

Enclosed please find certified check for sixteen hundred and thirty dollars ($1,630.00).

The only bet West could get down was $600 against $420 (10 to 7). Cobb did not get up a cent. He told us that and I believe him. Could have put up some at 5 to 2 on Detroit, but did not, as that would make us put up $1,000 to win $400.

We won the $420. I gave West $30 [as a tip], leaving $390, or $130 for each of us. Would not have cashed your check at all, but West thought he could get it up at 10 to 7, and I was going to put it all up at those odds. We could have won $1,750 for the $2,500 if we could have placed it.

If we ever have another chance like this we will know enough to try to get down early.

Let me hear from you, Dutch. With all good wishes to Mrs. Leonard and yourself, I am

JOE WOOD

Cobb's letter speaks for itself. While it shows his knowledge of the scheme, it reveals him to be a man uncomfortable with gambling. The articles and books that have quoted it in the past usually have edited out the small talk, but I present it here in unexpurgated form to show the friendly tone he took, at least on this occasion, with a teammate who was notoriously hard to like. To paraphrase something said earlier in this book, his legend notwithstanding, Cobb was not always the crankiest guy in the clubhouse.

Augusta, Ga., Oct. 23, 1919

Dear Dutch:

Well, old boy, guess you are out in old California by this time and enjoying life.

I arrived home and found Mrs. Cobb only fair, but the baby girl [Beverly] was fine and at this time Mrs. Cobb is very well, but I have been very busy getting acquainted with my family and have not tried to do any correspondence, hence my delay.

Wood and myself were considerably disappointed in our business

proposition, as we had $2,000 to put into it and the other side quoted
us $1,400, and when we finally secured that much money it was about
2 o'clock and they refused to deal with us as they had men in Chicago
take up the matter with and they had no time, so we completely fell down
and of course we felt badly over it.

Everything was open to Wood and he can tell you about it when we
get together. It was quite a responsibility and I don't care for it again,
I can tell you.

Well, I hope you found everything in fine shape at home and all your
troubles will be little ones. I made a this [sic] year's share of world series
in cotton since I came home and expect to make more.

I thought the White Sox should have won [the fixed World Series],
but I am satisfied they were too overconfident. Well, old scout, drop me
a line when you can. We have had some dandy fishing since I arrived
home.

With kindest regards to Mrs. Leonard, I remain,

Sincerely,
TY

Cobb would eventually admit that his letter "connected me to" the
plan to make a wager, but he insisted that in the end he acted only as
an intermediary, setting up Wood, an out-of-towner, with Fred West.
Speaker, though rumored to be a frequent gambler on baseball (and
horses), would claim he made no bet, and add in his own defense that
he was not even mentioned in either note. And he, Cobb, and Wood all
said there had never been a clandestine, beneath-the-stands meeting to
hatch a plot, but rather just casual, on-the-fly conversation about matters that at the time seemed of no major consequence. This rings true.
It is commonly and I think correctly assumed that baseball's garden was
then rampant with prototypical Pete Roses. Before the Black Sox scandal,
merely betting on a game, even one you participated in, was a mundane
thing and a venial sin at worst, a common violation of an unwritten rule
that was still not in the books seven years later, when Leonard came forward with his story, but for which a player might draw anything from a

warning to a suspension of several days. A much more serious crime was fixing a game in order to cash a bet. For undermining the integrity of the pastime in that particular way, players could and did receive lifetime suspensions as well as public scorn. Hal Chase, who would have been certain to win election to the Hall of Fame, once it was founded in 1936, was banned in 1919 for offering bribes to his teammates, and of course eight men connected with the Black Sox scandal, including the otherwise Cooperstown-worthy Shoeless Joe Jackson, were also exiled from baseball.

Did the game played on the chilly, windy afternoon of September 25, 1919, have a prearranged outcome? It certainly was odd in some ways. The daily newspaper accounts describe a sloppy slugfest won by the Tigers 9–5 in an hour and six minutes, the briefest game of the season. "Cleveland did its best to hurry the game through so it could make the 5 o'clock train for home, dodging the night boat trip," said the *Free Press*. Many batters on both sides swung at the first pitch. "Cleveland didn't care much whether it won or lost," wrote Harry Bullion in the story he filed that evening, "and the Tigers, catching the visitors in that mood, smashed their way to the top and held the advantage to the finish." The *Plain Dealer* felt the same way. "The best thing about this contest was its brevity," its writer said, noting that it "did not seem like a real championship game."

Even if you knew that players back then often coasted and jived their way through meaningless fall "friendship games," as they were known, the strange rhythm of the game still might raise an eyebrow. But what of the individuals singled out by Leonard as perpetrating or condoning a fix? Did they act suspiciously? It would be hard to convict them on the basis of their performances that day. Two of the men—Leonard himself and Wood—did not play (the former, finished for the year, was on his way back to California), while Cobb went a subpar 1-for-5, and Speaker, who was supposedly betting on his team to lose, smacked two triples that seemed to have been grooved into his wheelhouse by Detroit starter Bernie Boland. With so many players not participating in the "conspiracy," and the few insiders not playing their logical roles, it is difficult to see this as a classic example of a contest with a predetermined outcome, though clearly Speaker should never have spoken about a laydown and Cobb should never have even considered making a bet.

The quality of the evidence notwithstanding, Ban Johnson reacted strongly. He always took personally anything that even remotely threatened to besmirch the reputation of the league he had founded a quarter century before, and he wanted to mete out severe punishments—"guilty or innocent," he said later, inexplicably—but there were problems. Leonard and Wood, a planter and the baseball coach at Yale since 1923, respectively, were now beyond his jurisdictional reach. That left Cobb and Speaker, both all too involved, and synonymous with, the pastime, to discipline quietly—if that were possible. It would be tricky indeed to banish those stars from American League baseball without letting the world know that further evidence of gambling by players had surfaced. Since he didn't know what to do, Johnson did nothing about the matter for several months except hire private detectives to tail Speaker and Cobb and determine their betting habits (the Pinkertons discovered what was already known: that Speaker gambled frequently, and Cobb never did). In the meantime—probably in early June of 1926—Kenesaw Mountain Landis heard about Leonard's allegations, through the scuttlebutt, and also sat tight, no doubt enjoying the thought of Johnson agonizing the summer away in the AL president's more spacious Chicago digs.

The two baseball "czars" did not exactly go together like peanuts and Cracker Jack. Johnson openly resented Landis from the moment that the owners, in 1920, installed him as the first commissioner, with the command that he clean up the game in the wake of the Black Sox brouhaha, or at least give the impression that he was doing so. A clash between Johnson and Landis was inevitable because the new hierarchy was ambiguously defined—though it was clear that the commissioner superseded a league president—and both men were blatant egoists, more eager to claim territorial rights than to come up with coherent responses to the challenges at hand. Picking sides in this power grab would be difficult. We've already seen how mercurial and muddle-headed Johnson could be, even before he started to break down under the influence of drink. Landis—whose first name was a spelling variant of the Civil War battle where his father, a Union Army doctor, was wounded—had been a federal judge known for untoward pronouncements and outlandish decisions that were frequently overturned on appeal. No one ever accused him of being brilliant, or consistent—on the matter of the racial integration of the game, for example, he would in future years be, at turns, pro, neutral, and con—but he did enjoy the stage that baseball provided him, and it was sometimes entertaining to watch him hold forth at the center of it, dressed flamboyantly in nineteenth-century throwback style.

After keeping mum on the matter for almost four months, Johnson called a secret meeting of the American League owners in his Chicago office on September 9 and told them what he knew about Cobb and Speaker. It's not clear why he did this, but he may have felt that the gossip was reaching a level where it might soon spill into the press, and so the issue needed to be resolved quickly. It is also impossible to say what exactly he hoped might come of the meeting, but what did happen after some discussion was that Ernest Barnard of the Indians made a motion, seconded by Colonel Jacob Ruppert of the Yankees, that all of Johnson's files "pertaining to the charges made by Hubert Leonard . . . be submitted to Commissioner K. M. Landis for his consideration." This motion was passed unanimously. The owners also stipulated that they wanted Landis to conduct a hearing with Leonard, Cobb, Speaker, Wood, and West to investigate the charges.

Johnson, apparently angered by the resolution—*he* wanted to resolve the matter in *his* way—did not follow up on it for quite a while. The day of the meeting, his chief lawyer, Killilea, sent Landis copies of the 1919 letters from Cobb and Wood and promised in writing the full cooperation of the American League president, but the bulk of Johnson's information on the case seems to have remained in the American League offices for at least two additional months, if not longer. In the meantime, Johnson went to see Cobb and Speaker at their homes, to give them a status report—they both knew about the charges already, but Cobb, he said, "was heartbroken and maintained his innocence" when Johnson told him that he planned to banish him from the AL forever, no matter how Landis's hearing went. Meanwhile, the chagrined commissioner pursued his own investigation, inviting Leonard to come to his office for a discussion. When the ex-pitcher balked at that proposition, saying "they bump off people once in while around there [Chicago]," Landis went to Leonard's farm near Sanger, California, on October 29 to take his testimony himself. Landis scheduled a formal hearing for late November, which was postponed when Leonard refused to travel east to face the men he was accusing. When the hearing actually did occur, on December 20, Leonard, despite repeated requests for his presence, was still not among the dozen or so people crowded into Landis's small office.

There were no big surprises that day, just some interesting little revelations, such as Wood, to make the point that gambling by players had been an everyday thing, saying that the entire Washington Senators team once "went broke" betting on a game in which he out-pitched Walter Johnson. An attentive reader of the transcript might also have seen that Cobb could at times sound like an upper-class Brit: "All the players were *fagged out*," he told his inquisitor, Killilea, explaining why the September 25 game seemed so rushed. "*I dare say* every season there are games that slide along and are played off hurriedly on that account; it has been happening ever since baseball has been played." When Landis offered him the chance to slam his accuser, Cobb took it. Asked about Leonard's possible motive, he said "I cannot imagine a human being with any sort of honor or ideals having the spleen . . ." and so on for another five minutes. For the most part, though, the principals stuck to the stories they had been telling unofficially and behind closed doors all that spring, summer, and fall: Cobb and Speaker had not bet, the idea of them fixing a game was ridiculous, Leonard was just looking to make some money by threatening to go public with his slanders. They agreed that he had always been a troublemaker, or as Cobb called him, "a Bolshevik."

The hearing ended with Landis not giving a hint as to which way he was leaning in the case, but the next day he announced to the press what had been rumored for months: that he was investigating accusations made by Leonard involving Cobb and Speaker. At the same time he released 100 pages of related documents—everything he had on the matter, he said—and explained that as a result of the stories told about them the two player-managers had been "permitted to resign." That wasn't what Cobb and Speaker had been saying about their departures, but there were more contradictions to come. Asked by newspapermen why the public hadn't been informed previously, Landis said the delay was out of consideration for the baseball greats at the center of the controversy. But he also said, a few minutes later, that he had gone public at the *request* of Cobb and Speaker. As for when the world could expect a verdict, he at one point said he would not be rendering one since now *all* the men involved were out of organized baseball—and at another point noted that his decision could be expected sometime later that winter. Baseball must be a strong game to have survived its leaders. Only Leonard seemed happy with the judge's pronouncements. "I have had my revenge," he told Damon Runyon.

Johnson said he couldn't comment on the revelations because "I am dumbfounded" and "not over the shock" of Landis going public with them. In trying to keep the matter secret, he said, "we had thought of Ty Cobb's wonderful family, of Joe Wood's two sons at Yale University and of Tris Speaker's aged mother." Johnson, at this stage of his life, had a tendency to get garrulous, in a maudlin sort of way, like the man you regret sitting next to at a bar. He had never liked Speaker, who was a little too "cute" for his taste, he told the writers. But Cobb was another story. "I know Ty Cobb is not a crooked ballplayer," he said. "We let him go because he had written a peculiar letter about a betting deal that he couldn't explain and because I felt he had violated a position of trust." After more than twenty years of fining him, suspending him, and addressing countless letters of warning to him c/o the Detroit Tigers, "I love Ty Cobb!" Johnson declared.

To a lot of people, though, kicking Cobb out of the American League was a funny way of showing that affection. Both Johnson and Landis seemed caught off guard by the way the public instantly rallied around Cobb and Speaker, and denounced the lords of baseball for prosecuting them. "Fans Refuse to Believe Spoke or Ty Guilty" said a headline in the *Plain Dealer*, while sports columnist Joe Bang wrote, "Clevelanders believe in Tris. They are behind him almost to every last man and woman." At a rally for Cobb in Augusta, his wife, Charlie, told a crowd of about 500 people standing beneath a banner ("TY IS STILL OUR IDOL, AND THE IDOL OF AMERICA") on Broad Street, "above all persons I should know that Ty Cobb is absolutely fair and square. We have been married 19 years and have five children. My husband may have his faults, but dishonesty is not one of them." Detroit sportswriters, so recently ready to write good riddance when he resigned as manager, were unanimous in their support. So were most of the baseball people reached for comment by the press. "It's the bunk," said Harry Lunte, a shortstop for the 1919 Indians. Said Clark Griffith, owner of the Washington Senators: "I don't believe it." Even L. L. Scarborough, the druggist who owned the Anniston, Alabama, team that Cobb had played for briefly in 1904, chimed in: "When Ty came here he was just a youth, fresh from the countryside, but he had principles that were not to be overrun. Any man in Anniston who knew Ty when he played here doesn't believe these charges!" Navin had no comment, though clearly he could not bear the idea of Cobb still caught up in controversy at age forty. Of those who spoke for the record, only Hughie Jennings was not supportive, saying, "Judge Landis would not make such statements unless he had proof to back it up."

What undercut Jennings's observation a bit was that Landis had made no statement of any kind yet. He had both promised to make one and denied that he would ever do such a thing, so it was difficult to tell if anything was in the offing. But before he could clarify that matter, another old betting scandal knocked him sideways. "Won't these God damn things that happened before I came into baseball ever stop coming up?" Landis asked no one in particular after Charles "Swede" Risberg, an already banished Black Sox shortstop, came forward in the final days of 1926 to say he wanted to talk about a series of games the Tigers had allegedly thrown, or as he put it, "sloughed off," in 1917. "They pushed Ty Cobb and Tris Speaker out on a piker bet," Risberg told the press. "I think it's only fair that the 'white lilies' get the same treatment."

The lilies in his particular field were Eddie Collins, Ray Schalk, and other Chicago players who were believed not to have been involved with the fixing of the 1919 World Series. The Clean Sox, they were sometimes called. Risberg said that on this earlier occasion those fellows and other members of the Chicago club chipped in $45 each to create a purse of $1,100 for the Detroit pitchers, ensuring that they serve up slow fastballs and nonbreaking curves in back-to-back doubleheaders played in Chicago on September 2 and 3, ensuring a White Sox victory. Chicago, then battling Boston for first place, did win all four games (and eventually the pennant and the World Series), and for what it was worth, Risberg's fellow exile, Arnold "Chick" Gandil, spoke up to back his assertion that this was no accident. Fixed games were nothing unusual, the two Black Sox said. The St. Louis Browns also had sloughed off games against Chicago in 1917, and Chicago had purposely lost two against the Tigers late in 1919 so some White Sox players could cash bets on their opponents. If you don't believe us, the players said, ask White Sox owner Charlie Comiskey; he knew all about it.

This wasn't the first time these charges had been raised. Five years earlier, yet another Black Sox, conspirator Oscar "Happy" Felsch, had said the same thing and Landis had ignored him. This time, though, the commissioner brought in Risberg for an interview on New Year's Day and four days later brought in thirty-four players from the 1917 Tigers and White Sox for a two-day hearing. Pressed against the back wall, among the sports scribes, was the famous humorist Will Rogers, who considered himself a good friend of both Cobb's and Speaker's. Cobb testified on the first day while Risberg looked on, chain-smoking. While he had been polite and sincere at the hearing held two weeks earlier, Cobb's attitude toward Landis now seemed, depending on which newspaper you read, "cold" or "bitter." Like all of the players who had come before him, and would be called later, he flatly denied Risberg's charges. "There has never been a baseball game that I played in that I knew was fixed," he said. Risberg, speaking to the press between drags on his ever-present cigarette, backed him up on this. "There never was a better or straighter baseball player than Cobb, or Speaker, either, to my way of thinking," he said. Will Rogers agreed. "If Cobb and Speaker had been selling out all these years," he said, "I would like to have seen them when they wasn't selling."

Most of the players who testified over the course of the two days said that Risberg wasn't making up a story out of whole cloth exactly but was rather twisting one small truth. Money *was* collected from the White Sox, Collins admitted, but the fund it went into was used as a "reward" to the Tigers for beating the Red Sox in a doubleheader on September 19 and another game on the 20th, not as a bribe for lying down against Chicago. "It was nothing out of the ordinary," said Collins, "to give a player on another team some sort of a gift if he went out of the way to turn in a good performance against one of the team's leading rivals in the [pennant] race." Comiskey, when called to give his testimony, said, "I am not condoning anyone or any act, but this matter was known to every-body." Even Ban Johnson, speaking outside of the hearings, admitted he was aware of the practice. "It was simply a reward for a player to use extra effort against a pennant rival. Of course it was wrong doing, yet it was not a criminal act." On January 12, Landis, saying more or less the same thing as Johnson but taking 3,000 mostly multisyllabic words to do it, issued an opinion that exonerated all of the players involved in the "repre-hensible and censurable but not corrupt" practice of gift giving.

Meanwhile the status of Cobb and Speaker remained murky. While Landis had busied himself with the Risberg affair, they had traveled to Washington with a naive-sounding plan to "enlist the federal govern-ment's aid in the fight to clear their names from the taint of the latest baseball scandal," said the *Atlanta Constitution*. Not surprisingly, that didn't amount to much, but both men kept pleading their case with the newspapermen, saying now that they were seeking reinstatement. Cobb was especially adamant in insisting that his bad relations with the Tiger players had been exaggerated and that most men on the team had tele-graphed or written him to express their support. (However deserving he was of his reputation as a hard-ass, it greatly bothered him to be thought of as one.)

Johnson met the press, too—and in doing so enhanced the entertain-ment value of the controversy. There was no telling what he would say. While the Risberg case played out, he had been giving not-for-attribution interviews in which he, in the guise of "a leader of organized baseball" (he asked the scribes to use that particular locution), suggested that the Amer-ican League president was sitting on explosive information regarding Cobb and Speaker that had never been passed along to Landis. Then at a bizarrely gratuitous and disjointed press conference he called on January 17, Johnson came clean, admitting he was the source of those stories. He also claimed that the commissioner had stolen the credit for his, John-son's, investigation of the Black Sox scandal seven years earlier, and then mismanaged the outcome by not acting quickly enough—and he repeated his promise that whatever the commissioner decided about Cobb and Speaker they would never again play or manage in the American League. Asked why he thought Landis had gone public with Leonard's charges he said, "The only thing I could see behind it was a desire for personal pub-licity." Before he was finished, he mumbled something about a "financial matter" between him and Landis that he would rather not discuss. The suggestion was that the commissioner had acted less than honorably.

The sight and sound of a pompous suit self-destructing in public is both delicious and a little sad. Johnson had been formally warned by the AL owners two years earlier to quit criticizing Landis or lose his $40,000-a-year job, but he couldn't help himself. "I'm thoroughly tired of this," Jacob Ruppert said while on his way to Chicago for a January 23 "war council" Johnson had called to see just how much support he had. It was not a propitious time for the league president to check in with the owners, who had just shown their support for Landis by raising his salary $15,000 to $65,000 annually, and just read the accounts of Johnson saying embarrassing things, in an embarrassing way, not for the first time, to the press. Nor was the AL president finished making people cringe. Before the war council could convene, he called in the scribes to say that he had never said that Cobb and Speaker were "crooked"—no, not at all; they were forced out merely for being incompetent managers. As long as they didn't want to manage anymore, he now said, they could return to the American League as players anytime they desired. Physically and mentally Johnson was falling apart. It appears that he never spoke at his January 23 meeting, but his physician did, rising at the start to formally advise the assembled that "the president's health is such that he should immediately take a much-needed rest." A motion to grant him a leave of absence passed unanimously, and Frank Navin became the acting president of the league. Johnson left the room. His biographer, Eugene C. Murdock, wrote that Ban's "condition was considered 'pitiable,' and at several times he appeared near collapse. He was later seen wandering dazedly in the hotel lobby, where he seemed almost oblivious to what was going on around him."

Four days later, Landis issued his opinion on the Cobb-Speaker case: "These players have not been, nor are they now, found guilty of fixing a ball game. By no decent system of justice could such a finding be made."

Cobb returned to Augusta, picked up his dogs, and went duck hunting.

— CHAPTER TWENTY-EIGHT —

ONE OF THOSE DOGS WAS named Connie Mack.

That fact, little known beyond Cobb's circle of friends, would have been a useful clue for the many baseball fans wondering what the Peach planned to do next. For a while after Landis's decision came down, all he was certain of was that he didn't want to go out like this, a pawn in a game played by fools with fancy titles. But where to finish his career? Cobb was happy to relinquish the manager's responsibilities and become just a player again, but he couldn't play for just anyone. To take orders from some run-of-the-mill skipper would be unseemly. In November, more than a month before the general public even heard about Leonard's stories and letters, John McGraw, one of the insiders who knew about the case, had made it clear that there was a place for him on the New York Giants—and Landis had promptly slapped down McGraw, saying, "Lay off Cobb." It was too soon, and anyway under the rules the former Tiger couldn't play in the National League unless he cleared waivers, and that wasn't going to happen. Too many American League teams had expressed interest in him: the St. Louis Browns, the Yankees, the Philadelphia Athletics; the minor league Baltimore Orioles wanted him, too, and were offering $25,000. Only Detroit was completely out of the question. He liked the city, had friends and still went to the dentist there, but there were too many bad memories, one of them named Frank Navin. Cobb was looking for "vindication before the public," he would say years later in a letter to the two-legged Connie Mack. He wanted to start fresh and with someone he respected enough to name a dog after. (His other dog, by the way, he named after himself.)

Connie Mack, who was born a few days after the Battle of Freder-

icksburg and who would live long enough to manage a game called by
Vin Scully, had already been around a long time at that point. He first
came to the National League in 1886, the year Cobb was born, a tall,
blade-thin catcher for a Washington team known variously as the States-
men, Senators, and Nationals. He himself was in a larval stage known as
Cornelius McGillicuddy, or, sometimes, "Slats." By 1927, though, Mack
was sixty-four years old, the manager and part-owner of the Philadelphia
Athletics, and was generally regarded, along with McGraw, as one of the
game's great thinkers. Outside of their clash in the Baker Spiking Incident
in 1909, Cobb had only admiration for the natty sage of East Brookfield,
Massachusetts. "Think of the situations and how craftily manager Mack
analyzed every little detail," Cobb wrote in a syndicated column about the
1913 World Series (in which the Athletics beat the Giants four games to
one). "Think of the different angles and the thought which he put into
the problem." What impressed Cobb on that occasion was how Mack
disrupted his starting rotation to use Eddie Plank, "a pitcher of a nervous temperament, every action showing high tension," before a friendly
home crowd, where he'd be more at ease, and thus more effective. That
the A's lost that day didn't matter. Cobb and Mack shared the belief that
you should fit a pitcher to the particular circumstances he'd be facing—
batters, ballpark, weather, etc.—rather than worry about how rested he
might be.

More generally, Cobb liked the way Mack constantly employed psychology to gain an advantage or get the most out of his men. Mack's
motto—"If you get the other fellow worried, the battle is half won"—
closely resembled his own guiding principle. But what Cobb liked more
than anything about Mack was what most people liked: the sheer aes-
thetic pleasure of watching him work—seeing him standing in the dugout (or sometimes on top of the dugout), ramrod straight, dressed in suit,
tie, and hat, holding a rolled-up scorecard that he used like a conductor's
baton to signal his fielders to move this way or that in accordance with his
encyclopedic knowledge or golden gut.

Although it defied conventional wisdom in some ways, Mack had a
feeling that Cobb would be good for his club. The A's hadn't been in the
World Series since 1914, and had finished dead last every season from

1915 to 1921. But in 1925 and '26 they had helped make a race of it in the American League, and wound up, respectively, second and third. They lacked in two areas, as Mack saw it: pitching and passion. While he worked on the former, he figured, Cobb, along with a few other crafty veterans he signed that winter, would inspire the latter in the highly promising bunch of youngsters Mack had acquired—Al Simmons, Mickey Cochrane, Lefty Grove, Jimmie Foxx, future Hall of Famers all—just by being themselves. That Cobb was still fired up to play baseball at the age of forty might in fact make him a better role model than he'd ever been, though he would continue to be a most unconventional one: the last man to arrive in the clubhouse each day, and an inveterate heel-dragger when it came to spring training. He was never what we'd later call too cool for school, though; once he was suited up and ready to play, he pursued the typical baseball tasks, things like bunting, running, and sliding, as if they were as vital as sex. He could help Mack at the box office, too. With Sunday baseball against the law in Pennsylvania, the A's were hard-pressed to put up flashy attendance figures, and thus to show the profits being reaped by his fellow magnates. "I certainly would like to have *both* Cobb and Speaker," Mack said as soon as they were exonerated—though Spoke, he could sense, was hearing the Senators' siren song. The manager already had added forty-two-year-old Jack Quinn, forty-year-old Eddie Collins, and thirty-eight-year-old Zack Wheat to what James R. Harrison of the *New York Times* called "his interesting but not highly valuable collection of antiques." Mack thought they'd be useful both as teachers and as drawing cards. But those men took salary cuts to extend their careers. Cobb was something else again, much more than just a curiosity or a master coach, and for him Mack was willing to engage in a full-on courtship display.

What this meant was shining his shoes, putting on a sharp, dove-gray fedora, and taking a train from Philadelphia to Augusta. Cobb met Mack at the station on February 4, and drove him to the swanky Bon Air-Vanderbilt Hotel—where he ran into Dan Howley, once a coach under Cobb with the Tigers, and now manager of the St. Louis Browns. "You can't overemphasize my eagerness to sign Cobb," Mack told a reporter. Howley, too, had come to town to make his pitch. Both men took the awkwardness of the situation in stride, had dinner at Cobb's house that evening, and the next morning posed for a photographer from the *Augusta Chronicle* before getting a northbound train that would take them all to a writers dinner in New York City. When he had Cobb to himself for a moment in their private train compartment, Mack produced a contract with a salary area left blank. "Put down any amount you want, Ty," he said. Cobb demurred. He knew it would be the last baseball contract he would ever sign and he wanted to do it with a bit of ceremony, a few days hence in Philadelphia.

For anyone who accepts unquestioningly the notion that Cobb was a widely hated figure in his day—the "son of a bitch" Cobb from *Field of Dreams*—the fourth annual Baseball Writers Dinner, held in the East Ballroom of the Commodore Hotel on February 6, 1927, should serve as a bracing corrective. "When Bozeman Bulger, dean of New York sportswriters, reached the name of Cobb in reading the list of 20 Major League players present," said a wire service dispatch, "the gathering rose as a man and cheered the veteran outfielder until he was forced to speak to them. In a choked voice, he told them briefly of his appreciation of the tribute." Two nights later, at a similar gathering in Philadelphia, where he announced he was joining the Athletics, he basked in another standing ovation, punctuated by shouts of "You still have plenty left!" Mack, smiling in the audience, clearly agreed. The man who had said, in a fit of pique or perhaps a moment of posturing following the Baker Spiking Incident, that he would not have Cobb on my team if he played for nothing, was now paying him slightly more than $65,000, with another $10,000 to come if the Athletics won the pennant.

That was a lot of money for a man who had been falling apart in public for a while. "The last few years I played," Cobb said often in later life, "I was just tired, tired, tired." For Cobb, injuries starting cropping up with alarming frequency starting in 1920, the year that Hughie Jennings said in spring training, "Yeah, it's true—ole Ty is starting to slow down a little bit." On July 14, 1920, at Fenway, for example, he wrenched his right knee chasing a ball hit over his head. He had to be carried off the field by teammates and the scribes thought his career might be done. Hardly—he came back in the next game two days later and went 3-for-5, scoring the winning run from first on a 10th-inning double by Bobby

Veach. Just three days after *that*, though, he hurt the same knee again, sat out almost a week, and was never the same for the rest of the season. His 15 stolen bases tell the story.

The admirable—and maddening—thing about him was that he could never take it easy. In March of the following year, while playing an exhibition game in Americus, Georgia, against the Rochester Broncos of the International League, he stepped on a clod when trying to go from first to third on a single and tore ligaments in his right knee and ankle. The Tigers had been ahead 10–1 in the ninth inning of that meaningless contest, but Cobb said, as Joe DiMaggio supposedly would a decade or so later, that he had been playing for the spectators who might never see him again. At the same time he added, "I'm getting old and can no longer pull the stunts I once did. . . . I'm easier to hurt and harder to mend." He walked with a cane for a while afterward and didn't get into the regular lineup for several weeks. These were injuries you did not come all the way back from, not at his age. In 1922 and '23 he had a *combined total* of 18 steals.

In 1925 he was out two weeks with flu; had to be carried from the field after a second baseman fell on his leg; and a "troublesome hip" caused a 20-point drop in his batting average; all the while he was criticized for refusing to bench himself. He would go straight to bed after games, not getting up till morning. Eye surgery caused him to miss much of spring training in 1926 and a lame back hindered his play in May and June.

Cobb was almost injured again on his first day in an A's uniform, March 7, 1927—by Thomas Alva Edison. The eighty-year-old inventor paid a visit to the team's spring training camp in Fort Myers, Florida, and for the sake of the many photographers present took a turn at bat. Mack, wearing his usual suit and tie, acted as catcher while Cobb, standing halfway between the plate and the mound, lobbed the ball in. No one was expecting what the Wizard of Menlo Park delivered—a semi-wicked line drive that struck Cobb in the shoulder, knocking him down. Mack held his breath—until his most expensive player jumped to his feet, smiling, and strode plateward with his hand extended in greeting.

The Cobb of 1927 was a much sweeter Peach. He wanted to do whatever he could to help the Athletics. "I started out the year with an entirely different idea," he told Associated Press writer Alan J. Gould a few weeks into the season. "I would simply play the game, have the very best year I could, and work my head off for Connie Mack, one of the finest leaders this game has ever had. I made up my mind I wouldn't sir up any fuss or do anything that might arouse criticism." Fourteen-year-old Connie Mack Jr. was surprised to find that "Cobb was friendly right from the start. He often asked my father to let me sit with him on the train or on the bus. He told me stories and taught me card tricks and we became pals. I had thought he was some kind of ogre." Some of the younger A's had cherished Cobb's baseball card when they were kids, and they looked upon him with awe, which Cobb didn't mind in the slightest. "He could be a little bit crusty," Mickey Cochrane said, "but he gave me some fine advice and was an inspiration to me in every way." (Cobb and the feisty catcher bonded over their belief that home plate collisions were a necessary evil, and would later become close friends.)

One of Mack's projects on the A's was Al Simmons, an extremely promising young outfielder (he had hit .387 and .341 in the last two seasons) who had more than a bit of an attitude (the writer Donald Honig once called him "a testy character who bullied rookies and manifested a chilly disdain for lesser mortals") and an extremely odd batting stance for a right-hander (he pointed his left foot toward third base—"stepping into the bucket," it's still called—leaving himself vulnerable to an outside pitch). The manager asked Cobb if he would room with the twenty-four-year-old Simmons on the road, and talk to him in a fatherly way about the ins and outs of the ballplayer's life, and the older star readily agreed. Infielder Jimmy Dykes remembered eavesdropping on a lesson Cobb was giving Simmons one day. "Cobb is showing him how to hit lefthanders. He's telling Al to get up on the plate against them. The next day we're facing a lefty and *I* get up on the plate and go three for four. After the game I'm sitting in front of my locker all smiles. Cobb comes by, looks at me, and says, 'Well, rockhead, you're finally learning aren't you?'" Cobb was wise enough not to tinker too much with Simmons's stance, and no doubt in part because of that did he gain his respect and admiration. Before long Simmons adopted Cobb's habit of always wearing a long-sleeve jersey. "Bucketfoot Al," as they called him, hit .392 that year, his highest average ever. (Cochrane's average, meanwhile, jumped 65 points, to .338, in 1927.)

Cobb himself hit .357, doing it with what looked more and more like the old-fashioned way, i.e., meeting the ball up high and kind of paddling it beyond a fielder's reach—the "hit 'em where they ain't" style of the by now deceased Wee Willie Keeler. The year of Charles Lindbergh, the Great Mississippi Flood, and, alas for the Athletics, the 1927 Yankees cannot be called Cobb's best season, but it was perhaps a miraculous one, considering that it represented something like a complete rejuvenation. "Ty Cobb Vindicates Ponce de Leon Idea" said a headline in the *Times* that spring. Motivated by the notion of pleasing Mack, "Ty Cobb, the old warhorse," Richard Bak wrote, "galloped around the field like a young colt." He had 93 RBI, scored 104 runs, and struck out only 12 times in 490 plate appearances. He also had 22 stolen bases, tied for the third best in the league. In a column in the *New York Telegram* of April 13, Joe Williams wrote: of a game against the Yankees:

> *Ty Cobb went around the bases in the sixth inning, but more enlightening was the method he used—old-fashioned stuff scored in the Era of Ruth.*
>
> *He laid down a bunt, perfectly, which caught third baseman Joe Dugan totally by surprise. Cobb slid into first, beating Dugan's hasty throw. How long since you've seen a first base slide?*
>
> *Next, when Hale hit a short rap to center field, and when anyone else would have stopped at second, Cobb pumped his aged legs and went for third. Earle Combs' throw to Dugan had him out cold. Locating the ball with a quick glance over his shoulder, Cobb slid left, then contorted himself to the right. There was a geyser of dust and when it cleared, he was seen to have half-smothered the throw with his body, and as Dugan scrambled for the ball, Cobb was up and dusting himself off.*
>
> *The whole sequence was beautiful to see, a subtle, forgotten heritage from the romantic past.*

Cobb stole home three times that season, once on the front end of a rare and exhilarating triple steal. In Boston on April 26 he pulled off an unassisted double play, charging from right field to catch a sinking line drive, then continuing on at full speed to beat the tagging runner, William "Baby Doll" Jacobson, to first base. He put together a 21-game hitting streak, and got his 4,000th career hit (reaching a plateau that has since been achieved only by Pete Rose) and in late August had five hits in a game against St. Louis. He also had his worst-ever slump, going 20 games without a hit, but battled back the way he always did during a dry spell, by bunting, bunting, bunting until his stroke returned. During the Athletics' homestretch run, he put together a string of four games in which he had three or more hits, which helped his team stave off fast-closing Washington.

Two things spoiled what might have been a storybook season. One was the American League umpiring crew, which seemed to be lying in wait for Cobb after years of feeling they had been used by him to work out his numerous frustrations. At least a couple of umps didn't seem to notice that he had exhaled and become less confrontational. The problem first cropped up during a spring training game between the A's and Boston Braves. Umpire Frank Wilson was working the plate that day, and though he was employed by the National League he had previously worked for the American, where, prior to his being fired for oversensitivity, among other things, he had tussled frequently with Cobb. In the fifth inning of a game at St. Petersburg in March of 1927, with Eddie Collins up and Cobb swinging his three bats in the on-deck circle, Wilson whirled, whipped off his mask, and ordered Cobb to the showers. The fiery umpire had once been described by the *Times* as "an automatic ejector of the most efficient type," but could there have been cause for this action? Cobb said no, there absolutely wasn't, that he had said nothing, and when he tried to explain as much, "Wilson said something about beating my head in." Cobb then returned to the bench and took a seat but refused to go into the clubhouse, which caused Wilson to declare Boston the winners by forfeit. Commissioner Landis fined Cobb $100, but public sentiment was clearly with the player. Perhaps sensing this, Wilson, a few days later, ejected no fewer than fifteen A's for heckling him about the Cobb incident. Apart from the men on the field, only the team chaplain, a coach, and Connie Mack were left in the dugout. The next day, Wilson tossed nine Yankees for a similar offense—and when they razzed him for doing so, he announced that he was ejecting them *again* from the same game.

Cobb's mix-up with umpire Emmett "Red" Ormsby was less comical. With his team behind by a run in the eighth inning to the Red Sox at Shibe Park on May 5, Cobb saw a fat pitch coming, slid both hands down to the knob of his bat (a lighter model than he'd used in previous years to compensate for his slower swing), and stroked a shot over the right field wall, clearly to the left of the foul pole. To everyone in the park it appeared to be a game-tying homer. However, Ormsby, invoking a rarely applied and since abandoned rule, called it a long strike, because, he said, it had curved foul *after* it left the park. (Under the old rule a ball was either fair or foul depending where the umpire last saw it.) Cobb muttered something in response, but Simmons ran out and argued so vehemently that Ormsby ejected him. Cobb then resumed his turn at bat and either as he walked by the umpire, or in response to the next pitch (accounts vary), bumped him slightly. Before he could apologize—Cobb always maintained the contact was accidental—Ormsby said "You're out of the game!" The umpire later explained that an ejection for contact was automatic, that he'd no choice, but the fans got rowdy after the Athletics lost to Boston, and though no one came onto the field it seems, a few spectators threw objects from the stands. A flying seat cushion hit Ormsby in the head.

The umpire was not injured but by the time the story reached the league office a day or so later, it had grown into the tale of a full-scale riot, actively incited by Cobb and Simmons. Or so it seemed from the ruling of Ban Johnson, who had been reinstated as the AL president. A band of softhearted owners had felt sorry for a man in such an obviously sad state, and Johnson justified their pity by announcing in a deranged-sounding letter he wrote to Connie Mack, then released to the newspapers, that Cobb and Simmons were suspended indefinitely. Mack's biographer Norman Macht wrote, "Never a temperate man, Johnson had apparently lost some balance of mind and step since Ty Cobb and Tris Speaker [now with Washington] had been readmitted to *his* league over *his* ultimatum that they would never appear there again." In the letter he referred to "the throwing of a great number of murderous pop bottles" and said "the incident stamps the offender [Cobb] as entirely devoid of the highest principles of manhood." Much of what had happened, he added, "must be attributed to the lack of fairness, intelligence and true sportsmanship on the part of the Philadelphia management."

Cobb's suspension jeopardized his highly anticipated return to Detroit for his first ever game *against* the Tigers on Tuesday, May 10. Navin Field had been sold out for weeks in advance and, worried that Cobb wouldn't be able to play, thousands sent letters and telegrams to Johnson begging him to reinstate the star. Mack telephoned the league office several times but was always told the president was unavailable. It wasn't until the morning of the homecoming game, with Cobb already en route to the ballpark in a parade, that Johnson formally lifted the sanctions, allowing both men to play. At Navin Field, Cobb was treated like, as one local paper put it, "An Old Friend in a New Suit." During batting practice he signed autographs and lobbed baseballs into the stands. "Just before game time an automobile was driven out and presented to Cobb," said the *Times*. "There were other gifts, too, a sombrero, silverware and a floral piece. The presentation and Cobb's words of appreciation were radiocast from the plate through a microphone placed there." Announcer Edward Tyson did not try to speak over the thunderous ovation that greeted Cobb in his first turn at bat in the opening inning, when he smacked a double over the head of Harry Heilmann, knocking in the A's first two runs. He later walked, and made a fine catch in right to rob third baseman Jack Warner of a double, before retiring from the game—won by Philadelphia 6–3—in the seventh inning to rest the leg he'd injured a few days before in an exhibition game. The next day, after learning that Johnson was fining him and Simmons $200 each, he hit two more doubles in another Philadelphia victory.

As inspiring as Cobb was, though, and as well as Mack's A's played, no one that year could outrun the shadow of the Yankees, aka the best team ever assembled. The six members of New York's Murderers' Row—Ruth, Gehrig, Earle Combs, Bob Meusel, Tony Lazzeri, and Mark Koenig—hit for a combined average of .336. Ruth famously hit 60 homers and Gehrig drove in 173 runs. (Ruth had 165 RBI.) On the pitching side, Waite

Hoyt went 22–7 with a 2.63 ERA; Herb Pennock was 19–8. The Yankees won 110 that season, and lost 44. They were the only team better than Mack's Athletics, but they were 19 games better—and then they swept the Pirates in the World Series.

With Mack's permission and the pennant impossible, Cobb checked out of the season early, on September 21, with ten days and seven games to go. He and Charlie went to see the second Jack Dempsey–Gene Tunney fight at Soldier Field in Chicago—the famous "Battle of the Long Count" won by the champion, Tunney—then continued on to a hunting trip in the Grand Tetons. At the end of the year, in a letter to the agent Christy Walsh, he wrote, "I really and truly want to retire from the game—I am getting tired of the competition and being away from my family so much. I have had a lot of baseball and it's time that I step out." But he came back again and signed another contract with Mack, for an amount that was never revealed but which was assumed to be about half of what he got the previous season. He couldn't *not* stay a little too long. In this way, at least, Ty Cobb was like almost all the others.

And the Athletics almost caught the damn Yankees in 1928. They were a half game ahead of New York, in fact, when they came to Yankee Stadium on September 10 of that year. The biggest crowd in the history of baseball—more than 88,000—turned out for the doubleheader that would kick off the four-game set. "The stands rang with the cheers of the crowd," said the *Times*, "when Ty Cobb emerged from the Yankee dugout on his way to the A's bench." But that was where he stayed, for 18 innings of baseball, as the Yankees swept both halves of the twin bill. He wasn't injured, but that was the way it was by then, and had been for a while.

The year had started off fine. Mack had finally snagged Tris Speaker, also at a reduced rate, and the two of them, plus Simmons, added up to a ridiculously slow but classy outfield. But Speaker collided with a substitute right fielder named Bing Miller in late May and never came all the way back; Mack used him mostly as a third base coach, a demotion he graciously accepted. Cobb lasted two months longer, hitting comfortably above .300 all the way, until a condition described as "nervous indigestion," as well as general soreness and a fastball from White Sox pitcher

George Connally that struck him around the right pectoral muscle combined to force him out of the lineup. As July became August it became apparent that he, too, had a new role on the A's, as an occasional substitute. He was in some ways back to where he had started.

Mack put him in as a pinch hitter in the third game of the big series against the Yankees, on September 11, after Ruth (of course) had homered to put his club ahead 5–3 in the bottom of the eighth. We don't know if it influenced the manager, but just prior to the Peach's entry, a thunderous chant had swept through the stadium: "Cobb, Cobb, Cobb, Cobb!" finally turning into cheers when the man himself emerged. Facing Hank Johnson, a pitcher just about half his age, Cobb hit a benign little fly ball that Mark Koenig, a shortstop born the year Cobb joined the Augusta Tourists, drifted over and snagged behind third base. That brought his average for the season down a tick to a subpar .323, where it would stay. Cobb would play in two more exhibition games for the A's, but that mundane moment in the Bronx turned out to be *it*—that is, his 11,434th and last major league at-bat.

So this is how it ends, not with a bang but with a pop-up.

Of course in baseball you still have to play out the schedule. On September 22, Cobb made his last appearance as a player at Navin Field. There were no ceremonies or speeches, even though it was clear that he was tired (tired, tired) and surely wasn't coming back. During batting practice, he and Frank Navin passed each other on the field and said nothing. It was just another meaningless, end-of-the-season game that Cobb wasn't playing in; the Yankees had already clinched the pennant. There were a few extra reporters there to mark the occasion of Cobb's final visit, however, and one of them, a truly horrible fellow named Westbrook Pegler, who would later make a name for himself writing hard-hearted columns on assorted political topics, found Cobb's old friend and valet, Alex Rivers, in the stands. Lucky Alex! Pegler described him as a "niggerish blue gum colored boy" who dismissed his persistent questions about Cobb's many confrontations and ultimately had very little to say.

"I don't care what the crowd thinks of Mr. Ty," Rivers told him. "I don't care what the world says about him. I love him and I hate to see him go."

PART FOUR

ONE FINE SUMMER AFTERNOON WHEN I was about eight months into my Ty Cobb research I ran into a friend of mine, a fellow writer, on the F train heading from Brooklyn to Manhattan. She politely asked what I was working on these days, and from Bergen Street to the Broadway-Lafayette station I spun mesmerizing tales of the Georgia Peach that kept her awake for almost the entire fifteen-minute trip. Then something slightly odd happened. Just before she disembarked, a gray-haired man who had been sitting near us tapped me on the shoulder, apologized for listening in—and (only in New York, kiddies) said he had played Ty Cobb in a production of Lee Blessing's play *Cobb* about ten years before at the Lucille Lortel Theatre in downtown Manhattan. "He was a very complicated person," the actor, whose name I never got, informed me. "I'll never forget the time that one of his grandchildren, who had been in the audience, came backstage afterward and said to me, 'He was a man who needed a tremendous amount of love—but who nevertheless pushed everyone away.'" When I got home that evening I emailed Ty Cobb's granddaughter Peggy Cobb Shugg, who lives in North Carolina and with whom I'd been (sort of) in touch. "Does this ring any bells?" I asked, after telling her my subway story. "Yes!!" she wrote back almost immediately. "It happened!! That was me!!"

I found Peggy's response instructive. Although her assessment of her grandfather had come to me via a stranger on the subway, it was the first time in our several conversations that I had known her to say anything substantive about the man whom she had seen at reasonably regular intervals as a child and whom she had known well enough to have taken to show-and-tell at her grade school in Daytona Beach, Florida, when he was a heavyset and shambling man of nearly seventy. Usually, I got a gentle brush-off. Whenever I asked her something about Ty Cobb Sr. (her father had been Ty Cobb Jr.) her response had typically taken the form of a somewhat belated and brief note to the effect that I would be better off posing my question to one of a small list of independent experts she trusted, or one of the employees at the Ty Cobb Museum, in Royston, to which she had loaned some of her memorabilia. "They probably know better than I do about that," she often said in her emails, regardless of who the "they" or what the "that" was. Sometimes she didn't respond at all, perhaps unsure of whether I was just one of those many retirees who spent their time on the Internet doing "research." Or she simply may not have wanted to talk to someone outside the family about her grandfather, who lived for thirty-three years beyond that last Yankee Stadium fly-out and whose second act was something of a delicate subject in the family, to say the least. Before he died on July 17, 1961, Cobb lost two children and saw two marriages slip away, along with his last chance to shape his legacy. Considering all that many people seemed to know about him toward the end were some untrue stories about his sharpening his spikes and insanely sliding into rival infielders, his failure to correct the myths, and his sense that he had inadvertently wound up helping to propagate a distorted view of himself, brought him a profound sadness.

It is easy to get depressed watching a 1955 episode of the game show *I've Got a Secret* on which Cobb appeared as a "mystery guest." His secret was that he had the highest lifetime batting average in the history of baseball. The men on the panel—Bill Cullen and Henry Morgan—were asked to put on blindfolds before Cobb, identified as Mr. X, came out to answer a series of yes-or-no questions, but the women—1950s game show perennials Jayne Meadows and Kitty Carlisle—didn't have to. Women were assumed in those days to be ignorant about sports, but another factor, the reason he could be a guest on a show where people guessed identities, was that Cobb, at the age of sixty-eight, had long since slipped from the national spotlight. He looked reasonably healthy, if considerably overweight, in a light-colored double-breasted suit, and wasn't exactly a trivia answer yet, and would never be, but he was at that point in the twentieth century fading fast in that general direction.

In the end, the panelists did not guess as much as his identity, never mind his particular secret, in the allotted time; even after they were allowed to remove their blindfolds Cullen and Morgan didn't know who he was. For an awkward moment, the stars of the show stared at Cobb and sputtered. Morgan expressed a wait-wait-don't-tell-me sentiment as he pulled his curly hair. Finally the host, Garry Moore, who sat next to Cobb smoking a cigarette the whole time (the show's sponsor was Winston and Moore would die of emphysema in 1993) rushed into the breach. "This is probably the greatest baseball player we have in the world today—this is Mr. Ty Cobb!" Moore then ticked off a list of Cobb's records: "Highest average in an American League season; most bases stolen in one season, most total stolen bases; most seasons played; most games played; most times at bat; most hits; most runs scored; most years the batting champ; most years hitting over .300; most years hitting over .400—and that's only the beginning of the record!" The applause was tumultuous.

But it was almost as if the cast of the show were acting out an allegory about Cobb's public image, for over all that affirmation came the sound of Bill Cullen's voice saying, "He spiked a lot of second basemen, too!" To which Moore responded, "Yes, he was a mean one in his time!" Cobb chuckled along with everyone else, but something had registered. Instead of simply exiting stage left, as most guests did, he took his complimentary carton of Winstons from the host and walked over to the panel to say goodbye. Always the Southern gentlemen, he addressed the ladies first, bowing as he took their daintily presented hands. When he reached Morgan, however, the senior male member of the panel and thus to his mind perhaps in some way responsible for Cullen's mutterings, he stopped, and said a few things, which on the old clip are inaudible. It's likely he spoke in reaction to the spiking comment, though, offering a few corrective thoughts, because as Cobb, still smiling, moved along down the panel, Morgan appeared chastened and we clearly hear him respond, "Well, you're still okay, then!" I wouldn't be surprised if Cobb's appearance on *I've Got a Secret*, or the comment about spiking in particular, made before millions on national television, pushed him closer to the realization that he just *had* to write a book to explode the conventional wisdom about himself, and set the record straight for future generations.

Cobb's image problems, before he died, were to a great extent tied to technology. "The greatness of Ty Cobb was something that had to be seen," George Sisler said, "and to see him was to remember him forever." But relatively few actually did see him play because the only way to do that was to buy a ticket and watch him from the stands. Only a handful of his A's games were even broadcast on the radio, and there are, as I've mentioned, only a few brief film clips of him taking some cuts in batting practice or tossing a ball on the sidelines. While motion picture cameras existed when he arrived in the majors in 1905, virtually no one seemed to be using them to record baseball games, certainly not Cobb's baseball games. Even still photography was limited in Cobb's prime, and when it was employed it couldn't really capture the unpredictability and intimidation, the gracefulness and the (almost always strategic) violence that were inherent in his running game—although, as we've seen, it did once get him out of a jam regarding Home Run Baker. Cobb put up some of the best numbers ever, but with him perhaps more than anyone before or since, statistics don't tell the true story. So many of his best moments were invisible, often because they lived on in other people's memories, and most of his best performances are lost, like Sarah Bernhardt's. The human memory can hold proof of Cobb's singular greatness, true, but only so much and for only so long before it begins to fade. And without film to refer to, memory cannot be refreshed.

Fortunately, when the idea for a baseball Hall of Fame was first advanced in the mid-1930s by National League president Ford Frick and several others, many could still conjure a figurative movie of Cobb in their minds. Although he'd had no formal attachment to organized baseball for seven or so years by then (he never again would), everyone still knew who he was, by sight and by reputation. If there had been an *I've Got a Secret* in 1935, even the women would have had to be blindfolded, and *somebody* would have known who he was. It was de rigueur that his name be listed among the thirty-three players on the first ballot distributed to the Baseball Writers' Association of America, and hardly surprising that Cobb—who is referred to in recent books as "an avowed racist" (whatever that may mean) and "a near psychotic," though he clearly wasn't thought of that way in his day—got the most votes, 222, or four short of the maximum. Ruth and Honus Wagner tied for second, with 215; the only others who gained admission by being named on three quarters of the ballots were Christy Mathewson (205) and Walter Johnson (189). Cobb, who received the news while on a golf course in San Francisco, said he was "overwhelmed" by the honor, and in future years he would with obvious sincerity cite his admittance to the Hall as his proudest accomplishment in baseball.

But when the shrine finally opened in 1939, he seemed in no particular hurry to get there, eleven years retired but still a superstar charmingly oblivious to other people's schedules. By the time Cobb arrived in Cooperstown, late in the day, with his two youngest children, Beverly, nineteen, and Jimmy, eighteen, in tow, he had missed the induction and picture-taking ceremonies. Connie Mack said that Cobb must have thought he was heading for spring training. As usual, the tardy star blamed train delays. Some said he was late because he wanted to avoid having his picture taken with Commissioner Landis, but once Cobb got there, he was anything but a grudging participant. He genuinely liked being around most baseball people. He just didn't have such a strong need for their company, on a daily basis, that he ever found an agreeable way of getting back into the game.

From certain angles it looked like Cobb, in retirement, was living the dream. After toying with the idea of becoming a major league executive of some sort, or minor league team owner, he let such matters drop, and turned to a life of golfing, hunting, managing his financial portfolio, and griping to whoever would listen about the continuing decline of baseball, as evidenced by the slavish devotion to the long ball and the lost art of the bunt. He acted—and increasingly looked—like a typical prosperous (and cranky) retiree. His Coke and G.M. stocks had done well despite the Great Depression, and he was probably worth about $5 million on the day he almost didn't make it to Cooperstown. His success may have helped him bond there with Ruth, who had shown up on time for the festivities and with whom he no longer felt so competitive. Why should he? He was rich and seemingly content, after all, and Ruth was openly bitter about no one asking him to be a manager. Plus Ruth had received seven fewer Hall of Fame votes than he had—a fact that was very important to Cobb, and which he often mentioned.

From that point on, he and the Babe would get along just great. The series of three golf matches they played against each other for charity in 1941 was one of the highlights of Cobb's retirement. He beat Ruth 81–83 in the first, lost to him on a 19th-hole playoff in the second, then won the third after supposedly tricking the Babe into thinking he could break training (i.e., drink heavily) on the night before the rubber match (long, probably untrue, story), allowing him to win easily. "This 'exhibition golf' is more punishing than baseball," Cobb said afterward, obviously relishing the chance to once more address the press. "During my twenty-four years on the diamond I never was under such terrific pressure as I was while coming from behind to beat the Babe. Maybe it was because both of us were so gentlemanly. He was awfully nice to me." Not so nice, though, that he didn't push Cobb's buttons once or twice by saying, "Oh, Tyrus, remember how we used to sit around together and file our spikes?" (Neither ever had, of course, but Ruth couldn't help noticing how Cobb kept getting asked the Question and bridling at it.)

It sounds like the best part of their golf tournament was watching them tease and try to psych each other out. Cobb, like most people, considered playfulness, misdirection, and outright trickery to be much more interesting elements of competition than brute strength or a robotic reliance on technique. When he talked in his later years to young catchers, he liked to pass along, with a chuckle, Nig Clarke's old habit of throwing a handful of dirt on a batter's shoes just as a pitch was coming in so as to distract him. He also talked about how he would fake an injury after stealing second base—ask for a time-out so he could limp around a bit, and then when the game was resumed, take off for third on the first pitch. But a really good trickster had to know how to improvise. After Ruth was diagnosed with throat cancer in 1947, Cobb played at Yankee Stadium in a two-inning old-timers game staged to raise money for the Babe's charitable foundation. As he stepped into the box, Cobb told catcher Wally Schang that he hadn't swung a bat in ages and was afraid it might fly out of his hands; perhaps, he suggested, Schang should position himself back a few feet. As soon as he did, of course, Cobb laid down a dead-duck bunt a yard or two in the opposite direction from which the catcher had just moved, then hustled to first as fast as his sixty-three-year-old legs would carry him. He got thrown out by half a city block, but everyone, including him, had a good laugh about the maneuver. Cobb did indeed have a sense of humor, though he may have suppressed it during his career. Once he was done playing he could even be kind of goofy. The daughter of one of his neighbors in Lake Tahoe told me that after a few highballs at a local restaurant one night in the 1950s, Cobb tried to slip a pork chop into her mother's purse.

It was after more than a few highballs that things sometimes took a turn for the worse. Sadness, and the habits that attend and increase it, were the hallmarks of Cobb's retirement years. His mother died in 1936 at the age of sixty-five, and, in a decision that would suggest that he forgave her for shooting his father, he buried her beside W. H. Cobb at the Rose Hill Cemetery in Royston. Amanda's death left his sister, Florence, who had never married and who suffered from severe arthritis, on her own, and Cobb took her into his home for a while, though she would live out her short life—she died in 1944 at age fifty-one—mostly with their brother, Paul, in Sarasota, Florida. Paul had abandoned his baseball career in 1916, after more than a decade of trying in vain to make the major leagues (he had a lifetime average of .283), and was running a real estate brokerage and dabbling in local politics until he was partly paralyzed by a stroke in 1954. For years, though, nothing brought Cobb greater sorrow than the mention of his namesake. "Ty, Jr.," he wrote in a letter to a friend, "has been a very big disappointment to me."

Cobb's eldest boy had little interest in baseball, but that wasn't the problem. In 1919, when Cobb still had only two sons, Tyrus and Herschel, he told a sportswriter he didn't want them following in his path. "A ballplayer's fame is too fleeting," he said. "You are a star today and a has-been tomorrow. I wish that I had established myself along more permanent lines." Herschel did take to baseball anyway, and showed a talent for it. But Ty Jr. always preferred tennis. He had plenty of opportunity to play at the schools his father sent him to—Richmond Academy in Augusta, the tony Hun School in New Jersey, and Princeton University. At eighteen he was an alternate on the United States Davis Cup team, coached by Bill Tilden, a winner of 10 Grand Slams and the dominant player of the early 1920s. But just as his father was a trailblazer for future celebrities, Ty Jr. found himself in the first wave of overprivileged celebrity children, and behaved accordingly, drinking too much, driving too fast, and flunking out of college in his freshman year. Cobb yelled and maybe—probably—struck him; that in any case is what his younger sister Shirley said. Ty Jr. wasn't his only problem child. As a teenager Herschel was tried for what amounted to attempted rape (he was acquitted) and was later involved in an automobile mishap that resulted in a friend's death. But Ty Jr.'s screwups seemed to anger and embarrass Cobb more acutely, and he traced most of them to Charlie, since it was she who had the most influence on the boy while Cobb was away playing baseball. Years later the surviving Cobb children agreed that Charlie was not entirely blameless, since she spoiled Ty Jr., cleaned up all of his more youthful messes, and then concealed the facts from his father. Cobb also railed that she was never straight with him, even about simple domestic matters, like whether the laundry had been done. Eventually the marriage broke down under the strain and in 1931 Charlie filed for divorce, claiming "cruel treatment."

Cobb was "surprised and shocked," he told the newspapermen after they'd gotten wind of the action from Charlie's lawyer. Even though they slept in separate bedrooms by then he was probably telling the truth because they had been through so much together and come so far in the world that it was hard to imagine the family dissolving. Each spring the Cobbs had moved from Augusta to a rented house in Detroit for the long, emotionally exhausting baseball season, then back to Augusta each fall so the kids could go to school there. Along the way, Charlie had commenced thirteen pregnancies, eight of them ending in miscarriage, and she had needed surgeries a few times in between. When births or those other complications happened during the season, he always left the team to be with her. Meanwhile, it was she who had nursed Ty Sr. when he came home in the evening with his legs bleeding from sliding and from other men's spikes, using various homeopathic salves and ointments, then wrapped the wounds and sores in towels. The Cobbs went through a lot of towels. "I have always loved my wife, my children and my home," was about all he could muster for newsmen who came looking for a response to her divorce filing.

The Cobbs' home in 1931 had recently shifted from Augusta to

Atherton, California, a town about thirty miles south of San Francisco. His previous house had been more than comfortable, definitely upper-middle-class, but the new place was magnificent, a seven-bedroom Mission-style mansion, with pool and guesthouse, located on about four acres just off tree-lined Spencer Lane. They had named it El Roble, or the Oak, a nod, it would seem, to Charlie's family estate in Augusta, "The Oaks," where in 1908 they had been married. Cobb had become interested in the San Francisco area in the early 1920s, when he first came to California to play winter ball in the Pacific Coast League. Apart from a climate more benign than Georgia's, it offered what he hoped would be a fresh start. The old house in the last year or so had become unlivable for Charlie, who had moved out and into a rented place nearby with her children. In California, Ty and Charlie even moved back into the same bedroom.

The novelty of the new place wore off quickly, though, and the old tensions resurfaced. Ty Jr. by then had transferred to Yale, where he became captain of the tennis team, and his grades at first seemed marginally better. But then he suddenly quit tennis, saying that his coach, Tilden, who was known to be gay, had made flirty advances that disgusted him, and he could no longer be around the sport. Without tennis he seemed directionless, and he would soon leave college again.

Cobb took out his frustration with his son, and dissatisfaction with life in general, on his family, carrying on in a way that often made his children cower. Or maybe not; it depends on which sibling you talked to. Their descriptions of him varied significantly, from that of his elder daughter, Shirley, who told Don Rhodes, the author of *Ty Cobb: Safe at Home*, "I never spent five seconds with that man that I wasn't scared pea green," to that of his youngest boy, Jimmy, who said he could be intimidating, but that he was also the kind of father who routinely tucked in the children and told them bedtime stories. (Of the five Cobb children, Shirley, who ran a bookstore for many years in Palo Alto, was the most similar to her father, which may explain her particularly harsh assessments of him.) Jimmy was definitely the most pro-dad. "We were a very affectionate family," Jimmy told an NPR interviewer in 1995, about a year before he died. "Every time I saw my father it was always a hug. He wouldn't just shake your hand; it was an embrace." When Jimmy came home from the Navy at the end of World War II, Cobb was waiting on the dock in San Francisco with an ice-cold quart of milk and a bag of doughnuts, Jimmy's favorite childhood treat.

So which sibling is right, or most right, about what kind of father Cobb was? Perhaps it was Beverly, the younger daughter, who was born in 1919 and died in 1998, and who came down somewhere between Jimmy and Shirley, telling Rhodes that "Overall, it was happy living" in the Cobb house, but the kids had to learn to stand up for themselves. Once while she was home from college she offered a political opinion during a dinner at which her parents had several guests. This was not appreciated. Not only had she spoken up unbidden, but she'd said something her father didn't agree with. "Who gave you the right to think?" snapped Cobb. Beverly replied, "God gave me a brain, and you spent a lot of money developing it, and I hope you both haven't been failures!" Years later she remembered, "He never said anything like that to me again."

While they were never exactly estranged, Cobb ultimately had a troubled relationship with Herschel, who as a teenager was forced to abandon his baseball ambitions after he lost an eye in what Cobb once described as "a rock fight with hooligans down by the creek." Based on his grades and the cut of his jib, Herschel never did appear to be Ivy League material, the way Ty Jr. had. When he reached manhood, Cobb gave him a Coca-Cola distributorship in Idaho to run as his own business, so he could support himself and his family. Even with that jump-start, though, Herschel failed to find success. He abused alcohol, flew into rages, and struggled to keep his weight below 300 pounds. In his wrenching memoir, *Heart of a Tiger*, his son, also named Herschel, described a wretched childhood of abuse (both his parents drank themselves into a stupor more or less daily) relieved only by occasional visits from Ty, whom he saw as a typical loving grandfather. Herschel Jr. doesn't say this in so many words in his book, but when his father died suddenly of a heart attack in 1951 at the age of thirty-three, it seemed in some ways a relief as well as a shock and a sorrow.

The story of Ty Jr. seems even sadder. After things didn't work out at Yale, the tall, handsome ex-athlete pulled himself together and decided that he wanted to be what his grandfather W.H. had most earnestly wanted his father to become: a doctor. Ty Sr., however, would offer no financial help with medical school—in fact, according to family legend, Cobb was so angry at Ty Jr. for wasting his chances at two good schools, he sold all the G.M. stock he had in trust for him, and kept the money. In any case, they seldom spoke during the younger Cobb's years at Medical College of South Carolina in Charleston. It was only after Ty Jr. graduated in 1942 with a specialty in gynecology and obstetrics, married well, and set up a practice in Dublin, Georgia, that the two got back in touch. Wary of each other, they both proceeded with caution—more than was advisable, Cobb realized, when Ty Jr. was diagnosed with a brain tumor just a few months after Herschel's death. "His days are numbered," Cobb wrote in a letter to a friend. After that, apologies and explanations seemed beside the point; all they could do was sit with each other in the shade of a Dublin, Georgia, porch, son in a wheelchair, father in a rocker, and try to think of things to say. Ty Jr. died in September of 1952, at the age of forty-two. "My boys, my boys!" Cobb could sometimes be heard wailing in the time afterward.

By then Ty and Charlie's marriage was finally over. A few weeks after she had filed for divorce in 1931, she announced that she was rescinding the action. She would repeat this pattern three more times over the next sixteen years until, in 1947, she finally filed for good. Her lawyer in that instance was Melvin Belli, the flamboyant "King of Torts" whose clients would include Muhammad Ali, Zsa Zsa Gabor, and Jack Ruby. In her suit, Charlie estimated her husband's net worth at $7 million, which Ty naturally said was on the high side, but which sounds about right. They reached an agreement out of court, the terms of which were never disclosed.

Cobb was married to another women in the early 1950s, when he lost his two sons. Frances Fairburn Cass was the pretty daughter of an ear-nose-and-throat doctor whom Cobb knew, twice previously married but twenty-three years younger than he. After a brief courtship they wed in her hometown of Buffalo, and lived in Lake Tahoe, Nevada, mostly unhappily. Their divorce six years later was not exactly fodder for the scandal sheets. At their court hearing she accused him of occasionally "embarrassing me in front of my friends" due to his excessive drinking. He countered by saying she constantly criticized his choice of clothing. It was a low-stakes love affair. Frances did move back for a period a few years later when he became very sick—over his objections; he thought it was improper since they were no longer man and wife—but by the end she had faded from his life. When Cobb died in July of 1961, it was Charlie, along with his three surviving children, who stood around his bedside and wept.

CHAPTER THIRTY

WHEN I STARTED RESEARCHING THIS book I believed, like a lot of people, that Ty Cobb was a wonderful ballplayer but a maniac, meaning a racist and a mean, spikes-sharpening son of a bitch. This was not a professional opinion based on knowledge; it was an assumption based on stories I'd been hearing all my life. People said it in bars; Ken Burns said it in his baseball documentary, so it must be true—that sort of thing. That I'd come to this conclusion without investigating the matter myself made the myth more, not less, powerful for me.

I remember going to Royston very early in my research, when I was still deeply in this frame of mind, and peering into Cobb's crypt. What a pathetic scene, fit for a villain, I thought. The Rose Hill Cemetery is especially sad for being so nondescript, not ugly but unlovely. Propped on the steps of the Cobb mausoleum were a weathered pine wreath and a plastic pink lily, and in the space between a wrought iron grating and the window one or more people had stuffed four now sun-baked baseballs. A small handmade sign said "Thanks for the game, Ty." Everything looked as though it had been there a while, suggesting that the grave didn't get a lot of traffic. What did that sign even mean?

It was a beautiful April day in Georgia, though, very close to Masters Tournament time. I pressed my forehead to the warm glass and peered inside. *Very tidy!—just as you might expect*, I thought, though I would have thought the same thing if it had been very messy in there. Both order and disorder would have suggested evil to me in my prejudiced frame of mind.

There was room for six coffins in the crypt, which I knew was ordered and paid for by Cobb himself in the late 1950s when he felt that his days were numbered. Little plaques identified the residents. On the right side, from the top down, were his mother, Amanda, his father, William Herschel, and his sister, Florence Leslie Cobb. Directly across from W.H., in a space between two empty slots, was the evil genius himself. You know how they say that your hair and fingernails continue to grow after you die? As I stood squinting in through the window I imagined Cobb lying there in a kind of Howard Hughes–ian dishabille, hair and fingernails filling the casket like excelsior, the shrinking flesh forcing his lips into a zombie grin.

Since I had already devoured everything Al Stump had written about Cobb, I knew that writer and subject had visited this very spot together seven months before the Peach's passing. It was Christmas Eve, in fact, and a light snow was supposedly falling as darkness descended. In the distance, Stump wrote, "faintly, Yule chimes could be heard." It sounded like something out of an old movie. At first Cobb for some reason couldn't find what is probably the largest structure on the grounds, Stump said, but when he finally located the crypt "on a windswept hill" (which seemed to have flattened considerably in the years since) he asked Stump if he would like to pray with him, and dropped to his knees. After a silent moment he said, "My father had his head blown off with a shotgun when I was 18 years old—*by a member of my own family* [the italics are Stump's]. I didn't get over that. I've never gotten over that."

Indeed, the scene sounded *so much* like something from an old movie that it should have aroused my suspicions. But it didn't; not right then, anyway. Because Stump was confirming and enhancing my preconceived notions about Cobb and simultaneously appealing to my predilection for colorful bad guys who are not just interesting themselves, but who provide someone to feel superior to. I thought, instead, that it was cool to be standing in the spot where Cobb, more than fifty years before, had reenacted the Agony in the Garden.

After a while, though, it all got to be just a little too much. The more I reread and reconsidered the writings of Al Stump, the more the unrealness of his scenes and dialogue nagged at me. Then I saw, or saw again, something that I thought was really a step too far. It was something that occurred in Stump's infamous *True Magazine* article of late 1961, specifically in an anectdote about how Cobb had commissioned a portrait of himself just before his death. Stump's intention in this case was to illustrate Cobb's callousness toward the artist he'd promised to hire for the project, but it had a very different effect on me. I remember wondering why someone who, according to Stump, a) wouldn't part with a penny unless he absolutely had to, and b) couldn't sit up for more than a few minutes at a time because of numerous illnesses, would commission a portrait in oils, done from life. Wouldn't posing for a "noted Arizona artist" (Stump provides no name) both *necessitate* sitting and result in an unnecessary expense? What ultimately tipped the scales, though, was a quote that Stump used to finish the story. Stump's Cobb, after checking the preliminary sketches, and seeing a living corpse with "sagging cheeks and a thin neck," supposedly canceled the portrait, telling the artist, "I wouldn't let you recalcimine my toilet!"

I simply didn't believe that any human being ever said, "I wouldn't let you recalcimine my toilet!"

If one thing is a lie, how much else is? I decided to do a little random fact-checking, starting with the weather in Royston on December 24, 1960, the day Stump said he went to Rose Hill Cemetery with Cobb. It turned out that it didn't snow that day in Royston or for hundreds of miles around. Not even lightly. It was one tiny thread but when I tugged it, Stump's oeuvre unraveled. The more I checked, the more "mistakes" I found. It didn't take me long to realize that I could stop checking. Despite the audience Stump had attracted for his yarns about Cobb, and as influential as he had been in shaping the man's present-day image, most of what he wrote wasn't the truth. The degree to which his writing had been accepted (and embroidered upon by those who came after) had nothing to do with its dependability. He got both the finer details and the broader strokes wrong, and largely on purpose, for the sake of a more dramatic and thus more marketable story. The experience taught me a lesson about how assumptions can shape our thinking, and hence our lives. Just because you've heard something a thousand times doesn't mean it's true. Did you know that it's not even true that your hair and fingernails keep growing after you're dead?

• • •

Looking back at the way Cobb lived out his retirement years, it's hard to guess what he thought he was up to. In hindsight he looks very much like a man without a plan. Shortly after his last major league game he took off with his family for a six-week tour of Japan, playing (mostly first base, though he also pitched a bit) and coaching for several college teams in a series of games that routinely drew about 20,000 spectators. The following March, instead of going to spring training, he, Charlie, and the children set off on a months-long tour of Europe. He returned to a mostly blank appointment calendar. He played golf a lot, kept an eye on the stock market, and drove around with Grantland Rice visiting other old buddies. Some of these get-togethers went better than others. One night in the mid-1930s, when the columnist and Cobb were having dinner at the Detroit Athletic Club with ex-catcher Nig Clarke, Rice recalled in his memoir *The Tumult and the Shouting* that he mentioned "Clarke's rapid tag and immediate throwing of his glove aside, signifying the third out." When Clarke snickered and said, "I missed many a runner who was called out—I missed you at least ten times at the plate, Ty—times when you were called out," Cobb flew into a rage.

"You cost me 10 runs—runs I earned!" he said.

Rice wrote that "It was all I could do to pull him off and calm him down."

On another occasion about ten years later, when they were driving north after attending the Masters Tournament and passing through Greenville, South Carolina, Cobb said to Rice, "I've got an old friend in this town. Let's find him."

They proceeded to a small liquor store owned by Shoeless Joe Jackson. Cobb may not have seen him in more than twenty years, since his onetime rival for the batting title was barred from baseball in the wake of the Black Sox scandal.

"Waiting his turn," Rice wrote, "Cobb stepped up, looked the old boy in the eye and said, 'How's business?'

"'Just fine, sir,' replied Jackson, turning his back to rearrange a shelf.

"'Don't you know me, you old buzzard?' said Cobb.

"Jackson wheeled around. 'Christ, yes I know you!' grinned Joe. 'I just didn't know whether you knew me after all these years. I didn't want to embarrass you or nothin'.'"

An article in the *Sporting News* said that Jackson's response caused Cobb to smile. "I'll tell you how well I remember you, Joe," he said. "Whenever I got the idea that I was a good hitter I'd stop and take a good look at you. Then I knew I could stand some improvement."

Jackson insisted on giving Cobb and Rice a tour of the town, where he was a local celebrity. "It was a nice reunion," Rice concluded, "with three old gaffers fanning about the days that used to be."

With not enough to do in his retirement years, Cobb would butt into baseball, then butt out again, often getting somebody upset in the process. Even before Joe DiMaggio reached the Yankees, when he was still playing for the San Francisco Seals of the Pacific Coast League, Cobb sent him letters filled with miscellaneous advice, such as switching to a lighter bat during the dog days of August and not taking outfield practice, which would wear out his legs. "I still have those letters," DiMaggio said more than thirty years later. "I couldn't believe a man as great as Cobb would take the time to write to me." When Joe got his first contract from the Yankees in 1936, Cobb, as soon as he found out the amount—$5,625— invited him out to the house in Atherton to talk about it. "Sit down," he said, handing DiMaggio a piece of writing paper and a pen as soon as he walked through the door. Cobb then dictated a letter he wanted DiMaggio to send to Yankees general manager Ed Barrow, asking for a better offer. About a week later Joe called and said the New York club had sent a second contract, this one for $6,500. "That's not enough!" said Cobb, who then dictated another response. A few days later, DiMaggio got a third contract, for $8,500, but with a note saying, "Dear Joe, This is our final offer, so you can tell Ty Cobb he can stop writing those letters."

With Ted Williams things were a little different. Cobb tried to help Williams, too, but the Red Sox star was a big swinger and a dead pull hitter and less in awe of the Duke of Deadball. As he said in his book *My Turn at Bat*, "Cobb was a great athlete, in my estimate the greatest of all time, but he was an entirely different breed of cat. He was a push hitter. He choked up on the bat, two inches from the bottom, his hands four inches apart. He stood close to the plate, his hands forward. At bat he had the exact posture of the punch hitter that he was. Cobb was up high with his stance, slashing at the ball, pushing at it; I was down with a longer stroke. When he talked hitting, he talked Greek to me." Cobb and Williams never exchanged hot words, as has been alleged by Stump ("He's full of it," Williams said of Stump), but Cobb did criticize him to sportswriters for not adjusting to the defensive shift that left the left side of the infield wide open. Williams could never be considered a great hitter in his opinion, Cobb said, because he was "one dimensional."

And yet Williams *was* a great hitter, no matter what Cobb said. And so was DiMaggio, although Cobb criticized *him* harshly in a long-winded two-part piece about the decline of baseball that he wrote in 1952 for *Life* magazine. "Joe is another modern who made a name for himself without scratching the surface of his talents," Cobb said. "Joe, like Williams, never liked hitting to the opposite field. And even worse he was perhaps the outstanding example of how modern baseball players neglected to train and keep themselves in condition. He hated physical exertion, and as far as I know never took a lick of exercise from October till March. Naturally he went to spring training with his muscles weakened and soft . . ." and so on. Still, DiMaggio, if he was aware of such criticism, never seemed bothered by it. He revered Cobb, both as a great hitter and, like him, an artist of aloofness. One night in the 1950s when Cobb strolled into Toots Shor's, Joe, at the bar, turned to his drinking buddies and said, with no sarcasm, "Here comes God."

The problem for Cobb was that it was becoming increasingly necessary to have someone in the DiMaggio role, some latter-day saint pointing at him and saying how extraordinary he was. People were forgetting who he was. The game itself had changed so much by the 1950s that Cobb, with his push hitting and jittery base running, seemed like the hero of an extinct sport, something more akin to indoor baseball than what Mickey Mantle and Ted Williams were playing, something that couldn't be judged by modern standards, and so got dismissed, if it was thought of at all, as comically quaint. His lack of any formal connection to the major or minor leagues and even his physical appearance—rotund, grandfatherly—worked to render him as invisible as any other sixty-something individual. *Take off your blindfolds, panel! Do you know who this is?* When he spoke out publicly, Cobb was often his own worst enemy. Invited to testify in 1951 before a congressional committee investigating whether organized baseball violated antitrust laws, he came down—tediously—in defense of the reserve clause that still made it impossible for players to receive their true market value (though he did suggest some modifications that could shorten the path to free agency). In the *Life* diatribe—which attracted much attention at the time, as magazine articles then often did—he hit all the "old codger" bumpers, decrying virtually everything about post–World War I baseball, and going on about truly obscure players (like Dode Criss of the St. Louis Browns) whom he thought would have shone brightly in what he was still calling the age of the "rabbit ball." Jeez.

On some level Cobb seemed to sense he was suffering from logorrhea, and playing the old fool. He felt sheepish about his predictable ramblings even as he made them; in interviews from around this time he sometimes said things like, "I know I've been accused of sounding old-fashioned," and "I really don't think everything was better way back when, but . . ." He actually had some interesting things to say. "Back then baseball was a game played *within* certain confines," he said in a 1959 interview with Jeane Hoffman of the *Los Angeles Times*. "Today the emphasis is on blasting the ball *out* of those confines." His need to speak his piece concisely and not offhandedly, to create a statement that would be solid and enduring, something worthy of his signature, also pushed him in the direction of a book. But he was, as always, tired, tired, tired. The task of getting it all down and getting it right daunted him.

Cobb probably first heard the name Al Stump in late 1959 or very early 1960. Angered by yet another bad book about him—John D. McCallum's *The Tiger Wore Spikes*—and growing weaker every day (he had already been diagnosed with diabetes and hypertension, as well as heart and kidney problems, and would soon learn that he also had prostate cancer), he wanted more than ever to write a good and true autobiography. It is difficult at this remove to determine who approached whom but in early 1960 Doubleday agreed to publish Cobb's story. What *is* clear is that despite the author's lofty goals, the publisher didn't see *Ty Cobb: My Life in Baseball*, as it would come to be called, as anything more than just another baseball book. Of course, Doubleday would have been overjoyed if it topped the bestseller lists like Jack Paar's *I Kid You Not* or Pat Boone's *Between You, Me and the Gatepost*, both current bestsellers, but given Cobb's diminishing status, they didn't think it had that kind of potential. We know this because they paid him a very modest advance for the manuscript—$6,000 (he had gotten $25,000 for the two *Life* pieces)—and for the job of ghostwriter chose Al Stump.

Stump was a quantity not a quality guy. The little bio that appeared with his articles or on the jackets of books he'd banged out often bragged that he was "the author of more than 1,000 articles" and several works of nonfiction. In some ways Stump was not even slightly dependable, but in one way he was, and that way mattered very much to a major house like Doubleday: he always finished what he started—if only so he could move on expeditiously to the next unspectacular thing. He might not produce something that bore much scrutiny or made the short list for literary awards, but even if Cobb was as difficult to work with as some people said, as much of a perfectionist and a prima donna, Stump would come back with a book.

Cobb didn't have the energy to vet Stump's credentials, which included years of newspaper reporting in the Pacific Northwest (he was born in Colorado Springs) and a degree from the University of Wisconsin. He interviewed several prospective collaborators, but chose to go with the man whom the publisher recommended. It wasn't a tough decision. He was in a hurry and the writer who would likely have been his first choice, his old friend the Detroit sportswriter H. G. Salsinger, had died the year before (as had, by the way, Tris Speaker). Meanwhile Stump, at age forty-four, was charming, handsome, and smooth. Just as important, he knew when to keep silent. The writer's second wife, Jo Mosher, said Stump had a way of quietly disarming people, drinking with them and, with a minimum of prompting, "getting them to act up, to really be bad—he'd get good stories that way." Cobb, like a lot of his subjects, felt comfortable around Stump, at least at the start, and he liked the way their working relationship, as laid out by his coauthor, sounded. Writing to a friend (and evidencing a shaky grip on language that paralleled his weakening grasp on life) on June 8, 1960, he said that Stump "will do by tape, forming questions & answers a conversational procedure my part reciting from my early youth on to my retirement, select from all this what they think might be usable, the final composition continuity, polishing up which I insist Doubleday and myself will decide whats [*sic*] to be." Clearly, Cobb had a naively rosy view of the messy and tense process that ghostwriting often is.

Stump took himself seriously as a writer, and saw himself as a legitimate member of the vaguely Bohemian literary colony that worked and drank and lived at that time in Santa Barbara, California. He often dropped the name of the well-known crime writer Ross Macdonald, the colony's most prominent citizen. He wore a cardigan sweater, smoked a pipe, and in other ways tried to emulate Ernest Hemingway. He resented being thought of as just a guy grinding out stories for hairy-chested barber shop monthlies like *True*. But what neither Cobb nor Doubleday knew (or the publisher knew but chose to overlook) was that Stump had a reputation for inventing scenes and dialogue and otherwise stretching truth. On the advice of its research department *TV Guide* banned him, as did *The Saturday Evening Post*. "He got a lot of assignments," Melvin Durslag, a successful writer of that era told me, "but one by one he alienated the kind of magazines that had fact-checking departments. That's because he produced fiction."

Stump didn't just lie *in* the autobiography he wrote "with" Cobb, he lied *about* it. "For ten months I stuck to him like court plaster," he would say in his *True* piece. "I put him to bed, prepared his insulin, picked him up when he fell down, warded off irate taxi drivers, bartenders, waiters, clerks and private citizens whom Cobb was inclined to punch, cooked what food he could digest, drew his bath, got drunk with him and knelt with him in prayer on black nights when he knew death was near. I ducked a few bottles he threw, too." Stump may have done some of those things, but he didn't do any of them for very long. We know from Cobb's still busy schedule, as well from the guests—usually sportswriters and their wives—whom Cobb entertained at his Tahoe retreat during the same span of months that he and Stump spent relatively little time together: no more, in all likelihood, than a few days. Stump's goal as usual was to fill as many pages as possible as quickly as possible, and he correctly believed that actual reporting—interviewing Cobb and others—

was a relatively inefficient way to do that. He preferred to stay at home in Santa Barbara, puff his pipe, drink his drink—and cobble together an autobiography out of old newspaper clips, Cobb's *Life* article, and other previous books on his subject as well as his own flights of imagination. His interviews with Cobb were helpful only when they didn't contradict what Stump wanted to say.

The pages he was turning out had plenty of personality—"Al knew how to make up lively quotes," Durslag said. The ghostwriter was pleased with his work and happy to share it with Doubleday as it issued forth from his typewriter but he and the publisher conspired to keep the manuscript from Cobb for as long as possible, because he might object to having words put into his mouth—words that didn't sound like him and often contradicted his own opinions. If they could stall long enough, Cobb might die and that would both expedite the editing process and boost sales.

Somehow, though, perhaps by sheer persistence, Cobb got a look at what Stump and Doubleday were preparing to put out under his name. His anger, as might be expected, was volcanic. The manuscript teemed with errors of fact. Stump had Cy Young and Lou Criger on the wrong teams. He called the outfielder Danny Hoffman a second baseman. He referred to Rube Walberg as Rube Waddell. He had Buck Herzog catching and playing second base on the same play. He had Shoeless Joe Jackson playing in the major leagues when he was still in the minors. Cobb would have been mortified by such mistakes. But what bothered him even more were the egregious errors of tone and voice that would strike anyone who knew him as off-key. The very *fabric* of the book was faulty, and needed reweaving. Cobb's description of his rookie hazing sounded whiney and overwritten ("I'd stand shivering in a towel or bedsheet while they hogged the tub for hours. McIntyre and his chums began a systematic campaign to make me the fellow who picked his teeth with bench splinters while they made the money"). "Dubious" was the best that could be said of the baseball wisdom Stump put in Cobb's mouth. ("A defensive play is at least five times as hard to make as an offensive play.") Plenty of other passages just sounded weird. (Stump/Cobb said that he never held a grudge against fellow players "except when they decided to play beanbag with my slender 168-pound body.")

After reading the manuscript in what was probably June of 1961, three months before it was due to be published, Cobb got off a letter to Doubleday demanding that Stump be fired and the book be canceled or rewritten from scratch. By that time his cancer had spread to his brain, and he didn't have the strength to write himself, so he dictated the letter to Theresa Gailey, the daughter of his second cousin Harrison Gailey, in whose Royston house he'd recently lived for a while. When he got no response from the publisher, he asked Theresa Gailey to send off another letter, threatening a lawsuit if Doubleday didn't redo the book. Finally, Stump told Cobb to go ahead and mark up the galley proof as he saw fit, indicating areas that he thought needed changing. Although the problems were too extensive to be addressed this way, Cobb, in a shaky hand, did what he could and sent the galleys back. But no changes were ever made and in fact Stump continued to add to the book in his inimitable fashion. He never intended to heed Cobb's changes. His strategy was to stave off Cobb, who died on the 17th of July. *Ty Cobb: My Life in Baseball* came out two months later. "It is in its fourth printing, having sold furiously," Stump wrote in a letter to Sid Keener, director of the Hall of Fame in October. In reality it was selling only moderately well.

By that time Stump was already working on his piece for *True*, a piece that would shatter the code of silence that had previously prevailed between sportswriter and subject (this was nine years before Jim Bouton's groundbreaking book, *Ball Four*) and, in the process, undermine the credibility of his and Cobb's book. Stump always said that he'd pitched the piece to *True* because Cobb had wanted *My Life in Baseball* to be nothing more than a propaganda piece about himself and had ignored his coauthor's pleas to at last tell the full, honest truth. But of course that was nonsense; his real reason for writing the piece was that he saw a business opportunity. With Cobb safely dead he could portray him as he pleased. By remembering a little, and distorting or imagining the rest, he could fashion a yarn that fit perfectly into the pages of a monthly that paid $4,000 per piece, or $1,000 more than he'd realized from the autobiography.

Stump's article, which was given the ill-fitting title, "Ty Cobb's Wild 10-Month Fight to Live," came out in the December 1961 issue, between a lurid-looking crime story called "The Mystery of the Fiery Murders" and an exposé about slave traders who specialized in circus sideshow freaks.

Even by *True*'s standards Stump's piece was shockingly bold. From its opening lines—which describe a deathly sick but Scotch-sodden Cobb insisting that his houseguest, Stump, drive him from his luxurious lodge in Lake Tahoe into Reno in the midst of a post-midnight ice storm so he can meet up with Joe DiMaggio and shoot craps—the story presents Cobb as, to use Stump's phrase, "Tyrus the Terrible." Cobb's success on the field and in the stock market, as Stump sees it, has convinced him that he is superior to all other humans except his sainted father, and allowed his violently obnoxious streak to flourish. Everything is painted in lurid *Tales from the Crypt* comic book colors. At a motel in conveniently named Hangtown, California, Cobb fires his ever-present Luger out the window to scare noisy revelers. He speaks in a strange dialect: "What kind of pest house is this?" "Who gave you a license, you mugwump?" In the middle of the night he wakes Stump and forces him to drive twenty miles to Carson City where they in turn wake the president of the First National Bank of Nevada so Cobb can order him to stop payment on a $45 check. Together they visit Virginia City and its conveniently named Bucket of Blood Saloon, where Cobb decides the Scotch is watered and flings his drink in the direction of the bartender.

Stump's Cobb reels, stumbles, and grouses. He says his doctor told him that his tests came back and "they found urine in my whiskey." Cobb rails against the world, waves around his loaded Luger, and boasts of killing a man on the streets of Detroit in 1912, an incident that had previously gone unreported (and which Stump elects not to investigate). Stump's Cobb can barely rise to a standing position, or walk twenty feet "without clutching my shoulder," yet is fighting wars on any number of fronts—with the state of California over back taxes, with the Pacific Gas and Electric Company for allegedly overbilling, with doctors who want to charge too much for treating him, and with family members who seek his financial help. "Money was his idol," writes Stump. Cobb, he says, lived for part of the year with neither electricity nor water in his Atherton home, the services having been canceled months earlier when he refused to pay the utility company a few disputed dollars. The inconvenience hardly registers, though; a semi-ghoul at this stage, he doesn't need refrigeration because he doesn't eat. Cobb in his dotage always wore a $7,500 diamond ring and a top-of-the-line $600 hearing aid and bought $100 chips at the casinos, Stump tells us, but whenever someone wrote to request an autograph and included the return postage, the pitiless Peach would burn the fan letter ("Saves on firewood") and pocket the four-cent stamp.

Stump's *True* piece became a national sensation, another baseball bombshell in the year of Roger Maris's record 61 home runs. Bob Considine, the author of *Thirty Seconds over Tokyo* and a bad book about Babe Ruth, called it "perhaps the best sports piece I have ever read," and the Associated Press named it Best Sports Story of the Year. People talked about it in taverns, around the dinner table, and wherever newspapers were sold. Blame it on the sheer brashness of Stump's assertions (he called Cobb "the most violent, successful, thoroughly maladjusted personality ever to pass across American sports") and the bracing sting of his prose. Blame it also on the sportswriters who in trying to defend Cobb and pillory Stump disseminated the contents of the story far beyond *True*'s normal sphere of influence.

Clearly, it was Cobb's misfortune to have been known and liked by people who as columnists and beat writers had access to acres of newspaper space, but who were better at describing a baseball game than repairing a person's reputation. His defenders erred in two basic ways. Some of them said that whether Stump's depiction was accurate or not, it was wrong to disrespect the dead, especially the recently deceased, whose kith and kin should be spared the pain of seeing their loved one flayed in print. All this argument did was convince people that the article had been accurate—because if it hadn't been, after all, Cobb's old friends would be complaining about *that* and not the fact that hurtful stories were being circulated. To scold Stump for saying too much too soon only made him sound like a crusading journalist.

The other defense tactic, employed by the writers who'd had a more intimate knowledge of Cobb, was to contend that the monster stumbling through Stump's article bore no resemblance to their departed friend. San Francisco newspaperman Jack MacDonald wrote that he and his wife had visited Cobb in his Tahoe home during the period when Stump was supposedly doing his court-plaster impersonation, yet he found no evidence of the writer, nor heard any reference to him by their genial and generous host, who served the MacDonalds breakfast in bed. When MacDonald took a rare first edition of a Confederate military history down from a shelf in the cabin, Cobb noticed his interest, and insisted that he keep the book. When the three went to a restaurant, Cobb—though never a particularly big spender, MacDonald admitted—picked up the check and left the waitress $10, the equivalent of a 30 percent tip.

The *Sporting News* also had plenty to say about the Ty Cobb its publisher, J. G. Taylor Spink, had known for decades (and back in the 1920s had criticized for his managerial skills). The newspaper never once mentioned *True* by name, yet over the course of several weeks in late 1961 and early '62—immediately following the publication of "Ty Cobb's Wild 10-Month Fight to Live," in other words—it presented, by one scholar's count, forty-seven articles reminding readers that the real Cobb was, in addition to being a revolutionary ballplayer, the kind of man who quietly provided financial help to a number of former players (Cochrane, Lu Blue, and his old mentor George Leidy, among others) and who had campaigned hard to have Sam Crawford—who still had negative feelings about Cobb—admitted into the Hall of Fame.

The problem with this line of counterattack was that its proponents didn't know where to stop. As part of its fusillade of pro-Cobb pieces, the *Sporting News* ran an interview with the old comedian Joe E. Brown, an overly sentimental acquaintance of the deceased star's who was enjoying a comeback after appearing in *Some Like It Hot*. Brown said that he'd had a heart-to-heart with Cobb not long before he died and that Ty said that if he had it all to do over again he would have worked harder to make new friends and keep the ones he had. The old pitcher Urban "Red" Faber testified that he'd once hit Cobb in the groin with an errant spitball, and Cobb had acted with perfect equanimity, the litmus test for character, it seemed, in Faber's possibly too narrow universe. Clarence "Pants" Rowland swore that in all his days as an umpire he had never heard Cobb say anything worse than "I don't believe you" when disputing a call. ("Pants on Fire" might have been a better nickname.) These character witnesses were laying it on almost as thickly as Stump had, conjuring up a Cobb who was not only unbelievably saccharine but also unbelievably dull. One could hardly blame the public for preferring Stump's raving maniac to Cobb's pals' plaster saint.

How much better it would have been just to let the record speak for itself, to point out that though his several illnesses limited his appearances toward the end, Cobb in the late 1950s was a man out and about, available for inspection. Some of the things Stump saw anyone could have noticed, and they weren't pretty. Cobb drank too much and alcohol brought out the Southern cavalier in him, the man who believes quite passionately that everyone should act and be treated according to his proper station. It made him terribly sensitive to a world in which he was not recognized, or known only as That Guy Who Sharpened His Spikes. It also of course made him just plain drunk. It was true that Cobb was arrested in 1947 for DWI in Placerville, California, and that he slugged an old ballplayer (who subsequently sued him for damages and lost), as Stump has said. He got into pitched battles with the state of California over taxes he claimed he didn't owe, and with his utility company over a small alleged overbilling. (His power was shut off, as Stump claimed, but he appears to have been out of town when it happened.) But was cheapness at the root of his one-man rebellion? I don't think so. Like a lot of senior citizens, he took umbrage as if it were free pens at the bank, and stood strongly on principle. He went too far sometimes because there was no one around to temper his anger, to tell him, as his daughter Beverly had, when he asked her who gave her to the right to think, to just shut up. He was lonely in those final years. "In this house I'm just a lonesome old man," he told a *Sporting News* writer who visited him in Atherton in 1957. "What's the use of seven bedrooms when six are empty?"

But there were signs of health as well, signs of hope. He wasn't *just* getting stewed and stewing. When the *Sporting News* writer arrived, he had just returned from a four-mile hike. He was trying to keep fit. He was dating! He had a crush on an attractive middle-aged woman named Mabel Griegs back in Georgia (though he wrote her many letters, the relationship didn't progress). When he saw Carol Loomis, a pretty twenty-something *Fortune* magazine editor, on the game show *Tic-Tac-Dough* he managed to get in touch with her and asked her out to lunch at "21" in New York. Loomis, the longest-tenured Time, Inc., employee, still worked at the magazine while I was researching this book, and when I asked her about Cobb, with whom she'd also gone on a second date to an old-timers game at Yankee Stadium, she directed me toward a memoir she'd written in which she described him as "smart and gentlemanly." He'd been deeply impressed, she said, with her knowledge of baseball.

Except when cancer made him so, Cobb was never really a recluse. In the early 1950s he was a celebrity instructor at a baseball camp in the Ozarks, and he appeared at dozens of sports dinners, including one in January of 1960—the very time he was supposedly holed up with Stump in his cabin—at which he was cited as one of the "men in the age of sports" by B'nai B'rith. The reporters who covered these events often noted that he seemed in relatively good spirits as he struggled through his brief after-dinner speech.

Starting in 1950, Cobb made many trips back to Royston to oversee Cobb Memorial, a modern twenty-five-bed hospital that he built and kept going with his contributions. Stewart Brown Jr., the son of the pitcher who had accompanied Ty to his tryout with the Augusta Tourists in 1904, was the first head doctor. In 1953, Cobb announced that the W. H. Cobb Educational Fund, begun with his $100,000 endowment, would provide scholarships for Georgia residents of any race or creed who demonstrated determination and need. (As of July 2013, $15 million in scholarships had been awarded.) He still loved California, he said, but Georgia exerted a pull. In early 1957, Cobb decided he was giving up the too large house in Atherton and moving back to Royston. "I'm in the evening of my life," he said, "I want to build a house, hunt birds and just visit." By the end of the year, though, realizing there was no one left for him in Royston to visit anymore, he found a site he liked better, about thirty miles to the northwest, atop Chenocetah Mountain, just outside the little town of Cornelia. "It was an incredible piece of property, the highest point for miles around," Rod Gailey, a relative of his, told me. "You could see clear to the ocean. There was an old hotel on the property. Ty planned to raze it and build a house for himself." But he never did. His health waned and he abandoned his plan. All he ever built on the mountaintop was a kind of concrete bunker into which he put his numerous hunting trophies. Gailey remembers most vividly a giant grizzly bear standing on its hind legs—just like the one Cobb's Grandpa Johnnie had told him about so very long ago.

Time was running short, he sensed. In his last months, Cobb shuttled between Lake Tahoe and the little apartment he'd originally rented in Cornelia as a temporary base of operations. If we believe Stump, his Nevada life and his Georgia life were strikingly different. His Nevada life, as portrayed in *True* magazine, was Gothic, vampiric, even, except that he subsisted on a mix of Scotch and milk instead of blood. "I was like a steel spring with a growing and dangerous flaw in it," he supposedly told Stump. "If it is wound too tight or has the slightest weak point, the spring will fly apart and then it is done for." But in Cornelia, Cobb was a retiree puttering around town, going to Kiwanis and Chamber of Commerce luncheons, watching *Tic-Tac-Dough* and, on Saturday night, *The Lawrence Welk Show.* "He was like a grandfather to me," said Rod Gailey. "He watched me draw pictures, asked me about my Little League games. Never witnessed a fit of temper or heard him speak a racial slur. When he went into the hospital in Atlanta I was devastated."

Cobb didn't go to Emory University Hospital, though, until he visited the Hall of Fame one last time, in 1960, and then went to the Rome Olympics with Stewart Brown Jr. The following March he traveled to Scottsdale, Arizona, where a number of teams took spring training. He had no official role, but sat in the sun and players, managers, scouts, and executives came by to visit him. By then the cobalt treatments Cobb had been undergoing had run their course, and the cancer was still advancing. He was taking a combination of codeine, Darvon, and Demerol for the pain. Still, in an April 21 letter to Rex Teeslink, a first-year medical student, he insisted "doctors report good on my important organs." He was coming to Georgia on May 1, he said, "for quite a stay."

Indeed, he's still there. Cobb entered Emory University Hospital in mid-May. Teeslink had a job there to help pay his tuition, and the two immediately became close. "Somehow we clicked," he told *Sports Illustrated* in 1992. "I don't know what it was. I spent 24 hours a day with him, seven days a week, from 18 May 1961 until 17 July 1961, when he died." To a great degree this was a testament to Teeslink's patience. Cobb wasn't as nice with some of the nurses as he was with little Rod Gailey or the folks around town. "He was a real redhead with a hair-trigger temper," Teeslink told me when I interviewed him in 2012. It's not that Cobb was mean, exactly, he said; he just couldn't tolerate incompetence, or as Teeslink called it, "the lack of that drive for excellence that was so much a part of the Cobb philosophy. He was an unusual man with a keen mind and yet he could never put up with people who didn't, like him, strive to excel." The Tiger players whom he managed would have understood.

The difference between the real Cobb and the Stump Cobb was often a matter of degree. Cobb could be a difficult patient, but he wasn't a psychiatric patient. He didn't have a gun in his hospital room or a fortune in cash and securities on his nightstand, as Stump would say in his *True* article a few months hence. "Those things are just lies," Teeslink told me. "I was there, Stump wasn't. He wanted to portray Ty in a certain way, and so that's what he did. It wasn't about the truth; it was about Stump."

Just before Cobb entered Emory Hospital he asked Teeslink to accompany him to Rose Hill Cemetery. It was essentially the trip he had supposedly made with Stump, except Cobb was in a playful mood. He told the future doctor that they should work out a signal for when he came to visit him after his interment. "You knock six times," Cobb said, with a chuckle, smack in the middle of his wild ten-month fight to live. "I'll know it's you."

EVEN THOUGH I HAVE LEARNED much about Ty Cobb since my first visit to his grave, and no longer think of him as a monster, I would still like to have the proper authorities slip his coffin out of the niche it's been resting in for more than fifty years and pry it open, allowing the sun to shine in.

This is not as weird an idea as it may seem. In the nineteenth century people sometimes dug up their departed loved ones in the hopes of being shocked into what we now call "acceptance," a state that would allow the left-behind ones to, as we also say, "detach with love" and move on. Ralph Waldo Emerson arranged to have his first wife, Ellen, brought back to the surface for one last look in 1832, about a year after she died, so he could finally convince himself that she really wouldn't be coming through their front door again.

With Cobb I see the exhumation process as useful because it would show that he had actually lived, that there had been a flesh-and-blood Ty Cobb—not a man worthy of sympathy necessarily, but a historical figure about whom not just any old thing can be said. For quite a few people, as I've noted in earlier chapters, Ty Cobb is a character who has long since fallen into the public domain, a Wikipedia entry that can be edited at anyone's discretion. Some no doubt believe the Cobb stories they spin but feel that even if they aren't strictly true, he was such an evil man it doesn't matter. The world does not owe him accuracy, it seems. People also sense they have carte blanche about his legacy in a way they don't have with, say, Abraham Lincoln.

What would happen if you said that Lincoln once attacked a White House groundskeeper simply because he was black and that when the man's wife rushed to help her husband, Lincoln throttled her, too? Historians would demand to know your sources. But if you tell the exact same story about Cobb, people embrace it gleefully and do not ask for further details. The sheer oddness of Cobb's alleged behavior—if he attacked people simply for being black he would not have had time to eat, sleep, or play baseball, and he no doubt would have met his match somewhere along the line, quite a few times—never sparked further investigation. But then myths about Cobb have always been too useful to poke and probe. The reporters of his day liked the groundskeeper story because they wanted a wild character to write about. A bad boy who was not also a sloppy drunk was as rare to them as rubies and they had no desire to fact-check him out of existence. Latter-day baseball fans loved the tale, and others similar to it, because it was fascinating to imagine a racist psycho at large in the major leagues. This Cobb was someone they could shake their head at, denounce, and feel superior to. Spinning stories in a way that made him look immoral was a convenient way to say, "*I* am not a racist because *I* reject this man who is." Cultures change as values change, wars are waged and the harvest waxes and wanes, but a villain who inspires self-congratulation makes for one hell of a tenacious myth.

At the time of his death, Cobb was not a very controversial figure. The newspaper tributes that came in late July of 1961 were largely predictable and bland. Nobody said anything about race except those newspapers that noted he had spoken up in support of integration after Jackie Robinson broke the color barrier. A few papers mentioned Claude Lucker, the handicapped heckler he had beat up in 1912, but most avoided unpleasantness and instead fell back on his numbers, which conveyed at least something of his greatness to a populace that had largely forgotten or never knew who he was. Eulogizing him on its editorial page, the *New York Times* said he "epitomized the flaming spirit of youth. In Ty the will to win was ever uppermost. He set more records in baseball than any man who ever lived. . . . He drove himself from day to day to live by the only code he knew. That was to play each afternoon a little harder and a little better than he had the day before." And so on. This was the *Times*'s good gray way of saying to its readers, "Yes he was that famously overly aggressive fellow, but there's no point in going into that now; he's dead and that was long ago." In this way, the *Times* spoke for the majority of journalists who preferred to say something polite and move on. Only here and there in the flood of farewell columns and features does the real Cobb shine through, allowing mid-century fans to glimpse what all the commotion was about. "Ty Cobb could cause more excitement with a base on balls than Babe Ruth could with a home run," wrote Roger Birtwell of the *Boston Globe*. Another scribe from that paper, Jerry Nason, said Cobb was the first and only man he ever saw who could a) score from second on an outfield putout, b) go from first to third on a sacrifice bunt, and c) score from first on a single. A Toledo man named Carl J. Murphy wrote to the *Blade* to say that "As a boy I saw him bunt a ball down the first base line at a speed that was about as fast as he could run, then straddle the ball all the way so that no one could get at the ball, then slide in safely." Tracked down in Indianapolis, seventy-three-year-old Donie Bush, a longtime teammate of Cobb's, added a bit of much needed grit. "I can't envision anyone in baseball ever being as great as Cobb," he said, "but we didn't get along too well. The source of my trouble with Cobb was simple—he expected me to do the things he did, and I just couldn't be so perfect. Who could? I hit in front of him for 13 years and I scored lots of runs because I didn't want him to run me down on the base lines."

The autobiography that Stump wrote did not change the way its subject was perceived by the general public. To the extent that people talked about the book, they mostly talked about the many errors it contained. No one commented on the fact that in its pages Cobb sounded more like a jaded sportswriter than an old ballplayer. ("No, I didn't once attack Nap Rucker, the pitcher, in the bathroom and try to throw him out of the tub in which he was relaxing. That phony fable has dogged me for more than half a century and I doubt there are enough fans to fill a broom closet who don't believe it happened—which it never did. I don't know who first concocted that particular piece of Limburger, but it has an odor I seem to associate with certain New York writers—never exactly simpatico to me—who've made certain it appeared in every language but the Sanskrit.") That was just the way it went with ghostwritten baseball books after all. Since not many people knew that Cobb had hated everything about the autobiography, the tone and the organization and the corny

B-movie quotes that Stump had concocted, and was desperately trying to halt its publication in his dying days, it didn't have the sizzle of being "the book Ty Cobb tried to suppress." It had no dirt in it, no bombshells. And because it wasn't selling "furiously," as Stump claimed, there wasn't any money in it for him, either, beyond his original $3,000 share of the advance. And that right there was the key to the destruction of Cobb's good name. For if *My Life in Baseball* had been gushing royalties and looking like it was going to become a nice little annuity for Stump in his golden years, he likely would not have undermined its credibility, just two months later, by saying in *True* that the book had been a whitewash ordered up by Cobb, and that he now felt conscience-bound to come forward with the real story in *True* magazine.

When the culture has a mind to convict someone, facts are like gnats, annoyances to be swatted away. In the fullness of time, Ty the Ripper's body count only increased. "It is well known that Ty Cobb may have killed as many as three people," Ron Shelton, the director of the 1994 movie *Cobb*, told me in the course of an email conversation. Really? Who were his victims? What were his motives? When did these crimes happen? Shelton declined to say, beyond repeating "All this is well known." He was more forthcoming, though, about a squirm-inducing scene in his film in which Tommy Lee Jones, playing the sickly old Cobb, attempts to rape a cigarette girl at a Nevada casino but fails because of impotence. "What was that based on?" I asked.

"That actually was not in the original screenplay," he said—proudly, I thought. "That is something that Al and I came up with during the shoot. It felt like the sort of thing that Cobb might do."

"Al" of course was Al Stump, upon whose *True* story the movie was based, and who served as a consultant during the shoot and even made a cameo appearance. His first and last movie role, it would turn out. He died a few months later.

In the 1970s Al Stump noticed that the baseball memorabilia market was becoming lucrative. He thought seriously of again exploiting his connection to Cobb. He had a fair amount of material on hand, letters and personal effects such as a penknife, a corncob pipe given to Cobb by

General Douglas MacArthur, even a set of Cobb's false teeth—the kind of cool and quirky baseball-star-related things that were selling. How he'd acquired the items was a question Stump tried to avoid as he tested the waters of the new market, but if pressed he'd flash a note from Cobb— a warm and friendly note, addressed to "Alimony Al"—saying he could have certain of his effects, mostly clothing he'd left behind at Stump's house in Santa Barbara after he'd gone there for a couple of days to work on their book. That Stump's collection went far beyond the items mentioned in the note was never questioned.

Nor did the writer face much resistance when he decided to supercharge his new career as a seller of "Cobbibilia" by forging items, which he then claimed had been authenticated. Why not? He'd already created a fake Ty Cobb. In 1980 a respected authenticator named Mike Gutierrez signed off on between fifty and a hundred letters that Stump created by using his own typewriter and Cobb's personal stationery and trademark green ink. The letters were heavy on "baseball content," as the dealers say, which enhanced their value—though several things "Cobb" said in them were flagrantly inaccurate. Another collector said he knew something was amiss when he inspected the letters in a sales catalog and noticed that the content of one was exactly the same as a letter he already owned. Others noted that the signatures were strangely shaky. Gutierrez at first attributed this to Cobb's declining health, but it likely had more to do with Stump's delirium tremens. Ultimately, with other experts saying the letters were fraudulent, Gutierrez recanted his authentication, but by then it was too late to issue a recall, and a new batch of seventy-five or so forgeries had joined the hundreds of similar letters circulating through the marketplace. Ron Keurajian, the leading authority on the player's signature, told me that most of the Cobb autographs the average collector comes across these days were actually signed by Stump.

In the early 1990s Ron Shelton optioned the screen rights to "Ty Cobb's Wild 10-Month Fight to Live." Stump was a willing seller, and an eager listener when the filmmaker suggested that he expand the story into a book. Although he'd had a heart attack, the task was easier for Stump because Charles Alexander, John McCallum, and a few others had produced Cobb biographies in the interim. By repurposing his *True* story, borrowing the research of these other writers, and tricking out the old tale with his trademark touches, Stump could, with a minimum of energy, produce another volume that might both give a boost to and be boosted by Shelton's movie. *Cobb: A Biography* was published in November 1994. It suffered from all the predictable flaws: fake dialogue, tabloidy writing, and various kinds of inaccuracies—Stump has Casey Stengel complaining to Cobb about his years with the Mets, an expansion team that didn't play its first game until about nine months after Cobb died (the error was corrected in subsequent editions). But it also brought back the fascinatingly repellent character who had found such eager acceptance more than thirty years earlier—and the venom-spewing, gun-waving Cobb was at least as popular this time around, despite or maybe because of his being a raving racist. The reviews were mostly positive. Since the bulk of Stump's forgeries had not yet become known, his authority and accuracy went unquestioned. The critics opened wide and swallowed. "Spellbinding," said the *Washington Post*. "Stump has resurrected Cobb in all his terrifying malevolence." "A big, raw, rough-cut diamond of a book and the most powerful baseball biography I ever read," said Roger Kahn, author of *The Boys of Summer*. *Sports Illustrated*, which excerpted the book, was especially credulous: "A chilling biography," it said. "Cobb was fortunate not to have been locked up for life." The reading public loved the character Stump created. As a commercial venture, *Cobb* the book did exponentially better than *Cobb* the movie, which was hustled out of theaters shortly after it opened, its first week of national release having grossed less than a million dollars.

Perhaps the single meanest lie told about Ty Cobb is that nobody came to his funeral—or even more heartbreaking, because it is more specific—that only three people did. This story started with Stump, who said that just three people from the world of professional baseball traveled to Royston for the service, and it has been distorted in the process of mindless retellings, which since the advent of the Internet can happen at hyperspeed. In fact, there *were* very few baseball people there—just four—but that was because Charlie Cobb and her children had announced that it was a private service meant only for family and close friends. In the event, hundreds of mourners stood outside the Christian Church in Cornelia and thousands lined the road to Royston to witness the funeral cortege as it proceeded to Rose Hill Cemetery. The baseball people who did come— Hall of Fame director Sid Keener and former players Ray Schalk, Mickey Cochrane, and fellow Georgian boy Nap Rucker—all had a special connection to Cobb. Schalk, a catcher for the White Sox for seventeen years, no doubt got more than a few chances to use his favorite line about Cobb: "When Ty started to steal second, I would throw to third."

Another problem with the "nobody came to Cobb's funeral" myth, which I heard numerous times while researching this book, is that it misses the phenomenon of all the little spontaneous memorial services that broke out across the country in late July of 1961 as probably hundreds of old ballplayers and sportswriters sat down in front of typewriters and beer glasses and retold the old stories. A columnist for the *Detroit Free Press*, John C. Manning, recounted one that he'd heard from umpire Bill Dinneen. It probably happened around 1916 or so, in Detroit, in a game lost to history, and with good reason, it was so tediously one-sided—the Yankees were ahead of the Tigers by a score of 7 or 8 to 1, as Dinneen remembered it—and the field-level temperature so stifling. With two outs in the bottom of the ninth, Cobb came up and hit a single, prolonging the painful experience. Even the hometown fans groaned. As the next man got ready to hit, Wally Pipp, the Yankees first baseman, said to Cobb, "You must be as tired of this as I am," and suggested that he let himself get picked off so they could all go and take a cold shower. "Good idea," said Cobb. "I'll go along with that." He then took what Dinneen called "an accommodating lead," and the pitcher whipped the ball to Pipp, who reached out to make the tag. But Cobb pulled away. Pipp looked at him quizzically, and reached out with the ball again—at which point Cobb broke for second. As Manning wrote it, "A rundown ensued with Ty dodging back and forth between the converging infielders. One of them bobbled the ball momentarily and Cobb streaked for second. He rounded second full tilt and slid into third, safe by an eyelash. The next batter ended the game with a pop-up."

Dinneen, who'd overheard the conversation at first base, stopped Cobb as he left the field and asked him why he'd crossed up Pipp.

Cobb himself seemed surprised by what had happened, Dinneen said. "I simply couldn't help it," he told the umpire. "I give you my word I didn't mean to welsh on Wally. I intended to go through with it. But when he took that throw and reached, something exploded inside of me. I just couldn't stand there and take it without a fight."

— TY COBB'S LIFETIME STATISTICS —

Year	G	AB	R	H	RBI	SB	BA
1905	41	150	19	36	15	2	.240
1906	98	358	45	113	34	23	.316
1907	150	605	97	212	119	53	.350
1908	150	581	88	188	108	39	.324
1909	156	573	116	216	107	76	.377
1910	140	506	106	194	91	65	.383
1911	146	591	147	248	127	83	.420
1912	140	553	120	226	83	61	.409
1913	122	428	70	167	67	51	.390
1914	98	345	69	127	57	35	.368
1915	156	563	144	208	99	96	.369
1916	145	542	113	201	68	68	.371
1917	152	588	107	225	102	55	.383
1918	111	421	83	161	64	34	.382
1919	124	497	92	191	70	28	.384
1920	112	428	86	143	63	15	.334
1921*	128	507	124	197	101	22	.389
1922*	137	526	99	211	99	9	.401
1923*	145	556	103	189	88	9	.340
1924*	155	625	115	211	79	23	.338
1925*	121	415	97	157	102	13	.378
1926*	79	233	48	79	62	9	.339

(Detroit Tigers/*years as player-manager)

Year	G	AB	R	H	RBI	SB	BA
1927	133	490	104	175	93	22	.357
1928	95	353	54	114	40	6	.323

(Philadelphia Athletics)

24 Yrs	**3034**	**11434**	**2246**	**4189**	**1938**	**897**	**.366**

— ACKNOWLEDGMENTS —

Getting the thank-yous right is always impossible, but surely Wesley Fricks should be among the first to be acknowledged. A native of Royston, Georgia, and a longtime Ty Cobb scholar, he has a three-dimensional sense of our subject's early years, having grown up among the descendants of Cobb's friends and neighbors, and since reaching his majority has spent hundreds of hours collecting and studying personal and legal documents as well as news accounts related to the man that he and many others consider the greatest player in history. While at first understandably wary of someone who said he wanted to write a biography of Cobb, he quickly came to see that I was open to questioning the myths and he generously shared his trove of research, which included quite a few facts and stories that have never before been published. He also vetted the manuscript after it was completed and corrected several errors.

William R. Cobb—another Georgian, though no relation to Tyrus Raymond—was also a great help to me. Ron, as he's less formally known, is an award-winning writer and editor who has produced several books by and about the Peach (see Note on Sources) that guided and inspired me on my three-and-a-half-year journey. He is also a collector of Cobb's correspondence, and he shared many of his letters with me, and pointed me in the direction of others. I hope he likes this book, which wouldn't have been what it is without him.

My thanks to Roger Angell and Yogi Berra for the comments and insights they made. The Hertog Research Fellowship at Columbia University provided me with the services of Kevin Magruder, who did significant digging and interviewing. I'm also grateful for the help I received at the Baseball Hall of Fame in Cooperstown, New York, from librarian Jim Gates, as well as John Horne, Freddy Berowski, and Tim Wiles.

At the Detroit Public Library I was aided immensely over the course of several visits by Mark Bowden, the coordinator of special collections. The justifiably prominent Detroit attorney Gary Spicer received me warmly, advised me wisely, and took me to a Tigers game. Dan and Stephanie Wroblewski drove me around to various places Ty Cobb had lived in Detroit and became my friends.

Thanks also to two of Ty Cobb's grandchildren, Herschel Cobb and Peggy Cobb Shugg, as well as Julie Ridgeway at the Ty Cobb Museum in Royston, Rex Teeslink, Rod Gailey, Michele Merkel, and Carol Loomis. For the reporting on Al Stump, I owe a debt to J. Michael Kenyon, Melvin Durslag, Doug Kirkorian, Ron Keurajian, and John Stump.

I am grateful to the support and counsel I received from my agent at ICM, Kristine Dahl, and from Bob Bender, my editor at Simon & Schuster, superstars both. Kris's assistant, Caroline Eisenmann, and Bob's colleagues at S&S, Johanna Li, Jonathan Evans, Fred Chase, and Joy O'Meara, have also enriched my book-writing experiences. As always, my friend Karen Schneider was an early reader of my manuscript and an encouraging presence.

My wife, Sarah Saffian Leerhsen, is the love of my life *and* a superb editor. I can only thank God for that.

No truth was injured intentionally in the creation of this work of nonfiction. No quotes are made up, no scenes manufactured. The information is drawn mostly from hundreds of contemporary newspaper and magazine articles dating back to the late nineteenth century, but I also interviewed people who had known Ty Cobb and I relied on letters written by and to him, and recordings of radio and television appearances that he made following his days as a player, a number of websites—including Baseball -Fever.com—and the resources of the Baseball Hall of Fame and the Society of American Baseball Research (SABR).

Of the many previous books about Cobb, the ones I found most useful were, in no particular order, *The Ty Cobb Scrapbook* by Marc Okkonen; *Ty Cobb* by Charles C. Alexander; *My Twenty Years in Baseball* by Ty Cobb, edited by William R. Cobb; *Inside Baseball with Ty Cobb*, edited by Wesley Fricks; *Busting 'Em and Other Big League Stories* by Ty Cobb; *Ty Cobb: Safe at Home* by Don Rhodes; *The Georgia Peach: Stumped by the Storyteller* by William R. Cobb; *Heart of a Tiger: Growing Up with My Grandfather, Ty Cobb* by Herschel Cobb; and *Peach: Ty Cobb in His Time and Ours* by Richard Bak. The two most popular books about Cobb—*Ty Cobb: My Life in Baseball* by Ty Cobb with Al Stump, and *Cobb* by Al Stump contained too many inaccuracies to be useful. The movie *Cobb* was no help at all.

Other books I consulted:

The Glory of Their Times: The Story of the Early Days of Baseball Told by the Men Who Played It by Lawrence S. Ritter; *Baseball: The Golden Age* by Harold Seymour; *Touching Base: Professional Baseball and American Culture in the Progressive Era* by Steven A. Riess; *The Tumult and the Shouting* by Grantland Rice; *The New Bill James Historical Baseball Abstract*; *The Detroit Tigers* by Frederick G. Lieb; *The Chalmers Race: Ty Cobb, Napoleon Lajoie, and the Controversial 1910 Batting Title That Became a National Obsession* by Rick Huhn; *Ty Cobb: Two Biographies* by H. G. Salsinger, edited by William R. Cobb; *Ty Cobb* by John D. McCallum; *The Babe and I* by Mrs. Babe Ruth with Bill Slocum; *The Big Bam: The Life and Times of Babe Ruth* by Leigh Montville; *Babe: The Legend Comes to Life* by Robert W. Creamer; *Ty and the Babe: Baseball's Fiercest Rivals: A Surprising Friendship and the 1941 Has-Beens Golf Championship* by Tom Stanton; *Baseball Stars of the American League* edited by David Jones; *Ban Johnson, Czar of Baseball* by Eugene C. Murdock; *The American League Story* by Lee Allen; *Detroit Is My Own Home Town* by Malcolm W. Bingay; *History of Franklin County, Georgia* by the Franklin County Historical Society; *Southern Manhood: Perspectives on Masculinity in the Old South* edited by Craig Thompson Friend and Lorri Glover; *Brutes in Suits: Male Sensibility in America, 1890–1920* by John Pettigrew; *Honor and Slavery* by Kenneth S. Greenberg; *Culture of Honor: The Psychology of Violence in the South* by Richard E. Nesbitt and Dov Cohen; *Tris Speaker: The Rough-and-Tumble Life of a Baseball Legend* by Timothy M. Gay; *Ernie Harwell: My 60 Years in Baseball* by Tom Keegan; *Ee-Yah: The Life and Times of Hughie Jennings, Baseball Hall of Famer* by Jack Smiles; *Say It Ain't So, Joe!: The True Story of Shoeless Joe Jackson* by Donald Gropman and Alan M. Dershowitz; *Shoeless* by David L. Fleitz; *Walter Johnson: Baseball's Big Train* by Henry W. Thomas and Shirley Povich; *Baseball in the Garden of Eden: The Secret History of the Early Game* by John Thorn; *The Kid: The Immortal Life of Ted Williams* by Ben Bradlee Jr.; *Ted Williams: The Biography of an American Hero* by Leigh Montville; *Joe DiMaggio: The Hero's Life* by Richard Ben Cramer; *Connie Mack and the Early Years of Baseball* by Norman L. Macht; *Connie Mack: The Turbulent and Triumphant Years, 1915–1931* by Norman L. Macht; *Eight Men Out: The Black Sox and the 1919 World Series* by Eliot Asinof; *My Fifty Years in Baseball* by Edward Grant Barrow and James M. Kahn; *Touching Second: The Science of Baseball* by John J. Evers; *Cap Anson 3: Mugsy John McGraw and the Tricksters—Baseball's Fun Age of Rule-Bending* by Howard W. Rosenberg; *Guys, Dolls, and Curveballs: Damon Runyon on Baseball* edited by Jim Reisler; *How They Played the Game: The Life of Grantland Rice* by William A. Harper; *Baseball as I Have Known It* by Fred Lieb; *Cobb Would Have Caught It: The Golden Age of Baseball in Detroit* by Richard Bak; *Rogers Hornsby: A Biography* by Charles C. Alexander; *Ross Macdonald: A Biography* by Tom Nolan; *Going Their Way* by John D. McCallum; *Crazy '08* by Cait Murphy; *Where They Ain't: The Fabled Life and Untimely Death of the Original Baltimore Orioles, the Team That Gave Birth to Modern Baseball* by Burt Solomon; *Images of Forgotten Detroit* by Paul Vachon; *Georgia Boy* by Erskine Caldwell; *American Monsters: 44 Rats, Blackhats, and Plutocrats* edited by Jack Newfield and Mark Jacobson; *Ty Cobb: The Tiger Wore Spikes* by John McCallum.

— ENDNOTES —

Many sources are noted in the text. Those not so identified are listed below.

PRELUDE

This is an edited transcript of an *Opie and Anthony* radio broadcast from June 13, 2009.

CHAPTER ONE

The details and quotes from the dressing room scene were drawn from an article called "In Dressing Room Interview Cobb Sticks to Diamond Career" in the *Atlanta Constitution*, Nov. 26, 1911, p. D2. For sources on the 1909 incident at Cleveland's Euclid Hotel, see Chapter Eighteen. The Moe Berg quote about Cobb being an intellectual giant (p. 7) comes from an interview with the (I must admit not always trustworthy) John D. McCallum, date unknown; it appears in McCallum's 1975 book *Ty Cobb*. There are many references to Cobb as a good conversationalist, including one in *Baseball Digest*, Aug. 1985, p. 72. The Sam Crawford quote about Cobb outthinking the opposition (p. 10) comes from Lawrence S. Ritter's *The Glory of Their Times*, p. 60. Germany Schaefer's assessment of Cobb (p. 12) was reported in the *St. Louis Republic* of Sept. 9, 1915. The reference to Cobb's possibly having typhoid fever (p. 12) comes from the *Atlanta Constitution*, Aug. 4, 1911, p. 9. George Sisler's quote (p. 12) was published in the *American Mercury*, Sept. 1956, p. 104. Cobb admitted he sometimes lacked a sense of humor (p. 13) in the 1914 newspaper serial republished as *Busting 'Em and Other Big League Stories*; the subsequent quote, about base running, comes from the same series. The Eddie Collins comment about "compressed steam" (p. 13) was taken from *Baseball* magazine, Mar. 1924, pp. 435–36. Casey Stengel praised Cobb's base running in his autobiography *Casey at the Bat*, p. 244. The statement that "baseball is 50 percent brains . . ." (p. 15) is from the *Atlanta Constitution* of Feb. 25, 1912.

"I see no reason in the world why we shouldn't compete with colored athletes . . ." (p. 20) appears in an Associated Press story of Jan. 29, 1952. Cobb said that Roy Campanella was "the player who reminds me most of myself" (p. 21) in the *Huron* (South Dakota) *Daily Plainsman* of Dec. 1, 1955, among other places.

CHAPTER TWO

Cobb said "I was taken there to be born" (p. 23) in a radio interview with Grantland Rice, the tape of which was provided to me by the Cobb scholar Wesley Fricks; it is undated, but probably from the early 1930s. The quote "You saw it the minute you set eyes on him" (p. 24) is from an unsigned article in a special edition of the *Royston Record*, published in conjunction with the groundbreaking for the hospital that became the Ty Cobb Regional Medical Center in late March of 1950. The other quotes, from Joe Cunningham, about Cobb's boyhood adventures, come from the same piece. The quote about "a vying nature" (p. 25) appears in several places, including Richard Bak's *Ty Cobb: His Tumultuous Life and Times.* W. H. Cobb's quote about "harmony among the people" (p. 30) is from the *Atlanta Constitution*, July 9, 1899. Billy Bowers's claim to have been the only man in Georgia to have voted for Abe Lincoln (p. 32) comes from *Memoirs of Georgia Containing Historical Accounts of the State's Civil, Military, Industrial and Professional Interests, and Personal Sketches of Many of Its People, Vol. 2.* Nicholas Lemann's quote about Teddy Roosevelt is from the *New Yorker*, Nov. 18, 2013. The information on Ty Cobb's ancestors comes from documents provided by Wesley Fricks, Ancestry.com, Genealogy.com, the *Pittsburgh Press,* Dec. 10, 1911, and the *Atlanta Constitution,* Feb. 27, 1921. The excerpts from W.H.'s Cobb speech about educational opportunities for black children were taken from the *Columbus* (Georgia) *Enquirer-Sun,* Aug. 16, 1901. Cobb's quote about his father being a school commissioner and state senator is from *My Twenty Years in Baseball*, edited by William R. Cobb, p. 13.

CHAPTER THREE

Cobb's quote (p. 34) about Royston is from *My Twenty Years in Baseball*, p. 13. Much of the information about Royston is from *The History of Franklin County, Georgia,* published by the Franklin County Historical Society. Cobb's reminiscences about his boyhood years (p. 35) are drawn from my interviews with the Ty Cobb historian (and Royston native) Wesley Fricks, and the 1912 newspaper serial published in book form as *Inside Baseball with Ty Cobb*, edited by Fricks; the 1914 serial collected as *Busting 'Em and Other Big League Stories*; the 1925 serial, republished as *My Twenty Years in Baseball*, edited by William R. Cobb and from miscellaneous articles such as "Cobb Tells of Start and Secrets of Success in the American League," in the *Pittsburgh Press*, Dec. 10, 1911, p. 22; "Fighting and Baseball Were Cobb's Only Thoughts as a Boy; A Row Started His Bright Career" in the *Atlanta Constitution*, Feb. 18, 1912, p. D5; and "Bank Clerk Finds Ty Cobb," *Chicago Daily Tribune*, Feb. 25, 1912, p. C2. The medical student mentioned on p. 39 is Rex Teeslink, who spoke to me in 2013. My research assistant Kevin Magruder acted as an intermediary in the Yogi Berra interview mentioned on p. 40, as he was for the Roger Angell interview, cited on p. 42. Cobb made his observation (p. 45) about how we remember criticism better than praise in his 1914 newspaper memoir. The interview with Furman Bisher mentioned on p. 46 ran under the headline "A Visit with Ty Cobb" in the *Saturday Evening Post*, June 14, 1958, p. 53.

CHAPTER FOUR

Eddie Cantor frequently mentioned his grandmother's aversion to ballplayers (p. 50) in his comedy routines and in books such as *My Life Is in Your Hands*. Cobb's quote about baseball biographies (p. 51) is from *My Twenty Years in Baseball*, p. 13. That book, and Cobb's two other serialized memoirs, were used throughout this chapter. The information on early baseball demographics (p. 53) comes mostly from Chapter Six of Steven A. Riess's *Touching Base: Professional Baseball and American Culture in the Progressive Era*. The Rogers Hornsby article mentioned on p. 54 ran in *True* magazine, Aug. 1961, pp. 59–60. Hugh Fullerton's quote (p. 54) is taken from a series called "How to Play Baseball in 100 Lessons" that ran in the *Atlanta Constitution* during the summer of 1919. The Bill Veeck quote on p. 54 is from *The Hustler's Handbook* (1965). Sam Crawford's opinion of Ed Delahanty (p. 55) can be found on p. 65 of *The Glory of Their Times*. The Ned Garvin quote (p. 56) comes from *Pinstripe Empire: The New York Yankees from Before the Babe to After the Boss* by Marty Appel, p. 35.

CHAPTER FIVE

As noted in the text, the information about Cobb's experiences with Con Strouthers and the Augusta Tourists was taken largely from contemporary coverage in the *Augusta Chronicle*, which is available online. The Germany Schaefer quote about Cobb being the craziest runner he'd ever seen (p. 59) is from the *Sporting News*, Feb. 24, 1927, p. 8. Cobb's quote about being full of "life and pepper" (p. 59) and Strouthers's quote in reaction to his nervous energy (p. 59) are both taken from *Inside Baseball with Ty Cobb*, p. 47. The anecdote about Cobb encountering Oliver Hardy (p. 61) is from Grantland Rice's *The Tumult and the Shouting*, pp. 20–21. The information about Strouthers being arrested for theft (p. 62) comes from the *Detroit Free Press*, Dec. 3, 1902, p. 10. Cobb's quote about Strouthers not understanding "a boy's mind" (p. 64) comes from his 1914 newspaper serial. I obtained a copy of Cobb's first minor league contract, mentioned on p. 64, from Wesley Fricks.

CHAPTER SIX

As in Chapter Five, much of the information about the Augusta Tourists comes from the *Augusta Chronicle*. The information about the Jones sisters comes largely from material—newspaper accounts and court records—provided by Wesley Fricks. For information about the early Detroit Tigers I relied on the *Detroit Free Press*, *The Detroit Tigers* by Frederick G. Lieb, and *Baseball: The Golden Age* by Harold Seymour, as well as the letters in the Ernie Harwell Collection at the Detroit Public Library. Much of the information on Ed Barrow comes from his 1951 book *My Fifty Years in Baseball*. The catcher alluded to on p. 75 is Lew Drill, who later became the U.S. Attorney for Minnesota.

CHAPTER SEVEN

This chapter also relies on Cobb's three serialized memoirs and the *Augusta Chronicle*'s coverage, as well as materials provided by Wesley Fricks and discussions I had with Don Rhodes, author of *Ty Cobb: Safe at Home*. The best account of George Leidy and his interactions with Cobb comes from Cobb's *My Twenty Years in Baseball*, which is where the quotes about Leidy on pp. 80–81 come from. Cobb admitted he was not a good bunter (p. 81) in *My Twenty Years*. The quote about Cobb's "always doing something" to rattle the opposition (p. 82) comes from his undated radio interview with Grantland Rice. The letters written by Bill Armour (p. 84) are in the Ernie Harwell Collection at the Detroit Public Library.

CHAPTER EIGHT

Legal documents pertaining to the prosecution of Amanda Cobb, including the coroner's report on the shooting of William H. Cobb, were provided to me by Wesley Fricks, who also provided similar information on the Jones sisters' case. Charles Alexander's brief account of the death of W. H. Cobb (p. 90) can be found on pp. 20–21 of his biography *Ty Cobb*. Al Stump covers the same territory in Chapter Six of his book *Cobb*. The Fielder Jones quote about the Tigers (p. 94) is from the *Chicago Daily Tribune*, Apr. 19, 1905, p. 6. The information about

Cobb's negotiations to join the Tigers (pp. 95–96) is drawn from the letters in the Ernie Harwell Collection at the Detroit Public Library and from Cobb's newspaper memoirs, especially *My Twenty Years in Baseball*. For more on Jack Chesbro (p. 98), see *Before They Were the Bombers: The New York Yankees' Early Years, 1903–1915* by Jim Reisler, pp. 78–79, and *Greatness in Waiting: An Illustrated History of the Early New York Yankees* by Ray Istorico, pp. 29–30.

CHAPTER NINE

The letters I quote from are in the Ernie Harwell Collection at the Detroit Public Library. The quote about the cause of Kid Elberfeld's suspension (p. 102) is from *Sporting Life*, Aug. 20, 1905, p. 7. For more on Elberfeld, see *Before They Were the Bombers: The New York Yankees' Early Years, 1903–1915* by Jim Reisler, p. 144. Cobb's quote about how his initial success restored his self-confidence (p. 103) is from *Inside Baseball with Ty Cobb*, p. 61. The information about Mrs. Cobb's alleged lover, Joshua Chambers (p. 103), was provided by Wesley Fricks. In this chapter, information on Cobb's performance in big league games is drawn largely from contemporary coverage in the *Detroit Free Press*, the *Detroit Daily News*, the *New York Times*, the *Sporting News*, *Sporting Life*, and the other major papers in American League cities, especially Boston, Washington, and Chicago. Clark Griffith's quote about Cobb probably not surviving a second trip "around the circuit" (p. 106) comes from the *Detroit Free Press*, Dec. 8, 1912, p. 12.

CHAPTER TEN

The letters referenced in this chapter are in the Ernie Harwell Collection at the Detroit Public Library. Al Stump, for example, mistakenly refers to a "Bungy Davis" (p. 110) on p. 141 of Cobb's biography. The information on the Cobb family's finances (p. 110) came from documents provided by Wesley Fricks. Cobb's quotes about being shocked by McIntyre's epithets (p. 115) come from *My Twenty Years in Baseball*, p. 50. Cobb's observation that ballplayers were a higher class of men than in the "olden days" (p. 115) can be found in *Inside Baseball with Ty Cobb*, p. 65. The quote about a "tragedy" (p. 116) is on p. 50 of *My Twenty Years in Baseball*. The Albert Beveridge quote about the "male animal" (p. 117) is from his 1905 book *The Young Man and the World*, p. 34. Charles Foster Kent's defense of hazing (p. 117) was reported in the *Boston Evening Transcript*, Mar. 13, 1902, p. 23. Shoeless Joe Jackson's quote (p. 118) about how "It don't take school stuff to help a fella play ball" appears in many places, including Donald Gropman's 1979 book *Say It Ain't So, Joe: The True Story of Shoeless Joe Jackson*, p. 101. Cobb's quote about crying (p. 120) comes from a special commemorative issue of the *Royston Record* published in 1950 in conjunction with the dedication of Cobb Memorial Hospital, no specific date or page number available. The quote "They sort of formed a gang . . ." (p. 120) comes from *My Twenty Years in Baseball,* p. 53. Cobb's statement about liking opposition (p. 120) appears in *Busting 'Em and Other Big League Stories,* p. 81. Connie Mack advised his players not to get Cobb mad on many occasions over the years, but the remark (p. 121) is reported most authoritatively in volume 2 of Norman L. Macht's majestic biography of Mack, published in 2012, *Connie Mack: The Turbulent and Triumphant Years: 1915–1931,* p. 376. Cobb's quote about gritting his teeth (p. 121) comes from *My Twenty Years in Baseball,* p. 51, as does the quote from Bill Donovan (p. 121). Some of the information about Amanda Cobb's trial comes from a document called "The State of Georgia vs. Amanda Cobb: A Timeline of Justice," prepared by Wesley Fricks.

CHAPTER ELEVEN

The quote from Joe Cantillon (p. 126) can be found in the *Washington Star,* Feb. 2, 1930. The mention of umpire Tom Connor being roughly handled (p. 128) comes from the *Detroit Free Press,* May 15, 1906, p. 10. The quote from Louis Menand (p. 128) comes from his book *Discovering Modernism: T. S. Eliot and His Context,* p. 4. The quote from Nap Lajoie (p. 129) comes from the *Weirton* (West Virginia) *Daily Times,* July 18, 1961, p. 8. Cobb's account of Schmidt falling over a barrel (p. 132) is from *My Twenty Years in Baseball,* p. 52. Armour's advice to Schaefer about taking a dose of olive oil (p. 133) comes from a letter in the Ernie Harwell Collection at the Detroit Public Library.

CHAPTER TWELVE

Margaret Sangster's article on nervous disorders (p. 136) ran in the *Detroit Free Press* on Dec. 9, 1906, p. C2. The quote (p. 136) about the "sanatorium" in Al Stump's book *Cobb* is on p. 129. The quote from Richard Bak's book *Peach* (p. 136) is on p. 41. The quote from the Charles Alexander book (p. 136) is on p. 45. Bill Armour's statement about being practically out of major league ball (p. 140) comes from the *Cleveland Plain Dealer,* Sept. 21, 1906. The information about Armour's death (p. 140) comes from the *Plain Dealer,* Dec. 3, 1922. The term "You threw me down" (p. 143) can be found in *Busting 'Em and Other Big League Stories,* p. 122. The quote from Bill Donovan (p. 143) appears on p. 53 of *My Twenty Years in Baseball.*

CHAPTER THIRTEEN

Some of the information about the old Baltimore Orioles (p. 145) comes from *Where They Ain't: The Fabled Life and Untimely Death of the Original Baltimore Orioles, the Team That Gave Birth to Modern Baseball*, by Burt Solomon, and *Cap Anson 3: Mugsy John McGraw and the Tricksters—Baseball's Fun Age of Rule-Bending* by Howard W. Rosenberg. Some of the information about Jennings, including the Ban Johnson quote about "the old Oriole stamp (p. 146), can be found in *Ee-Yah: The Life and Times of Hughie Jennings, Baseball Hall of Famer*, by Jack Smiles. Similar information appears in Fred Lieb's book *The Detroit Tigers*, p. 85. Frank Navin's quote about dealing with players (p. 148) and his dialogue with Cobb, McIntyre, and Jennings are from a letter in the Ernie Harwell Collection at the Detroit Public Library. Information about Cobb's dispute with Putnam (p. 149) comes from documents provided to me by Wesley Fricks. The anecdote about Cobb stealing a list of salaries from Navin's desk (p. 151) comes from a letter in the Ernie Harwell Collection at the Detroit Public Library. Hugh Fullerton's description of how Jennings conducted a frame-up of Cobb (p. 153) appeared in the *Washington Post,* Feb. 18, 1921, p. 10. The quotes about Cobb being "quiet as a lamb," and Jennings being "plainly wrought up" (p. 153) come from the *Detroit Free Press*, Mar. 17, 1907, p. 17. Navin's letters to Jennings (pp. 154–55) are in the Ernie Harwell Collection at the Detroit Public Library, as is Navin's letter to Ban Johnson (p. 157). Cobb's quote about his collision with Elberfeld (p. 159) is on p. 42 of *My Twenty Years in Baseball*. A copy of Cobb's 1907 letter to Elberfeld (p. 159) was provided to me by William R. (Ron) Cobb.

CHAPTER FOURTEEN

The quote from Hughie Jennings about stupid ballplayers (p. 166) can be found on p. 470 of *Connie Mack and the Early Years of Baseball*, by Norman L. Macht. Cobb's quote about rarely taking a chance that he had not figured out in advance (p. 167) is from *My Twenty Years in Baseball*, p. 89. Navin's wistful quote about baseball salaries (p. 174) is from a letter in the Ernie Harwell Collection at the Detroit Public Libary. Connie Mack's observation about Jennings's managing style (p. 173) can be found in Lieb's book, *The Detroit Tigers*, p. 90. The quote about a fan chewing off "one side of his drooping mustache" (p. 175) appeared in the *Detroit Free Press*, Oct. 1, 1907, p. 5. Cobb's statement about "bodily harm" (p. 176) is from *Busting 'Em and Other Big League Stories*, p. 134.

CHAPTER FIFTEEN

The writer to whom Cobb expressed his disappointment (p. 179) was Paul Bruske of the *Detroit Daily News*. The description of the Tigers dinner (p. 179) comes from the *Detroit Free Press*, Oct. 17, 1907, p. 1. The description of the wrestling match Cobb refereed (p. 180) comes from the *Waterloo* (Iowa) *Semi-Weekly Reporter*, Dec. 27, 1907. The letters referred to (p. 180) are in the Ernie Harwell Collection at the Detroit Public Library. Cobb's quote about how baseball has cut into his reading (p. 181) appears on p. 38 of Don Rhodes's *Ty Cobb: Safe at Home*, and probably came originally from the *Augusta Herald*. Navin's letter to Jennings (p. 182) is in the Ernie Harwell Collection at the Detroit Public Library. The report of everyone abandoning hope about Cobb's re-signing (p. 183) is from the *Detroit Free Press*, Mar. 21, 1908, pp. 1–2. The quote from Mark Okkonen (p. 184) appears in his *Ty Cobb Scrapbook*, p. 20. The Broun quote about Cobb giving more "for their hard-earned money" (p. 184) appeared in the *Telegraph* in October of 1910. The quote from Hugh Fullerton that starts "He fought for every point" (p. 185) appeared in an article called "Baseball's Best" in the *North American Review*, May 1930, p. 605. The quote from Cobb (p. 185) that begins, "I would think, 'I haven't tried to score from second base'" is from the undated radio interview with Grantland Rice provided by Wesley Fricks. Cobb's quote about being thought of as a "barroom gladiator" (p. 185) ran in several newspapers including the *Fort Wayne Sentinel,* Dec. 2, 1914, p. 8. Walter Johnson's quotes about Cobb (p. 185) come from a newspaper series called "My Pitching Years" that ran in the *Washington Times* and other outlets in early 1925. Salsinger's comment about Cobb being Harrison's "main defender and patron" (p. 190) appeared in his "Our Ty" series that ran in the *Detroit News* throughout 1924.

CHAPTER SIXTEEN

The description of Cobb's wedding (p. 193) comes from the Society page of the *Augusta Chronicle*, Aug. 7, 1908. The reference to Charlie Cobb's being "heavily veiled" (p. 194) comes from the *Augusta Herald*, Aug. 10, 1908, via Don Rhode's *Ty Cobb: Safe at Home*, p. 37. The quote about "actors, politicians and barbers" (p. 198) comes from Fred Lieb's *The Detroit Tigers*, p. 118, as does the Hugh Fullerton quote (p. 198) about Louis Mann. Will Wreford (p. 199) wrote for the *Detroit Free Press*. Cobb expressed his hopes for the 1909 season (p. 200) in *Sporting Life,* Dec. 26, 1908, p. 5.

CHAPTER SEVENTEEN

I found the Fred Mitchell story about Cobb stealing home (p. 204) in the *Winnipeg Tribune*, Dec. 16, 1924, but it probably appeared first in H. G. Salsinger's "Our Ty" series in the *Detroit Daily News*. Hughie Jennings made his comments about Cobb's running and sliding (p. 204) in *Baseball Magazine*, Mar. 1921, p. 468. Shotton's comments about Cobb (p. 205 and 207) appeared in the *Tuscaloosa News*, Apr. 6, 1950, p. 7. Paul Krichell's quotes (p. 205) come from the *Sporting News*, June 12, 1957, p. 28. Cobb talks about the "swoop slide" and his small ankles (p. 205) on p. 39 of *My Twenty Years in Baseball*. One place Cobb talks about sliding as if you enjoy it (p. 206) is on p. 171 of *Busting 'Em and Other Big League Stories*. The quote from Wally Schang about Cobb being "too pretty a slider" to hurt anyone intentionally (p. 206) comes from the *Washington Post*, Mar. 19, 1940, p. 20. Roger Peckinpaugh's comments about Cobb never hurting him (p. 206) ran in the *Sporting News*, Apr. 13, 1944, p. 17. Steve O'Neill's assessment (p. 207 and p. 211) ran in the *Sporting News*, Apr. 2, 1942, as part of a "Greatest Player" survey. Ben Hunt expressed his thoughts about Cobb's base running (p. 207) in the *Los Angeles Times*, Feb. 16, 1911, Sec. 3, p. 1. Red Farber's 1961 quote about Cobb never hurting anyone (p. 207) appeared in a collection of quotes aggregated by the Cobb scholar Bill Burgess on the *Baseball Fever* website. Cobb's letter to Ban Johnson about spikes (p. 209) is quoted in the *Boston Daily Globe*, Jan. 14, 1910, p. 5. O'Loughlin's defense of Cobb (p. 209) ran in the *Pittsburgh Press*, July 24, 1911, p. 13. Ossie Bluege spoke to Donald Honig about Cobb (p. 209) for Honig's 1977 *The Man in the Dugout*, p. 152. George Burns made his remarks about Cobb (p. 210) in the *Los Angeles Times*, May 14, 1931, p. F4. Tinker's remarks about Cobb (p. 210) appeared in the *Pittsburgh Press,* Jan. 5, 1910, p. 14. O'Leary's quote about Cobb not being a crybaby (p. 211) comes from the *Sporting News*, Dec. 26, 1935, p. 2. Cobb vehemently denied being a spiker (p. 211) in a United Press story that ran, among other places, in the *Huron* (South Dakota) *Daily Plainsman*, July 31, 1955, p. 10.

CHAPTER EIGHTEEN

Connie Mack's angry statement about Cobb (p. 214) is reported in *Connie Mack and the Early Years of Baseball* by Norman L. Macht, p. 453. It appeared originally in *Sporting Life,* Sept. 4, 1909, p. 6. Jennings's testy response to Connie Mack (p. 214) ran in the *Cincinnati Enquirer*, Aug. 28, 1909, page unknown. One place Cobb's response (p. 215) appeared was alongside Mack's statement in *Sporting Life,* Sept. 4, 1909, p. 6. Collins's statement (p. 215) about Cobb's base running appeared in the *Sporting News*, Oct. 18, 1950, p. 14. Charlie Murphy defended Cobb (p. 216) in *Sporting Life*, Oct. 2, 1909, p. 13, and in a syndicated story that ran in the *Cincinnati Enquirer* and other papers on or just after Sept. 8, 1909. Frank Navin's letter to Ban Johnson (p. 216) is in the Ernie Harwell Collection at the Detroit Public Library. Cohan's comment about Cobb being "a Yankee Doodle boy" (p. 218) appeared in the *Detroit News*, Sept. 4, 1909, p. 8. Avery's statement that Cobb was "roaring drunk" when he entered the Euclid (p. 218) appeared in the *Cleveland News*, Sept. 6, 1909, p. 1. (Vaughn Glaser denied Cobb was drunk when he came back to the Euclid Hotel in the *Detroit Free Press*, Sept. 8, 1909, p. 10.) Cobb's version of what happened that night in Cleveland (p. 218) comes from the *Sporting News*, Oct. 28, 1909, p. 3. George Stanfield's version (p. 219) appeared in the *Detroit Free Press*, Sept. 8, 1909, p. 9. Hughie Jennings's brief speech and the "ragtime chorus" (p. 221) are mentioned in the *Free Press* of Sept. 17, 1909, p. 8. Cobb made his comment about street clothes (p. 222) on several occasions, including in *Busting 'Em*, p. 42. Lieb's quote (p. 227) comes from *The Detroit Tigers*, p. 127. Navin said "If Cobb were less impetuous . . ." (p. 227), in the *Detroit Free Press*, Aug. 7, 1910, p. 26. Comiskey's article praising Cobb (p. 228), which also ran in the *Chicago Daily Tribune* (Apr. 17, 1910, pp. C1–2), is reproduced in full in *Inside Baseball with Ty Cobb*, edited by Wesley Fricks. Cobb's quote about walking with his head down and shoulders hunched (p. 228) comes from the undated radio interview provided by Wesley Fricks.

CHAPTER NINETEEN

Koosma Tarasoff's comments about Cobb (p. 230) appeared in the *Ottawa Citizen*, Dec. 26, 2004. Navin's comments to Charlie Schmidt about Cobb (p. 231) are from a letter in the Ernie Harwell Collection at the Detroit Public Library. Cobb's comment about training trips (p. 232) appeared, among other places, in the *El Paso Herald*, Jan. 16, 1912, p. 12. Jennings's letter to Cobb urging him to come to spring training (p. 233) is also in the Ernie Harwell Collection at the Detroit Public Library. Cobb's remarks about the strawberry shortcake (p. 234) appeared in the *Charlotte Observer*, May 27, 1910, p. 9. Cobb's interactions with President Taft (p. 234) were reported in the same edition of the *Observer*, p. 3. E. A. Batchelor (p. 235) assisted and succeeded Joe Jackson as sports editor of the *Detroit Free Press*. He wrote about Jones's lack of popularity in the editorial of Aug. 6, 1910, p. 8. Cobb's "open letter" to the press and public (p. 236) was reported in and quoted from *Sporting Life*, Aug. 13, 1910, p. 5. Red Nelson's account of Lajoie's hitting performance (p. 238) appeared in the *Cleveland Plain Dealer*, Oct. 12, 1910, p. 8.

O'Connor's widely reported quote about "tearing your head off" with line drives (p. 238) also appeared in "The Amazing Race" by L. Jon Wertheim, *Sports Illustrated*, Sept. 20, 2010. O'Connor's lame explanation for Lajoie's hits (p. 241) was reported in the *Detroit Free Press*, Oct. 11, 1910, p. 9. Lajoie's testy response to Navin's suspicions (p. 242) appeared in the *New York Times*, Oct. 11, 1910. Cobb expressed surprise at Lajoie's performance in the doubleheader (p. 243) in the *Detroit Free Press*, Oct. 12, 1910, p. 9. Ban Johnson's statement (p. 243) can be found, among other places, in the *Winnipeg Free Press*, Oct. 17, 1910, p. 14. Batchelor made his comment about a "nasty mess" (p. 244) in the *Detroit Free Press*, Oct. 13, 1910, p. 9.

CHAPTER TWENTY

The story of Ty Cobb's encounter with a fake policeman in Central Park (p. 246) appeared in an article titled "Ty Cobb, Actor" in *The National Pastime*, a publication of the Society for American Baseball Research. Batchelor's article about Cobb and *The College Widow* (p. 247) ran in the *Detroit Free Press*, Dec. 18, 1911, p. 8. Frank Navin's letters to Cobb and Burske (p. 247) are in the Ernie Harwell Collection at the Detroit Public Library. Cobb feeling "pretty punk" (p. 251) comes from the *Atlanta Constitution*, Aug. 4, 1911, p. 9. Cobb made his joke about not being able to run for office (p. 253) in the *Augusta Herald*, Nov. 19, 1911.

CHAPTER TWENTY-ONE

The quote about the "exacting and depressing nature of the work" (p. 255) comes from a published decision on an arbitration case involving the New York Newspaper Web Pressmen's Union No. 25 and the Publishers' Association of New York City rendered on Feb. 21, 1921. The photo of Lucker (p. 255) ran, among other places, in the *Meridian* (Miss.) *Daily Journal*, May 21, 1912, p. 7. Jack Fournier's reference to "ugly epithets" (p. 257) appears on p. 113 of Harold Seymour's *Baseball: The Golden Age*. Callahan's remarks about being "protected from insult" (p. 257) appeared in the *New York Times*, May 19, 1912. Lucker's comments about Cobb getting peevish (p. 259) appeared in *Sporting Life*, May 25, 1912, p. 4; Lucker's statement about being told that the league would take "immediate action" (p. 260) appears in the same article. Cobb's complaint of an injustice (p. 261) comes from *Baseball Magazine*, July 1912, p. 8. Mayor Thompson's statement about being "perfectly right" to express his resentment with his fists (p. 261) appeared, among other places, in the *Pittsburgh Press*, May 19, 1912, p. 22. Connolly's and Phelan's comments about Ban Johnson (p. 261) appeared in the *New York Times*, May 19, 1912, p. 2. Hugh Fullerton's statement in defense of Cobb (p. 261) was quoted by Jerome Holtzman in the *Chicago Tribune* Jan. 24, 1995, p. 3. Cobb's statement about baseball having a "higher class of men" than previously (p. 262) appears in *Inside Baseball with Ty Cobb*, p. 65. Mathewson's views (p. 262) appeared in the *New York Times*, May 19, 1912. The trouble at the Chicago Beach Hotel (p. 264) was related in the *Detroit Free Press*, Apr. 16, 1912, p. 10. The story about Cobb's teammates honoring him with a gift (p. 264) appeared in the *Detroit Free Press*, Dec. 24, 1911, p. 13. Navin's broad grin (p. 265) was noted in the *Detroit Daily News*, May 19, 1912. The telegram in support of Cobb (p. 265) was quoted in *Sporting Life*, May 25, 1912, p. 1. Cobb's statement about sticking together (p. 265) can be found in the same edition of *Sporting Life*, p. 6. Baer (p. 266) is quoted in John McCallum's *The Tiger Wore Spikes*, p. 231. The quote about "slashing away" at the man's face (p. 269) is from Al Stump's book *Cobb*, p. 212.

CHAPTER TWENTY-TWO

Cobb's comments about how he didn't think people wanted to watch healthy men play baseball while their sons and brothers were fighting "the Huns" (p. 273) appeared, among other places, in the *Bisbee* (Arizona) *Daily Review*, July 14, 1918, p. 12. Cobb's quotes about helping in the war effort (p. 274) come from the *Milwaukee Sentinel*, Aug. 26, 1918, p. 6. Navin's quote beginning "Mr. Cobb did not make baseball . . ." (p. 275) appeared in many papers including the *Richmond Times Dispatch*, Apr. 17, 1913, p. 7. Cobb's response to Navin (p. 276) appeared in the *Detroit Free Press*, Apr. 17, 1913, p. 8. Cobb's statement about the holdout of 1913 being his last (p. 276) ran in the *San Francisco Call*, Apr. 26, 1913. The "love note" to Frank Navin (p. 277) was published in a number of papers including the *Jeffersonville* (Indiana) *Daily Reflector*, Dec. 4, p. 4. The reference to a fight with Joe Engel (p. 277) was in the *Washington Post*, Aug. 25, 1914, p. 8. The account of Cobb's fight with the college student (p. 278) appeared in the *Pittsburgh Post-Gazette*, Apr. 9, 1913, p. 13. The account of the fight with Herzog (p. 278) is drawn from several sources including the *New York Times* of Apr. 1, 1917, the *Boston Globe* of Apr. 8, 1917, the *Detroit Free Press* of Apr. 1, 1917, p. 21, and the *Spokane Spokesman-Review* of Apr. 12, 1917, p. 18. The butcher's quote "I'm glad of it . . ." (p. 280), appeared in the *Boston Globe*, June 24, 1914, p. 1. Cobb's statement about the butcher seeming to want trouble (p. 280) appeared in *Sporting Life*, June 17, 1914, p. 10. Alexander's mistake about Harding (p. 281) appears on page 119 of his biography *Ty Cobb*. The story about Cobb's regretting the fight with the butcher (p. 281) ran in the *New York Times*, June 22, 1914. Heilmann's quote about Cobb being a great teacher of batting (p. 283) ran in the *Ironwood* (Michigan) *Daily Globe*, July 13, 1951, p. 7. Fitch's comments about Cobb (p. 283) appeared in the *New London* (Connecticut) *Day*, Sept. 9, 1915, p. 6.

CHAPTER TWENTY-THREE

The comment about Jennings losing "hold on his men" (p. 285) appears in Jack Smiles *"Ee-Yah": The Life and Times of Hughie Jennings, Baseball Hall of Famer*, p. 172. Ruth's comment about Bill Carrigan (p. 288) comes from a biography of Carrigan published by the Society for American Baseball Research (SABR); the piece originally ran in *Deadball Stars of the American League*, edited by David Jones, pp. 451–52. Jones's description of Dutch Leonard (p. 288) comes from that same book, pp. 453–56. The information about Boston fans "blowing horns and carrying policemen's rattles" (p. 293) appeared in the *Boston Globe*, Aug. 25, 1915, p. 1. The line about Cobb being late because he attended a concert (p. 296) comes from *Baseball Magazine*, Apr. 1916, p. 51. Fielder's line about preaching Cobb to his players (p. 296) appeared in the *Chicago Tribune*, June 6, 1917, p. 14. Ehmke's quote about Cobb talking baseball with him (p. 297) ran in the *Los Angeles Times*, Jan. 18, 1917, p. III 1. Cobb's comments about wanting to become a composer (p. 297) are taken from *Baseball Magazine*, Apr. 1916, p. 51. Bressler's quote about never seeing anyone like Cobb (p. 298) appears in *The Glory of Their Times*, page 205. Cobb's quote about being tired of baseball (p. 298) appeared in the *Detroit Free Press*, Dec. 17, 1918, p. 13.

CHAPTER TWENTY-FOUR

Maxwell's piece (p. 299), originally written for the *Philadelphia Daily Ledger*, also ran in the *Detroit Free Press* on Oct. 10, 1918, p. 13. The quote from Cobb's postcard to Navin (p. 300) appeared in the *Kansas City Star*, Nov. 1, 1918, p. 13. Cobb's quote about going to Augusta to rest (p. 300) ran in the *Augusta Chronicle*, Dec. 17, 1918. The information about Cobb making a speech during a minstrel show (p. 301) was taken from the *Providence News*, Dec. 16, 1918, p. 14. Cobb's quote about his "terrible fascination" with baseball (p. 301) was taken from the *Border Cities Star*, Dec. 18, 1918, p. 12. Cobb's comments about Campanella (p. 305) are from a letter Cobb wrote to Walter O'Malley dated May 8, 1959, a copy of which was provided to me by Ron Cobb. Nick Wilson's book (p. 305) is called *Voices from the Pastime: Oral Histories of Surviving Major Leaguers, Negro*

Leaguers, Cuban Leaguers and Writers. Rivers's quote about naming his child after Cobb (p. 305) comes from a PowerPoint article called "Alec Rivers Detroit Tigers Batman" put together by Patricia Zacharias of the *Detroit News*. Rivers expressed his love for Cobb (p. 306) in the *Chicago Tribune*, Sept. 23, 1928, p. A1. Cobb's letter to Walsh (p. 308) is dated Sept. 17, 1953, and was provided to me by Ron Cobb. Ty Cobb's comment about Ruth not having to protect the plate (p. 308) appears in Robert Creamer's *Babe: The Legend Comes to Life*, Kindle location 1434. Yawkey's comment about taking Cobb over Ruth (p. 309) was published in the *Sporting News*, Mar. 9, 1933.

CHAPTER TWENTY-FIVE

Hughie Jennings declared war on alibis (p. 312) in the *Atlanta Constitution*, Mar. 12, 1920, p. 15. Cobb's alleged demand for summary measures (p. 313) was reported in the *Reading Eagle*, Aug. 17, 1920, p. 9. Carl Mays's comments about Cobb (p. 314) appeared in the *Eugene Register-Guard*, July 14, 1962, p. 1. Damon Runyon's thoughts on Cobb as a manager (p. 315) appeared on p. 1 of the *Detroit Free Press*, Dec. 26, 1920.

CHAPTER TWENTY-SIX

Ty Cobb made his comment about ballplayers being "full of sentiment" (p. 318) in a piece by Robert Edgren of the *Chicago Tribune* that ran on May 21, 1921, p. 18. Bullion compared Cobb's popularity to Hughie Jennings's (p. 319) in the *Detroit Free Press*, Mar. 2, 1921, p. 11. Buranelli's long feature (p. 319) did not run in the *Free Press* until Sept. 25, 1921; it appeared on p. E1. The at-home piece (p. 321) ran without a byline in the *Milwaukee Journal*, Oct. 28, 1921, p. 1. Alexander's observation about Heilmann (p. 322) is on p. 161 of his *Ty Cobb*. Harry Heilmann's quote about Cobb teaching him about hitting (p. 322) appeared in the *Ellensburg* (Washington) *Daily Record*, June 10, 1951, p. 8. Bill Moore's quote about Heilmann not thinking too much of Cobb (p. 323) appears on p. 169 of *Cobb Would Have Caught It: The Golden Age of Baseball in Detroit* by Richard Bak. Moore's memory of being yanked out of the only major league game he ever played (p. 323) appears on p. 173 of the same book. The story about Dauss's beer drinking (p. 323) appears on p. 153 of *Cobb Would Have Caught It*. The story about Gehringer and Cobb (p. 324) is related in several places including *Charlie Gehringer: A Biography of the Hall of Fame Tigers Second Baseman* by John C. Skipper, p. 20. The Alexander quote (p. 326) is from his *Ty Cobb*, p. 164. Tigers team doctor Keane's comments on Babe Ruth (p. 327) are reported in *Ty and the Babe: Baseball's Fiercest*

Rivals: A Surprising Friendship and the 1941 Has-Beens Golf Championship by Tom Stanton, p. 66. Miller Huggin's statement about Cobb (p. 327) appeared originally in the *Sporting News*, Aug. 12, 1920, p. 3. The line about Ruth "taking it as a challenge" (p. 328) appeared in the *Detroit Free Press*, June 13, 1921, p. 9; the other quotes about confrontation between the Tigers and Yankees come from the same piece. The quote about Ruth from Lanier (p. 329) appeared in *Baseball Digest*, Jan. 7, 2007, p. 1. The description of Cobb's fight with Evans (p. 330) comes from the *Kansas City Kansan*, Sept. 25, 1921, p. 8. Abe Pollock dined out on his story about the mad dog (p. 331), which appears in print perhaps for the first time in *Touching Second: The Science of Baseball* by John J. Evers and Hugh Fullerton, p. 192. Lanier's quotes about Cobb's relations with umpires (p. 331) are from the same issue of *Baseball Digest* mentioned above.

CHAPTER TWENTY-SEVEN

Fred Lieb's account of his conversation with Cobb in San Francisco (p. 336) appears on pp. 178–79 of his *The Detroit Tigers*. Batchelor's anecdote about Cobb encountering "countrymen" (p. 337) comes from an unsourced clipping in the Ty Cobb folder of the library at the Baseball Hall of Fame in Cooperstown, NY. Navin's comments about Cobb's tenure as a manager (p. 338) are taken from an undated clip from the *Detroit News* in the Cobb folder at the Hall of Fame. Wood's statement about the mysterious "man from Cleveland," as well as his and Cobb's letters and statements (pp. 341–43), appear in the transcript of the hearing I obtained at the Baseball Hall of Fame. Virtually every newspaper in the country covered the Cobb-Speaker-Leonard scandal, but Ban Johnson's statements (p. 346) are presented at length in the *Cleveland Plain Dealer*, Jan. 21, 1927, pp. 1 and 10. The quote about Cobb being heartbroken (p. 346) appeared in the *Reading Times*, Jan. 18, 1927, p. 12. Leonard's statement about getting bumped off occasionally (p. 346) appeared in the transcript of the hearing, as well as the *Bluefield* (West Virginia) *Daily Telegraph*, Dec. 22, 1925, p. 5. Cobb's quotes about the Sept. 25 game (p. 347) come from the hearing transcript, which I obtained at the Baseball Hall of Fame. Damon Runyon's interview with Leonard (p. 348) was syndicated by Universal Service; I saw it in an unsourced clipping in the Cobb file at the Baseball Hall of Fame, dated Dec. 22, 1926. Johnson's quotes about Cobb and Speaker (p. 348) were reported by many papers including the editions of the *Plain Dealer* and *Bluefield Daily Telegraph* mentioned above. Charlie Cobb's quote about her husband (p. 348) from the *Augusta Chronicle* is cited in Don Rhodes's *Ty Cobb: Safe at Home*, p. 102. Lundt's and Griffith's quotes (p. 349) appeared in the *Ogden Standard-Examiner*, Dec. 28, 1926, p. 8. Jennings statement about Judge Landis (p. 349) is taken from the *Palm Beach Daily News*, Dec. 20, 1926, p. 24. Landis's complaint (p. 349) is cited in many places including *Judge and Jury: The Life and Times of Judge Kenesaw Mountain Landis* by David Pietrusza, p. 302. Risberg's quote about a "piker bet" (p. 349) appeared in the *Reading Times*, Jan. 3, 1927, p. 13. Cobb's denial that he ever played in a fixed game (p. 350) can be found in many places including *Baseball: An Illustrated History* by Geoffrey C. Ward and Ken Burns, p. 182. Risberg's quote about Cobb being a straight player (p. 350) comes from Alexander's *Ty Cobb*, p. 192. Will Rogers's quip (p. 350) can be found on page 182 of *Baseball: An Illustrated History*. Collins's quote about it being nothing out of the ordinary for a team to give gifts (p. 350) appears, among other places, on p. 147 of *Tales from the Deadball Era: Ty Cobb, Home Run Baker, Shoeless Joe Jackson, and the Wildest Times in Baseball History* by Mark S. Halfon. Comiskey's statement about the matter being known to everyone (p. 351) comes from the hearing transcript. Landis's statement (p. 351) was in the Ty Cobb folder at the Baseball Hall of Fame. Johnson's quotes about Landis seeking publicity and being involved with him in a "financial matter" (p. 352) were taken from the article in the *Bluefield Daily Telegraph* mentioned above. Jacob Ruppert said he was tired of Ban Johnson's behavior (p. 352) in the *Belvidere* (Illinois) *Daily Republican*, Jan. 19, 1927, p. 5. Johnson's opinion on the Cobb-Speaker case (p. 352) was in the Cobb file in the library of the Baseball Hall of Fame.

CHAPTER TWENTY-EIGHT

Landis's order to McGraw to "Lay off Cobb" (p. 353) is cited in *Tris Speaker: The Rough-and-Tumble Life of a Baseball Legend* by Timothy M. Gay, p. 242. Cobb's statement about wanting "vindication before the public" (p. 353) is taken from a letter Cobb wrote to Connie Mack dated Feb. 22, 1955, and provided to me by Ron Cobb. Connie Mack's philosophy about "getting the other fellow worried" (p. 354) appears on p. 448 of Norman Macht's *Connie Mack: The Turbulent and Triumphant Years, 1915–1931*. Mack's quote about wanting both Cobb and Speaker (p. 355) ran in the *Uniontown* (Pennsylvania) *Morning Herald*, Jan. 28, 1927, p. 10. Mack expressed his eagerness to sign Cobb (p. 355) in the *Augusta Chronicle*, Feb. 5, 1927, p. 1. One of the places Cobb said he was tired (p. 356) was on the undated radio interview with Grantland Rice, provided by Wesley Fricks. Jennings's quote about Cobb slowing down a bit (p. 356) appeared in the *Detroit Free Press*, Feb. 23, 1920, p. 14. Cobb made his comment about getting old (p. 357) in the *Sporting News*, Apr. 13, 1922, p. 1. Connie Mack Jr.'s quote about being surprised about Cobb's niceness (p. 358) appears on p. 444 of Macht's *Connie Mack: The Turbulent and Triumphant Years*. Mickey Cochrane's quote about Cobb being "a little bit crusty" (p. 358) appears in several places including *Mickey Cochrane: The Life of a Baseball Hall of Fame Catcher* by Charlie Bevis, p. 47. Donald Honig's comment about Al Simmons (p. 358) appears in Honig's *Baseball America*, p. 173. Jimmy Dykes's story about snooping on a hitting lesson Cobb was giving to Simmons (p. 358) appears in *Connie Mack: The Turbulent and Triumphant Years*, p. 445. The Macht quote that begins "Never a temperate man . . ." (p. 361) appears on p. 462 of *Connie Mack: The Turbulent and Triumphant Years*. Cobb's letter to Walsh about retiring (p. 363) is dated Dec. 15, 1927, and was provided to me by Ron Cobb. Westbrook Pegler's article quoting Rivers (p. 364) appeared in the *Detroit Free Press*, Sept. 23, 1928, p. A1.

CHAPTER TWENTY-NINE

Ty Cobb's quote about "exhibition golf" being more punishing than baseball (p. 372) comes from *Ty and the Babe: Baseball's Fiercest Rivals: A Surprising Friendship and the 1941 Has-Beens Golf Championship* by Tom Stanton, p. 181. Cobb's quotes about a ballplayer's fame being too fleeting (p. 375) ran in the *Toronto World*, Feb. 11, 1919, p. 9. Cobb's surprise and shock over the news of his divorce (p. 374) was noted in the *Chicago Daily Tribune*, Apr. 6, 1931, p. 23. Cobb's quote about his son Herschel getting in a fight with "hooligans" (p. 376) appears in *Heart of a Tiger: Growing Up with My Grandfather, Ty Cobb* by Herschel Cobb, p. 126. The quote "My boys, my boys!" (p. 377) appears on p. 86 of *Heart of a Tiger*. The quotes about Cobb's second divorce (p. 378) were taken from the hearing transcripts.

CHAPTER THIRTY

The quote about "yule chimes" (p. 380) appears on p. 22 of Al Stump's book *Cobb*, as do the quotes about the "windswept hill" and his father's head being "blown off." Joe DiMaggio's quote about holding on to Cobb's letters (p. 383) appeared in an article in *Baseball Digest* called "Use Heavier Bat with Thick Handle Is DiMag's Advice" by Phil Elderkin; my clip says 1968 but is otherwise undated. The story about Cobb helping DiMaggio negotiate (p. 383) appears in Richard Ben Cramer's *DiMaggio: The Hero's Life*, p. 73. The Jo Mosher quote about Stump getting people to "act up" (p. 386) appeared in William R. (Ron) Cobb's article "The Georgia Peach: Stumped by the Storyteller," which ran in the summer 2010 edition of *The National Pastime*, published by the Society for American Baseball Research; it has since been republished as a small book. Cobb's quote about being in the evening of his life (p. 394) comes from the *Sporting News*, Apr. 3, 1957, pp. 3–4.

EPILOGUE

Donie Bush's comment about Cobb (p. 399) appeared in the *New York Times*, July 17, 1961. The quote about Nap Rucker (p. 399) is from *My Life in Baseball*, p. 143.

— INDEX —